T0369705

THE COMMON FREEDOM
OF THE PEOPLE

THE
COMMON
FREEDOM
of the PEPLE

John Lilburne & the English Revolution

MICHAEL BRADDICK

OXFORD
UNIVERSITY PRESS

OXFORD
UNIVERSITY PRESS

Great Clarendon Street, Oxford, OX2 6DP,
United Kingdom

Oxford University Press is a department of the University of Oxford.
It furthers the University's objective of excellence in research, scholarship,
and education by publishing worldwide. Oxford is a registered trade mark of
Oxford University Press in the UK and in certain other countries

© Michael Braddick 2018

First Edition published in 2018

Impression: 1

Published in the United States of America by Oxford University Press
198 Madison Avenue, New York, NY 10016, United States of America

British Library Cataloguing in Publication Data
Data available

Library of Congress Control Number: 2017960662

ISBN 978–0–19–880323–2

Printed in Great Britain by
Clays Ltd, St Ives plc

For Cora and Melissa

[My] great love and respect [are] justly due unto you, for your constant zealous affection to the Common Wealth, and for your undaunted resolution in defence of the common freedome of the People

William Walwyn to John Lilburne, 1645
Quoted from *The Levellers in the English Revolution*,
ed. G. E. Aylmer (London, 1975), p. 64

Preface

At the heart of this book is a remarkable life. The second son of a modest gentry family in the north-east, John Lilburne was apprenticed to a London woollen merchant in 1632. Through his master's connections he became involved in opposition to the religious policies of Charles I, and in the publication of dangerous books, leading to a first arrest in 1637. He was eventually to be accused of treason four times, and was on trial for his life three times. Over twenty years he was subjected to brutal physical punishment, harsh prison conditions, and lonely exile, but he also managed to fit in active military service in the civil war. He fought bravely at a number of the key battles, was shot through the arm, nearly lost an eye in a pike accident, and rose to the rank of lieutenant colonel. Initially in trouble for his opposition to Charles I's regime, he was subsequently at odds with every government under which he lived. He died in his early forties, having spent the major part of his adult life in prison or exile.

In the course of this dramatic life he fought some important legal battles: for the right to remain silent (one of the issues on which he has been cited by US constitutional lawyers) and to an open trial (an issue on which he has been cited in the US Supreme Court), while his argument that juries were judges of law as well as of fact long outlived him. He made ample use of habeas corpus, and his example became central to the image of the freeborn Englishman of the eighteenth and nineteenth centuries.[1] Most strikingly of all, he was closely associated with the Leveller-led campaign for a written constitution, an *Agreement of the People*, which would have established a government answerable to the will of the people two centuries before the advent of mass representative democracy in Europe.

This was a remarkably courageous career, but the strength of character on which it drew made Lilburne an unreliable friend. It was Oliver Cromwell, in his first recorded parliamentary speech, who called for Lilburne's release from imprisonment imposed by Charles I's regime. Yet Lilburne was also tried for treason in the first year of republican rule, and Cromwell was probably

instrumental in his banishment from England two years after that. Towards
the end of his life a number of epitaphs and anagrams circulated, all with
essentially the same theme—bury John in one place and Lilburne in another,
for if they ever meet in the afterlife they will argue for eternity. He was, for
his opponents, the archetypal figure capable of starting an argument in an
empty room. In fact, at the time of his final trial, in 1653, this test of character
was literally a matter of life and death: central to that trial was the battle to
persuade the jury that he was either a champion of legal freedoms or simply
a troublemaker, a turbulent spirit who posed a threat to political stability.

This book traces Lilburne's political life, his journey to the articulation of
these powerful legal principles and revolutionary ideas. Central to that story
is the force of his personality: wholly admirable for his political commitment,
there is nonetheless something maniacal and destructive about Lilburne
the man. A serial martyr to religious and political causes, he was careless of his
own safety and, no doubt infuriatingly, cussedly committed to his opinions.

This is not simply a study of an extraordinary man, therefore: it is also
about the genesis of the big ideas with which he is linked. He is most popu-
larly associated with the attempt to establish a government based on the
principle that governors should be answerable to those they govern. But this
is not the only big idea for which he campaigned. Over the full twenty years
of his public activism he was more consistently concerned with the preservation of the legal rights that were his native inheritance as an Englishman,
particularly against the actions of a tyrannous and corrupt government:
writing in 1649, he said that in all his many publications he had '*constantly
and fearelessely opposed himself against the Tyrannie of the times, not in the least, in
opposition to a just Government, having alwaies … had the* Law *of England on his
side*'.[2] Just governments had nothing to fear from honest John; it was unfor-
tunate that he seems never to have lived under one.

It was this commitment to the shared rights of Englishmen, the 'common
freedom of the people', that led him into battle. In his descriptions of himself and his life such verbs predominate—battle, struggle, suffering, and
defence, for example. The object of this struggle is consistently described in
terms of legal rights, fundamental liberties, and the shared freedoms that were
an Englishman's inheritance. The protection of this common freedom was
central to the Leveller campaigns, leading to the call for annual parliaments
and securing for the Levellers a place among the champions of democracy.
But we might just as easily associate Lilburne with the development of the
idea of the rule of law, something equally fundamental to the way we now

live. In language nearer his own, however, William Walwyn probably offers
the best (sympathetic) characterization of Lilburne's career, by acknowledging the 'great love and respect justly due unto you, for your constant zealous
affection to the Common Wealth, and for your undaunted resolution in
defence of the common freedome of the People'.[3]

For his role in these revolutionary politics Lilburne has become a hero of
the left, particularly as perhaps the most prominent of the Leveller leaders.
The Levellers stand proudly in the British radical pantheon, and star particularly as forerunners of the Chartists and others. But Lilburne's central
ideas are not the property of the left. Rather, as he might have put it, he
fought for the birthright of all Englishmen. His core commitments were to
the ideals, not his friends or political allies. That is really the point: his commitment to individual legal rights as a defence against tyranny is now shared
across the political spectrum; his defence of those rights would have made
him just as much a pain in the neck for twenty-first-century politicians,
engaged in compromise and negotiation, as he was for those in the seventeenth. It is for this reason that Michael Foot thought he should have a national
monument, and that Geoffrey Bindman described him as his 'legal hero'.[4]
His interpretation of his legal rights, and the implications for the authority
of governments, were outlandish at the time Lilburne entered his adulthood
in early Stuart London: this book seeks to recover their importance and to
explore how they emerged from the politics of revolutionary England.

Of course these decades gave rise not just to John Lilburne, but to John
Milton's and Thomas Hobbes's greatest works, as well as others only slightly
less renowned, such as those of James Harrington and Andrew Marvell.
Lilburne's ideas are particular threads in a rich, even chaotic, world of public
debate, in which prophets set up camp on Blackheath to await Armageddon,
or ploughed the common lands, and a republic was declared. The debates
that emerged stimulated a longer argument, reaching across the Atlantic and
the English Channel in the eighteenth century and, in Britain, forward into
that other period of heroic political reform, the nineteenth century.

Other elements of that debate, however, now seem strange. Lilburne
shared with many contemporaries an intense religiosity that is often difficult
for us to comprehend, and the immediacy with which he felt God's presence
can appear very alien. In focussing on his commitment to secular legal rights
we are stripping away much of what he himself would have thought most
important and much of what he shared with his contemporaries. Nonetheless,
something about how he entered these seventeenth-century debates survived

the immediate context, appealing not just at the time but to subsequent generations. His writing, and the example of his actions, appealed more easily to less zealous restoration and eighteenth-century audiences than that of other mid-century radicals: his arguments were more easily comprehensible to subsequent generations than some of the more directly inspired writing of his contemporaries. As a result, he has been remembered, read, and imitated more often between then and now.

Lilburne was a highly unusual man, then, but his experiences reveal more general features of life in revolutionary England. Through the tumultuous decades of rebellion, civil war, and revolution, his thinking was clarified, leading him to some certainties which resonated powerfully with later reformers and activists. Many others were forced by the same events and dilemmas to think more carefully about what they believed, and why. They reached other conclusions, but they were often equally innovative, even if they were pointing to roads which in the end we have not taken, at least yet. According to one scholar, these were the 'epic years' of the English political imagination[5] and in that context Lilburne is a richly documented example of a much more general phenomenon.

Moreover, Lilburne took advantage of new opportunities to mobilize support for his ideas, and to act on them. This too reveals broader features of life in revolutionary England, a world of expanding possibilities for political engagement. Many others took up these opportunities to argue with or against him, or about other issues altogether. Lilburne was a master of these political arts, as well as an unusually creative thinker; but understanding his career throws light on to a broader experience in both respects. To understand intellectual creativity, and how ideas took hold, is at the same time to understand the conditions from which they arose.

Lilburne placed his own experiences at the centre of his political campaigns and his image was constructed using the newly liberated presses by him and by others—his fame and carefully constructed public image were key political weapons. That creates problems for the biographer, of course. He and others described his serial battles with authority in detail, often with a very immediate sense of place or of crucial personal encounters. By doing this, abstract battles were given a very concrete reality, and by publicizing his life Lilburne became a figurehead for larger causes. But this public account is interestingly partial, and those gaps which we can identify help to demonstrate how Lilburne set about constructing it: the names he does not mention, the boundaries around what he reveals of his private life (he was not above publishing letters addressed to his wife, and yet never mentions any of his children by name), the details of his biography that he mis-states, or the emphasis he places on his own action rather than that of all those that supported him. It is possible to get some distance on the crafted narrative of his life presented to contemporaries, testing it against the views of his critics and, where possible, the more neutral records of government. It is a seductive, embracing view, though, and many of his contemporaries would contest the picture of them that emerges from this telling of Lilburne's story. More frustratingly, some parts of his life remain almost entirely hidden from view—key personal relationships (such as that with his equally extraordinary but far less visible wife) or explicit reflection on what really motivated him.

There have been two previous biographies of this singular man. Both are fine works of scholarship but they share a desire to recruit Lilburne to what were at the time current political battles—in 1947 Muriel Gibb wrote about him as a model Christian democrat whose ideas offered an alternative to both state authoritarianism and to free market politics in the early years of the cold war; and in 1961 Pauline Gregg recovered the story of an early democrat in a native English radical tradition. Otherwise Lilburne's life and writing appears most often as an element of a broader study of Leveller thought and action. The emphasis on those Leveller campaigns leads to a focus on the constitutional proposals for a peace settlement in 1649—and notably who the Levellers thought should be enfranchised.[6]

The Leveller movement has been out of fashion with historians for a long time now, and that is one reason why there has been no biography of Lilburne for nearly sixty years. At the high point of their historical fortunes they could be considered key political players, 'the first model of a democratically organized political party',[7] pursuing 'precociously' modern ideas. Over the last thirty years they have been cut down to size: placed more at the margins of the main political action; more likely to be regarded as a loose coalition or movement than a party, and inconsistent in their political theory; and holding views that are quite alien to us, no matter how familiar their constitutional proposals seem.[8]

Their fortunes are now perhaps reviving, but my main purpose here is not to revisit those arguments about the Levellers, or to position Lilburne in relation to them. In fact, he always resisted the label Leveller and, writing in 1649, he characterized his own career rather differently: as a series of struggles, in succession, against first the bishops, then the House of Lords, then the Lords and Commons together, and finally the Council of State. A key moment in the evolution of his thought came when he saw that his commanders in the parliamentary army could be just as oppressive as the royalists he had joined up to fight. What we might call his '*Animal Farm* moment' led him to see that the war was not really between king and Parliament, but between the people and tyranny. It was this that led him into the partisan battles within the parliamentary alliance and to join the Leveller campaign, as well as to oppose all the regimes after 1649. The thread that connected them was the protection of an Englishman's inherited legal rights; it was a cause he pursued through the Leveller mobilization and in other campaigns before and after those dramatic years.

By looking at the whole of his career we get a different sense of his key political concerns and their evolution. More importantly, though, we can also see how he was able to mobilize people in support of their legal rights, and how the possibilities for that kind of mobilization were changed by war and revolution. Through print, petitioning campaigns, tavern meetings, and free religious congregations, he forged ties with people who shared his beliefs, around concrete political objectives and practical plans for mobilization. The conscious construction and manipulation of his image—by him, his friends, and his opponents—reveals something important about how politics worked in revolutionary England: the use of print, changes in popular politics, and the relationship between Parliament and the nation, for example. Although he had no landed estate and no established profession, and never held public office, he was nonetheless able to mobilize support on a scale that threatened governments—making it seem worthwhile to imprison him, charge him with treason, or send him into exile. It would not have been possible to have sustained such a career twenty years earlier, but his model was much imitated in the following centuries—consciously so, in fact.

Rather than revisit his life primarily as an element of the history of the Levellers, therefore, this book explores what this dramatic and lavishly documented life tells us about revolutionary England more broadly. These decades saw a deeply traumatic conflict, whether we measure that in terms of lives lost, property destroyed, or political and religious certainties unravelled; but it was also, and perhaps for the same reason, a period of remarkable intellectual creativity. Lilburne's life reveals emerging opportunities for political action and also something about the relationship between that political engagement, his own sufferings (as he saw them), and his political creativity. The surviving evidence, while flawed for biography, provides rich materials with which to study this political life. That story reveals how the unfolding crisis prompted Lilburne to creative thought, and innovative political action: it takes us into the world of illegal print, street demonstrations, dawn raids, military campaigns, and the courtroom. In doing so it does not claim that what he thought or how he lived somehow epitomizes what was really at stake in this crisis, but rather that it reveals some of the core dynamics of the revolution. This is not a biography, then, but a political life, and one that explores the life not just of John Lilburne but also of revolutionary England.

Acknowledgements

This book had a long gestation, in a period when I had heavy administrative commitments. During that time Sir Keith Burnett and Suzanne Hubbard encouraged and facilitated my attempts to retain contact with my scholarly field. A number of fellowships during and after that period allowed me the time for space and reflection in which it took shape and was eventually finished. I am grateful to have been a Professeur Invité at the École des Hautes Études at the invitation of Philippe Minard and a Distinguished Research Fellow in the ARC Centre for the History of Emotions, which I held at the University of Adelaide. I am also grateful to the Leverhulme Trust for the generous award of an international network grant on 'The Comparative History of Political Engagement', which shaped how I wrote this book. The book was written during a period of institutional leave generously granted by the University of Sheffield and as a Leverhulme/British Academy Senior Research Fellow. I completed the final draft at the Huntington Library, as a Fletcher Jones Fellow, enjoying facilities that are ideal for this kind of work and the intellectual generosity and hospitality of Steve Hindle, the Director of Research.

I am also grateful to the organizers of a number of conferences and workshops which gave me the opportunity to try out my ideas, and to the audiences who helped me to refine them: at the Lilburne 400 conference at the Bishopsgate Centre in 2015, and at Penn State University, the Institute of Historical Research, London, as well as the universities of Cambridge, Durham, Leicester, Newcastle, Oxford, and Sheffield. Participation in a number of collaborative projects took me to Barcelona, Le Mans, Nice, New York, and Pretoria, where my ideas about mobilization and political engagement were also extensively trailed.

I am very grateful for the help and expertise available at the Amsterdam City Archives, Bedfordshire and Luton Archives Service, British Library, Bodleian Library, the Clothworkers' Company, Durham University Special Collections, the London Metropolitan Archives, and the Parliamentary

Archives. Joy Lloyd undertook extensive and fundamental preparatory research for me in the printed materials, and I have drawn heavily on her unpublished study of the manor of Epworth in trying to understand what Lilburne was up to in the Lincolnshire Fens. Tim Wales also did valuable work, particularly on Thomas Hewson's will and the connections it reveals. I am also grateful to Colin Merrony who kindly put down his trowel at a busy time and drew one of the maps.

Jason Peacey and John Morrill read a draft of the book and made a number of very helpful suggestions for improvement, as did Jill Pritchard, John Walter, and two anonymous reviewers at another press. As ever I am grateful to colleagues in the excellent Department of History at the University of Sheffield and I have benefitted greatly from the advice, insight, and encouragement of many other scholars. I would particularly like to thank David Adams, Alex Barber, John Coffey, Ken Fincham, Paul Halliday, Roeland Harms, Karen Harvey, Alex Hitchman, Helmer Helmers, Ann Hughes, Joanna Innes, Mark Kishlansky, Mark Knights, Peter Lake, David Lemmings, Tom Leng, Simon Middleton, Anthony Milton, John Morrill, Melissa Mowry, Kent Olson, Jason Peacey, Ismini Pells, Hunter Powell, Joad Raymond, John Rees, Gary Rivett, Harman Snel, Ted Vallance, Elliot Vernon, John Walter, and Phil Withington. It has been a pleasure working with OUP, and I am particularly grateful to Luciana O'Flaherty, Martha Cunneen, Fiona Orbell, and Dan Harding. Above all, though, I am grateful to Sarah, who never volunteered for life with Lilburne.

Contents

List of Illustrations and Maps

Illustrations

Maps

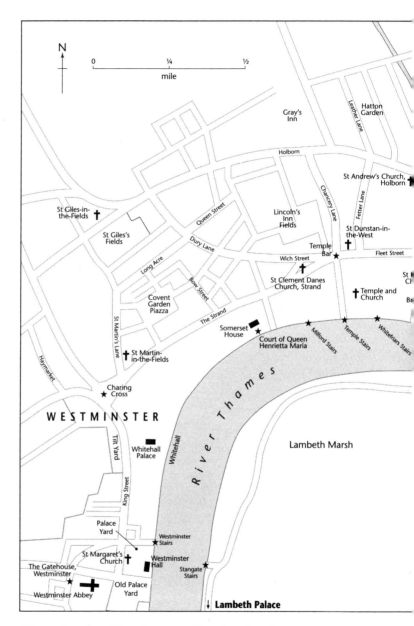

Map 1. London, Westminster, and Southwark *c.*1640

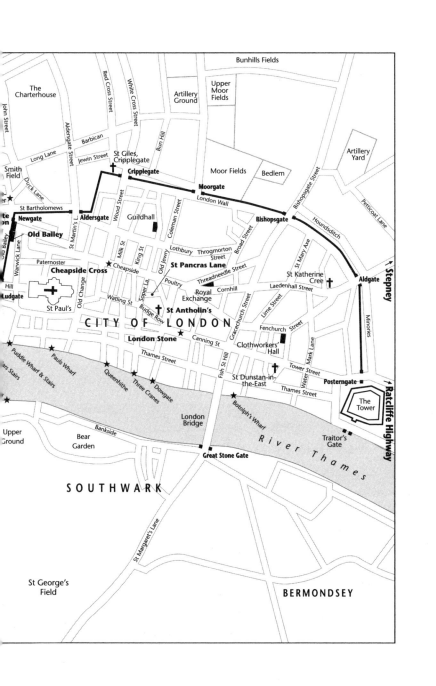

Bunhills Fields

The Charterhouse

John Street

Red Cross Street

White Cross Street

Artillery Ground

Upper Moor Fields

Long Lane

Aldersgate Street

Barbican

Jewin Street

Bun Hill

St Giles, Cripplegate

Moor Fields

Bedlem

Artillery Yard

Smith Field

Duck Lane

St Bartholomews

Cripplegate

Moorgate

London Wall

Bishopsgate Street

Petticoat Lane

Newgate

Aldersgate

Wood Street

Guildhall

Coleman Street

London Wall

Bishopsgate

Houndsditch

Old Bailey

St Martin's L.

Milk St

King St

Old Jewry

Lothbury

Throgmorton Street

Broad Street

St Mary Axe

Paternoster

Cheapside

St Pancras Lane

Threadneedle Street

St Katherine Cree

Aldgate

STEPNEY

Cheapside Cross

Old Change

La. Jacobs

Poultry

Cornhill

Laedenhall Street

Hill

Ludgate

Watling St

Budge Row

Royal Exchange

Gracechurch Street

Lime Street

Minories

St Paul's

CITY OF LONDON

† St Antholin's

Fenchurch Street

London Stone

Canning St

Clothworkers' Hall

Tower Street

Posterngate

Puddle Wharf & Stairs

Pauls Wharf

Thames Street

Queenhithe

Three Cranes

Dowgate

Fish St Hill

St Dunstan-in-the-East

Water Lane

Mark Lane

Thames Street

Ratcliffe Highway

s Stairs

London Bridge

Botolph's Wharf

Traitor's Gate

The Tower

Upper Ground

Bankside

Bear Garden

Great Stone Gate

River Thames

SOUTHWARK

St Margaret's Lane

St George's Field

BERMONDSEY

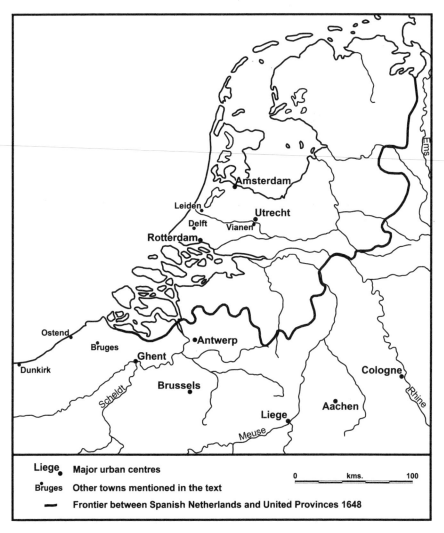

Amsterdam

Leiden

Utrecht

Delft

Vianen

Rotterdam

Ostend

Bruges

Antwerp

Ghent

Dunkirk

Scheldt

Brussels

Cologne

Aachen

Liege

Rhine

Meuse

Ems

Liege•   Major urban centres

Bruges•   Other towns mentioned in the text

—   Frontier between Spanish Netherlands and United Provinces 1648

0   kms.   100

Map 2. The low countries, *c.*1648

I

Apprentice, 1632–40

Apprentice to Thomas Hewson, 1632–7

John Lilburne arrived back in London from Amsterdam in early December 1637. He was hoping, among other things, to visit an old acquaintance, John Wharton, at his house on Soper Lane (or Bow Lane into which it ran). This was just around the corner from the house at London Stone in which Lilburne had lived as an apprentice.[1] Wharton was a dangerous man to know. Now into his eighties, he was a hot presser, someone who worked in the textile trades finishing cloth, but he also dealt in politically dangerous books. Well known to the authorities, he had been before the Court of High Commission in December 1635, and was only recently returned from prison.[2]

Lilburne was with a servant of Wharton's, John Chilliburne, whose behaviour over the course of the afternoon had left him increasingly unnerved. They had been due to meet earlier at the Exchange but at 2.00 p.m., the appointed hour, Chilliburne was nowhere to be seen. Instead two other men appeared, who Lilburne recognized as religious opponents of his ('Arminians') from Cornhill. He thought afterwards that they had been sent to size him up, 'vewing very narrowly my apparell, visage and countenance'. They were, he thought, too interested in him: 'when J sat downe, they would passe by, and goe a little from me and fix their eyes upon me'. Anxious, Lilburne had left, and when he did next meet Chilliburne he told him about it, adding that it had crossed his mind that Chilliburne was in the process of betraying him.[3]

Later that afternoon Lilburne was on his way to meet someone else at Temple. Learning about this, Chilliburne intercepted him on Fleet Street and as they walked together Chilliburne assured him that it would be safe to visit Wharton, although Lilburne was clearly worried he would be arrested. Reassured, though, he agreed to meet later at the stairs between

Bridewell and Blackfriars, and in the meantime Chilliburne would make sure the coast was clear. Lilburne waited for some time before Chilliburne arrived, and when he did arrive it was not from the direction of Bridewell, where Lilburne had sent him to visit another unnamed person. Instead he came from the opposite direction—Lilburne later deduced that he had come from the house of Flamsted, a pursuivant (an officer of the ecclesiastical authorities). Once more he and Chilliburne walked together, this time towards Wharton's house, before parting company again, with agreement to meet at Tantlins Church. As he approached for this final meeting Lilburne thought Chilliburne was with another man, someone he did not recognize.[4]

By the time they entered Soper Lane, then, Lilburne was more than a little uneasy. He immediately 'saw a fellow stand in a corner, very suspiciously, who looked very wishfully at me, and I at him; and therefore I desired [Chilliburne] to goe and see who it was, and whether I might goe safely to his Masters'. Lilburne followed at a distance with his sword half drawn, passing by two 'great fellowes' in the 'narrow Lane' without taking much notice of them. Once he had passed, however, they came up behind him, seizing him by the back and shoulders, crying out for help in the King's name, and that they had the 'Rogues *Whartons* men'. A third man (who he identified as Chilliburne) took him by his left shoulder, and together they pulled his cloak around him so that he could not draw his sword. His pride was perhaps wounded at being taken: had he not been caught unawares in this way, he later claimed, he could have looked after himself, 'for though had fast hold of me, they quaked and trembled for feare; and though they were five or sixe, yet they cryed out for more helpe to assist them'. He was certain that he had been betrayed since they spoke to him by name, even though it was now dark.[5] Surprised and overpowered, he was forced into a nearby shop, thrown over a sugar chest, and his sword was taken from him. His captors once again called for help, claiming to have taken one of the 'notioriousest dispersers of scandalous bookes that was in the kingdom'.[6]

Flamsted, the pursuivant, took Lilburne to the Pole-Head Tavern near Doctors' Commons, where they were met by Bonntragge, the 'Prelate's pursevant', that is a servant of the Archbishop of Canterbury himself. Bonntragge ordered sack to celebrate meeting Lilburne at last, although Lilburne refused to join him in drink: in the circumstances, perhaps, an assertion of his greater godliness, or a refusal of the insult. From there he was taken to Flamsted's house and, at midday the next day was committed to the Gatehouse prison by order of the Archbishop of Canterbury's chancellor,

Sir John Lambe. Without examination he was charged with 'sending of factious and scandalous books out of *Holland* into *England*'.[7] It was his first arrest, the beginning of a series of battles with authority that lasted for the rest of his life.

★   ★   ★

In more normal times John Lilburne could have hoped for a life of respectable obscurity. Certainly, as the second son of an established gentry family, he was born with some advantages. His mother and father had been employed at court and as John later proclaimed, they represented the most distinguished house of a family that traced its roots back to the conquest. His father, Richard, had a younger brother, George, who was to be an important influence at crucial moments in John's life, and was one of the more powerful men in Sunderland: he had been a Justice of the Peace under Charles I and served three terms as Mayor of Sunderland in the late 1630s and early 1640s.[8] According to later family tradition, in fact, Lilburne was born at his uncle's house, although Lilburne himself said that he was born in Greenwich, where 'my Father and mother [were] both Courtiers, and her Father for the greatest part of twice 20. yeares before'.[9] He moved back to the north-east at an early age and grew up at Thickley Punchardon, going to school in Auckland and then in Newcastle where 'I did not only know, but also was knowne of the prinicipall men there'.[10] At school in Newcastle his master had been Thomas Gibson, 'a very good man, and a godly man....I boarded in his house, we had prayers twice a day in the School: & every night in his family'.[11]

Like many younger sons before him, Lilburne entered an apprenticeship. His master, Thomas Hewson, was a London clothier, but came originally from Aycliffe, county Durham, the village next to Thickley Punchardon. It was a place to which Hewson retained some loyalty: he made provision for the poor of the parish in his will.[12] He took on five apprentices between 1611 and 1622, three of them from the north-east and two of them apparently kinsmen from Aycliffe. The other north-easterner, William Leedham, came from Darlington, half a dozen miles to the south. These apprenticeships had been evenly spaced, and John Lilburne was clearly a latecomer to Hewson's house—ten years after his most recent predecessor, taken on in 1632 perhaps as a particular favour reflecting those local connections.[13]

When Lilburne came to London he was on his own account a serious, industrious, and religious young man. Arriving as a teenager, he spent six years in Hewson's service, serving him 'as faithfully...as ever Apprentice served a Master'. He drove a wholesale trade, and was proud that although he had 'many thousands of Pounds' going through his hands he had never, as far as he could remember, 'wronged him of a Groat'. Neither was he a difficult young man, 'although I had then as much mettle, life and spirit as most young men in London had'. He certainly had pride in his family, and his family certainly displayed mettle: Richard, his father, was the last man in England to demand settlement of a property dispute by trial by battle, while his uncle George, and brothers Robert and Henry, were all bold men of action. Nonetheless, John claimed that in all his time as an apprentice he could not remember ever giving or receiving a box on the ear, or any quarrel with anyone, although he did take a dispute with his master to the Chamberlain. Their relationship was clearly mended by the time of Lilburne's troubles with the regime, though: Lilburne then had 'the truest and cordiallest friend of him, that ever servant had of a *Master* in the day of his tryall'.[14] On his death in the autumn of 1641 Hewson remembered Lilburne in his will— the only one of his apprentices to be so remembered.[15]

There may have been some religious sympathy as well as local connection behind this apprenticeship, and these religious sympathies led John into the 'puritan underground', a world of informal religious fellowship that sometimes shaded into opposition to the national government and its church. We don't know much about Richard, John's father, but he was clearly a friend of the parliamentarian regime during the 1640s, and had probably been an opponent of Charles I's church in the 1630s. John's schoolmaster in Newcastle, Thomas Gibson, seems likely to have been at least broadly speaking puritan in his views, although he later changed his religious opinions, and in the 1640s was clearly seen as an enemy of the parliamentary cause.[16] John's uncle George was certainly a vocal opponent of Charles I's church policies, the 'clergy innovations' during the 1630s, and had an apparently puritan insistence on the primacy of scripture. These sympathies put him on the wrong side of the regime: as we will see, he sympathized with the Scots when they rebelled against Charles I over religion and was investigated by the Court of High Commission in 1640 for his anti-episcopal views. In fact he was imprisoned twice.[17]

Hewson certainly shared these sympathies, and had important friends in puritan circles. They included the Gurdon family, prominent puritans in Suffolk, one of whom married Hewson's daughter. In fact Hewson's will reveals an impressive roll call of prominent puritan friends, including Lady Anne Montague, wife of a powerful patron to puritan ministers in Northamptonshire.[18] Hewson also invested in the Massachusetts Bay Company and clearly knew John Winthrop, a prominent puritan and key figure in the early history of America, who also had roots in Suffolk.[19] A financial stake in rents at Banbury connected Hewson with Robert Vivers, and through him the circles of Viscount Saye and Sele, also a powerful puritan figure whose family seat was at Broughton just outside Banbury. Vivers was at odds with the church in the 1630s and defended Saye from local opponents.[20] Saye was, like Hewson, a colonial investor and with other prominent puritans supported the settlement at Providence Island in the Caribbean. With Robert Greville, Lord Brooke, he had been a sponsor of the Saybrook settlement at the mouth of the Connecticut River and Hewson had some connection to that enterprise through the Massachusetts Bay Company.[21]

Brooke and Vivers were to be important to Lilburne's story in the coming years. Hewson's connections also included Henry Jessey, who was chaplain to the Gurdon's and who also knew relatives of Anne Montague's first husband. Jessey was an important figure in London's separatist churches, and was later active in London's civil war politics. His circles in turn overlapped with those of Edmund Rosier and William Kiffin, also important early connections for Lilburne.[22] Rosier led a separatist congregation in London—a religious group meeting outside the national church—which perhaps met in or near Soper Lane. He was to hold civic office and take an active role in the politics of the revolution, and Lilburne later said they enjoyed religious fellowship for several years, although they took different views of the execution of Charles I and the establishment of the Commonwealth. Kiffin and Lilburne were close correspondents throughout Lilburne's life, and Kiffin later published some of his writing, although they were also to fall out in 1649.[23] One of Hewson's executors, George Willingham, seems to have been of interest to the authorities in the late 1630s, since letters to his son survive among the state papers, apparently having been intercepted. They reveal that he was familiar with some dangerous reading material and he was later to be a prominent figure in the parliamentary war effort.[24]

Close examination reveals a dense network of such connections, many of them rooted in the cramped streets around Hewson's house at London Stone. Hewson's friendship and kin networks clearly took him close to some very prominent puritans with whom he shared interests in colonial ventures. Some of them were also, or were to become, prominent opponents of the regime. These were formative influences for Lilburne, offering crucial connections which added to the advantages of his gentry background, and which enabled and supported his entry into the religious politics of the 1630s.

John was not very busy in Hewson's service, 'keeping only a Ware-house', enjoying spare time several days a week, and he used his time to study. He read the Bible, of course, but also Foxe's '*Book of martyrs*' and the work of leading Protestant writers: Martin Luther, Jean Calvin, Theodor Beza, 'Molins' (Peter du Moulin?) as well as Thomas Cartwright, William Perkins, Henry Burton, and Richard Rogers, all prominent English reformers of a broadly puritan stripe whose views would not stand easily with the religious policies of Charles I.[25] Many of these recollections come from the summer of 1649, when Lilburne was in open conflict with the republican regime, and he had a strong incentive to claim that he was a respectable, sober, and godly man who did not seek out conflict.[26] He may not have been quite as peaceable as he claimed, therefore, but it is clear that by the end of his apprenticeship he had profound religious commitments, and that they were at odds with those of the regime.

Several years later John Bastwick, another eminent figure in these circles, claimed that he had schooled Lilburne for polite society, helping him to lose his rough country language and dialect and to acquire some of the social graces necessary for acceptance in metropolitan society.[27] At times it suited Lilburne to conform to this image of the simple man, but he was also clear about the social value of his family background: 'I am a sonne of a Gentle man, and my Friends are of rancke and quality in the Countrie where they live'.[28] He did not claim any formal expertise in theological matters ('It is true J am a yong man and noe Scoller, according to that which the world counts Schollership'),[29] but in response to a later gibe that he had been raised from obscurity, he was assertive about his background and education. Living at his father's hereditary seat 'beside other education, the best which the Country afforded, I was brought up well nigh 10. yeares together, in the best Schooles in the North, namely at *Auckland*, and New Castle'. Ten years in good schools, and being 'not one of the dronessest [least able or conscientious] Schoole Boyes there', meant that he had 'besides my knowledge in the Latin tongue,... a little entred into the Greeke also'. He took pride in his family background and social status throughout his life, and was greatly offended by a later claim that he had been a servant.[30] When he entered Hewson's house he added to these advantages, gaining access to a potentially powerful puritan network including men who were important to him over the coming years. Lilburne was, then, better connected than he sometimes liked to let on, and was apprenticed to a man in whose house he was free to read godly works.

★   ★   ★

Lilburne had arrived in London at a moment of rising religious tensions, and as he neared the end of his apprenticeship they were reaching a crescendo. As trouble began to erupt, Hewson's connections led him into a puritan underground of resistance to official church policy.

The arguments at stake were the latest round in England of a long debate in European Protestantism about what was required to purify the church. The Reformation had sought to strip the church of corrupt papistical practices but it was not clear exactly how far that should proceed. Scripture was the touchstone, but the account of early church practice was not easily applied to the more complex world of Christian practice 1,600 years later. A persecuted sect, gathering in a world dominated by other religions and authorities, lived by different rules than an established church claiming the loyalty of the whole community. Some particularly austere reformers wanted to return to the pristine form of early Christianity, throwing out any practices that were not explicitly sanctioned in scripture. A more mainstream view, though, was that there were many helpful traditions that had developed over the centuries, which guided belief and practice and which were not in conflict with scripture—it was important to defend them while throwing out those practices which were corrupt.

This middle position was a difficult one of course, and it related not just to what Christians should believe about their own conduct and salvation, but also how the Christian community should be organized, and what Christians should do when they gathered for worship. These were interrelated questions too, since corrupt organization or religious practice might lead to corrupt individual belief and conduct, and might ultimately therefore jeopardize salvation. What was actually useful from these received traditions was therefore a fraught question. On the other hand, there was plenty of evidence from the century since Luther's reformation that individual Christians, left to their own devices, could go horribly wrong in their views about good Christian practice and belief. Just letting people lead their own lives based on their reading of scriptures seemed to many Christians a recipe for disaster.

Under Charles I, and particularly associated with William Laud, official policy in England had taken a turn towards respect for tradition, even if it was not explicitly described in scripture, and to asserting the special importance of the clergy to the health of the Christian community. Ordinary Christians, on this view, needed guidance in seeking God's will and that guidance should come from the accumulated wisdom of the church, embedded in its traditions, and from men learned in those traditions and in biblical interpretation.

Official policy also emphasized the beauty of holiness—ceremonial practice at times of worship that alerted members of the congregation to the presence of the divine, 'edified' them, and made them ready to receive the Christian message.

These policies, known as Arminianism (after a Dutch reformer) or Laudianism (after the Archbishop), while very well intentioned, posed a direct challenge to the more purely scripturalist views that had dominated the English church over the previous two generations. These views were also broadly Calvinist, following the inspiration of Jean Calvin. Central to this strand of thought was the doctrine of predestination: the belief that salvation was at God's will, and could not be affected by human action. Our fate rests on God's grace, not our own free will in choosing to be virtuous and worthy of salvation. It followed that our own good works or the intercession of the clergy could not affect God's judgement: we are simply dependent on God's will for us. The role of worship was to expose Christians to scripture, and congregations, organized into a Presbyterian structure, gave the clergy at best a limited role in mediating between individuals and God: the relationship was much more direct and intimate. Laudianism, by emphasizing the power of the clergy, the beauty of holiness, and the value of wholesome tradition, posed a direct challenge to these core scripturalist and Calvinist commitments.

All this had a serious and directly political dimension. The power of kings had become closely connected to their religious authority: a king who defended his subjects' faith enjoyed a double loyalty as a result; one whose religion was thought false, however, enjoyed a very compromised political authority. Kings often favoured clerical authority, seeing it as a way of promoting unity and ensuring their subjects did not end up on the wilder shores of reformation thought. As Charles's father, James I, had famously put it, 'No bishop, no King'. On the other hand, Calvinist or hotter Protestants questioned the bolder claims of the clergy (especially the bishops) to spiritual authority, since they rested more clearly on tradition than on scripture. On this view, bishops had often proved obstacles to authentic Christian practice, notably of course the Bishop of Rome, and the Reformation had been prompted by exactly this desire to prevent clerical authority corrupting the church. For English Calvinists the dangers of clerical authority seemed to be clearly demonstrated in Laudian policy on Christian belief and practice.

These arguments were not matters simply of learned theological debate either, since they affected what kind of religion was practised in parish churches, and therefore the lives of ordinary people. While there was a national church, appointments to individual parishes often depended on the patronage of private individuals: bishops and the king could not simply impose their version of the church by imposing their preferred ministers. Similarly, the prosecution of dissent, or nonconformity, depended on the active participation of local people—willing to bring offenders before the ecclesiastical courts, and to see punishments imposed. As a result the detail of the religion people experienced varied according to where they lived, and was even to some extent sensitive to local opinion.[31]

Nor were the politics of these disputes inaccessible to ordinary people. England was a small society, of around five million people, in which there were often few degrees of separation between relatively ordinary people and those at the heart of power. There was an elaborate system of government which depended on the voluntary participation of a surprisingly broad section of society, particularly in Lilburne's London. In the crowded streets of the City, rich and poor lived alongside each other, while through the organization of the City's government (the wards), the parishes, and the various guilds and companies, men were integrated into institutions which brought them close to people with real influence in national government. In fact, in some wards one in three householders might hold some kind of public office at any one time: such offices brought people into contact with Aldermen who were themselves not far removed from connections to the Royal Court or Parliament. London was also at the heart of networks of news and gossip, stretching not just across England but the whole of Europe, through which the future fates of nations and churches were widely discussed. Innumerable churches served the City, many of them also supporting lecturers—men paid by charitable foundations or individual philanthropists to deliver improving sermons. Walking the two or three hundred yards down Soper Lane, along Budge Row and up to his own church, St Swithin's by London Stone, that afternoon in December 1637, Lilburne would have passed within yards of six other churches as well as the Mercers', Skinners', and Tallow Chandlers' Halls, all important institutions in London's rich civic life. On his walk from Cheapside to Soper Lane via the Exchange, Temple, and Blackfriar's steps, Lilburne would have been close to the Cross at Cheapside— where London's Catholics were said to surreptitiously cross themselves as they passed—and the radical Protestant congregation at St Stephen's, Colemanstreet, while not far across the city was the Queen's Chapel, where Catholic mass was celebrated. Turning right rather than left at the end of

Soper Lane would, within a similar distance, have brought him to St Paul's Cathedral, and its many bookshops. The Exchange, centre of international trade, news, and gossip, was not far off.[32] These cramped streets housed, in microcosm, the larger religious debates that had fractured western Christendom in the aftermath of the reformation (Fig. 1.1).

We know that Lilburne's London had well-established networks of people gathering outside the established church to discuss their religion, and its future. These forms of voluntary religion existed in an uneasy relationship with the established church, in some ways supplementing official religion, but in others shading into a puritan underground that might subvert it. Occasionally figures from this world fell foul of the authorities, for what they said or did in informal meetings, or for what they wrote, and this encouraged a view among the godly that they were persecuted. The authorities, on the other hand, could be suspicious to the point of paranoia about what was going on in these circles. There was a gradient along which a committed Protestant might move, from attending meetings intended to supplement official religion into a separatist congregation, defined in opposition to it. Much depended on what was going on in the official church, of course: the further it diverged from these voluntary forms of belief and practice, the more likely it was that an individual might want to abandon the official practice altogether and separate. But that in itself, the decision to separate, was a profound challenge to the religious conscience, and the subject of much informed discussion.[33]

Many of Lilburne's future associates had experience of this puritan underground. Kiffin and Rosier we have already mentioned, but perhaps the most notorious example is St Stephens, Colemanstreet, where the parishioners had acquired the right to elect their own minister at the dissolution of the monasteries. During the 1630s they were in the care of John Goodwin, a very hot Protestant, and the ward was also home to a Baptist conventicle, as well as numerous individuals who were later to become important to parliamentarian politics—printers working without licences, staunch parliamentarian administrators, and politicians. It was here that John Lilburne's first publisher, John Canne, had organized a conventicle before he left for Amsterdam, and future Levellers Richard Overton and Nicholas Tew had run secret presses.[34]

During the 1630s there were no parliaments in which to air concerns about Laudian policy. In the first five years of his reign, from 1625 onwards, Charles had resorted to Parliament frequently, primarily for money to support his foreign policy. His experience of parliaments had not been a happy one,

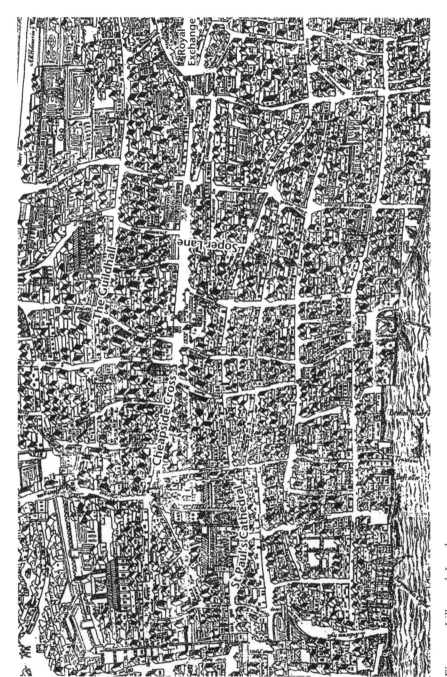

Fig. 1.1. Lilburne's London

however—he encountered criticism of his religious and foreign policy and of his key advisers, as well as a lack of realism about the costs of modern war. Parliaments yielded very little money, and lots of headaches, and by 1629 he had had enough, at least for the time being. He continued to promote Laudianism and in the meantime tried to raise money using legal powers that did not depend on Parliament. He raised cash by imposing fines, raising rents, or imposing obligations that could be met in cash, for example using his prerogative powers to regulate trade, to police the boundaries of royal forests, or to demand military service in times of emergency. To many of his subjects this looked like taxation without consent, and a threat to property rights. For many critics of his church, these legal and religious concerns were related, since the English Church had been established through the break with Rome in 1530s, which was achieved by parliamentary statute. It was widely believed that those who wanted to return to Rome would have to undermine parliaments, and hence that undermining parliaments weakened the resistance to Rome. It was in the house of a godly master with good puritan connections that Lilburne first entered this world, and he emerged a strong critic of Charles's regime.

★   ★   ★

By the mid-1630s the advance of Laudianism, dubious financial policies, and the absence of parliaments were creating more than a little disquiet in England. For hotter Protestants this was creating pressure towards separation or even migration—the New World looked like a more hopeful place than England. For those who stayed home, it made active opposition to Charles's policies seem increasingly worth the risk, and as the worries increased, Lilburne followed some of Hewson's connections into this puritan underground. Through his master he had become Edmund Rosier's 'familiar friend and neighbor, and fellow-professor of religion', and in 1636, as he approached the end of his apprenticeship, Rosier introduced him to John Bastwick (Fig. 1.2), who was then in prison in the Gatehouse. Bastwick came from a relatively modest background on the fringes of gentility, but had been at Cambridge, Leiden, and Padua, training as a doctor and absorbing radical Protestant views. By the 1630s he was known for his hostility to bishops and record of controversial publication. Having been introduced to him, Lilburne became a devoted follower, visiting Bastwick 'constantly', later recalling that he 'could have laid down my life' in his service.[35] This friendship was to lead Lilburne directly into serious trouble.

Fig. 1.2. John Bastwick (1595?–1654)

In the mid-1630s, the government went after Bastwick, along with William Prynne (Fig. 1.3) and Henry Burton, scandalized by some of their writing. Prynne, also from a background on the fringes of gentility, had been at Oxford and was a lawyer. He had been in trouble a few years earlier for denunciations of the stage, and female actors in particular, just at the time that the queen was appearing in a court masque. This was simply one of what became 200 publications engaging in religious controversies. Burton was a minister, with connections among London's separatists and a strong line on the popishness of Charles I's Church.[36] In trouble with the regime, the three of them chose confrontation, acting in ways that were bound to force a government response and refusing opportunities to mitigate their punishment, to evade or avoid the rigorous application of the law.[37]

Eventually, on 30 June 1637, they were subject to painful and humiliating public punishment, an ordeal which they embraced bravely and freely. They had been sentenced to stand in the pillory and have their ears cropped. Prynne's ears had already been cropped, but the remaining stumps came off

Fig. 1.3. William Prynne (1600–69)

nonetheless, and his cheeks were branded. Burton's left ear was cut so close to the head, and so clumsily, that he lost a lot of blood. Lilburne was at his feet as he suffered, and in the course of all this Burton looked down at the young man, asking 'Son, son, what is the matter, you look so pale?' During and after their brutal public mutilations these men enjoyed public support, and won a significant moral victory. It seems that many of London's separatists were present, in a crowd that was sympathetic. In the eyes of the godly, no doubt, they had forced the regime to reveal its fundamental nature; for others their fortitude helped to erode support for the government's position. As Sir Thomas Wentworth, powerful adviser to Charles I, put it to Laud: 'A Prince that loseth the force and example of his punishments loseth withal the greatest part of his domain'.[38] It was a lesson that Lilburne fully absorbed: for the rest of his life he never flinched from similar confrontations.

These punishments were part of a major turn of events in official policy in England and Scotland, which did not end well for Charles's government. Eleven days after the punishment of these 'puritan martyrs' the government instituted a major clampdown on seditious publication. The press was regulated by the Stationers' Company which had a monopoly on printing, and the government now sought to tighten up enforcement of the monopoly, and to ensure that what the company licensed was acceptable to the regime. The regulation was to be enforced in the courts of the Star Chamber or High Commission.[39] That same day the Star Chamber fined John Williams, Bishop of Lincoln, and suspended him from his living. It was the resolution of a complex set of disputes that had dragged out over a decade but behind which lay Williams's relatively open dislike for the ecclesiastical policies of Laud and the king. In Laud's words, the sentence was intended to have 'that fierce mastiv tyed up ... until [the king] finds means to secure him from doing more hurt to himself, the state and the church'. It was a notoriously political trial.[40]

Increased pressure was also being exerted on the opponents of Charles's fiscal policies. In February the judges had been asked to rule on the legality of Ship Money in response to marked reluctance to pay. It exploited the king's power to raise ships from coastal towns in times of imminent danger, commuting it into a payment raised from the whole country. Since it was simply up to the king to decide if there was such a danger or not, this seemed to many people to give the king an unlimited power to interfere with the property of his subjects. The Lilburnes were among those who resisted— John boasted that his father and his uncle George were the only two men in County Durham who had dared to oppose the king's will in the matter, and George was certainly prominent in resistance in the north-east in 1635. As we have seen, there was a connection for many people between respect for the law and the English Church, since one depended on the other, and George was also an opponent of Charles's religious policies. He may, though, have had more directly secular objections. He had prospered in the coal trade, initially as a merchant based in Sunderland, and then, during the 1620s and 1630s, by building up a stake in a number of collieries. This led him into direct competition with the Newcastle coal merchants, the Hostmen, and he was influential in the challenge to their monopoly of the region's coal trade during the 1630s. The Crown's support for the monopoly may have informed his dislike of prerogative rule. The judges' verdict in February had not been enough to bring an end to such grumbling. In the face of continued complaint, and refusals to pay, a test case was brought against John Hampden in August 1637, weeks after the prosecutions of the puritan martyrs and Bishop Williams, and the tightening of press controls.[41]

Finally, and most fatefully, a new prayer book was introduced in Scotland in July, a month later. It was the product of a long gestation, aiming to bring greater formal order to worship, and intended to bring Scottish and English practice closer together under the authority of their shared king. It proved instead to be the beginning of the unravelling of the king's authority. A riot greeted the attempt to use it for the first time, on 23 July at St Giles' Cathedral in Edinburgh. The Scottish Privy Council, perhaps misreading the situation, moved slowly, and as the agitation escalated they felt increasing pressure from the streets. As the situation worsened it was not just the prayer book but the future organization of the Scottish church that was at stake—momentum developed for a campaign to finally and conclusively exclude bishops from authority in the Scottish Church.

As events took a turn towards religious confrontation in Scotland, and closer restriction in England, Lilburne went to Holland. Quite why he went is not clear. Writing in 1645, after they had become enemies, Bastwick claimed that as Lilburne approached the end of his apprenticeship, he had lacked the means to set up in trade, and was hoping instead to make money by publishing some of Bastwick's writings. There was, it seems, good money to be had: Bastwick claimed that Lilburne had made £60 in a few days when the books were brought to London, and might have hoped to make £500 in time.[42] William Prynne, writing at the same time and by then also hostile to Lilburne, likewise claimed that this had been a commercial favour—Bastwick had freely given him the *Letany* to publish, and at the time this was the most valuable asset Lilburne possessed. Enemies were later to claim that he had only been interested in money, in fact. At the time Lilburne's father was embroiled in a long-running property dispute which was coming to a head, and so it is plausible that he could not at that point help him set up in business as a younger son might normally have hoped. Certainly Lilburne did not challenge the claim that he hoped to make a profit, even though he did dispute other claims from the same pages, saying a little more coyly that in Holland he 'was like to have settled my selfe in a Course of trading, that might have brought me in a pretty large portion of earthlie things'. Bastwick said that the whole idea was Wharton's, a man well known for his involvement in the world of illicit publishing.[43]

Perhaps, then, he was hoping to enter into the illegal print trade as an alternative to cloth wholesaling, and his trip to Holland was a commercial venture. This is somewhat at odds with, although does not contradict, a claim he made in 1649 that the bishops and their catchpoles had forced him to 'fly into the Low-Countreys for refuge, just about the time of his banishment' as a result of his friendship with Bastwick.[44]

Holland had become an attractive place of refuge for Protestants. In the course of the long revolt against Hapsburg rule the northern parts of the Low Countries emerged as an independent Protestant state, the United Provinces, with relatively weak central powers and toleration of a wide variety of religious belief and practice. Peace came in 1618 and with it increasing commercial prosperity, and there were close trading connections with England, not least through the cloth trades in which Lilburne had been apprenticed. There was also a well-established puritan connection with the radical churches in the Low Countries, particularly Amsterdam. Dutch presses could handle material that could not be printed elsewhere, and were difficult to regulate—even when pressure was successfully brought to bear on English-language printing in Amsterdam, for example, much of the work simply moved to Rotterdam and Delft. It was claimed that books were regularly smuggled into England by merchants of all kinds—easily concealed amid the cargoes and presumably of relatively high value in relation to their weight and the space they took up. There were English-speaking congregations in several Dutch towns and the great cloth company, the Merchant Adventurers, also supported a church. These churches were riven by a number of the disputes that fractured Protestantism across the whole of Europe, but for this very reason they were not reliably conformable to Laud and Charles's vision of Protestantism, and they were in a position to debate these issues more openly. As a result they were important for the broader development of Protestantism in the English-speaking world. Many of the key figures in them were Scottish, too, and the disputes with Charles's government in Scotland were also of great interest to these congregations: this too fed the presses.[45]

The English authorities clearly thought Lilburne was up to no good in Holland, and tried to bring some pressure to bear. He evidently felt he was now a marked man, claiming that while he was in the Low Countries the king's ambassador constantly tried to trick him on board a ship, so that he could be taken back to England, 'which forced me continually to wear my sword about me'.[46] We do know that the English Crown was trying to restrict publishing activity in the Low Countries, particularly in Amsterdam: the Star Chamber decree on printing had aimed at publishing 'beyond the Seas' as well as at home.[47]

Having been drawn into the puritan underground by his beliefs and connections, Lilburne seems to have gone to the Netherlands in the summer of

1637 as the Stuart Crown was trying to tighten its grip on religious practice and political dissent in England, Scotland, and overseas. It is not exactly clear what he was doing there: pursuing a career in publishing or fleeing persecution. It was probably both. Given these friendships and connections, however, it is easy to see how the authorities could believe that Lilburne was in the Netherlands to discuss the publication of subversive books; easy to see how he had become involved in the networks of John Wharton, formerly a near neighbour and a man well known to the authorities; in short, why he was the cause of such excitement to the pursuivants and their men as he walked into Soper Lane that December day. In any case, whatever had lain behind his flight to Holland, we know that the authorities were ready for him on his return. Three days after his dramatic arrest he was sent to the Fleet Prison, where he was to remain for nearly three years.

Trial and punishment, 1637-8

This first prosecution and punishment revealed Lilburne's extraordinary courage and sense of purpose. The Star Chamber decree of July 1637 set out punishments not just for those who actually printed subversive books, but anyone who imported, sold, or even bound them. Exemplary punishments were clearly envisaged: offenders should 'suffer such Correction, and severe punishment . . . as . . . shall be thought fit . . . for such their Offence and Contempt'.[48] Lilburne was in deep trouble but, as events would prove, he was undaunted.

On 14 January 1638, a month after his arrest, he was examined before Sir John Banks, the Attorney General. The examination began in a friendly tone: the two men sat side by side and Banks invited Lilburne to put his hat back on his head. Banks concentrated on what Lilburne knew about the publication and sale of English books in Amsterdam, in particular four books of Bastwick's: his *Letany*, his *Answer to Sir John Bancks*, his *Answer to Certaine Objections*, and the *Vanities and Impiety of the old Letany*. He was also asked about other 'factious books', including two by Prynne (*The Unbishoping of Timothy and Titus* and *A breviate of Bishops late proceedings*), and another book referred to as *Sixteen new queries*.[49] The Bastwick titles were all published by Willem Christiaensz in Leiden in 1637.[50] Those by Prynne were published in Amsterdam by Jan Fredericksz Stam. The *Sixteen new queries* was probably a pamphlet arguing against the taking of the *ex officio* oath, something which Lilburne was shortly to refuse to do. If this identification is correct, it was produced by the Richt Right Press in Amsterdam, which became Lilburne's first publisher the following year.[51] It is at least plausible that Lilburne was interested in the printing and circulation of these works.

Lilburne admitted that he had seen these works in the bookshops, but said that he did not know who had paid for their printing, or who had published them. Banks was also interested in Lilburne's dealings with 'Hargust', who Lilburne admitted to meeting twice in Amsterdam and also in Rotterdam. Under examination, though, he seems to have been careful in his choice of words: asked, for example, if he had asked Hargust to write a letter back to London he replied, slightly at a tangent, 'what he writ, I know no more than you'. Challenged by Lilburne that this was nothing to do with the accusations against him, Banks replied that they were; but Lilburne refused to discuss other people: 'What other men did, doth not belong to me to know or search into, sufficient it is for me to looke well to my owne occasions'.[52]

Despite this, questioning then turned to John Wharton and Edmund Chillenden (not to be confused with Chilliburne, the man who had led him to his arrest in Soper Lane). Chillenden was thought to have handled books arriving from Amsterdam, while Wharton was clearly suspected of being behind their import. Chillenden had been arrested in April and named in the Star Chamber as one of the people helping to distribute scandalous books by Bastwick and Prynne. At this point Lilburne became more resistant: 'why doe you aske me all these questions, these are nothing pertinent to my imprisonment, for I am not imprisoned for knowing and talking with such and such men: But for sending over *Bookes*'. He therefore refused to answer any more such questions, designed to 'insnare' him.[53]

This prompted Banks to reveal the detail of the accusations, made in fact by Chillenden: that Lilburne had printed 10,000 or 12,000 books in Holland, and that they were kept in Delft in a property belonging to Mr John Foote, where Lilburne had rented a room. Foote was an outspoken critic of the new Scottish Prayer Book, and sympathetic to the gathering campaign in Scotland against episcopal authority.[54] Lilburne was also accused of hoping to publish an earlier work by Bastwick, the *Unmasking of the mystery of iniquity*, if he had been able to find a true copy of it.[55] Lilburne would not believe that Chillenden had said this, asserting that if he had, it was all lies,[56] and while he did not deny receiving money from Wharton, he would not say if it was for books. Threatened with a return to prison, he was still more defiant in his refusal to answer questions: 'if I had thought you would have insisted on such impertinent [irrelevant] questions, I would not have given . . . so many answers'. Banks wrote out a statement that Lilburne had refused to answer questions and asked him to sign it; Lilburne took the pen and began to write 'the answer of me John Lilburne', but as soon as his name was on the paper Banks took it and sent the prisoner back to the Fleet prison.[57]

About ten or twelve days later he was brought before the Star Chamber where he was to be examined again. Quizzing the clerk about the process, he discovered that no bill (formal charge) would be presented against him until after his examination, which Lilburne interpreted as meaning 'they had no grounded matter against me . . . and therefore they went about to make me betray my owne innocency, that so they might ground the Bill upon my owne words'. John thanked God, who showed his goodness by preserving him from this snare, but his own strength of purpose was no little part of it: he refused to pay a fee to have his name entered as having appeared, and refused to swear to answer questions truthfully—since he did not know what he was going to be asked, he would be swearing to something in ignorance. He wanted legal counsel since he needed better advice, he said.[58]

This caught the attention of those present, since it was the first time that anyone had refused the Star Chamber oath. The use of the 'ex officio oath' was a well-established grievance with the Court of High Commission—a court established under Elizabeth I with jurisdiction in ecclesiastical affairs. Cases could be brought before the court by either a plaintiff or by court officials (procedures known technically as either ex officio promoto or ex officio mero), who presented an information against the accused. The defendant was then summoned to answer, being required to swear to do so truthfully—the ex officio oath. In effect, the accused had to swear before God to answer truthfully to accusations they had yet to hear. Lilburne later expressed his objection as a matter of fundamental legal right: 'this Oath is against the uery law of nature, for nature is alwaies a preserver of it selfe, and not a distroyer'. The right not to incriminate oneself, as later generations would know it, was a natural right, which had to be respected by human laws. Lawyers and religious radicals had in fact been hostile to the oath since the reign of James I, but despite this in 1637, the year in which policy seemed to tighten in so many respects, Charles I restated his commitment to the use of the oath not only in the High Commission but also in the Star Chamber and the Court of Requests and Chancery.[59]

These procedural questions became the subject of a verbal accusation laid against Lilburne by Banks in the Star Chamber the following Friday, where he appeared alongside John Wharton. Lilburne was now face-to-face with the most powerful figures in the land but was apparently unfazed. Chillenden's affidavit was read, which clearly accused both Lilburne and Wharton. Lilburne now claimed that he had answered the accusation in his first examination—that he had sent books out of Holland—and repeated that he would not answer questions about other things, and other men, under oath. Laud himself commanded Lilburne to take the oath but with no greater success than Banks. The earl of Dorset seems to have been infuriated: 'My Lords, this is one of their private spirits; Do you heare him, how he stands in his owne justification?' Laud was convinced that they had in front of them two key figures in the puritan underground: 'this fellow [Lilburne]...hath been one of the noto-riousest disperser of Libellous *bookes* that is in the Kingdome, and that is the father of them all (pointing to old Mr *Wharton*)'. In an exchange Lilburne would refer to again in future publications, he issued a direct challenge to the Archbishop:

Sir, I know you are not able to prove and make good which you have said. 'I have testimony of it' said he. Then said I produce them in the face of the open Court, that wee may see what they have to accuse me of; And I am ready here to answer for my selfe, and to make my just defence. With this he was silent, and said not one word more to me.

Lilburne revelled in this victory: 'I to your face did silence you in the presence of the open Court', causing Laud to sit down, red-faced and 'as it seemed to me, in a great chafe & rage'.[60]

Wharton also refused to swear the oath, and had written to Dr John Lambe in December saying that the *ex officio* oath was illegal, citing a number of authorities in his support.[61] Faced with this refusal the court considered charges on the precedent of Jesuits and Catholic seminary priests, who also refused to take oaths, but for Lilburne the comparison was fundamentally flawed: whereas those papists were traitors his position was 'neither against the glory of God, the honour of the King, the Lawes of the Land, nor the good of the commonwealth, but rather for the maintaining of the honour of them all'. He pursued this line of argument with remarkable consistency over the next twenty years, in each of his brushes with the law: by defending his rights he was serving the Commonwealth. In this context it made him a loyal subject of the king.

Pending their next appearance, Wharton and Lilburne were committed to prison for their contempt and held 'close prisoners', subject to greater than usual restrictions. At his final examination, at Grays Inn, no further progress was made. Lilburne drew a direct comparison with the High Commission oath and both he and Wharton continued to refuse to swear. As a result they were summoned to the Star Chamber at 7.00 a.m. the next morning. There, Chillenden's affidavit was read in detail. Lilburne denied all charges, again perhaps with carefully chosen words: he did not send the books over and had not knowingly seen the ship or anything belonging to it 'with my eyes'.[62] He denounced his accusers as perjured and false witnesses, and refused the oath once more, denouncing it and other oaths which were, he said, against the law of the land. As a result he and Wharton were censured: Lilburne to be whipped through the City and pilloried, Wharton (in view of his age) merely pilloried. Wharton then treated James Ingram, the warden of the Fleet Prison, to a lecture on the popishness of bishops, and the absence of any scriptural warrant for their authority.[63]

At this distance in time it is not clear whether or not Lilburne was guilty of the charges the government wanted him to answer. The books in which the authorities were interested were published in Leiden and Amsterdam, by Willem Christiaensz and Jan Fredericksz Stam, but Lilburne was asked about Rotterdam and Delft, and questions about his dealings in Amsterdam and Rotterdam concentrated on Hargust not Stam. In his denials of the details in the charges he would not have been perjuring himself about any other involvement he might have had. He was also asked if Wharton had put up the money for the publishing, which he denied, but we know that Christiaensz, who was married to an English woman, felt sufficiently strongly about English affairs to make his own translations: perhaps he financed his own work.[64] Lilburne did, though, have money from Wharton for a purpose which he did not reveal: it is of course quite possible that it was to pay for some other aspect of the publication or distribution of these books. Later, in the pillory, his statements were again ambiguous. At one point he appeared unequivocal: 'That *Mr Wharton* and I never joyned together in printing, either these or any other Bookes whatsoever. Neither did I receive any money from him, toward the printing any'. Printing, of course, was only one part of the enterprise. At other times he seems to stick closely to denying the detail of the accusation: 'I never in all my daies either printed, or caused to be printed, either for myself or *Mr. Wharton* any Bookes at *Rotterdam*. Neither did I come into any Printing house all the time I was in the Citty'.[65] Such apparently unambiguous statements do not mean that he had no involvement with the broader publishing enterprise undertaken in Leiden and Amsterdam by Christiaensz and Stam.

This account of these proceedings depends primarily on Lilburne's own retrospective testimony, which was intended for public consumption to promote his cause. It is possible, therefore, that he did not cut quite such an impressive figure, but there is no counter-testimony that he did not. We do certainly know that he did not take the oath, so never answered his accusers in court, preferring instead to stay in prison, which he did until the autumn of 1640.[66]

★   ★   ★

The day of his punishment seems to have gone as badly for the government as the mutilation of Burton, Bastwick, and Prynne had done the previous summer. On 18 April he and John Wharton were brought from the Fleet and it was only then that Lilburne was told he was to be whipped through the City. He was treated well by the porters at the Fleet, who told him they regretted his treatment and wished him strength in enduring it. The executioner, who was to whip him with a knotted chord, was also sympathetic: he was used, he said, to whipping rogues, but this was the first time he had been required to punish an honest man. He urged Lilburne to bear in mind that it would not last long. Stripped to the waist and tied at the 'Carts Arsse', Lilburne exclaimed, '*Wellcome be the Crosse of Christ*'. Friends (none of them named) greeted him and wished him courage at various points along the route: as he came out of the Fleet, all along the Strand, in an encounter at the middle of the Strand, passing through the gate into Westminster and along King's Street. This kindness contrasted with the cruelty of the Tipstaff overseeing the punishment, who refused him a hat as protection from the sun, and who ordered that the cart be driven slowly, to prolong his suffering in the heat.

Throughout, it was the strength given to him by God and by his faith that allowed Lilburne to endure these cruelties:

> I must confesse, if I had had no more but mine owne naturall strength, I had suncke under the burden of my punishment; for to the flesh the paine was uery grievous & heavie: But my God in whom I did trust was higher and stronger than my selfe, whoe strengthened and enabled mee not onely to undergoe the punishment with cherefulnes: but made me Triumph, & with a holy disdaine to insult over my torments.[67]

Lilburne was bearing his cross, and he cast his experience in ways that recalled Christ's journey to Calgary and his encounters along the way: this account is clearly shaped by standard martyrological stories in which Lilburne had become interested as an apprentice, and having witnessed the mutilation of Burton, Bastwick, and Prynne. But whatever exaggerations or poetic licence lie behind this crafting of the story, there is no doubting Lilburne's strength of purpose. The executioner clearly did his job: according to the later testimony of Thomas Smith, a merchant, Lilburne was whipped every two or three paces with a whip of two or three chords. He thought Lilburne was probably right to say that he had received 500 lashes. Mr Higs, the chirurgeon who dressed Lilburne's wounds, testified that they were among 'the miserablest that ever he did see: for the wheales on his back, made by his cruel whipping, were bigger then Tobacco-pipes'. Mary Dorman, another witness, thought that both his shoulders had swollen to the size of penny loaves and confirmed that throughout this ordeal the sun was 'shining very hot', as did Thomas Haws.[68]

At Westminster, Lilburne was taken to a tavern, where he withdrew from the crowd that had gathered there. It was here that his wounds were dressed, and he was brought a message that if he would submit to the Star Chamber he would be spared the pillory. He refused. Taking the pillory, he was once again refused a hat, while some of the Lords of Star Chamber, which was then in session nearby, craned from a window to get a view of him.

Now was his chance to speak and he took the opportunity to deny the charges against him, to denounce his betrayers, to justify his refusal of the Star Chamber oath, and then, guided by the power of the Lord, to declare his mind on other matters. He denounced the power of bishops, and said that Christians were obliged not to obey them. At one point a 'fat *lawier*' who he did not know interrupted him, commanding him to hold his peace, but Lilburne refused and continued in the same vein until the lawyer returned, this time with the warden of the Fleet: they gagged him. Thomas Haws later testified that the gagging had been done cruelly, 'as if he would have torne his jawes in peeces', and both he and Mary Dorman agreed that it had made Lilburne's mouth bleed. Gagging was not just a practical measure, but a humiliation from which a gentleman should have been immune: 'an unmanly and barbarous cruelty, to be exercised upon beasts'. In the meantime, though, Lilburne had taken copies of three of Bastwick's books from his pockets and passed them to the crowd. He later testified that they were the *Letany*, his *Answer to Sir John Bancks*, and his *Answer to Certaine Objections*:

three of the books Lilburne was accused of having helped into print in the Low Countries. Now, gagged and threatened with a further whipping if he spoke again, he stood for an hour and a half in the pillory. Unable to move or speak, he stamped his feet, the only gesture of resistance open to him. As he was taken down from the pillory, however, he declared, 'Vivat Rex. Let the King live for ever'.[69] He was then taken back to the tavern with Wharton, dressed, and returned to the Fleet. There he was again shown kindness by the porters and others who dealt with him.

There can be little doubt that this exemplary punishment had backfired, just as it had with the puritan martyrs. The same day the Star Chamber expressed outrage that while undergoing punishment he not only 'audaciously and wickedly' uttered 'sundry scandalous speeches', but also distributed copies of 'seditious bookes among the people that beheld the said execution'. After all, this latter offence was the 'very thing', with other offences, that had led to his censure. This outrage led to further punishment. Lilburne was not simply sent to prison, but it was ordered that he be 'laid alone, with yrons on his hands and legges, in the *Wards* of the *Fleet*, where the basest and meanest sort of Prisoners are used to be put; and that the *Warden* of the *Fleet* take especiall care to hinder resort of any persons whatsoever unto him'. In particular he should not be supplied with money, all letters, writings, or books brought to him should be delivered to the Star Chamber, and all those attending the prison to try to speak to him should be identified to the court.[70] This second order, about the conditions of his imprisonment, was later agreed to be a cruel abuse of power, exacerbating the injustice of the initial sentence. His extraordinary fortitude had another consequence, too. The court ordered that in future all those undergoing similar punishment should be searched and 'neither writing nor other thing suffered to be about them; and their hands likewise to be bound, during the time they are under punishment'.[71] So thoroughly had Lilburne undermined the spectacle of retribution that he had caused its directors to change the choreography.

His behaviour during his punishment reveals not just his extraordinary fortitude but also a gift for political theatre. There is no doubt that he had phenomenal reserves of strength, but there were perhaps two other factors at work in his self-presentation as a man alone before his persecutors: a reluctance to name others for their own protection; and a reading of the martyrological literature, which emphasized the centrality of personal suffering as testimony of the justice of the cause. Between the lines, however, we can see the importance of his network of friends, and not just in the support offered to him at key points along the way. For example, on his own account he had been stripped to the waist and whipped through the city, but in the pillory had books concealed about him. It seems likely then that in the tavern, when he sought solitude away from the crowds before going into the pillory, someone had brought him the books to distribute. His prosecutors were certainly interested in this detail.[72]

Key and recurrent features of his writings were already present: how he drew strength in the face of suffering from his faith and justness of his cause, and how his loyalty was to the laws of the land, not to any particular person. In the pillory he had spoken of the ungodliness of the bishops, and his later publications spared nothing in their criticism of Laud and his creatures, but he had only spoken about his religious beliefs *after* speaking about the actual cause of his imprisonment, which he claimed was wholly secular. He had been imprisoned for refusing to take an oath, something he said was contrary to the legal freedoms he enjoyed under the king. As he left the pillory he declared his loyalty to the king, and he was to claim that he was being a good subject in opposing the abuse of legal process. As it seemed to him later, 'all this contestation was but for maintaining my legall rights due to me by the Petition of Right'.[73] This self-presentation was to set him apart from all those of his contemporaries who suffered in the name of their religious faith, and it was to make his cause more comprehensible to subsequent generations too.

Prison writings, 1638–40

Prison in seventeenth-century England constrained the prisoner, but did not necessarily isolate him or her from the world. Prisons were privately run, and considerable sums changed hands for leases and annual rents. Inmates had to support themselves, paying fees and the costs of their food, while those working in the prisons often depended on tips and fees. Officers could be very willing to accept payment in return for permissions of various kinds and the profitability of the lease depended on these transactions. As a consequence, conditions varied between and within prisons—for example, in the grounds of the Fleet, where Lilburne was now sent, wardens had built dwellings for rent to the prisoners. If the inmates were up to date with their rent then the warden had no right to enter their dwellings without permission.

An elaborate schedule of rates survives from 1625, specifying what people would pay in fees, and what diet and accommodation they would get in return, according to their social standing (setting particular rates for earls or gentlemen, for example). Those able to make these financial arrangements could live in some comfort: there was a garden, for example, in which the prisoners could play bowls. By contrast the common wards of the Fleet were 500 years old, and there were at least eight prisoners to each ward, two in a bed. A report made to Parliament in 1621 revealed that men were packed so tight in the wards that they could not spit without spitting on someone else, and that the prisoners were in danger of being poisoned by the smell. One man they saw had no bed, but had slept with his head on a trunk, his body on a stool and his legs on a block. Some of them could not get their food for a week at a time and (quite shockingly for contemporaries) the inmates enduring these conditions included men of quality. In Newgate, another prison with which Lilburne was to become familiar, a five-storey building from the fifteenth century stood over dark cellars in which prisoners endured much worse conditions than those in other parts of the prison.[74]

To modern eyes this way of running prisons had some remarkable consequences. For example, in 1588, the year of the Armada, Catholics had been worshipping openly at the Tower. More generally, prisoners often had family or servants with them and there was movement of people in and out. In these circumstances people could write in prison and get published. By Lilburne's time this was a well-established genre, which allowed political prisoners the opportunity to make their case to a reading public.[75]

At first, however, Lilburne was kept in the wards of the Fleet, where he suffered isolation and considerable hardship, further punishment inflicted as revenge for his performance in the pillory. Examined in May about that performance, he refused to name those who had helped him, reaffirmed that he thought the bishops had their calling from the devil, and endorsed the record of the examination 'and this I will sealle with my dearest blood'. The signature included a little flourish (Fig. 1.4).[76] In December 1638, still denied visitors and running short of money, he petitioned for better conditions. The warden of the Fleet, however, would not forward the petition unless he recanted, something Lilburne naturally refused to do. Since he was not allowed to dispute his case he would not submit, even though 'J had rather (I professe vnto you) chuse to morrow to dy at Tyburne or Smithfield, than to bee still induring my Constant Extraordinarie bodily paines and

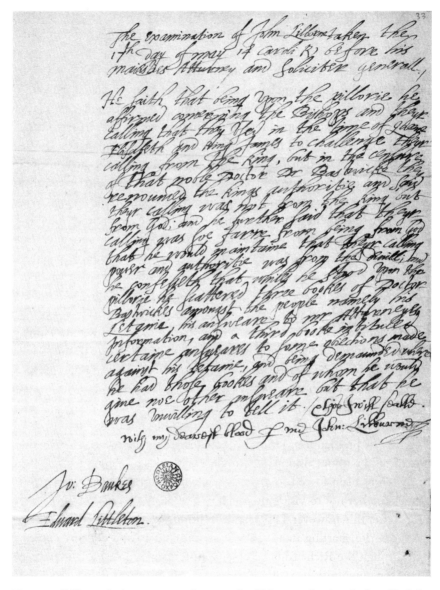

Fig. 1.4. Lilburne's signature on the record of his examination before Sir John Banks and Sir Edward Littleton, 1638

torments'. He was not allowed to take the air more than one hour a day, wearing the same stockings and boots for days on end and held constantly in irons. A doctor had warned him that the coldness of the irons was a threat to his health, but he had been refused bigger ones, having instead to try to wrap them in cloth to avoid this danger. All this for a 'faithfull subject to the

King [who] neuer broke any of his lawes'. Independent testimony was later given to support these claims, presented to the House of Lords by John Bradshaw, the eminent parliamentarian lawyer.[77]

He was also denied the support of his family. Richard, his father, was still embroiled in the land dispute relating to the family home at Thickley Punchardon. His opponent, Ralph Claxton, had petitioned the Privy Council in 1630 seeking settlement of the dispute, which had origins a century earlier and which had been actively contested since the 1590s. In the course of the dispute Richard's house had been occupied and, later, burned down, and important records had been destroyed. As a result he felt that legal trial of the title was impossible for him to win, and in November 1636 he sued for a settlement by trial by battle, engaging a champion for the purpose. He seems to have arrived at Durham assizes more than once with his champion, and the rules of engagement have been preserved. The embarrassed judges, urged in part by the king, found reasons for postponement while seeking a way of stopping it altogether, something they found difficult since the plea had been entered in a legal form. No one, of course, wanted property disputes settled this way, including the king, who now found himself involved in an obscure provincial land dispute. In late 1638 the Privy Council, the king, and judges were actively considering how to prevent the trial by battle and John claimed that the case was being vindictively influenced by Laud, also a member of the Privy Council. It may have been these problems that prevented Richard from helping his son set up in trade. Now, following his prosecution, John said that his father could not show sympathy for him without risking the outcome of these land disputes. His father had therefore been forced to avoid contact with him and had warned his younger brother not to visit either.[78]

Soon after this, however, Lilburne's conditions seem to have eased, and he began to write. Starting in 1639 he published as part of a concerted campaign through the Richt Right Press in Amsterdam, which took advantage of the deepening crisis in Scotland. The story of the injustice visited on him was used to indict the tyranny of the regime that was being challenged in Scotland and, increasingly, undermined in England: his sufferings were the vehicle for an ongoing and increasingly public campaign.

Scotland's rebellion had escalated dramatically between the riots in July 1637 and the time of Lilburne's punishment, the cause extending rapidly beyond the new Prayer Book to the constitution of the Scottish Church, and in particular the need to finally rid Scotland of the power of the bishops. A national body, the Tables, had been established to promote a National

Covenant, binding the people and the king together to preserve the Scottish Church and the king's 'person and estate'. The Tables, though, appeared to claim that it was they who knew the correct form of the church, basing their view on historical agreements about its constitution. This and the order in which the Covenant set out the obligations (as well as the Covenanters' actual behaviour) gave at least a very strong hint that their primary loyalty was to a particular constitution of the Scottish Church, and to the king only in so far as he supported that. The Covenanters of course claimed there was no problem, because true worship and royal authority were so closely connected that 'they had the same friends and common enemies, and did stand and fall together', but the implication was not lost on Charles. He wrote to the Marquis of Hamilton that so long as this Covenant was in force he had no more authority in Scotland than the Doge had in Venice.[79] He felt he had no choice but to face down this rebellion.

This issue, of the relationship between religious and political authority, was no less a problem in England: it was a key reason for the clampdown on the puritan underground, after all. Lilburne's first prison pamphlet, *A light for the ignorant*, stands out among his writings for its tone: carefully and almost academically argued. In it he claimed, like the Covenanters, that he was a loyal subject, but he made his case quite differently, arguing for a radical separation of religious and secular authority. He drew a distinction between the ecclesiastical state, governed by scripture, and the civil state, established after the time of Christ and governed by its own laws, books, and charters. In the time of the apostles there had been no Christian kings, only human laws distinguished by Paul as the ordinances of men, distinct from the divine law. Secular laws and traditions were therefore to be respected in the civil state, since they had emerged after Christ to regulate what was Caesar's. Obedience to these laws was a Christian duty.[80] He was, on his own account, a loyal subject, willing to submit to the legal order of the civil state.

The ecclesiastical state, by contrast, was established by Christ and the apostles, and should be governed by scripture. In ecclesiastical matters human laws, or national traditions and charters, were an intrusion, the result of the machinations of the false ecclesiastical state: that 'smoaky pollitique State of the Crowned Locusts or Roman Clergy' governed not by scripture, but by its own distinct books, canons, and so on, in place of scripture.[81] The problem Lilburne (and all Englishmen) faced was that the false ecclesiastical state had established dominion in England. This corrupted the church, of course, but these crowned locusts were also preserving themselves by corrupting the civil state: only by denying people their rights could they hold on to power. Lilburne claimed his troubles were civil—about his rights as an Englishman—and that these rights were jeopardized by men busy corrupting the ecclesiastical state.

For Lilburne, then, his cause was a secular one. In a sense this position mirrored the official position, that religious critics were prosecuted for civil offences not for their religious beliefs—a claim common since the Elizabethan period and the prosecution of Catholics for civil offences, such as treason.[82] Inverting this claim, Lilburne was able to say that by refusing to swear an illegal oath, urged on him by Laud and his cronies, he was defending Englishmen from the corruption spread by the false ecclesiastical state. In the *Poore man's cry* he said the bishops who had prosecuted Bastwick were effectively guilty of treason—an offence against secular government. In later years he was to argue that opposing illegal government was a Christian obligation, but in these early pamphlets he does not seem to have gone quite so far. There are many assertions that he was willing to obey earthly powers so long as they were acting lawfully, but he does not seem to have argued directly that God required him to oppose civil tyranny.[83] Of his prosecution he said quite plainly that 'if I had beene proceeded against by a Bill, J would haue answered & justified all that they coulde have proved against me';[84] but he would not swear an oath to incriminate himself. When he threw Bastwick's books to the crowd at his feet before the pillory, he challenged them to 'see if you finde any thing in them, against the Law of God, the Law of the Land, the glory of God, the honour of the King or state'.[85]

His quarrel then was not with the king but with the false ecclesiastical state. By arguing this way he avoided the implication of the Covenanter position that the king's authority was conditional on keeping a bargain with his people, but in another sense, of course, this was also a profoundly subversive argument about the church. His distinction between the civil and ecclesiastical states could easily imply that the king had no role at all in religious matters—'These divine things are due to Christ Iesus, and to him, & to him onely belongs this visible worship'.[86]

There was a further very radical implication, therefore: he denied the validity of national churches altogether. According to Lilburne, Christ had left his power 'in the bodies of his particular (not Nationall) Churches': Christians should gather, as the Apostles had, and find the authority to minister from within that body, not derive it from a national church.[87] Since the sixteenth-century Reformation, Christians had been faced with increasingly religious pluralism, and to any particular Christian some of this practice was bound to appear wrong-headed. They confronted the fact of religious error, therefore, but also the difficulty of finding grounds to define what was and what was not acceptable, since it was impossible truly to know God's mind. In dealing with this problem, contemporaries drew a distinction between the invisible church of all true believers (known to God) and the visible churches in this world. This gave some licence to variety, but still left a problem of knowing which visible churches were corrupt and a danger to the souls of those attending them and to the society around them. It was still important to know which of these visible churches were 'true' churches, in which the Word of God could be heard.

Lilburne took a very permissive view of this: 'every true visible Church of Christ are a company of people, called and separated out of the world . . . By the word of God ioyned . . . together in fellowship of the Gospell . . . by voluntery profession of fayth and obedience of Christ'.[88] In other words, he argued for voluntary religion, and full congregational independence: church practice and belief was a matter for the congregation and God, not for any national authority. Lilburne said that he had not been a separatist prior to his imprisonment, but he now committed to that position.[89] This was a highly controversial stance, and one which Bastwick and Prynne, for example, were strenuously opposed to. It was plainly quite dangerous territory—suppose groups came together in such voluntary professions of faith but were in fact deeply misled? Heresy, blasphemy, and lost souls were dangers that led many contemporaries to think there should be some form of discipline over the regulation of visible churches. Had the Reformation not started, in fact, in the attempt to free Christians from a corrupt visible church? Might not congregational independence threaten authentic religious practice as much as popery had?

In arguing as he did, Lilburne was going much further on these issues than many of his friends in the puritan underground. On the separation of the civil and ecclesiastical states he made arguments like those made by Bastwick and Prynne in the pamphlets he had been accused of helping to get printed.[90] On this issue of religious independency, however, he was later to be divided from them. He seemed in fact to want not just to overturn the power of bishops within the Church of England, but to be able to separate from it. In 1638, intervening in an argument about the legitimacy of the churches in New England, Lilburne had argued they did not derive from the Church of

England, since it was not a true church. This may not have been published at the time, but when it was published in 1645 it enraged Prynne—who wanted to reform rather than dismantle the Church of England.[91]

Despite the shared hostility to Charles's church, it was also an argument quite distinct from that of the Covenanters: the National Covenant took it for granted that theirs was a national church, governed in part by tradition, national laws, and charters. For the moment, however, they were united by their hostility to the bishops: the epistle to the reader in *A light for the ignorant* noted approvingly that 'many of Gods deare Servants both haue and still doe, refuse to yield any Reuerance, Honour, Service, &c. vnto *Archbishops, Bishops*: and their dependent Offices'.[92]

Such prison writing drew on well-established networks in the puritan underground. *A light for the ignorant* was published in Amsterdam, through the Richt Right press, run by John Canne, a veteran of that world. He had been a member of an independent church in London but by 1632 he was in Amsterdam, working as a printer. During the 1630s he had himself published in favour of total separation of like-minded Christians from the national church, and had argued that Christians had a duty not to hear the preaching of ministers who had been ordained by bishops. In 1638 he was fined 300 guilders by the Amsterdam authorities for printing material disliked by the English government, part of the broader campaign to restrict hostile print in Holland. His press, though, remained active in promoting opposition to the Laudian Church and publicizing the Covenanters' campaign, and Lilburne's plight was a key part of that.[93]

As the Scottish crisis escalated in 1638–9, the Richt Right press published not only *A light for the ignorant*, but also *The beast is wounded. Or Information from Scotland concerning their reformation*, which included observations by Bastwick's younger brother.[94] A second Lilburne pamphlet from the same press, *A Worke of the Beast*, also claimed to be 'printed in the yeare the Beast was Wounded', and spoke to the same political context. It recounted his trial and punishment in detail, not to explain his religious beliefs but to demonstrate the tyranny of the bishops: it was they who had 'so cruellie and butcherlie dealt with' the puritan martyrs. It was this false church that misled the king: 'For in their Sermons that they preach before his Majestie: how doe they incense the King & nobles against the people of God... though they be the most harmelesse generation of all others'. There was hope, however: 'Their end and ruine is at hand'.[95]

The *Poore man's cry*, again published in 1639, contained marginal comments by 'a backe friend of the English Popish Prelates' which directly
linked the tyranny exercised on Lilburne to the grievances of the Scots. For
example, alongside Lilburne's claim that he would rather die than endure
the treatment he experienced in prison ran the comment: 'It is no marvaille
that the Scotsmen will haue no Bishops among them. Considering that it is
better, that a man were put to the cruel'st death that could be devised, then
to be under their hands'.[96] The pamphlet refers to both *The beast is wounded*
and *A light for the ignorant*: it was an integral part of the broader campaign
being conducted by the Richt Right press. It made Lilburne's suffering
emblematic of this wider problem, of episcopal authority in both England
and Scotland: it was not simply a cry of pain at a point where Lilburne's
treatment had become unsupportable.

This publication campaign seems also to have been quite large in scale.
Writing in 1640, Lilburne claimed to have been out of pocket and unable
to support himself partly because of the disruption of his printing activities:
the government had seized 2,000 of his books, depriving him of his livelihood. He was able to bear the loss of his books with a laugh when he discovered that the archbishop's servants had cheated their master, and sent
most of the confiscated books to Scotland 'for filthy lucres sake'. There they
were 'sold as publique as *Martin Parker* (the Bishops champion ballad maker)
Ballads are sould here at *London*'.[97]

At times during 1639, Lilburne had clearly been kept in conditions that
allowed him to write and to publish. At other times, however, he was
returned to the harsh conditions of his initial imprisonment. Katherine
Hadley later testified that she had been Lilburne's servant while he was
again being kept a close prisoner during 1639, tending and watching him
'in his extreordenary sicknes occasioned by his two severall tymes longe
l[y]inge in Irones, w[i]th divers other great cruelties'. At the time, she said he
was experiencing 'extremytie of payne in his head & braynes'. His physician
had prescribed a medicine to be applied fresh once a day, hoping to alleviate
his great distress, but also to prevent 'the losse of his senses w[hi]ch his
Physitian with others were afrayde of'. Such was the inhumanity of his
keeper, however, that on 19 May 1639 she was denied access to dress his head
or do other services. Lilburne was so weak at the time that he could not
help himself or walk alone, and Robert Ellis, another prisoner, led him
by the arm, but Hadley was kept from him by force. He was threatened with
a dungeon isolated from his servant, diet, and linen where he would be

clapped head and heels together in irons and 'to hamper him as he was never soe hampered since he came to the Fleet'.[98]

Remarkably, despite these conditions, Lilburne was able to agitate directly on London's streets, using his treatment to indict the regime. Hadley was accused of helping him in this. In the early summer of 1639 Lilburne wrote a letter in two sheets, one addressed to the magistrates of London, and the other to the apprentices. The latter 'was thrown among them one day when they were at their recreations in *Moor-fields*, which had like to have occasioned the Bishop of *Canterburies* ruine'. Laud in fact received copies of both. A later printed version of the letter to the apprentices sets out his sufferings, his vulnerability in the absence of family and friends to support him in prison, claiming that he feared a plan to kill him, and also his desire to enjoy the benefit of a proper legal hearing and incarceration in safe conditions.[99] The king was told by a senior councillor that the papers had incited the apprentices to attack Laud's house and to be revenged on the Lord Keeper, 'who had shewed himself an unjust Judge in that sentence against Lillborne in Starchamber'. Lilburne later claimed that '*many thousands of [apprentices] were got together with an intention to go to* Lambeth', and apprentices did indeed attack Laud's palace there the following May, prompted to it by similar means.[100]

In the face of the 'transcendent dangerousness' of this mobilization, 'which might have set the whole City and Kingdom in a flame', the mayor imprisoned Hadley. She too complained of arbitrary and cruel treatment: in prison for three days and three nights by authority only of a verbal command of the mayor, she applied to the Privy Council to be given a hearing or set free. Instead, she was transferred without hearing to Bridewell, where she remained until December 1640. The matron there treated her 'hardly and churlishly', perhaps encouraged by Lilburne's adversaries, so that she had endured cruel treatment even despite the fact that she had 'honestly & uprightly behaved herselfe & w[i]th her fingers [had] truly laboured to earne the bread she eates being not chargable in the least to the house'. The matron had turned her out of her lodging and put her instead 'amongst the com[m]on slutts and whores, whose societye is a heall upon earth to one that feares the Lord', forcing her to pay a shilling a week for the privilege. When Parliament finally met, Hadley petitioned the House of Lords for reparations for false imprisonment, with the support of Lord Brooke and Lord Robarts, who cited the Petition of Right in her favour. She was released immediately.[101] Lilburne's campaign clearly rested on the support and sufferings of a wider circle, for all the martyrological emphasis of his self-presentation.

Periods of better treatment in prison allowed Lilburne to use the press, publicizing his sufferings to illustrate the tyranny of bishops. He was also able to use it to campaign to improve his own treatment. He threatened his captors that if conditions did not get better then 'J shall be forced to proc-lame abroad & make the Kingdome ring with [the warden's] and Prela[te]s cruelty towards mee'. Although few would be at his death 'yet you knowe not what great troupes may com to my burial'. He made good on the threat, since our copy of this is in print. In the meantime he called on the people to work peaceably for his petition for better treatment to be heard, despite the machinations of the warden and archbishop in preventing that. He urged his supporters 'that some of you would dailie come to my pittifull Purgatorie & inquire how 'tis with me' to act as a restraint on his persecu-tors.[102] Such was the force of his reputation in fact that when there was a fire near where he was being kept, it 'gave the jealousy that he being desperate had set the prison on fire'. Thereupon the people living near the prison, and the other prisoners, 'all cryed, *Release* Lilburne, *or we shall all be burnt*, and…made the *Warden* remove him…[to] a place where he had some more Air'.[103] He also enjoyed the support of Sir Richard Gravenner (Grosvenor), also at the time in the Fleet. A substantial Cheshire gentleman with puritan sympathies who had sat in the parliaments of the 1620s, he wrote to the warden on Lilburne's behalf.[104]

Lilburne's political education seems to have continued in prison, therefore, having started with Bastwick in the Gatehouse. In those early years he stud-ied the martyrological literature, and the reformed theological tradition: in the *Poore man's cry* he claimed that nothing in Foxe's *Book of martyrs* com-pared with his own treatment and that even the notorious Bishop Bonner had allowed prisoners to have visitors, and had entered into disputations with them.[105] Now, in the Fleet, he was in conversation with Sir Richard Grosvenor, a man of affairs, and appealing directly to a London audience while becom-ing active as a politically engaged author, commenting in his own name on current policy in church and state. His first publications had used his own circumstances to illustrate what was wrong in the kingdom, and he was clearly aware of the power of publicity to secure change. He was able to mobilize opinion on London's streets too, causing anxiety to those in power.

By late 1639 the prospects for men of Lilburne's beliefs had improved still further. The First Bishop's War, fought against the Covenanters, failed disastrously but, worse still, Charles had raised, equipped, and fed his army without calling a Parliament. This had avoided public dispute with his Parliament, but had stoked up grievances against the regime: the campaign had depended on conscription, forced service from the militia, as well as the imposition of free quarter and billeting. Considerable political friction was generated in the service of a military failure.

In an increasingly helpful atmosphere, Lilburne spoke more boldly. The title page of *Come out of her my people* proclaimed that this was 'the yeare of hope, of ENGLANDS purgation & the Prelates dissolution'. It gave a full account of what he had said, and what he would have liked to have said, from the pillory. Lilburne challenged his persecutors to dispute with him at St Paul's Cross about the nature of the true church, and he detailed all the times his persecutors had ducked the argument. He promised in fact to wager his life on an open argument: 'letting the word of God be the sole Judge of the controversie' and promised to 'preach a Recanting Sermon in every Citty in the Kingdome' if he lost.[106] A clear sign of the changing times was that for the first time a Lilburne pamphlet was produced which did not carry the Richt Right imprint: this may have come from a London press.

Things got no better for Charles I the following year, and as his regime in England unravelled, John Lilburne was able to speak increasingly freely. A Parliament was called in the early summer of 1640 which failed to provide military and financial support for a renewed military campaign against the Covenanters, and instead rehearsed grievances about Charles's government in England, particularly about the trend of religious policy and threats to legal process. Charles and his close advisers suspected the Parliament had been subverted by powerful men of puritan sympathies—notably the earl of Warwick, and Lords Brooke and Saye, all of whom were subject to searches in May 1640. Saye's son, Nathaniel Fiennes, was also implicated, and John Pym, soon to be a leading figure in parliamentary opposition in the Long Parliament, was close to the top of the list too. The cumulative evidence of sympathy for the Scots among sections of the English political elite is clear.[107] Parliament was quickly dissolved, Charles perhaps feeling that he had managed to avert a plot to subvert the military campaign,[108] and another army was set on foot. This time, however, the military defeat was total. It was said that many English soldiers sympathized with the Covenanter's cause, and there is evidence of popular hostility to Charles's campaign too.[109]

A number of Lilburne's acquaintances were certainly among those English sympathizers. His master had connections close to Saye and Brooke, for example. Other connections were more direct. Early in 1639, Daniel Butler, Hewson's son-in-law, had been imprisoned for importing Scottish books, an intercepted letter revealing that he had tried to bring in a copy of a Prayer Book. His defence has a ring of Lilburne about it, in fact. He claimed that he had got himself a copy for his own use while in Scotland and brought it home with him. When his father-in-law, Thomas Hewson, had seen it he had been so taken by the print that he wanted a copy of his own. The regime was sufficiently jumpy to have ordered a search of Butler's house in February.[110] As the crisis deepened, one of George Lilburne's servants had challenged a soldier in a tavern in Sunderland, saying that soldiers did nothing but drink and swear, and that no honest man 'would take up arms against those in Scotland'. George defended his man, and was referred to by Thomas Triplett as one of the 'most arrant Covenanters and Boutefeus [incendiaries] that are in these parts'. Triplett also complained that the prominent local officehold-ers had failed to act on information about these seditious words, and they had to answer questions about their treatment of this offence along with George.[111] Later in the year Triplett claimed that George, who had previ-ously refused to pay Ship Money, was now refusing to pay the Coat and Conduct money (a rate imposed to support the king's campaign in the second Bishop's War) and was encouraging others to resist as well. George, he told Laud, 'sure is a Covenanter, if we could discover him'.[112] In some eyes, of course, to consort with a foreign enemy in this way was treasonous, and Lilburne was not immune from the charge. One night during his close imprisonment he was moved to some meditations *after the reading of a pamphlet sung in the streets of London, in which I was joyned as a* Traytour *with the* Scots *at their first comeing into England*'.[113]

The military campaign in 1640 ended in complete military defeat, after which the Covenanters occupied Newcastle, more or less unopposed. Charles was forced to agree to a humiliating ceasefire in the Treaty of Ripon, and had to call an English Parliament from a position of great political weakness. Not the least of his problems was the need to find money to pay the £850 per day promised to support the Covenanter army while it occupied the north of England. For Lilburne and his friends this was by no means a dis-aster; in fact, the defeat of their king at the hands of the Scots was good news. This was surely a position in which few Englishmen had found them-selves before. On 24 September, Charles summoned his Great Council at York and announced his intention to call a Parliament.

A little over a week later, Lilburne moved more aggressively against his tormentors. In *A coppy of a letter*, written on 4 October, he promised them vengeance in the new Parliament, linking their cruelty with the corruption of the tyrannous regime it served, retailing stories that are hard to credit: that the Wardens had him set upon and assaulted, by large groups of men, and refused to treat his wounds, and had been indifferent to the dreadful effects of his close confinement. Those who helped him, such as an honest gentleman who had given him three bottles of water, were themselves in danger: 'how can a Man live when all resort of persons shall bee kept from him, and that necessary subsistence from his Friends, and yet his enemies will not allow him a bit of bread, or a drop of drinke'.[114]

The publication, and the threat it carried, reflected Lilburne's confidence that he had effective connections in the City and the international print trade:

> therfore know...that if there be but a Printing-house in any of the Cities in the Provinces of Holland, I will cause this Letter to be printed that so (if it be possible) it may be claimed up upon the Posts,...so you may (if you will) read it in the Streets, as you goe to the Parliament House.

This seems to have been part of a battle for opinion on the streets: Lilburne claimed he could have the same impact as a pamphlet called *The Coblers Sermon* had apparently had for his opponents. Like many others, Lilburne thought that the new Parliament would bring him justice: 'therfore know, that the more cruelty you exercise upon me, the more notches you set upon the tally, to make the Bill of my complaint in Parliament the larger against you'. And this growing potential for public redress was associated with language about Laud that would have been extremely dangerous only a few years earlier: 'the King, and head of the blacke Regiment of Locusts in this Kingdome'.[115]

Charles had seen in the Covenanter campaign the threat that he might be reduced to the status of a Doge of Venice. By 1640 a well-connected group of English aristocrats seem to have been trying to use this crisis to achieve exactly that. Saye, Brooke, and others had certainly been in correspondence with the Covenanters, and were in the forthcoming Parliament to attempt to use Charles's weakness to impose limits on his power.[116] Through Hewson, Lilburne can be placed at the fringes of these networks: not just Brooke and Saye, but also Daniel Butler, who had been a member of the Artillery Company, one of the civic bodies that connected aristocratic opponents of the regime; and George Willingham, who by 1641 was in correspondence with Burton, Bastwick, and Prynne, and with Oliver Cromwell, to whom he wrote about Scottish affairs.[117]

Lilburne had undergone persecution for a cause that was soon to be championed in Parliament. His case had been the focus of a targeted print campaign against the bishops, coordinated initially from Amsterdam via the Richt Right press. He did not name those who helped him, for obvious reasons, and that compounds an impression that he was a simple man caught up in the arms of a tyrannous regime, an impression he no doubt wanted to cultivate. The truth is clearly more complicated, but by late 1640 the provincial younger son, grammar school-educated but no more, who Bastwick later claimed had required schooling in his speech and manners, had through his convictions and his connections acquired a degree of public fame (or notoriety). He now clearly understood the power delivered by print, publicity, and parliaments: they offered the possibility of overthrowing the tyranny of gaolers and prelates. The Star Chamber had changed the rules of its punishments in the light of his bravery, and from prison he had been able to exert some political influence, even managing to agitate directly among the apprentices to the evident alarm of the government. His release was made parliamentary business early in the next session. By that time his punishment, imprisonment, and publication, as well as his agitation among the apprentices, all supported by his connections in a puritan underground with contacts in Scotland and which reached across the north sea to Holland, had already made him something of a public figure. His apprenticeship did not lead to a career in the cloth trade, but had established the basis for a lifetime of shrewd political activism.

2

Soldier, 1640–5

Choosing sides, 1640–2

The meeting of the new Parliament, which could not easily be dissolved, encouraged extravagant hopes for reform, and not just of religion. One informed observer reckoned that Parliament very quickly set up more than forty committees to handle the flow of complaints.[1] The House of Lords, meanwhile, was rejuvenated as a court of appeal, and reports of all sorts of injustice flooded in: during the 1620s, on a rising trend, a total of 207 petitions for redress had been sent up to the Lords. This now became a flood: 400 were received in the first six months of the new Parliament alone. Many of them related to misconduct by officials and courts, illegality in the collection of non-parliamentary revenues, or the prosecution of religious nonconformity.[2]

There was a very public element to all this. These committees heard complaints from comparatively humble people, while outside Parliament petitions were drawn up and circulated in the counties, some of them gathering tens of thousands of signatures, before being brought to London for theatrical presentation by crowds of supporters. From the start of proceedings it was common to canvass support outside Parliament in order to influence the business within, something made increasingly easy and effective by the total breakdown of pre-publication censorship. The monopoly of the Stationers' Company, so central to the licensing system, began to totter amid a much more general attack on monopolies. The courts of the Star Chamber and High Commission, both widely associated with unpopular aspects of Charles's government, were under acute political pressure from 1640 onwards and were in fact abolished the following summer. The Stationers' Company was therefore left for a while toothless in enforcing its monopoly, which was in any case under threat. In the absence of effective control there was a huge increase in the number of titles coming from the presses, the result of a rapid shift towards the production of short, cheap pamphlets dealing with current affairs. Resort to the Dutch presses became unnecessary.

Over the next year, however, as grievances were settled, new anxieties emerged. It began to seem that in opposing particular policies activists were going beyond reform, and in fact were themselves bending the constitution, indulging in a dangerous populism and entertaining, for example, religious radicalism rather than simply rolling back the Laudian reforms. The openness of politics to obscure and humble people reinforced this sense that the cure might be worse than the disease—the complaints to committees, petitions, and crowds, and the flood of cheap print, could seem a real threat to political decency. To some people, even erstwhile critics of Charles I, parliamentary reform, in its substance and the means by which it was being pursued, seemed to be running out of control. Unprecedented political measures prompted increasing polarization and forced people to make difficult choices, and ultimately to choose between two armed camps. Lilburne's path, however, took him unhesitatingly into the parliamentary army.

★ ★ ★

One symptom of the early mood of exuberant reform was the liberation of the victims of the 1630s. Very soon after it opened, Parliament voted to bring Burton, Bastwick, and Prynne back from exile. Following their mutilation they had been sent to prisons off the mainland—Prynne to Jersey, Bastwick to the Isles of Scilly, and Burton to Guernsey—but they were now released and entered London in triumph. Their return was managed in order to demonstrate a political point. Prynne and Burton arrived together, having been met several miles from town by 'multitudes of people of several conditions, some on horseback, others on foot'. Arriving at Charing Cross at about 2.00 p.m., they were carried into the city by more than 10,000 people, 'the common people strewing flowers and herbs in the ways as they passed, making great noise and expressions of joy for their deliverance and return, and in those acclamations mingling loud and virulent exclamations against the bishops'. Bastwick, returning separately five or six days later, was greeted with similar rapture.[3]

Writing much later, the earl of Clarendon thought these scenes revealed the dark potential of populism and religious radicalism on London's streets: 'this insurrection (for it was no better) and phrensy of the people was an effect of great industry and policy, to try and publish the temper of the people'. It was soon followed, he said, by much greater licence in 'preaching and printing...to that degree that all pulpits were freely delivered to the schismatical and silenced preachers, who till then had lurked in corners or lived in New England; and the presses [were] at liberty for the publishing the most invective, seditious and scurrilous pamphlets that their wit and malice could invent'.[4] But it was not only puritans who made populist appeals or who exploited the transformation of the print business: pamphlets were soon in circulation ridiculing radical religion, or seeking to scare respectable opinion with lurid tales of sectarian excess. Over the next two years, increasingly public invective served to polarize opinion.

In the short term, however, hopes were high. Lilburne was another bene-ficiary of the general mood of reform. On 9 November, only six days into the session, Oliver Cromwell, in his first recorded speech in Parliament, spoke in support of a petition from Lilburne about his sufferings. Lilburne and others were released so that they could present their cases to Parliament, and he left the Fleet on 13 November, two weeks before the puritan mar-tyrs' triumphal re-entry into London.[5] The broader progress of reform was slow, however—the flow of business overwhelmed Parliament's cap-acity to deal with it, while a settlement on who should govern with the king and the negotiation of a permanent peace with the Scots proved tricky. A triennial Act passed in February obliged the king to summon a Parliament every three years, securing the future of parliamentary govern-ment, but the evidence was that Parliament would not easily settle all these political problems.[6]

In the meantime, Lilburne was establishing himself as an independent man. He became a freeman of the Company of Clothworkers in 1641, although he never seems to have pursued that trade. As we have seen, at the time of his first arrest he may have been interested in making a living from print because he lacked the capital to enter the cloth trade, his interest in Bastwick's work being a means to more than one end.[7] If that had been his plan, imprisonment had put paid to it. His father's lawsuit had been endan-gered by John's agitation, and as a result John did not 'aske him for any por-tion, neither did I in all my life receive 6. d. of him'. This left him with no capital with which to establish himself, though he did have some hopes of reparations for his sufferings at the hands of the Star Chamber. In the mean-time, with the help of significant financial investment from his uncle George, he set up as a brewer. George was himself said to have included brewing in what was by then a portfolio career, and in addition to the £1,000 investment

he may have provided important trade contacts, since John later said that
much of his business was with the north-east. Brewing also required access
to coal, a trade in which his uncle had an increasingly significant interest, and
it is clear from later comments that John sometimes had significant capital
tied up in coal.[8]

He also made what seems to have been a good marriage to Elizabeth
Dewell, daughter of Henry Dewell, a merchant, about whom little is
known.[9] Lilburne had evidently fallen for Elizabeth during his imprisonment, a time in which she had shown him some kindness. Their connection
probably came therefore from the puritan underground, the network of
fellow travellers from which Lilburne drew support during his imprisonment. He later wrote that he had had an eye on her for some time, that
she was 'an object so deare in my affections, severall yeares before from
me she knew any thing of it'. As she was to demonstrate in the coming
years, she was clearly a strong person capable of independent thought and
action, and was among twenty-nine people arrested for attending John
Spilsbury's conventicle in Ratcliffe in the autumn of 1641. She hardly figures,
though, in John's numerous accounts of himself, or the associated records,
although she was to play a crucial role at a number of critical junctures. In
a rare glimpse of their relationship, Lilburne later recalled the dotage of
those first years of marriage and expressed his debt to her 'who now for
about 12. years, hath many times with a good proportion of strength & resolution, gon through so many miseries with me'.[10] For much of the time,
though, she is beyond the historian's reach, as now, when she is recorded
simply as the wife of John Lilburne of Stepney, brewer.

★   ★   ★

The desire to see justice for the victims of the 1630s had been accompanied
by a purge of the regime's leading figures. Early and bitter speeches attacking
the policies of the previous decade had been a prelude to the impeachment
of the earl of Strafford (one of the king's key advisers) for high treason, in
fact on the same day that Lilburne's petition for release from prison had
been heard. By December the same charge had been brought against Laud.
Secretary Windebank also faced charges, while Lord Keeper Finch and
other chief ministers fled abroad. More minor officials in the counties were
denounced before parliamentary committees. The most controversial of
these prosecutions was that of Strafford, which certainly demonstrated the
vengeful potential of this populist mood.

Strafford had been the king's Lord Deputy in Ireland, and among other things was accused of having offered to raise an army in 1640 that could be used not only against the Scottish Covenanters but also to bring the English Parliament to heel. His impeachment had come early in the session but his prosecution had not run smoothly. Impeachment required Parliament to prove the case against him, and Strafford had run a very effective defence against the charge of treason. Anxious about the outcome, parliamentary managers had resorted instead to attainder—an antiquated procedure which allowed them simply to declare him guilty by a vote. Even this had not gone well, however, and it was not clear that the vote would be in favour of execution. As a result crowds pressed round Parliament calling for 'justice' on Strafford, so that it seemed increasingly likely that he would be killed partly at the behest of London's crowds.[11]

Lilburne was caught up in this, and was hauled before the Lords on suspicion of uttering treasonous words. On 3 May Eusebius Andrewe, in conversation with Francis Littleton and Lilburne, had asked Lilburne about the crowd that had gathered. Lilburne 'Answered they come for Justice, & were about the number of six, or seaven thousand, & that there would bee forty, or fifty thousand the next day, or wordes implyeing as much, & that they came then w[i]th their cloakes, butt the next day they would come w[i]th their swords by their sydes, or armed'. When Andrewe asked what they wanted, or hoped to achieve, 'Lylbon answered, there is a report or Rumour that they will either have the Deputy or the Kyng'. These were serious claims and Andrewe had Lilburne taken into custody, at which point 'Lylbon recollected ye words of his own accord, & confessed them'.[12]

This apparent threat to the king was treated very seriously, and the following day Lilburne was brought before the House of Lords. Littleton was a personal servant to Prince Charles (the future Charles II): on several later occasions Lilburne claimed that his appearance was directly instigated by the king and that his life was at stake in this hearing.[13] Lilburne's defence was that these were not his own words, he 'only spake them as the Words which were generally spoken of the Multitude of People which came out of *London*, and told them only as News, which he heard reported abroad'. The witnesses against him did not agree on the details, and he was of course known to many in Parliament: not only was he a public figure, but his connections brought him close to a number of members—Brooke and Saye in the Lords, Cromwell in the Commons. He was not just an obscure apprentice swept up from the streets, therefore, and this helps perhaps explain why he was discharged. Nonetheless, this was a serious matter, and the Lords ordered that 'the Cause to be retained in this House, and an Account to be given to His Majesty hereof'.[14]

In general, though, the mood in Parliament clearly favoured men like Lilburne, rather than Strafford or the king. On 4 May, the same day that the Lords dismissed the case for want of evidence, the Commons also quashed Lilburne's Star Chamber conviction of 13 February 1638, declaring it 'illegal, and gainst the liberty of the subject, and also bloody, wicked, cruel, barbarous & tyrannicall'. This was a significant legal victory, at least in subsequent interpretation. Lilburne (and Wharton) had been imprisoned for contempt because they refused to answer questions under oath—the quashing of the sentence has been cited as precedent for the right to remain silent, not least in the United States in relation to the 5th Amendment. The Star Chamber order of 18 April, which had imposed harsh prison conditions on him following his performance in the pillory, was also quashed.[15]

Lilburne was also awarded reparations for his 'Sufferings and Losses sustained by that illegal Sentence', although no sum was specified. This too was of longer-term significance—Lilburne spent much of the following decade trying to secure payment of these reparations, and his serial disappointments in that quest added to his sense that the later parliamentary regimes did not honour their commitments, or those who had served them. Finally, Lilburne's case formed part of a broader scrutiny of the Star Chamber by a parliamentary committee which prepared a report on his case for the House of Lords, alongside (among others) Bastwick's case. The court was eventually abolished by an Act of 5 July 1641.[16]

On 4 May, a key date in so many of these respects, Parliament had also tendered an oath, the Protestation, to all its members. It committed them to defend 'the true reformed Protestant religion expressed in the doctrine of the Church of England', and 'His Majesty's royal person and estate, as also the power and privilege of Parliament, the lawful rights and liberties of the subjects'.[17] Sir Philip Warwick thought this another very bad sign: 'thus protestations and Covenants are introduced in England as well as Scotland, that the Subjects might not have too great veneration for the Oath of Allegiance, but thinke themselves as much tyed to the two Houses [of Parliament] as to the King'.[18] The point, for some, was that the king was sworn to defend religion and law, and his subjects were sworn to obey him. The Protestation implied a quite different view of things.[19]

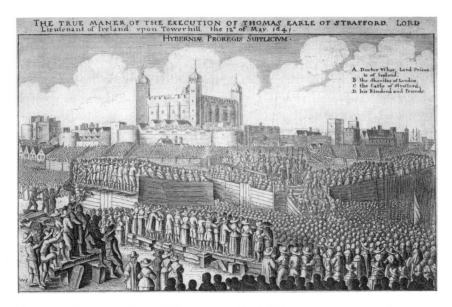

THE TRUE MANER OF THE EXECUTION OF THOMAS EARLE OF STRAFFORD, LORD Lieutenant of Ireland, vpon Tower hill, the 12ᵗ of May, 1641.

HYBERNIÆ PROREGIS SUPPLICIVM

A Doctor Vsher, Lord Prima-
te of Ireland.
B the sheriffes of London
C the Earle of Strafford,
D his Kindred and Friends.

Fig. 2.1. The execution of Thomas Strafford: Lilburne was among the crowd (1641)

With the tide running against him in this way, Charles reluctantly gave his assent to the Act of Attainder. Strafford was executed a little over a week later, on 12 May, before a huge crowd, Lilburne among them: 'I saw him lose his head upon Tower-Hill' (Fig. 2.1).[20] While plenty of people were happy to see Strafford dead, he had been declared guilty on a charge of dubious legality under pressure from crowds on the street: however welcome the end, the means prompted considerable unease.[21] As Warwick noted in his memoirs, 'many, that came up to Towne on purpose to see the Execution, rode in Triumph back, waving their Hatts, & with all expressions of Joy through every Towne, they went crying His Head is off, His Head is off, & in many places committing insolencyes upon & breaking the windows of those persons who would not solemnize this Festivall with Bonfires: soe ignorant, & brutish is a Multitude'.[22] This reinforced fears that puritan populism—of the kind that had turned Burton, Bastwick, and Prynne into living saints—was now posing a serious threat to legal propriety and social decency. Lilburne, however, seems to have suffered no qualms about it at the time, or later, despite his own repeated insistence on his right to due and transparent process under the known laws. He returned to Strafford's fate on many subsequent occasions, but never to question its legitimacy: his point was invariably that someone else was in danger of meeting the same end, and often because in his opinion they deserved it.

Fear of puritan populism had a long history, and even those who wanted further religious reform might be unnerved by it. On the other hand, there was an equally long-standing fear of a popish plot to undermine church and state and to re-establish the authority of Rome in England.[23] Strafford's execution was something of a lightning conductor for these tensions: what some thought was judicial murder to satisfy the multitude looked to others like a moment when resolve had been maintained in the face of the popish plot.

In his own way, Lilburne's fortunes offered an index of the balance of the political mood—a charge of treason dropped in the Lords (perhaps despite the personal interest of the king) on the same day that his Star Chamber conviction was quashed by the Commons and moves to abolish the court were begun. Lilburne himself does not seem to have hesitated either. Whereas at the end of the decade he stood trial for his life for pointing to the potential for parliamentary tyranny, there is no evidence that he suffered such anxieties in 1641. His legal rhetoric against the tyranny of the Star Chamber, High Commission and bishops had resonated strongly with those alarmed by aspects of Charles's secular policy and he demonstrated in favour of 'justice' on Strafford, possibly went much further, and attended the execution. He was at the hotter end of the pressure for reform of religion too: his anti-episcopal declarations aligned him with an increasingly powerful pressure for reform that was beginning to seem to some people more threatening to English Protestantism than Laudianism had been. The balance of forces permitted the execution of Strafford, but not without the deep misgivings of many observers. For some opponents of the 1630s regime it was becoming clearer that Lilburne and his like had been their enemy's enemy, rather than a friend.

★ ★ ★

By the summer of 1641 much had been achieved—particular policies had been reversed, malign institutions abolished, the future of parliaments secured, and unpopular ministers were dead, in custody, or forced out of the country. Reformers continued to be plagued by fears about the future, though. Charles was believed to have supported an attempt to spring Strafford from jail—what was known as the first army plot—and had clearly been reluctant to sign the bill of Attainder. In August, during the recess, he travelled to Scotland, apparently hoping to build support there. In the light of continuing fears about popery and the king's intentions, the Ten Propositions were drawn up stating that, for example, Parliament should have a veto power over the appointment of crown ministers, should have oversight of the education of the royal children, and that the militia should be put in a posture of defence under the command of lieutenants chosen by Parliament, not the king.[24] Here it seemed clear that the remedies for the country's grievances were threatening fundamental change to the monarchy, not just resistance to the policies of this particular king.

When Parliament met again in the autumn of 1641 following the summer recess, these forces seemed evenly balanced—between, on the one hand, the hope that settlement might soon be achieved and, on the other, the fear that these political victories might all be swept away by a popish plot. The balance shifted decisively as news reached London of an uprising in Ireland. What had started as an elite movement to take control of the Irish government, driven in part by fear of gathering anti-Catholicism in London, had ended up as a popular movement, over which no identifiable group had control. Ordinary Catholics rose up against Protestant settlers, and greatly exaggerated stories of atrocities quickly reached England and Scotland. Worst of all, leading figures in the initial rising had claimed to be acting on a royal commission—this seemed to be evidence of a direct connection between a popish plot against Protestantism and the very heart of royal government, and one that had led, so the reports claimed, to the slaughter of thousands of ordinary Protestants. Responses to the rising created a spiral of escalating distrust at Westminster, as Parliament pushed for strong measures to protect the country from the popish threat and the king sought ways to retain or re-establish his authority.

Elections in London in December filled the City's institutions with men convinced that popery posed an immediate threat, and of the imperative need to defend Parliament. Soldiers from the now-disbanded northern army raised to fight the Covenanters had been gathering around the king, and as a response to the threat this seemed to pose, the city's Trained Bands became the focus of a political battle. Charles then made a serious miscalculation in replacing Sir William Balfour as lieutenant of the Tower—a man who was thought to have acted steadfastly in the face of the army plot in June to get Strafford out of jail. In his place he put Colonel Lunsford, a notorious swordsman, widely regarded as a threat to the parliamentary cause.[25]

Colonell Lunsford assaulting the Londoners at Westminster Hall, with a great rout of ruffinly Cavaleires

Fig. 2.2. Colonel Thomas Lunsford at Westminster Hall in December 1641

Crowds were gathering around Westminster too, where moves to exclude the bishops from Parliament had led to active demonstrations. On 28 December, Archbishop Williams was jostled by apprentices as he tried to enter the House, and this led the Lords to call for a joint declaration of both Houses against riotous assemblies. As the political temperature continued to rise, jostling came to blows at Westminster, and on 27 December defenders of Parliament fought with Colonel Lunsford's men (Fig. 2.2). So disastrous had been the effect of his appointment that he had been dismissed only four days later, but the crowds at Westminster did not know this. Lilburne was among them 'with my sword in my hand', one of those 'two or three men' who took up arms to resist Lunsford, believing he and his men 'intended to cut the throats of the chiefest men then sitting in the House of Commons'. Lilburne had, he later claimed, 'ventured his life for [Parliament's] preservation, against *Lunsford* and his crue of Ruffians at Westminster, where the Parliament of England that had preserved him, was by his speciall means (under God) preserved'.[26]

A week later Charles launched the most disastrous of his adventures—an attempt to round up five members of the Commons and one of the House of Lords on a charge of treason. Arriving at Parliament with armed men, he famously found that the birds had flown, and in the meantime he had seemed to demonstrate a very real menace to the freedom of parliaments. At 10.00 a.m. the following morning he was at the Guildhall to address the Corporation of London, convinced that his intended targets were still in London. A crowd had gathered before he arrived, and after Charles had addressed the Corporation and taken lunch with the Sheriff of London next door, the atmosphere became quite confrontational. As he left there were shouts of 'privilege of parliament' and crowds surged towards his carriage. Taking his chance, Henry Walker, an 'ironmonger' in his late twenties, threw a text through his window. It has not survived, but it is known as 'To your Tents, O Israel', since it carried the text of 1 Kings 12:16, which tells the story of how King Rehoboam had imposed heavy taxes and harsh punishments on his people, and how the ten northern tribes had rebelled. The contemporary resonance was plain. It had been hastily printed overnight and scattered about the streets that morning: we know this because the printer, Thomas Payne, was later to regret his role in it, and reported Walker to the authorities. A newspaper published anonymously by Walker during 1644 reprinted what it claimed was the text, in the form of a petition, asking Charles to bear in mind the lesson of King Rehoboam, and to relieve his people. It was a threat of rebellion, or at least of the people turning away from their king, but also expressed the hope that more of his subjects could be persuaded to loyalty if he mended his ways.[27]

Walker had spent some time at Queen's College, Cambridge, and claimed to have been ordained. He was later both a significant publisher and a preacher, and was claimed to have secured a church living by the late 1640s.[28] Like Lilburne, then, he was not an innocent abroad, but there is no question that the times were creating the reason and opportunity for otherwise relatively obscure men to carve out new careers in political activism. It was certainly a remarkable state of affairs—a young man with no real claims to political authority using the presses to distribute a warning from the Bible to his king around the streets of the capital, before delivering it personally through the window of his carriage. The presses had become central to these populist street politics more generally: the rival conspiracy theories— of popery and of puritan populism—were sharpened and broadcast, helping to stoke up the conflict; petitions were the focus for mobilization in the city and beyond, and here, a way of communicating directly with the king.

Lilburne, active in London's crowds, had served an apprenticeship in the politics of press and street: he was clearly part of this world too. In 1641, *A light for the ignorant* had been republished by William Kiffin. A near

Fig. 2.3. Portrait of John Lilburne by George Glover (1641)

contemporary of Lilburne's, Kiffin was born in 1616 and apprenticed in a mean trade in London. He had been tempted to run away but immersed himself in a critical, godly Protestant culture in the early 1630s, having heard preaching in the churches around Coleman Street and Budge Row.[29] It is not unlikely that they knew one another in those early years, and Lilburne later mentioned him alongside Edmund Rosier, the man who had introduced him to Bastwick: *'with whom as Teacher to the Congregation where I was a Member*, I walked many yeares in fellowship, and Master *William Kiffin who was once my servant*, and unto both whom the indearadest of my affections run out unto'.[30] The same year, William Larner, who was to become a prominent figure in the print trade over the next decade, republished *The Christian mans triall*, complete with an expensive engraving of Lilburne by George Glover which made him recognizable, as it still does (Fig. 2.3). Larner was of the same generation, apprenticed in 1630 as a Merchant Taylor, although three years later he entered a different apprenticeship as a stationer. By the early 1640s, Larner was publishing from an unlicensed press, specializing in works by religious nonconformists. The new edition of *The Christian mans triall* was probably printed in December, an early fruit of the new freedoms of the press, and a contribution to the early debates excited by the new Parliament.[31] The puritan underground, so crucial to his formation, now provided developing means to participate in the deepening political crisis, giving men like Lilburne and Henry Walker new routes to political influence.

★   ★   ★

Following the attempt to arrest the five members Charles lost control of London, and early in January he left the capital for Windsor, arranging for his queen to leave for France. In these tense weeks the whole nation was called on to take the Protestation. It had been imposed on MPs and Lords the previous May, but was now a national commitment: a further, dramatic, escalation, which made the people the defenders of the law and religion. It divided communities, but also induced crises of conscience, and this was to be an important feature of the politics of the spring and summer of 1642: it was worn in hats and carried as an emblem of commitment to the defence of Parliament and the true religion.[32]

No certain record has been found that Lilburne swore the Protestation. It is not obvious, in fact, that he would have done so, since one thing we really do know about him was that he was opposed to oaths. He had spent the best part of three years in prison for refusing one, and was later to denounce those who made them, or demanded them, rashly: 'be not rash with thy mouth, and let not they heart by hasty to utter any thing before God; but when thou vowest a vow unto God, deferre not to pay it: for he hath no pleasure in fools' (Ecclesiastes, 5:2–4). In that tract, *Rash Oaths unwarrantable*, he cited the Protestation (along with later state oaths) against Parliament, referring to it as one of 'your' oaths and covenants: he was holding them to account for failing to meet the obligations it implied rather than claiming it as a commitment of his own.[33] He certainly did not take later state oaths, and preferred that people be judged by their actions, not their words.

It is possible, though, that Lilburne did take the Protestation. In *An Anatomy of the Lords Tyranny*, published in 1646, Lilburne points out that all Commoners were bound by the Protestation to maintain their liberties and adds, perhaps ambiguously, 'I am resolved by the strength of God, in a just and legal way' to do just that (in this case, by defending himself against

injustice exercised by the House of Lords). In another slightly ambiguous
passage, in *On the 150th page*, published the previous year, he had defended
his actions in revealing evidence of treason by the Speaker of the House of
Commons as the obligation of a freeborn Englishman according his 'duty,
oath and Protestation'.[34] We know that a John Lilbarne took the Protestation
on 23 January 1642 at Childerditch, in Essex, and it is possible this is our
man.[35] Lilburne or Lilbarne was not a common name in Essex, and a search
of the name indexes for the county archives does not reveal this man again,
or many others of that name. Childerditch is close to Brentwood, then an
important centre for malting and brewing, and not far from the capital, in
fact less than twenty miles from Lilburne's home in Stepney. It is quite plausible that Lilburne's trade took him that way, and there were more immediate
reasons why he might have been there that day. George Willingham's son
John was at school in Doddinghurst, a couple of miles the other side of
Brentwood, and he was clearly causing concern to those at home in these
weeks. Willingham, friend of Lilburne's master, wrote to the minister of
Doddinghurst on the same day that the Protestation was taken, sending
clothes for his son and hoping that he would prove obedient and ingenious
in his studies. A few days later he and his wife wrote separately to their son,
expressing some concern about his behaviour, and a week later Abraham
Molyne, curate and lecturer at St Swithin, Hewson's church, also wrote,
albeit in slightly more emollient terms.[36]

The family was clearly worried that all was not well with their son and it
is not impossible that Lilburne had reason to be in those parts that January,
perhaps combining business with some personal favour to a fellow parishioner and friend of his former master. If he had been there, he might have
been drawn to Childerditch, a notably puritan parish, whose presentments
in the 1650s were in the gift of Sir Thomas Cheeke, a zealous puritan. The
vicar at the time, Daniel Duckfield, whose name is at the head of those
taking the Protestation, was a 'godly and preaching minister', and several of
his predecessors had been in trouble in the early seventeenth century for
their opposition to ceremonial religion. Childerditch later had a notable
Presbyterian presence.[37]

Whether he took it or not, however, the Protestation was clearly a statement of the parliamentary cause of which Lilburne approved, later using it
as a benchmark against which he measured Parliament's falling away from
its primitive purity. In the following months Parliament took more and more
radical measures to preserve its position. Without the king's consent Parliament

could not pass acts, and so used ordinances instead. A key justification for this was that they were acting as the Great Council, serving the king's authority in his absence. Those who had gone with the king found it easy to question the legality of ordinances, and the plausibility of Parliament's self-presentation as representatives of the king's authority: indeed it is fairly obvious that Parliament was in new political territory. As the paper war unfolded, Parliament's propagandists also set out a theory of parliamentary sovereignty—that within the mixed constitution Parliament was a sovereign power. A dozen other, semi-official publications produced from the same press went further, anxious that royalists were deceiving the people, and making arguments that were significant for Lilburne later—for example that scripture did not govern the civil constitution. Among the authors was William Walwyn, with whom Lilburne was later very closely allied.[38]

On these questionable grounds, Parliament passed measures which significantly affected individual rights and the constitution: to disarm Catholics, for example, or to take control of the militia. This latter measure was supposedly defensive—to protect against the danger of popish conspiracy—but could easily be seen as an aggressive move. It was met by a straightforward challenge. The king summoned the militia by his own authority, through a Commission of Array. This was another key moment, creating a stark choice between answering a summons to arms by order of the king or of Parliament. In the face of these and other choices many fell away from the parliamentary cause. Edward Montagu, for example, a puritan grandee whose wife at least was well known to Hewson, was driven to royalism by a sense of personal honour, and political decency: when a choice was forced he felt he had a personal obligation to the king which outweighed all other considerations.[39] Lord Brooke, another grandee at the edges of Hewson's acquaintance, made a very different choice, taking on the earl of Northampton in a battle for control of the militia in Warwickshire and drawing Lilburne into his service.

From June, when rival militia orders began to be executed in Warwickshire, until August, there was confused jockeying for position. Northampton moved first, supported by a greater proportion of the leading gentry in the county, prompting Brooke to hold musters starting at Stratford on 30 June. He seemed to enjoy more support from those below the ranks of the gentry having, according to one pamphleteer, 'gained the hearts of all the people unless it be a few of the Gentlemen that never were known to do any good to the Commonwealth'. At Coleshill the turnout was impressive, spurred by the fear that Northampton would bring 500 men to oppose

Brooke's muster. The struggle continued, however: in July there was an attempt to indict Brooke at the Assizes for executing the militia ordinance, while the king summoned the mayor and sheriffs of Coventry to Leicester to explain why they had not executed his Commission of Array. As the summer went on the gentry of the county seem to have favoured the king's call to arms as the better guarantee of social and political order, a pattern which has been seen in other areas too.[40]

By late summer, though, the military struggle had moved beyond the control of the militia, and on 18 July Brooke received a warrant to garrison Warwick Castle and nine pieces of ordnance were sent to defend it. In August, as the position of the parliamentarians in the county deteriorated, Brooke left for London for further consultation and to seek reinforcements. In his absence John Fiennes delivered up the ordnance of Northampton to the royalists, something which was later blamed on his weakness, rather than that of the cause as a whole. Nonetheless, it was reinforcements from London, and Brooke's apparent popularity below the level of the gentry, that secured the vital strongholds of Coventry and Warwick for Parliament.[41]

In his search for recruits in London, Brooke seems to have drawn on his reputation as a godly man, and on connections among the London godly. Among them was William Kiffin, who had sought Brooke's intercession in March 1642, when in trouble with Parliament for seditious preaching.[42] Given the strength of his own convictions, and his connection with Kiffin and men like him, it is no surprise that Lilburne also accepted a commission as captain of a troop of horse. Lilburne's brothers Robert and Henry also signed up with Brooke, Robert as a cornet in a troop of horse and Henry signed off on the first month's pay for John's company.[43] John claimed that he had worked to persuade 'all the friends he had, one way or other to ingage' in Parliament's cause: the Lilburne connection may have been quite significant for Brooke in securing recruits in London.[44] In all, about 400 of Brooke's men came from London, and alongside the professional soldiers among his junior officers were radicals, such as John Okey, the future regicide, and Thomas Fitch, future governor of the Tower.[45]

George Lilburne, like John, seems to have suffered few doubts about his allegiances in these crucial months. When the royalist earl of Newcastle had arrived in the county, George refused to attend prayers, and was put out of the Commission of the Peace. He was reported to Newcastle as his 'greatest enemy in those parts' and put under restraint and much abused 'as puritan, rogue, and roundhead'. He stole away to Edinburgh to talk to Parliament's 'agent' there, and having 'vehemently' opposed the Commission of Array he tried to escape the county to join John Hotham. He was captured, though, and endured fourteen months imprisonment, resisting attempts to get him to submit to the royalist cause, before the Commons arranged a prisoner exchange for him.[46] This decisive commitment contrasted with others who were drawn into the parliamentary cause, but perhaps with less firm conviction. Sir Henry Vane the elder, for example, who had been part of the Star Chamber court that sentenced Lilburne in 1638, nonetheless chose the parliamentary cause when war came. A number of local gentlemen, though, blamed the loss of Durham and Northumberland on his hesitancy. They claimed that George Lilburne had visited Vane's house in Charing Cross in July, calling for urgent action, but had not been heeded. As a result, the north-east was lost the following month. The charge against Vane was repeated to the earl of Essex in February 1643. This royalist success cost John's father dear since all his lands lay under their military control until early in 1644,[47] and this was the start of what became a festering grievance against Vane and his son held by several members of the Lilburne family.

In later publications, John Lilburne made much of his steadfast commitment the justness of the parliamentary cause, partly as a rebuke to Parliament for failing to live up to those ideals or to reward those who made these sacrifices. His personal connections and convictions had led him into the puritan underground during the 1630s, and then out into the open once conditions changed. He had, like Prynne before him, used the courts and the press to challenge the regime, and was able to do so increasingly openly during 1641, with the help of the wider godly network of which he was clearly a part. These convictions and connections seem also to have led him on to the streets. While others had qualms about the constitutional and legal propriety of Parliament's actions, about populism, and about radical religion, Lilburne showed no hesitation, joining the crowds calling for Strafford's death, fighting Lunsford's men, perhaps taking the Protestation, and signing up with a famously godly commander. Choosing sides had apparently given Lilburne no difficulty.

Edgehill, Brentford, and prison, 1642–3

The outbreak of war introduced the country to new terrors. We have no record of Lilburne's movements prior to the battle of Edgehill, although it seems he took up his commission too late to have been part of Brooke's march from London to secure Coventry and Warwick: the warrant for payment of the first month's pay for his troops reveals that he was still in London planning to join a rendezvous in Knightsbridge on 24 August, the day after the siege of Warwick had been lifted.[48]

While Lilburne has left no record of his experiences of the descent to war, the letters of Nehemiah Wharton, a contemporary of Lilburne's living in the same London streets, have survived. Apprenticed to George Willingham, the friend of Lilburne's master, Wharton signed up that summer under Denzil Holles (one of the five MPs Charles had attempted to arrest).[49] His letters conjure the feelings of a godly apprentice in the weeks before the war started in earnest, out to see the world, or on 'pilgrimage' as Wharton put it. He often commented on local antiquities, for example.[50] But they also show how the outbreak of active hostilities raised the political stakes once again: how apparently minor differences of language—were you for the king or for the king and Parliament, for example—signalled fundamental differences with violent consequences; how the march was punctuated by the experience of casual violence; and how the early skirmishes vividly illustrated the horrors of war—the injuries and the treatment of prisoners, the dead, and the wounded. In the face of this local people, like those at Long Bugby in Northamptonshire, 'were glad to leave the town and hide themselves in ditches and corn fields'.[51]

Wharton's marches were punctuated not just by these military encounters, but by a practical reformation: burning altar rails, defacing images, breaking windows. This was potentially alarming in a different way: as hostile commentators put it, this amounted to abolishing superstition with sedition. The soldiers were encouraged in this by godly preaching, for which Wharton obviously had a taste: men like Stephen Marshall, Simeon Ash, and Obadiah Sedgwick 'have already subdued and satisfied the more malignante spirits amongst us than a thousand armed men could have done'.[52] On the march, church services were disrupted, vestments abused, and individuals and towns appraised for their religious and political acceptability.

This last aspect of the march—political partisanship—was clearly a threat to social order and decency. As Sir Philip Warwick noted, prior to the summer of 1642 the story of the civil war could at each stage be recounted in relation to 'one part of the Nation alone, as in Parliament, Whitehall, Citty &c.' But now 'Civill war…spread itself…like an Vniversall Fire, & seyzed upon the whole Nation…[like] a conflagration all att once, which broke out in every part of the Kingdome'.[53] Partisan identities gave cause to refuse the normal courtesies, and studied deference, of a highly unequal society. A recurring expression of this was the spoliation of deer parks—a highly transgressive act of hostility against genteel order. Early in the march Wharton's men had gone to Sir Alexander Denton's park 'who is a malignant fellow, and killed a fat buck, fastened his head upon my halbert, and commaunded two of my pickes to bring the body after me to Buckingham'. Even the earl of Northampton was not safe from these gross breaches of deference: 'we could not restraine our soildiers from entringe his park and killinge his deer, and had not the Lord Grey and our Sergeant Major General withstood them they had pillaged his house'. At Coventry, soldiers went to Lord Dunsmore's park, returning with 'great store of venison, which is as good as ever I tasted; and ever since they make it their dayly practise, so that venison is almost as common with us as beefe with you'. By September, in Northampton 'All the venison belonging to malignants in the country are destroyed.'[54] In Coventry, soldiers returning from a sally 'brought in with them two Cavaleeres, and with them an old base priest, the parson of Sowe, near us, and led him ridiculously about the City unto the chiefe commaunders'. These troops had earlier made handkerchiefs from surplices. Near Holmby, 'our soildiers sallyed out about the cuntrey, and returned in state clothed with a surplisse, hood, and cap, representing the Bishop of Canterbury'. It was not only priests who were mocked. Soldiers who took asses from Lord Dunsmore's park, 'dignified them with the name of the Lord Dunsmore'.[55] Brooke and Essex both saw the dangers of this misrule, threatening dire consequences for those involved, and it became part of the propaganda used to firm up resistance to the parliamentarians' march.[56]

Wharton too had misgivings about the army, noting the threat of some soldiers to throw down their arms if they were not paid, and their acts of plunder, including his own loss of goods to men from the same army. He approved of attempts to restrain the ordinary soldiery at the earl of Northampton's house, and he noted without comment that at Coventry 'a whore, which had followed our campe from London, was taken by the soildiers, and first led about the city, then set in the pillory, after in the cage, then duckt in a river, and at the last banisht the city'. At another point he noted the conduct of 'the ruder sort of soildiers, whose society, blessed be God, I hate and avoide'.[57]

These experiences of war—the violence, and the threat of it; the suffering; the humiliation of enemies and the exaltation of being on top—became an additional issue in the testing of commitment. Over the summer of 1642, Bruno Ryves began publishing a regular newspaper with stories of outrages committed by parliamentarians around the country, while the word 'plunder' was absorbed into the English language—each side claiming it was the other that had introduced the word, and the thing, to England. An important element of this was social transgression: the denial of the normal civilities of social life. England was a highly unequal society, in which gestures of respect and deference were expected. Appropriate dress, manner, and deportment marked out distinctions between men and women, and rich and poor, but the gentry could now be heard complaining that partisan insults had been thrown at them, even to their face. People wrote shocked letters and published accounts of open breaches of deference. Anxiety that the social order was breaking down was palpable. The breach of political order allowed the expression of class hostilities, and for apprentices to 'triumph' over priests.[58]

What political and religious demands were worth this? Over the next four years the fighting escalated so that a greater proportion of the population died than were to die in the First World War, huge amounts of property were destroyed, crops and livestock seized, and unprecedented strain placed on normal decencies. Not all those who were able to choose sides in 1642 continued to support the war thereafter.

★   ★   ★

Lilburne's experience, as a godly apprentice from similar circles to those of Wharton, cannot have been very different, but there is no evidence that it did anything to shake his convictions. He was at Worcester, one of the first encounters between the field armies, while at Edgehill he claimed he 'ventured his life freely' for Parliament and his country, 'so that he gained very much respect from all who observed his faithfulnesse and valour'.[59] It was there that the two armies faced each other in full strength for the first time: around 14,000 on each side. Successful cavalry charges by the royalist flanks became a pursuit as the parliamentarian cavalry fled. This left the two bodies of infantry to advance on one another, coming to a grim 'push of pike' and hand-to-hand combat. Wharton was in Holles's infantry regiment, here, in the thick of the battle. Brooke himself was not there, but his regiment, Lilburne among them, was also at the heart of this bloody infantry tussle. Brooke's regiment appears to have suffered heavy losses, and Lilburne was commended for his conduct by others. The earl of Warwick noted his 'valour at the battell of Kenton [Edgehill]', and another observer reported that 'he kept the Field all Night'.[60] By nightfall the two sides had fought themselves to a standstill, without a decisive outcome. About 1,500 died, with numbers roughly even on both sides. A cold night followed, in which the regrouped armies could hear the groans of the wounded and dying out on the battlefield.

Edgehill certainly tested the resolution of many people on both sides, but not Lilburne's. In fact he later said that at Worcester and Edgehill, he saw things which made him 'doubt that there was no intention of a speedy end to the war': it was the lack of commitment among his commanders rather than the magnitude of the suffering that he remembered.[61] Following the battle, Lilburne withdrew with Brooke's troops to Warwick and then Northampton, from where he was sent to London with a message from Brooke. Back in London his reputation was clearly strong: he was offered command of a troop of horse in a new army of 16,000 men being put together from the London Trained Bands. Brooke, though, persuaded him to return to his side, in the hope that a victory could be secured quickly, more quickly in fact than a new troop of horse could be put together. Lilburne agreed to rejoin Brooke at Brentford, on the western approaches to London.[62]

Brentford proved to be a military disaster for the parliamentarians, and another experience that tested the resolve of partisans. The royalist infantry, attacking out of thick mist, surprised the parliamentarian forces and inflicted heavy losses on Holles's regiment, which was in front of the town. Much of the fighting concentrated on two barricades, the first of which, on the bridge over the river Brent, fell after an hour or so. Brooke's men were quartered in the town, and defended the second barricade. According to Lilburne many of them thought that retreat was the best option in the face of the assault, and it was his personal intervention that made them turn back and stand alongside Holles's regiment and other defenders of the town. Seven hundred men, significantly outnumbered and with limited cover, managed to hold their ground for another five or six hours (other accounts say less). As the parliamentary position was overrun, men fled through the town or jumped into the river. Many were drowned, killed, or captured. Lilburne, nearly drowned several times, was among those captured and taken to Oxford.[63] Wharton has often been assumed to have died at Edgehill, since his correspondence stopped at that point, but he may in fact have survived and married a few years later.[64]

It was a defeat, of course, but a brave one, and this dogged defence had served a significant military purpose, allowing the parliamentary artillery train to make its escape.[65] Lilburne was justifiably proud: 'about 700 men . . . withstood the King's whole army . . . about five houres together, and fought it out to very Swords point, and to the Butt end of the Musket, and thereby hindered the King from his then possessing the Parliament's Train of Artillery, and by consequence the City of *London*'.[66]

Edgehill and Brentford had brought the realities of seventeenth-century warfare into clear view, and war stories were part of the wider propaganda battle. It was said to have been a dishonourable and perfidious attack, and the damages caused were publicized, partly as a warning about what might be expected from a triumphant Cavalier army. The royalists felt obliged to answer these charges.[67] For others, it demonstrated the costs of war, and the dangers of arming men of low principle in the service of political arguments.[68] One of those whose commitment to war was now shaken was Denzil Holles, whose regiment had fought with distinction at Edgehill and Brentford. A contemporary noted on 24 November that Holles 'was much cooled in his fierceness by the great slaughter made in his regiment at Brentford' and he refused the offer of command of the western forces. He subsequently advocated an essentially defensive military effort: lukewarm about war as the solution to the kingdom's problems, he became a prominent 'peace party' parliamentarian, alert to any opportunity to negotiate a peaceful settlement rather than a man committed first to securing an outright military victory.[69]

The royal army now advanced on London, but a rapid, panicky mobilization among the Trained Bands and apprentices of the City on the day of the engagement at Brentford allowed an army of 24,000 men to be drawn up at Turnham Green. There, on 13 November, the two armies faced each other, but after a tense day battle was avoided, and the royal army retreated to Oxford. It was as close as a royal army came to capturing London, often regarded by historians as a crucial failure of nerve on the king's part.[70] What is clear is that the war had not been won in a single confrontation, as Brooke and many others had hoped. As the two armies withdrew to winter quarters peace negotiations were set in train alongside preparations for a more sustained war.

England had been introduced to a new world over the summer of 1642— open conflict between the kingdom's natural governors in Parliament and local institutions such as the militia and the assizes; the movement of troops, bringing with them class conflict, or at least an absence of proper deference, unruly reformation, casual and tragic violence, and eventually the horrors of war. These experiences had a profound effect on many on both sides. The complexity of events, and the moral dilemmas posed in conditions of extreme and polarized political life, continued to force people to decide what their core commitments really were. For Lilburne, clearly, there was honour in these engagements: 'for many houres . . . an inconsiderable party of men that can never be too much honoured' held up the royalists at Brentford and allowed London time to prepare its defences. For him going to war was an inspiring experience, which gave him strength as he 'underwent a long and loathsome imprisonment . . . and a most dangerous triall for his life'.[71]

★   ★   ★

Following his capture, Lilburne was taken to Oxford and put on trial for treason. He later said that he had withstood blandishments from four Lords to change sides, preferring to face his trial.[72] Robert Vivers, one of his prominent co-defendants, was a man with whom he had connections going back before the war, to the network of the godly into which Lilburne had been apprenticed.[73] Edmund Chillenden, who under duress in 1638 had turned informer against Lilburne, was also among them; Lilburne had apparently forgiven him.[74]

The political point of the trial was that all those in arms against the king were guilty of treason—they were rebels whatever warrant they might claim from Parliament. Since they had no legitimate cause, they could expect no mercy. As Lilburne himself was later to emphasize, however, the hearing on 17 December was conducted with propriety—it was a show case, not a show trial. Lilburne was brought to the bar in the Oxford Guildhall where Lord Chief Justice Heath told him that the court would not take advantage of the fact that he had been taken in arms to proceed by martial laws 'or any other arbitrary ways; but we will try you by the good old laws of England'. Heath encouraged him to claim whatever rights and privileges he could 'as your birth right and inheritance'. This was a matter of propriety, duty, and professional pride, of course, but also of political calculation: this way 'your friends shall not have any just cause to say, we murdered you with cruelty, or denied you the benefit of law'.[75] At the time he reported these words Lilburne had in mind a contrast with the conduct of the republican regime in 1649, and Heath's language is remarkably close to his own, but if this is what Heath actually said the contrast in *his* mind might well have been with the conduct of the treason charge against Strafford.

Lilburne was defiant. He bridled, for example, at the assertion that he was no gentleman. One (sympathetic) pamphlet thought Lilburne 'but a man of low fortunes, [who] arose to the degree of Captaine, by the boldnesse of his spirit',[76] and when he was introduced as yeoman he refused to answer the indictment 'for that he'd admit nothing on Record so much to the prejudice of his family . . . as to answer to the name of Yeomen'. Heath agreed to amend the indictment. Lilburne's defence was plain—he was following the orders of Parliament to defend Brentford, arguing that 'he did nothing but in his own Defence and that he never did nor would bear Arms against his King'.[77] He spoke at length in his own defence, more than the others accused, claiming that he honoured the king as much as any present, and was indeed acting to preserve his sacred person. His only purpose 'was by the losse of his bloud to secure safety to his Maiesty, and peace unto the Kingdome, by endeavouring what in him lay to pluck him from the hands of those who infused bad counsaile into his sacred eares'.[78] Challenged by the earl of Northampton whether his conscience had convicted him of the crime he had committed, he asked if the abuse of the law (prior to the war) had convicted their consciences. Asked by Prince Rupert if it was honourable to shed innocent blood, he asked in reply if it was honourable to shed innocent blood by abuse of the law. When the prince asked him how he chose to die, he 'demanded a swoord telling them he desired to die in single opposition man to man with any there, or if they feared the triall, any two so he might die with honour'.[79]

Lilburne's strength of purpose was remarkable, and characteristic, but it was not what saved his neck. A few days prior to the trial Lilburne, Vivers, and Catesby, another defendant, had written a letter to the Commons reporting the royalists' intention. Four solicitors (including Edmund Prideaux, who was himself to lead a treason prosecution against Lilburne seven years later) were ordered to draft a declaration threatening similar reprisals against all royalist prisoners. It was to be sent to the judges and to royalist prisoners to allow them to begin to prepare their defence, and provision was made for it to be printed.[80] The parliamentarian prisoners in Oxford were all condemned, but this threat of retaliation (*lex talionis*, an eye for an eye) prevented their execution. Both sides stepped back from the brink and in so doing probably saved the war from a ruinous descent. Elizabeth Lilburne was crucial in persuading the Commons to intervene, soliciting them daily and hourly 'to interpose their power for his preservation, and when by ordinary solicitation she could not prevaile' she presented herself at the Commons bar 'there begging and importuning their care of her husbands life'. Having secured an order and letter to Heath, '(big with child as she was) she undergoes a task through all the strong Courts of Guard, which none else (as things then stood) durst undertake', and delivered the letter. In doing so, 'she met with so many sad and difficult accidents, to a woman in her condition, as would force tears from the hardest heart'.[81]

All this was clearly part of a broader propaganda battle about the justifiability of the war, and the conditions in which the royalists kept their prisoners were cited as evidence of what kind of men were around the king. One published letter publicizing this petty tyranny asked Lord Brooke to intervene by inducing the earl of Lindsey to bring these conditions to the notice of the king.[82] A number of these pamphlets used reports of these events to call for peace, but it was to no avail. Peace negotiations over the winter of 1642/3 failed, and the following spring hostilities were resumed in greater earnest.[83] Lilburne himself wrote asking to be part of a prisoner exchange, and was eventually exchanged in May 1643 for Sir John Smith, who had high status, having regained the king's standard when it had been lost during the battle at Edgehill. Lilburne remained grateful to the earl of Essex thereafter for having secured this exchange 'upon odds'.[84] This was, perhaps, the high point of his championship of the parliamentary cause: a prisoner of high value, with a record of active, perhaps even heroic, service.

The army of the Eastern Association, 1643–4

Lilburne claimed that on his return to London from Oxford he was offered 'a place of honour and profit…then reputed worth about 1000 l. per annum', an offer relayed via Elizabeth. He preferred, though, 8 pence per day, to 'see the Liberties and Peace of *England* setled', and returned to arms.[85] He did so, however, in changed and changing conditions. In the autumn of 1642 the fighting had been an extension of the defensive manoeuvres of earlier in the year, and there had been some hope that a short war, or even a single battle, might settle the issues. Nothing much had been resolved, however, as the disappointing peace talks held in Oxford over the winter revealed. As spring and renewed fighting approached, it was with a different tone—Parliament was organizing for a more sustained and more demanding campaign. New committees, with extensive powers over persons and property and new taxes now underpinned an active military campaign on several fronts, and were impressively (or worryingly) effective. Counties were gathered into regional associations, again under committees, while in London a more radical reformation was launched, moving beyond the reaction to Laud's religious policies and towards a new reformation. Yet another committee, this one led by Sir Robert Harley, began to purge London of superstitious icons, pulling down Cheapside Cross, for example. All of this was done by the authority of ordinances passed by a Parliament from which many MPs and Lords had withdrawn. Unsurprisingly there was an escalating public debate about Parliament's cause, and whether the measures now being taken were justifiable in terms of the arguments made the previous year: the defence of the constitution under the king and Parliament, and of the Protestant religion.[86]

By the summer, Parliament had negotiated a military alliance with the Scottish Covenanters, the Solemn League and Covenant, and this had introduced significant further complications into the religious debate. For the Covenanters the outcome of the English war would have significant implications for the security of their own victory over Charles's religious policy, but the potential tension here was clear: were the English opponents of Charles I's religious policy seeking the same kind of replacement for it? For some the answer was yes, but for many others not. The key passage in the Solemn League and Covenant committed those who took it to pursue the reform of the English Church according to the best examples. It is clear that the Covenanters had a particular example in mind, but many of their English allies would prefer to have read that clause differently.

This clearly tested Lilburne's conscience. In *A light for the ignorant* Lilburne had acknowledged that the true clerical state might include positions of authority: it had a constitution, and five offices in the church were recognized in the New Testament. While he clearly favoured congregational independence, therefore, he also acknowledged the legitimacy of some kind of church government. He had clearly said, though, in print, that in his view Christ had left his power in particular, not national, churches,[87] and it is no surprise therefore that he saw Scottish Presbyterianism as a threat—a form of organization which restricted the ability of individual Christians to gather themselves in congregations, responding freely to God's word. Some of the men alongside whom he was fighting (including, as it turned out, his commander) took a different view—that too much congregational

Fig. 2.4. Edward Montagu, 2nd earl of Manchester (1602–71)

independence threatened spiritual anarchy and might licence all kinds of religious error.

When Lilburne returned to the fighting, therefore, new tensions were emerging about what kind of church settlement was being fought for, and what costs were acceptable in achieving it. Over the following two years the politics of the parliamentary coalition became more complex and Lilburne identified increasingly strongly with some strands of opinion against others. Holding a strongly partisan view within the parliamentary side led him to see that it was not just royalists who posed a threat to a just and appropriate outcome.

Oliver Cromwell, 'my old friend that got me my libertie from the Bishops Captivitie', recruited Lilburne into the Eastern Association army in October 1643, under the command of the earl of Manchester (Fig. 2.4). Cromwell was, by virtue of his military success, an increasingly important figure in Parliament's Eastern Association army. Manchester had been a prominent supporter of the godly opponents of Charles I during the 1630s, and was, like Cromwell, a prominent and active parliamentarian: together they were Lilburne's 'two Darlings, and familiar friends'.[88] He also later claimed that he had preferred not to join Essex's army, despite his personal debt to the earl, because he had heard there was a persecuting spirit in its ranks.[89]

Lilburne found life with his immediate commander, Colonel Edward King, far from comfortable, however. King was a controversial figure, who had led a prolonged campaign against the County Committee of Lincoln and the military commander in the county, Lord Willoughby. He had championed the formation of the Eastern Association, which amalgamated the forces of several counties, in the name of military effectiveness and had secured appointment as governor of Boston. In this office people found him jealous of his authority and casual of the authority of the County Committee with which his powers were in uneasy tension. As a result, his relationship with the County Committee remained very strained.[90] He was also an uncompromising Presbyterian, anxious about the ungodly, anarchic potential of religious independency. In the autumn of 1643 he broke up a religious gathering at Boston and imprisoned the congregation, including some of his own officers and some of Lilburne's troops.[91] According to Lilburne, they had met 'for exercising the very power of godliness', but to King this seemed instead an opportunity to 'vent theirown [*sic*] novelties'.[92]

Lilburne claimed at first to have been a moderating influence, helping to smooth over the tensions caused by King's religious intolerance, and speaking as well as he could of the man to the earl of Manchester when he was considering enlarging King's commission. At that point King was apparently sufficiently grateful to have given Lilburne's brother a commission.[93] Lilburne also apparently defended his former schoolmaster, Thomas Gibson, from persecution by King. Gibson, now vicar of Horncastle in Lincolnshire, had by the 1630s become a prominent supporter of Laudian religion, and his sermon in 1640 at the return of Clerks to the Convocation had nettled the local puritans, making him a prime target once the Laudian regime had fallen. He was imprisoned in Hull and his parishioners denounced him to the parliamentary committee for his Arminian views. Early in 1644, King ordered a party of horse to take him prisoner and plunder his house. According to later local legend, having heard that a party of horse was being sent to Horncastle, Lilburne immediately went to see his commander '& desires to be inform'd Whether he had order'd a Party to HornCastle, & for what'. King told him:

It was to fetch away one Gibson, a notorious Malignant Priest. What (sayes Lilborn) with a deep accent (according to his usual fervor) ---- Gibson! Hees a very good man, and a godly man. . . . I cann't endure that my master should be a prisoner or be plunder'd. Well replyes the Governor, but hee's a dangerous man, and preaches against the Cause we are engag'd in, & if we let such men alone, the warr will never have an end, and we may fight till Dooms=day. Verely (qouth John) if you do send for him, I'le march along with 'em, & com[m]and the Party, and I'le cut that Rogues Crown that shall lay hands upon my Master, or offer to touch so much as a Dish or a spoon in his house.

'This Huffyness of Lilborn sav'd Mr Gibson from imprison[en]t for the pres[en]t'. When, having fallen out with King, Lilburne left the army at the end of 1645, Gibson suffered mightily: he was imprisoned, plundered, and deprived of his living, surviving and providing for his wife and six children until the Restoration by serving as a schoolmaster to sympathetic patrons in Newark and Sleaford.[94]

This incident is perhaps revealing of the deep personal loyalties that Lilburne could feel towards people with whom he did not share a religious sensibility. His respect for godliness later extended to royalist divines and others with whom he differed fundamentally, suggesting a capacity to put aside such differences on the basis of personal respect, and to respect sincere godliness which found expression in forms he disliked. In this he was clearly at odds with men like King.

The re-emergence of persecution within the parliamentary coalition must therefore have given Lilburne pause for thought about where this war was leading, particularly if the Solemn League and Covenant had indeed committed Parliament to a settlement in England along Scottish Presbyterian lines. Nevertheless, when he began a sustained attempt to get King court-martialled, in early 1644, it was on military not overtly partisan grounds. A key accusation related to King's conduct at the siege of Newark in March 1644. John was later credited with having led a charge in which Prince Rupert had almost been captured, but in the end Rupert's forces were able to relieve the siege and capture the parliamentary forces. The articles of agreement following this defeat had called for the parliamentarians to march away without their arms, but King had commanded Lilburne, indeed forced him, to march away with his regiment armed. As a result the royalist horse fell upon them, and they were plundered, almost to a man. Lilburne himself claimed to have lost £100. King, however, 'fled the danger, and had a care of himselfe' with the result that he 'scaped better than we did'.[95] This, and claims that King refused to take advice from his fellow officers and was quarrelsome, fuelled an attack that was sustained throughout 1644. There clearly were religious tensions, though. Lilburne complained that King's chaplains promoted dissension, and that King persecuted 'all honest zealous and conscientious men' without cause. For his part, King complained that he was 'madded' by Lilburne's constant reports on him to Cromwell, and that his 'bitter invective against the church and ministers of England' were intolerable.[96]

Lilburne was not Colonel King's only enemy on the parliamentary side, however. King was also involved in mutual recriminations with Lord Willoughby over conduct at Newark, in the course of which he was summoned to the House of Lords for censure. He and his fellow accused, Rous, refused to kneel and accept the censure, claiming that the cause was in the process of being heard in the Commons. King was committed to the Fleet for his refusal, and there was clearly some tense discussion between the two Houses about their respective privileges.[97]

Following his escape from Newark in March, over eight miles of hedges and ditches, Lilburne had briefly appeared in Suffolk, alongside his brother Robert, but his discontent with life in the parliamentary army led to his resignation shortly after. In May 1644, however, he was persuaded back into service once more and promoted to command of a troop of dragoons under Manchester's command.[98] In the following months the fighting went well for the Eastern Association army as Scottish intervention helped turn the tide of the war in the north of England. Between January and March the Scots moved south. As a result, the earl of Newcastle's royalist forces were caught between the Covenanters and the parliamentary armies to their south, and Newcastle withdrew from Northumberland and Durham in the face of the Scottish advance. By the summer of 1644 he had made York his base, and it was under siege by parliamentary forces. Prince Rupert was sent to relieve the city. In response a parliamentary army was also sent, including Manchester's Eastern Association troops and, in their first major contribution to the English war, Scottish Covenanter troops. Rupert, perhaps misinterpreting his orders, chose not simply to relieve York but also to engage these parliamentary armies in battle. The result, on 2 July, was military disaster at Marston Moor, the battle that gave control of the north to Parliament. Two weeks later York fell, although in the course of the storm of the city a number of lives had been lost unnecessarily as a result of a misjudgement by Crawford, one of the Covenanter commanders. Lilburne was unsparing in his criticism of this misjudgement.[99] He himself had been a vigorous participant in these campaigns. It was later said that Lilburne had been an 'emminent actor in that famous Battle at Marston Moor', and in the course of these campaigns he was shot through the arm taking Sir Francis Wortley's house in South Yorkshire.[100]

This change of military fortunes exacerbated some of the tensions in the parliamentary coalition—victories for the Scots and their allies gave added political weight to the calls for a Presbyterian Church settlement, and there were some rather mean-spirited exchanges about who had really earned parliamentary victories over the coming year. Oliver Cromwell played a crucial role at Marston Moor, more important than that played by the Covenanters or the earl of Manchester, but his association with Independency led many parliamentarian Presbyterians to downplay this, while Lilburne and others made much of Crawford's misjudgement at York. In addition to differences about what kind of church a victorious Parliament might establish, a widening disagreement developed not just about tactics in particular situations but about the overall military strategy. There were those, like Lilburne and Cromwell, who sought an outright military victory as the basis from which to impose terms; while others were sceptical that a lasting settlement could be achieved that way, and alarmed by the costs of securing such a victory. They tried instead to sustain the pressure while seeking a peaceful settlement. Vigorous prosecution of the war, and a suspicion of Presbyterianism, set Lilburne at odds with such 'peace party' politicians and, increasingly, Presbyterian parliamentarians like Manchester. By the same token it made him a more comfortable ally of religious Independents who wanted a clear military victory as a prelude to a settled peace.

Lilburne had continued his campaign against his former commander, Colonel King, pressing ceaselessly to get him court-martialled. Eventually he got support in the form of a petition from the townsmen of Boston, and a formal charge presented to the earl of Manchester by the County Committee for Lincoln.[101] This battle with King was increasingly connected with national politics and wider problems within the command of the Eastern Association army. Cromwell did not support Lilburne in getting King court-martialled, but as a vigorous and effective soldier, and as a protector of tender consciences, he was clearly a political ally on this broader front: Lilburne 'was so faithfull, resolute, and successefull, that he became the darling and bosome-friend to [Oliver] *Cromwell*'.[102]

These tensions over the conduct of the war and the shape of the peace also led to Lilburne's growing estrangement from Manchester. The earl seemed oddly reluctant to press home the advantage after these significant victories. He was a 'sweet meek man' and the loss of life at the siege of York may have marked him, as it did his chaplain Simeon Ash. There was more than simple war weariness behind his increasingly cautious approach to the campaign, however: it also reflected his belief 'that it would not be well for the kingdom if it wer ended by the sword'. Manchester had joined the conflict to perfect religious reformation in England, but no longer felt that the war would lead to that: a parliamentary military victory would not create a new Jerusalem but perhaps instead a religious chaos, a sure guarantee of further strife.[103] Neither would it establish a sound government under a secure monarchy. Following the fall of York the parliamentary armies had taken the castles at Sheffield, Welbeck, and Bolsover, but Manchester had passed by Pontefract without trying to summon it, and he now fell out with Lilburne, who remained committed to vigorous action. As a consequence Lilburne came to believe that Manchester had 'visibly degenerated, and would have hanged me, for being over honest and over active in taking *Tikel Castle* too soon'.[104]

Lilburne had gone to Tickhill at Cromwell's command a week after Marston Moor. He was at the head of four troops of dragoons looking for quarter and aiming to do their best to stop the royalist garrison from launching damaging sallies against the parliamentarian forces. Lilburne set guards to prevent people moving between the town and the castle, at points around the town, and took control of a mill and dam which allowed him to empty the moat. All of this was in line with his orders from Cromwell. What changed the nature of the encounter, at least according to Lilburne, was the evident willingness of the castle's defenders to surrender. Some of the sentries in the castle called to Lilburne's men that they 'would not shoot a bullet against them, for their commanders used them bas[e]ly and kept their pay from them'. He also discovered from his landlord that they had very limited supplies of powder and that the men inside were 'no great fighters but were altogether given to their pleasures'. As a result he gave permission to some of his men to call to them over the wall, and to agree a ceasefire. Soon after the talking started he was invited into the castle to 'be merrie with them'. This offer he refused, saying he had no commission for it; in response they asked if instead they could come out 'to be merrie at the Ale-house a little'.[105]

Convinced that they 'had no mind to fight, but were rather desirous, upon reasonable terms to be rid of the castle', Lilburne told them he would go to Doncaster to get permission to talk to them. This he did, but Manchester's response was very unwelcoming. Lilburne met him while he was out taking the air, with Cromwell and many of his other chief officers. When Lilburne told him about the chance of taking Tickhill Manchester seemed 'to slight'. Lilburne also told him that there were many such small garrisons in the area, causing a lot of damage, and that taking one of them might lead to the taking of others, but Manchester was not interested. He thought summoning it would engage his army, since it was said to be a strongpoint, and that it would therefore be a distraction. 'I will not loose ten men for the gayning of it, in regard I doe not Iudge it worth such losse'.[106]

Taken aback, Lilburne asked permission to summon it, promising that if he did not then succeed in taking the castle Manchester could hang him. Rather than give an explicit command, could he not just wink at it? That way Manchester's honour would not be engaged if the castle did not surrender, but Lilburne would be free to accept a surrender should that be the outcome. Manchester responded 'get thee gone, thou art a mad fellow', which Lilburne interpreted as agreement. He also asked the opinion of a senior officer present who confirmed that it was reasonable to believe that Lilburne now had permission to summon the castle. Lilburne was careful on this point, knowing that important people in the army now bore him grudges, including Manchester's chaplains, Ash and Good, who were friends of King's and of Crawford, whom Lilburne had publicly criticized for his recklessness at York. Conscious then that he was a 'great...eye sore' to important people in the army, he rode away, confident that he had covered his back.[107]

Once back at Tickhill he wrote out a summons and the very next morning the governor, 'very fairly and like a man willing to yield' sent out articles of surrender. Lilburne rode with them and two garrison commanders to Doncaster, to deliver them to Manchester and see the terms of surrender performed. They found him once again taking the air, and the news did not improve his mood:

> without any more adoe, in the presence of the companie (which were many) and the presence, and hearing of the Cavaileers,...fell a calling me Rogue, Rascall, and base fellow, and asked me wither he or I was Generall, and told me, the Armie was to much troubled with such busie Rogues as I was, and he

would send me farre enough from it, and also told me I deserved to be hanged, and would not suffer me to speake one word in my owne defence, but turned away from me in greater fury than ever I see him in, in my days.

Manchester's response, he was sure, was 'a cleere Demonstration . . . that he in a manner scorned to accept of the Castle because I had taken it'.[108]

Part of Manchester's embarrassment, presumably, was that he could not very well refuse to accept the surrender, and with Cromwell's intercession it was accordingly done. All the provision, arms, ammunition, and horses (save only twelve for the officers) were taken. As a result Manchester acquired around sixty horses, and a large amount of wheat, rye, peas, cheese, and bacon as well as butter, beef, and bread. Lilburne and his men received no reward for this haul, saving some hay, coals, and 'lumbering odd things'.[109]

Cromwell agreed that Manchester had been 'very unwilling' to summon the castle, 'and expressed much anger and threates against him that (being sent to quarter in the towne) did summon it, though upon the bare summons it was surrendered'. Manchester, though, had written to the Committee of Both Kingdoms (the body in charge of the war) on 27 July, claiming credit. Since arriving in Doncaster 'I have intended as much as in mee lyes, the freeing of these parts from the violence and oppressions which they suffered under the garrisons of the enemy'. Tickhill was one such, 'being the nearest and most prejudiciall to the Isle of Axholme', and claimed to have summoned it at his first arrival. He reported the haul of horse and men, and that the gentlemen had been allowed to go to their dwellings 'because they referred themselves very much to my disposall'. Quite contrary to what Lilburne reported him to have said, he now boasted: 'The place is of consequence, in respect it lyes to hinder all commerce betwixt Derbyshire and these parts'.[110]

This episode clearly left Lilburne disillusioned. Worse still, and despite having taken credit from his political masters for capturing the castle, Manchester continued to bear a grudge against him. Lilburne had heard that Manchester continued to threaten revenge on him, and that at a meeting in a London tavern, 'the Beare at bridgefoot, before two Lords and five eminent men of the House of Commons, his honour spoke both very great, high and disgracefull words of me, about that very businesse'.[111]

Divisions such as these were growing, and intersected with religious differences. Cromwell was accused, with some justification, of trying to fill the army's ranks with Independents. Lilburne had been one of his recruits and, as we have seen, took up the cudgels against Colonel King.

He was pressing for the court martial of King at the same time that other Presbyterian officers were under attack from Independent opponents, including Crawford who was now in Lilburne's sights. From the summer of 1644 these tensions were increasingly difficult to manage. Cromwell's hostility to the Presbyterian interest was reinforced by his growing sense of the rigidity of Scots Presbyterian convictions and the grudging recognition he had got from the Presbyterian interest for his contribution to the great victory at Marston Moor. This led him, in August, to try to rid the army of Presbyterians. He and 'his Colonels' threatened to resign their commissions if their opponents were not dismissed.[112]

Manchester's inactivity was now very apparent. Since Marston Moor he had ignored an order to follow Prince Rupert's retreating army into Lancashire, and did not listen to calls from his own officers to put pressure on the royalist strongpoint at Newark. Instead, the army rested at Lincoln, during which time Tickhill was taken against his will. Between August and October he ignored sixteen orders from the Committee of Both Kingdoms and three from the House of Commons. When he did eventually move it was to go to the relief of Reading, where he arrived too late. Having joined up with the forces of Sir William Waller and the earl of Essex, he was engaged at the second battle of Newbury, on 28 October, but he delayed his attack until late in the day, and it failed. The royalist forces were able to withdraw without significant losses under cover of darkness. Ignoring advice to follow them, he preferred instead to summon Donnington Castle, but when his attempt to storm it failed he withdrew, allowing a royalist force to arrive for its relief unchallenged within, as one contemporary put it, not much more than a musket shot from his troops. He left, apparently to relieve parliamentary forces besieging Basing House, but never got there, and the siege was subsequently abandoned.[113]

This was the background to broader recriminations in the parliamentary coalition that autumn. At Donnington, challenged by Cromwell about his failure to prevent the arrival of the relieving force, Manchester had said 'if we beat the king ninety and nine times yet he is king still, and so will his posterity be after him; but if the King beat us once we shall all be hanged, and our posterity made slaves'. Cromwell's response has also earned fame: 'My lord, if this be so, why did we take up arms at first?'[114] The argument was aired before the Commons in late November, when the House heard Cromwell's accusations about the earl's weak commitment. Manchester responded in the Lords, accusing Cromwell of failing to respect nobility, and of fostering religious radicalism.

At the same time the earl of Essex was under similar pressure for failing to press home the military advantage, and the result was the proposal of a self-denying ordinance—that no member of the Houses should hold a commission in the army or a civil office. The formal justification was that doing so gave them a vested interest in the war, and about discussions of its progress. However, the ordinance would also have the effect of barring all the Lords, including obviously Essex and Manchester, from military command. In an associated measure, a new army was formed, taking orders and supply directly from the Committee of Both Kingdoms—the New Model. The disputes had at least achieved clarity on that—the war would now be pursued vigorously to its conclusion.

Lilburne was certainly clear where he stood on all this: Manchester had visibly turned 'Knave, and apparently betraying his trust at *Dunnington*, in designing his Army, or the best part of it, a sacrifice to the Kings fury'. This convinced Lilburne to 'engage against him, and others of his Associates, with *Cromwel*, who thereunto solicited me'.[115] In this context it was significant that Manchester had accused Lilburne of being too 'busie' in taking Tickhill Castle: it was a term used of minor officials who were too literal-minded in their interpretation of their office. For Lilburne what the army said it was doing was clear, and he was wholehearted in pursuit of that aim; for Manchester it was a much more subtle and nuanced undertaking.

When it came to formal accusations against Manchester, Lilburne's testimony had been important, he having such close knowledge of Colonel King's behaviour that Cromwell had not had 'so materiall a witnesse (or that durst so effectually appeare)' as Lilburne, who testified fully 'not knowing what belonged to fear or distrust'.[116] Where others had found their commitments challenged by the hardships and suffering, coming like Manchester to the view that the war could have no victor, it was Lilburne's disillusion with his commander that led him to consider what really mattered.

Nonetheless, he had also apparently lost his stomach for the fight. His encounters with the internal politics of the high command, particularly the argument about Tickhill, had left him disillusioned. These events did 'so vex and perplex my very soule … and so cooled my courage in fighting, that I could never from that day to this present houre, draw my sword, nor ingage my life in the way of a Souldier, with that freenesse, alacrity and cheerfullnesse, as formerlie I had'.[117] Cromwell urged him to join the New Model, but

Lilburne said he could not, since he would be required to take the Solemn League and Covenant, which he could not do. He had served Parliament out of conscience, which was a greater tie than any human covenant, and had never given his Parliament any reason to distrust his commitment. If after all this they nonetheless 'distrusted me, I was resolved not to serve a Jealous master'.[118] He 'threw up [his] Commission', as he later claimed, 'upon a just dislike of the corrupt managing [of the war]' and left military service on 30 April 1645.[119]

3

Partisan, 1645–6

New enmities: Presbyterians and Independents, 1643–5

The divisions afflicting the army had developed more quickly and more openly on London's streets and in the presses. In fact, the most heated arguments about the future of the English Church and its government were now taking place *within* the parliamentary coalition rather than between the royalists and parliamentarians. In 1641, leading London divines had met at the house of Edmund Calamy and agreed not to debate church government in public, emphasizing instead the need for unity in the face of the threat of popery.[1] By 1643, however, it was increasingly difficult to put off the argument, and in June that year Parliament passed an ordinance empowering a new body, the Westminster Assembly, to meet to define a new religious settlement. The suggestion had first been made in 1641, so it was not an expedient measure, and the assembly went about its work carefully and conscientiously, eventually producing the Westminster Confession, which is still a spiritual guide for millions of Presbyterians. In 1643, though, many Independents saw here a threat to what they had been fighting for. The agreement of the Solemn League and Covenant in the early autumn really brought these issues to the fore, and they became ever more pressing over the following two years as military victory seemed increasingly likely.

The absence of effective press controls and the breakdown in the silence agreed at Calamy's house meant that these issues were being thrashed out at length and in public. In the process opinions hardened and more radical positions evolved. Some people, like Cheney Culpeper, a minor Kentish gentleman, found this an exhilarating prospect: 'I cannot but conceiue...that men are like (by a reassuminge theire owne judgementes from the vassilage of former ages) to caste off all blinde reuerence of suche pretended powers as…cannot proue themselues grownded upon publike consente'. For Culpeper these arguments were an invitation to debate all matters—political, theological, and scientific—in order to discover real, fundamental, and universal truths.[2] For others, though, this chaotic debate threatened the collapse of cultural order, tradition, and learning.

Certainly some very challenging voices were now being heard. Roger Williams had gone to settle in Massachusetts during the 1630s but had fallen foul of religious discipline there. In 1644 he came back to England seeking parliamentary protection, and published his *Bloudy Tenant of Persecution*. It recounted his troubles, and argued that civil authorities had no role in policing religious life: civil government came from the people, and so had no authority from God in spiritual affairs. The primitive church had not been persecuting, but had in fact endured unjust persecution. Religious persecution by the civil state was clearly unjustifiable: the claim that secular authorities had any role in religious discipline was a bloody tenet because it led to the punishment of men and women trying to follow their own conscience in worshipping God.[3]

For many respectable puritans such Independency seemed not just wrong-headed but a danger to true religion. There was by 1644 a well-established polemical literature demonstrating how the lack of discipline led to error—behaviour so obviously sinful that it could not be God's will—but it was not just a press scare. Some of the ideas now circulating seemed to threaten the social order, not just the spiritual health of individual Christians. John Milton had married in the summer of 1642, but the marriage had suffered 'almost instantaneous collapse', leading him to speculate on what might be just grounds for divorce. Rejecting the six traditional grounds for divorce, he argued, in *The Doctrine and Discipline of Divorce* (1643), that if there was no spiritual or emotional life in a marriage then a man should be able to get it dissolved.[4] The following year Richard Overton, soon to be a close ally of Lilburne's, challenged a central tenet of orthodox Christian belief. He was probably around the same age as Lilburne, and may have attended Queens College, Cambridge, but he had not graduated or attended one of the Inns of Court. An opponent of the Laudian Church, he had sympathized with the Scots and had high hopes of Parliament, but he had also been a member of a congregation in Amsterdam at some point before 1640. There he had heard unorthodox speculation about the relationship between body and soul—was the latter really eternal? In *Mans Mortalitie* he argued that souls would be resurrected at the Last Judgement, but in the meantime had died: mortalism, to give it its theological name, was regarded by many Christians not simply as an error, but as a heresy, something plainly contrary to essential Christian belief. Then and now it was suspected that people who think this do not really believe the Christian message of sin and redemption, although the counter-case was that thinking soul and body were resurrected together made redemption even more compelling.[5] While not as outlandish and atheistical as has sometimes been suggested, the ideas themselves were very alarming, and perhaps even more alarming was that they should be laid out by men such as Overton—who had no formal qualifications—for anyone who cared to read them. The break-down of church government could seem to threaten the breakdown of religious decency, and even Christian orthodoxy.

In this context the Solemn League and Covenant, with its apparent promise of a Presbyterian settlement in England, seemed a way of restrain-ing heterodox thought; others, Lilburne among them, saw it as a redefinition of the war aims, and a prize for which they had not thought they were fighting. A test of loyalty for those in arms, and a means for excluding people from office, it became a new touchstone of loyalty to the parliamentary cause. This penalized many of those who had served the parliamentary cause well over the preceding few years.

There had also been a concerted attempt to restore greater control over the presses during and after 1643. Pre-publication licensing had been lost as collateral damage in the attack on the courts of the Star Chamber and High Commission and on monopolies like that of the Stationers' Company. A new ordinance to restore controls had been passed in June 1643, around the same time that the Westminster Assembly had been summoned. This had not attracted much adverse comment, or in fact much comment at all: there was no principled case for the removal of pre-publication licensing at this point.[6] However, it was widely believed by Independents that regu-lation had not been a neutral governmental measure, but one being used against them.

In fact this clampdown does seem to reveal with particular clarity net-works of printers promoting the Independent cause. For example, days after the passage of the ordinance, Peter Cole's house had been raided. He was a stationer and sympathetic to the separatists, acting as a trustee for Richard Overton when the latter's press was confiscated. Cole was required to enter a large bond to get his keys back, promising not to publish unlicensed material, and not to move the presses.[7] Overton himself had been very

Fig. 3.1. William Walwyn (1600–81)

active, without license and outside the Stationers' Company, and willing to publish highly controversial texts. He was also in the headlights when control was reimposed.[8] In December 1643 Lawrence Sanders was arrested. He was a business associate of Clement Writer, who was by then a close friend of William Walwyn's, who championed Sanders' case.[9] Walwyn (Fig. 3.1) had been publishing in favour of religious toleration since 1641 and was another man soon to be closely allied with Lilburne. In February 1644 there was another raid on Cole's house and another independent printer, Dexter, left for America.[10]

There were connections among the authors too. It was Milton who had introduced Roger Williams to his printer and inquiries into the authorship and publication of *Mans Mortalitie* and *The Doctrine and Discipline of Divorce* were launched at the same time by the House of Commons on 26 August 1644.[11] Many of these men, now falling foul of the parliamentarian authorities—Overton, Walwyn, Sanders, Cole, and Writer—were to be important to Lilburne's activism over the next few years.

Although this was clearly a problem for some individuals, it would be an exaggeration to say that there was an effective clampdown—there is no very obvious change in what was available on London's bookstalls. Polemical battles, and attempts to restrain printing, induced caution in men like Overton and Walwyn, but did not stop them publishing. Walwyn's name appears on only seven publications, but he clearly authored many more. Nor did these attempts at control stop the escalation and clarification of the arguments either. In 1643 and 1644, Walwyn had developed a wholly novel view of necessary constitutional change, promoting it first through direct agitation around a Remonstrance and then, the following year, in anonymous publications.[12] Arguments for toleration were refined in Henry Robinson's *Liberty of Conscience*, William Walwyn's *Compassionate Samaritane*, and, as we have seen, in Williams's *Bloudy Tenent*. Because of their immediate context they touched also on freedom of the press, something which was now championed by Milton in *Areopagitica*.[13] Nonetheless, the looming possibility of a Presbyterian settlement, and a sense that the presses were being closed to proponents of Independency, increased the perception that a wing of the parliamentary coalition might be offered a settlement that did not repay their loyalty to the cause.

★   ★   ★

Over the coming year, Lilburne's disillusionment with army service was redoubled by his exposure to these increasingly rancorous arguments and by what he felt was a more immediate and practical denial of his dues.

This more immediate personal injustice was a pressing matter. Released from prison in 1640 he had gone into brewing, supported by an investment of £1,000 from his uncle George. He had, he said, with God's blessing and his own 'industry and paines,...in short time raised a compitent trade in a house, that had none in it before, and within a short time after upon agreement betwixt us, he turned it all over to me'. He had laid out £1,500 on stock and equipment, but was so successful that he met all debts and charges, despite deteriorating conditions on the eve of war: he had lost £200 on a single load of coals, for example, that he had to sell in haste and which were worth far more only two months later.[14] But military service had interrupted this, and brought him no material reward or security. As a result, when he left the army, 'I was robd of my trade, and in greater bondage by my fighting for justice, liberty and freedome, then I was before: I was at a mighty stand with my selfe what to do to provide for my selfe and family'.[15]

While he was away fighting his brewing business had been let at an annual rent to one Binmon, 'but during the time of my imprisonment at *Oxford*, he let the house run to decay, and gave over brewing in it, and run away I doe not know whether'. When John got back part of the roof had collapsed, rain was getting in, and much of the equipment had been damaged. Forced to lease the house once more at a low rate on his return to the army, he also had many bad debts: numerous debtors had taken advantage of the charge for treason in 1642, some of them saying they would not pay anything to a traitor. The business may have drawn on his uncle's connections in the north-east, and that was also badly affected by the war. As a result, 'when J came home I found about [£400–£500] of my debts become altogether desperate'.[16]

Renewed military service had not helped. It was not only that his vigorous service had not been recognized ('the best requitall that *I* got at [Manchester's] hand, was an earnest endeavor by him to hang me'[17]), he had not been paid either. He had undergone considerable costs, in plunder, quarter, and care for his men, and was himself owed around £700 in arrears but 'for any thing I can perceive am likely to be paid at *Domes-day* in the afternoone'. Colonel King, he thought, had at least £20,000 at his disposal, but had refused to pay any of it out.[18] Disappointed in his quest for reparations, his brewing business run into the ground, and owed significant arrears of pay from the army, Lilburne now needed a fresh start. Finding some money from somewhere (he did not say where, perhaps not wishing to complicate his claims for reparations and arrears), he had hoped to invest in the cloth trade with Holland, but had been thwarted in this by '*the Prerogative-Pattentee monopolizing Merchant adventurers*'.[19]

The evidence of these private financial affairs is difficult to verify of course, but much of it was recounted in debates with his enemies in which he was clearly challenged on details, and refuted claims that he was lying. He expected such challenges, and produced copies of orders, committee papers, and so on where possible, and promised to authenticate his claims before parliamentary committees; he also repeated many of these details in a petition to the Commons.[20] It seems true then that he faced serious financial difficulties. Behind them lay some figures with whom Lilburne had very little political sympathy—not least of course King, who would not pay him arrears and costs from military service, and Manchester, who was clearly no ally.

Lilburne's wider family had similar complaints. The loss of the north-east had caused ruin to his father, Richard: 'our Country was betrayed by those that should have preserved it'. As a result, 'for my affection to the publique, I lost all that ever the enemy could finger of mine' for the whole time the region was under royalist control. By the same token, when the Scots took the north-east from the royalists in the early spring of 1644, there were opportunities for the wider Lilburne family to recover their fortunes. Both John's father Richard and his uncle George began to strengthen their local position through service in Parliament's committees and commissions, while his elder brother Robert's military service was putting him on a course that eventually secured him the governorship of Newcastle, and some political prominence during the 1650s.[21] In this, however, they rubbed up against the ambitions of Sir Henry Vane and others who were building up their fortunes at the same time. To add insult to injury, it was Vane that George Lilburne and others blamed for the loss of the north-east in the first place, as we have seen.[22]

In any case, their recovery was not complete by 1645, and Richard complained that 'though I have my land, yet being in the Bishopprick of *Durham*, I can make little or nothing of it'. In a twist that was irritatingly familiar to John, this was in some contrast to the fortunes of other, less virtuous men: his father complained that he had not enjoyed any reparation for his losses from the estates of those who should have protected the region, but did not, and who now enjoyed their own estates 'with advantage'. The injustice seems to have rankled as much as the loss, but in any case it meant he could not help his son out of his problems either: having suffered these losses 'I in a manner, am as new to begin the world as thy selfe'.[23] Despite a reconciliation with his father, John could get no more help from him now than had been available five years earlier.

Over the coming years John's own quest for reparations, and his family's ambitions to establish or repair their fortunes in the north-east, were obstructed by political opponents or rivals. These frictions were exacerbated by differences over religion, of course, but Lilburne was increasingly prompted to a more secular argument—that they represented an abuse of political position, and a failure to reward honest political service. Lilburne's own fidelity to the parliamentary cause was manifest in his actions, but he was now suspect because he was on the wrong side of the arguments about the Solemn League and Covenant; in the meantime, some of those whose fidelity he doubted had been able to take the Covenant without any difficulty and so could now prosper: notably Sir Henry Vane. Unsurprisingly, given his formation in the martyrological tradition, Lilburne saw the proof of his commitment in his steadfastness and suffering in the parliamentary cause and he was not impressed by fine words from those who could not match his record. Failure to reward that loyalty was proof of the corruption and bankruptcy of the parliamentary leadership.

These issues of virtue and reward were central to the tensions which increasingly threatened to break apart the parliamentary coalition. The shape of the church settlement was also, in a way, an issue about reward for the suffering, since a Presbyterian settlement might lead to the persecution of some of those who had been loyal servants of Parliament during the war and the bravest opponents of the bishops: Colonel King had, after all, imprisoned officers of the Eastern Association, having broken up an Independent meeting in Boston.[24] These intertwining issues, and the difficulties he encountered in resolving them, began to prompt Lilburne to think carefully about what the war was really about.

★   ★   ★

When Lilburne returned to London at the end of 1644 he had been 'expecting a joyfull and cheerfull entertainment, and good acceptation both of my selfe and all other the like conscientious persons', but he was gravely disappointed. '[T]o my exceeding grief and astonishment, I found a very sad and frowning countenance from most of those that formerly had had us in great and good esteeme'.[25] The city was full of stories of the hard usage suffered by Independents, as the Solemn League and Covenant was used against them as vigorously as against Neutrals and Malignants 'though their faithfulnesse were no whit doubtfull'. Behind these persecutions, and a palpable popular hostility, lay 'sundrie invective and provoking language divulged both from the Pulpit and Presse'. A key figure in this was one of his former friends: 'Wherein I found none to exceed or to come neer unto my old fellow-sufferer Mr *Prinne*, from whom I least expected such bitter expressions'.[26]

In early January 1645, Prynne was fresh from his labours in the trial of William Laud. This had ended successfully in the archbishop's execution and Prynne had played a key role, going through Laud's papers and publishing an edited version of his diary, in a prosecution marked by particular malice. Yet this hostility to Laudianism did not make him a friend of Independency: he now published *Truth Triumphing*, a sustained assault on the dangers posed by Independency to what he saw as the core of the parliamentary cause.

In order to defend his view of the church, Prynne had also to defend tradition and authority, since much of what he treasured was not laid out explicitly in the scriptures. It is a lengthy tract, larded with citations from the

Bible, but also from legal and antiquarian sources. It also makes direct comment on contemporary writers, both in approval and reproof. He mounted a learned defence of the role of princes, parliaments, and magistrates in religious matters, but also of 'Antiquity over Novelty': he was addressing both the question in hand—church discipline and its relation to civil authority—but also how such arguments should be settled. Perhaps a little hypocritically given his own combative style, he had in his sights 'Polemicall School-divinity'.[27] His main worry though was that by undercutting the religious role of the secular authorities the Independents were doing the work of Arminians and Papists—attacking the fundamental laws and liberties of the English church: indeed 'the very Malignant Prelates, and Anti-Parliamentary Cavaliers, having not proceeded, in this kind, so farre as [the Independents]'. In brief, Prynne had not supported the parliamentary war effort in order to sweep away the Church of England, but to defend it, and in order to defend it he now had to defend scholarship, custom, tradition, and established authorities.[28] Having dispatched Laud he clearly felt this was the moment to turn his attention towards these dangers within the parliamentary coalition—both the substantive arguments of the Independents and their lack of respect for established ways of arguing.

Truth Triumphing was a contribution to a much wider debate. For example, John Goodwin, named as one of the targets on Prynne's title page, had within a week published a ninety-nine-page reply to an earlier Prynne pamphlet.[29] Although Lilburne was not at the centre of these exchanges, he nonetheless entered into paper combat as eagerly as he had gone to war, claiming that he was dragged into it by the Presbyterians. This is perhaps an exaggeration, but it is certainly true that his quarrels with Manchester and Colonel King were picked up by Presbyterians outside the army as part of this wider argument.[30] 'Here began' a later pamphlet claimed 'Mr. *Lilburne* and all other honest mens overthrow'. The means for this overthrow were 'railing & lying pamphlets' which abused and provoked him to a response that got him in trouble with the Committee of Examinations, the Commons committee responsible for policing the presses.[31]

Lilburne wrote to Prynne on 7 January, a few days after the publication of *Truth Triumphing*. Having received no answer he had his letter printed, without licence, on 15 January. *A copie of a letter* complained about the 'bitter and unsavory Language against the poore Saints of God', and wished that they could contend 'upon even ground and equall termes, namely that the

Presse might be as open for us as for you'. Bridling at the suggestion that Independents had betrayed the cause, he denounced the 'Blacke-Coates in the Synod' (the presbyters).[32] Later in the year he was to claim that the monopoly of printing, which had allowed 'Canterbury and his Malignant party [to pursue] their Arbitrary Designes', had simply changed hands. Many of the same men in the Stationers' Company were now 'invested with an Arbitrary unlimmited Power, even by generall Ordinance of Parliament' and printed what they liked, even lies and things tending 'to the poysoning of the Kingdom with unjust and Tyrannicall Principles'. At the same time they censored other publications, effectively suppressing knowledge of rights and liberties, while scurrilous royalist pamphlets circulated freely in the capital.[33]

Those who took the Solemn League and Covenant were obliged to discover enemies to its purposes.[34] Lilburne acknowledged the implicit threat that Prynne might see this as obliging him to denounce him, but was unperturbed: 'I weigh it not'. Although the Presbyterians were dominating the presses, and securing influence over the course of affairs, Lilburne claimed, as he had done in opposition to Laud, that he had strong arguments on his side: 'finding your confidence very great but your Arguments very weak and unsound'. He challenged Prynne and his allies to public disputation, just as he had Laud in 1641.[35]

There was obviously a strictly religious element to this conflict with Prynne, over the nature of the church, and the sources of authority which could guide Christian behaviour. The publishers who Lilburne worked with were clearly motivated by these religious controversies: Overton (whose press published the Copie of a letter), Walwyn, and Thomas Paine.[36] Overton's own writing had turned away from knotty philosophical and theological problems like the nature of the soul, and towards a more direct and satirical attack on clerical pretensions in the so-called Marpriest tracts.[37] This campaign was coordinated with that of Thomas Paine, who was also publishing Walwyn, and it was around this time that Lilburne and Walwyn first met.[38]

Clearly Lilburne's religious sympathies were with these opponents of the Presbyterians. When A light for the ignorant had been republished in 1641 it was virtually identical, but the passage relating to the nature of a true church had been revised in ways that made his commitment to Independency stronger. Presumably, with bishops now tottering, the differences he had with his Presbyterian allies were becoming more significant.[39] After that,

however, he said very little about his vision for church government, and in
fact seemed offended that the agreement at Calamy's house in 1641 not to
dispute these issues in public had not been respected: he correctly pointed
out that 'he had not in print medled or made with the Controversies of the
Church'.[40] What he did say, though, was that he did not oppose a state church
'to make the generality of the Land-members of', but he would not be
compelled to attend himself: his conscience should be left 'free to the Law
and Will of my Lord and King [i.e. God]'.[41] Such freedom of conscience
was an important issue for Overton's press in these months, and it now
republished Lilburne's pamphlet *An answer to nine arguments*, first written in
1638. This spoke directly to the escalating conflict of the church settlement,
although Lilburne claimed to be surprised that it was proving inflammatory,
having been written 'in the Fleet above 6. yeares agoe, in the hight of the
Bishops tyrannie'.[42]

Unsurprisingly, given his conclusions on these issues, Lilburne was dismissive of tradition and learning in exactly the ways that Prynne had identified as a danger to respectable order:

> you spend a great deale of paines in citing old rusty Authours, to prove that
> Kings, Councels Synods and States have for so many hundred yeares medled
> with matters of Religion, I grant you they have; but I demand of you, by what
> Right or by what Authority out of the Word of God they have done so?

If the test was simply that established governments could govern their
churches, did this not prove that Queen Mary had been within her rights in
sending the godly to their deaths? For Lilburne, popery lay in the conjoin-
ing of civil and ecclesiastical power: the work of the Pope was 'to joyne the
Ecclesiasticall and *Civil State* together, making the golden Lawes of Christ to
depend upon the leaden Lawes of men'.[43]

This was clearly an argument about the government of the Christian
community. Perhaps equally importantly, though, Prynne emphasized the
need to preserve the legal rights and liberties of princes and parliaments,
whereas Lilburne said he was fighting for the 'subject's liberty'.[44] He was
drawn into the fight by the attacks on what Prynne 'stiles Independants,
&c.' primarily because of the injustice this represented as a return on his
'integrity and uprightness (as also the rest of those he defames) towards
our native Country'.[45] This was the real damage done by the Solemn
League and Covenant. It had been intended to produce unity, but the sad
experience had been that it had in fact set 'us at as bitter a Warre and

contestation amongst ourselves', a war almost as bitter as that 'we have with our professed enemies'.[46]

In any case, when Lilburne entered into battle with Prynne in 1645 it was not simply as an advocate of religious Independency: there was also a more secular claim about just reward for his sufferings, related to his freedom of religious conscience, but also to his freedom to defend his views in print, and to secure his dues from Parliament. He was clearly motivated by his religious views, and continued to draw on the martyrological tradition to make his sufferings stand for a more general cause. He claimed too that his proficiency in public disputation came as a 'Talent from the Lord', and that as a consequence 'I conceived my selfe bound in Conscience to imploy it'.[47] But in the coming year, it was the denial of his legal rights, not freedom of conscience, that came to predominate his public self-presentation.

Having published his letter to Prynne, Lilburne was immediately in trouble with his political enemies, and on 17 January the Committee of Examinations asked the Stationers' Company to investigate who had published the pamphlet. The Stationers' had that day found Nicholas Tew publishing illegally from Coleman Street, and committed him to the Fleet. Tew had initially refused to name his accomplices, but once in the Fleet he confessed that the press had been brought to his house. Although he could not say by whom, about the same time he had taken a lodger, Overton, whose christian name Tew claimed to think was Robert. People arrived to use the press usually in the morning, before Tew was awake, and the type, he claimed, was not set there. Two texts by Lilburne had been produced there, including the letter to Prynne.[48] The proceedings against Lilburne, though, were dismissed, in all likelihood reflecting the influence of powerful friends, including Oliver Cromwell.[49]

He seems to have had some protectors in May, too, when he was taken into custody once more, this time alongside Jane Coe and Henry Robinson to answer for the printing of the *Copie of a letter*. At the conclusion of the hearing Lawrence Whitaker, the chair, commended him for his valour and good service, but advised him 'as a friend, to be moderate and wise, that so you may not loose that good repute that hetherto you have deserved from us'. He was also warned to 'publish nothing', although he could now go home as a free man. Thus, 'for all *William Prinns* mallice' his fidelity and honesty had been recognized.[50] Back in London he had quickly found himself back in the political spotlight. In fact, with some help, he might be said to have put himself there.

New solidarities: the changing world of political mobilization, 1645

Out of the army and into these paper combats, Lilburne was clearly closely connected with some influential figures in the world of secret printing, and these men were very active in the 'Controversies of the Church'. He was hardly an innocent abroad, of course: a veteran of the puritan underground of the 1630s and well connected in the emerging world of Independent political mobilization. In the weeks after his appearance before the Committee of Examinations he had printed copies of the articles of accusation against Colonel King, distributing them in London before riding to Lincolnshire to do the same. In the meantime, the printer had been apprehended, and admitted that Lilburne had ordered and paid for them, reserving 200 copies 'to disperse privately among his friends'. Prynne claimed that in August Lilburne's 'Emissaries' had been distributing his publications 'in Kent, and elsewhere, no doubt to excite them to a new Rebellion'. There is no particular reason to believe Prynne—he and Lilburne continually contested the accuracy of each other's claims—and in the same publication he had falsely claimed, for example, that Lilburne had been cashiered by Colonel King. In contrast to many other details, however, Lilburne did not contest these particular claims about his uses of print for active mobilization.[51] It is clear, in any case, that he was well known, skilled in his use of the presses, and fast developing an understanding of the world of parliamentary politics.

He had been schooled in the puritan underground by some of the men who now opposed him, but also retained some friends from those days: both Larner and Kiffin had reprinted work by him in 1641, and four years later he was printing with Larner again. These connections had expanded: Larner also seems to have had connections with Overton.[52] While Lilburne had been in prison in Oxford, and at war, Walwyn had been active in London, raising money and putting pressure on the parliamentary authorities to pursue the war vigorously. In this he had cooperated with Sir Henry Marten, mobilizing the London citizenry through, for example, the Committee for the General Rising. Marten was the son of a judge, and himself a graduate of Oxford who had attended the Inns of Court. Elected in 1640, he was a convinced parliamentarian during the war, and his work on the Committee for a General Rising formed part of the background to the assault on aristocratic military leadership in which Lilburne's testimony about Manchester had played a significant part. Marten was to prove a friend of Lilburne's over the long term, despite some moments of friction.[53] Although Marten's route to these alliances had been different, the networks of Independent authors with whom Lilburne was now working had grown in the same soil as him—a world of voluntary religion and Independency, of mobilization and knowing the law and how to use committees and the presses. He was quickly able to forge strong connections of his own with new contacts like Walwyn and Overton.

He did this not simply to promote his own views, but to defend this pattern of political activity: not just the publication of political argument, but the use of the presses to mobilize concrete political action through petitions, articles of accusation, and so on. The war had transformed government, creating new opportunities and demanding new skills in political mobilization. Parliament was in permanent session and had developed an elaborate committee structure, with extensive powers. This created new political grievances, but also new opportunities. It was porous too, and people were at the door of the House and its committees every day, pressing their case. The presses were much more open than they had been before the war, despite attempts at regulation, and they were used in creative ways. Pamphlets were printed and sold, but not all printing was commercial: fliers were printed to spread on the streets and in the armies. Public disputes allowed conversations to occur which would otherwise not have happened, and to take place in enormous detail. Following a public controversy in the 1640s could be a wearying experience, as claim and counter-claim were thrashed out by multiple authors all arguing across one another. This kind of print brought together networks of fellow travellers, people who became acquainted not as neighbours, or members of the same congregation or guild, but as people who shared an ideological position or a particular policy aim.[54]

These partisan communities were clearly being mobilized through public meetings in London's taverns too. For example, in 1645 the early performance of the New Model Army caused acute anxiety. It had been forged out of the recriminations over the apparent hesitancy and incompetence of the earls of Manchester and Essex, but was initially derided by the royalists. When the campaign season started in earnest, Parliament suffered a major setback when Leicester fell, causing consternation and soul-searching in London. In the wake of this disaster, Lilburne attended a meeting of 200 or 300 people at the Windmill Tavern which discussed what was to be done, and a committee was elected which drew up a petition to London's

Common Council. The aim, according to Lilburne, was to discuss what military steps were necessary (the Eastern Association should be prepared to resist a major royalist advance) and what the clergy might do to help (they could take a six-week break from the Westminster Assembly to go down to the Eastern Association to stiffen the people's resolve). Prynne claimed, however, that this was a conspiracy, led by Lilburne and Hugh Peter, to dissolve the assembly. Lilburne's response is revealing in several ways. He said that Peter had not been there, that he himself had not been in the chair, and that he had been elected to a committee of sixteen, at least a third of whom he hardly knew: it would have been very foolish to enter a conspiracy with men to whom he had hardly spoken before. He claimed that the suggestion did not come from an Independent and that it had support from a Presbyterian member of the assembly.

There is no suggestion in Lilburne's account that such a large meeting in a tavern, the election of a committee, and the drawing up of a petition was in itself unusual practice. In fact, he seems to suggest that there had been other meetings at the Windmill: as well as saying that Peter had not been present on that occasion, Lilburne also said 'to my remembrance, I never saw him there in my life'. Tavern meetings, committees to make proposals to Parliament and City about military strategy and the activity of the clergy, and accusations and counter-accusations in print about these things: in this emerging world petitions were not simply the expression of the voice of a local community, or some other established interest such as a guild, but offered a way to forge and express partisan solidarities. In this case, for example, Lilburne joined a committee consisting in part of people he hardly knew, and worked with people not known for their commitment to Independency.[55]

The acute anxiety caused by the loss of Leicester quickly dissipated following what proved to be the decisive victory of the war at Naseby in June. In the aftermath of that great victory, Sir Thomas Fairfax led the New Model Army on a triumphant campaign in the West Country, and by the late summer the royalist field armies were in tatters. The New Model was associated with religious Independency, and at Langport, as the royalists had scattered before a parliamentarian charge, Colonel Harrison, watching from a hill, had thrown back his head and cried out in religious rapture. Royalist garrisons and strongholds held out around the country, so the war was not over, but the king's field armies had been destroyed and his chance of a military victory had gone.

The approaching parliamentary military victory raised the stakes in arguments about what the peace should bring. Thomas Edwards, the Presbyterian polemicist, claimed that following Naseby the sectaries became more bold in their challenges to the established order.[56] Lilburne was certainly a party to the arguments, having had a key role in the attacks on Manchester. Most recently, he had been at Langport to meet Cromwell and, following the battle, had done further signal service. He had ridden '*post from Summerset-shire* through twenty dangers to bring you the first news of *Lord Gorings Army being routed*'.[57] In return for this service, however, he 'enjoyed nothing but jeares, scoffes and abuses'.[58]

As he entered this battle, the obstructions he found in the world of parliamentary committees—in the regulation of printing and in pursuit of his own financial interests—led him to ask increasingly clearly why the opponents of Charles I's rule had made legal challenges to policies such as Ship Money or unseated his evil advisers, like the earl of Strafford. 'I desire him [Prynne] and the rest of his freinds, to take heed they doe not walke in their steps, if they doe,...they are as accountable for their actions & doings'. Many people who had done little to bring down that regime were now in great places with rich rewards, 'and live in as great pompe, superfluity and bravery, as ever they did in their dayes, by the ruines of the people, when thousands, that have spent all they have in the world, and done the Kingdom good service, have not a bit of bread to put in their mouths'.[59] His experience of renewed persecution made him a focal point for those convinced that Parliament was betraying the cause for which it had originally fought, and his public role reflected the new possibilities for political mobilization in civil war London.

Lilburne's political style was highly personalized—he continually drew on his own experience as evidence of what was wrong with government. As a consequence, his opponents obviously had him in their sights, and much of the biographical information we have about him comes from very personalized attacks on him and his friends. Since he put his record of service at the heart of his account of injustice his opponents naturally tried to undercut it, and it is from these exchanges that we get his emphasis on his gentry background and solid education; his peaceableness as an apprentice and in prison; or his conduct at Tickhill. All of this came in direct response to barbs and accusations from Prynne, Bastwick, and others. Other details of his life are only really known from these sources. For example, Prynne noted that proceedings against Lilburne had been delayed because he had been 'casually run into the eye with the head of a Pike about *Moore-fields*, which for a time endangered both the loss of his life, and eye too'. For Vicars this was a providential punishment for his spiritual pride: like other Independents, Lilburne had cried up his own sufferings and vilified reformed churches by comparison to his own preferences. Lilburne's unjust assault on Prynne had been justly punished by the wound to his eye, sustained immediately after his publishing of 'that most shallow and silly *Letter*'. These attacks were intended to render him ridiculous as a figure of political or religious significance—they sought to rob him of his dignity and make him implausible as a figure of natural authority—and for that reason his allies disputed, for example, the seriousness of his wound.[60] There was also a relatively involved discussion about whether he played cards, for example, and a dissection of the exact wording of his denials.[61] The purpose was also to undercut his claims of injustice, presenting him not as an innocent man of principle undone by injustice, but as a quarrelsome and troublesome man, an unquiet spirit, or a religious hypocrite.

These practices drew on networks and techniques familiar from before the war, but which had rapidly developed beyond what had then been possible, and were now out in the open. One continuity in Lilburne's practice was his habit of dramatizing his own experience as a way of exemplifying what was wrong with the world, but this broadly martyrological reflex was increasingly used to dramatize a legal claim, not a religious one. Lilburne was to prove highly skilled in these arts, and his self-presentation was very powerful, but he was far from unique in his political practice: the Presbyterians worked in exactly the same way, of course. What set Lilburne and his friends apart was the argument they were beginning to make.

A new cause: *England's birthright justified*, 1645

Lilburne had escaped censure earlier in the year for publishing his letter to Prynne, but pursued the fight over the summer of 1645, bringing a second accusation to the Committee for Examinations. When Lilburne appeared, on 11 June, 'I found not so faire play as before, for they would neither heare me nor tell me the cause, nor ground to this day, wherefore they imprisoned me'. The charge was, however, dismissed on 19 July.[62]

Nonetheless, this proved a prelude to more serious trouble. While at Westminster Hall that day he had played some role in promoting rumours that the Speaker, William Lenthall, had been in treasonous correspondence with the royalists, and even that he had sent £60,000 to Oxford. Not only were the disputes in the parliamentary coalition now rancorous, they were marked by an acute suspicion of the motives and integrity of opponents. Lilburne, for example, blamed Bastwick and King for procuring the charge against him in order to divert attention from the treason charge Lilburne was at the same time laying against King. Lilburne's enemies, by contrast, claimed this was part of a conspiracy, and that Lilburne had visited Cromwell at Langport in order to hatch it.[63]

Lilburne was careful to deny this conspiracy: his only purpose at Langport had been to get Cromwell's letter of support for his claim for reparations (which Cromwell did indeed write and which Lilburne published several times); and he had never had any discussion of the accusation about Lenthall before that day at Westminster. He also downplayed his role in spreading the rumours on the day itself: they were already common gossip, 'known to thousands of Citizens by hearing of the eare', and in any case three witnesses had said the same thing to the committee earlier in the day. Lilburne claimed that when William Pendred had started to tell him about it, he had not wanted to hear any more. The only role he would admit to playing in spreading the story was taking Colonel Roe to meet the three citizens who had appeared before the committee. In any case, finally, if he had said these things, should he not have had a legal hearing? The Speaker, however, had convinced the Commons to send Lilburne to prison on the basis of information given to him by Bastwick, although Bastwick and Lilburne had not exchanged a single word about it.[64] To Lilburne this seemed a fundamental contravention of Magna Carta, since he had not been allowed to hear a charge, or to speak in his own defence.[65]

The upshot was another appearance before the Committee of Examinations five days later, this time on a charge of slandering the Speaker.[66] In response he did not so much answer the charge as denounce his enemies in the regime, likening his treatment to that he had suffered at the hands of the bishops. *A coppie of a letter . . . to a freind*, published by Overton's press the day after his arrest, gave details of his hearing, but also claimed Magna Carta as a defence against Parliament—an argument was crystallizing here that the enemy was not the king, but tyranny. He narrated his various sufferings in the parliamentary cause, claiming that he had been rewarded with arbitrary treatment. This tyranny was a matter both of religious conscience and legal rights. He had been hauled before committees three times that year and imprisoned without charge, a striking echo of his sufferings under the Star Chamber, which Parliament itself had denounced. Parliament had in the past offered him protection and justice, but was now denying him these things, and the claim that Parliament's reputation had to be defended was in this case no more than a defence of tyranny. As in his fight against the bishops, he was willing to suffer in defence of his rights.[67]

Around the account of his sufferings Lilburne had developed an argument about the betrayal of Parliament's cause by backsliding and corruption: '*I have been in the field with my sword in my hand, to venter my life and my blood (against Tyrants) for the preservation of my Freedome, and J doe not know that ever J did an act in all my life that disfranchised me of my Freedome*'. The privileges contained in Magna Carta were his '*Birth-right* and Inheritance, which Priviledges have been ratified and confirmed to the free People of *England* this present Parliament, and many Declarations put out against the King, for violating of them.' He was now, however, imprisoned by a vote of the whole House, again for a cause he did not know. He could make no sense of this, he said, in one of his most resonant phrases, unless it was because 'I neither love a slave nor fear a Tyrant'.[68] Parliament needed to be called back to the cause that had led its supporters to take up arms in 1642. This pamphlet was published in several editions, suggesting perhaps that Lilburne had found a significant audience for his case.[69]

These arguments were set out increasingly plainly. His broadsheet, *On the 150th page*, took one of the key parliamentary commitments of the summer of 1642, which had persuaded so many to take up arms, and juxtaposed it with his own treatment. In the spring of 1642, Parliament's declarations and ordinances had been collected and published by Edward Husbands, setting out, cumulatively, the key reasons for taking up arms for Parliament and not the king. On page 150 of the *Book of Declarations* was an argument justifying obedience to the militia ordinance rather than the king's Commission of Array: how could that not be rebellion? Well, ran the answer, law has a literal sense and an equitable meaning, 'For it cannot be supposed that the parliament would ever by law entrust the king with the militia against themselves, or the commonwealth that entrusts *them*, to provide for their weal'. This might not appear in any statute, but such equitable principles need not be openly stated—just as there is no need for a positive law that a general should not turn his cannon on his own army. It is this equity that prevents tyranny by qualifying the letter of the law.[70]

Lilburne now turned these arguments to his own defence. He had probably read the *Book of Declarations* in Newgate in August 1645, although he does not seem to have acquired his own copy until April 1647. Certainly, from around 1645 he began to quote from it more frequently—more often in fact than any source other than the Bible.[71] Was not Parliament itself bound by these principles? And if not, should they not extend this principle to all freemen 'that in all their actions and expressions have declared faithfulness to the commonwealth?' If not, surely they were lawless, and able to rule by their own will, in just the way they had suggested an unrestrained monarch would. Were they free to flout their own ordinances? Lilburne claimed that reporting suspicions about Lenthall was a duty according to the Protestation, which had enjoined those taking it to oppose and bring condign punishment on all those who plotted or acted against the Protestation. Could it be right for Parliament to punish or imprison a man 'for doing what they command him and by oath enjoin him?' This was the same argument that Prynne had used against him: the Protestation *required* him to report Lenthall's treason just as Prynne had felt the Solemn League and Covenant obliged him to denounce Lilburne. Finally, he called for Lenthall to be tried by court martial.[72]

More immediately, the cause for which he fought was the defence of legal rights and liberties, set out in the Protestation and the paper war of 1642; it was not the cause of the Solemn League and Covenant, which he had refused to take. Parliament was the guardian of those rights, not in itself the body for which the war was being fought. First-hand experience of this new Presbyterian persecuting spirit led him not to oppose Parliament, but to decry the corrupting influence of his enemies over its committees. It was not just the suppression of his publications about the impending peace, however. Over the previous six months he had been at some expense trying to get his petition for reparations and arrears heard. To that end he had 'made all the freinds J could in the House' with no effect and Lenthall had been part of the problem: Lilburne had twice gone to his house to solicit his help 'But so lofty and high was hee, that hee would not so much as looke upon me or speak with me though I waighted upon him to his very Coach'.[73] Without favour, he wanted his readers to understand, ordinary men could not get fair treatment from this parliamentary regime.

Lilburne was dealing with a sophisticated political culture in which activists moved between the street, press, and lobbying, and secured influence over the conduct of government. His experience of lobbying was pushing him to an argument that Parliament was open to influence and corruption, and had to be answerable to the Commonwealth it served; so too its individual members. In the terms he had set out from prison in the late 1630s we might say that the laws governing the civil state in England enshrined principles of natural right and reason which were his inheritance.[74] In the 1630s it was the bishops who had threatened those rights, but now it seems that there was a similar potential in the current regime.

Lilburne was before the Committee of Examinations again on 9 August, summoned to answer whether he was the author of a book that had his name on it. He refused to answer, speaking instead about the serial denial of his rights by parliamentary committees. This committee had been given power to imprison him if he did not answer, and he was accordingly committed to Newgate on 11 August, pending trial at Quarter Sessions. Elizabeth, who was expecting another child, joined him there.[75] A petition was promoted on his behalf, in which he said he had no hand, but which kept him in the heat of the polemical battle. Prynne, Bastwick, and King 'with the assistance of their base and rascally agents . . . goe about to make an uproare in the Citie, by framing, posting, and dispersing scandalous paper libells, concerning myselfe, thereby to make me odious, and destroy me'. As a result he wrote to the Lord Mayor on 21 August denying any role in the circulation of a paper claiming that there would be a rising in the city.[76]

In the meantime his house was searched by the Stationers' beadle, Hunscott, one of 'the Bishops old Theeves and Roagues'. He could now argue not just that figures in this new regime *resembled* those of the discredited Laudian regime, they were in some cases literally the same people. As one outraged commentator put it, Hunscott and his cronies, using their warrant to search for 'dangerous Bookes', had instead robbed the houses of honest men, including some of 'the Parliaments best freinds and servants' including 'Lievtenant Colonell *Lilburnes* house': the military title was significant evidence about the injustice of this. While he was in Newgate, and his wife was 'great with Childe, & neer her time', they took their chance. Finding only 'an old Gentle-woman' at the house, who they frightened, and another younger gentlewoman, who was scared that she was in danger of her life, crying out 'in her extreame-Fever, *Hunscott, Hunscott*'. Decency was clearly on the side of the radicals here: these men, formerly creatures of Laud's, did not respect the expectations of class or gender, nor of privacy. '[T]hey ranne up into the Chambers, & stole out of his wives Drawers, divers pieces of her Child-bed linnen and such other things as they pleased', refusing to show the old woman what they had taken 'though shee earnestly intreated them'.[77]

Lilburne's cause attracted some public sympathy: it was said that Mr Knowles had led public prayers for him at St Helen's church.[78] More significantly, perhaps, the 'well-affected citizens of London, Westminster and Southwark' presented a petition on his behalf which had 2,000–3,000 signatures. This was significant pressure, the product of the civic culture glimpsed in the Windmill meeting in June, and the Commons ordered that the case be heard at the next general sessions. In the meantime, he would be given £100 for his maintenance while awaiting trial. The petitioners were told this, but also to mind their own business while common law proceeded.[79] Several pamphleteers took up his case, including William Walwyn and Richard Overton, cementing their emerging alliance. By contrast he continued to drift apart from some old friends—Bastwick and Prynne of course were long gone as allies, and his estrangement from Edmund Rosier, for example, was under way.[80]

While Lilburne was in Newgate two Quarter Sessions had met without his case having been heard. As a result, he wrote to the Lord Mayor asking for his release, and the House of Commons discharged him on 11 October. He was finally released on 14 October, no formal charge having been presented. During 1645 he had experienced apparently arbitrary government at the hands of those who had promised citizens their legal rights and liberties. Lilburne had no reparations, and had been detained or imprisoned by parliamentary committees five times (18 January, 16 May, 18 June, 19 July, and 9 August) on the basis of reports about his publishing activities or what he had said. It is not entirely clear how long he spent in prison or in what conditions, but he had been in safe custody prior to the hearings in May, June, and July, and had just spent three months in Newgate without, in the end, facing any charge.[81] His house had been searched by beadles who had served Charles I. It was easy to believe that this was scant reward for his sufferings.

England's birthright justified had been published four days before his release. This is often attributed to Lilburne, but seems more likely to be the result of a collaboration with his new friends: it is a long rambling text which stitches together a number of different arguments. Taken together, though, it was the most fully articulated argument so far for the institutional changes necessary to put Englishmen in possession of their fundamental legal rights. It opens by juxtaposing the very visible service of those well affected to the

cause with the equally visible injustices now being committed. The opening
pages are the broadsheet *On the 150th page*, setting actual conduct against its
avowed principles, and this leads into a sustained critique of the Solemn
League and Covenant as the test of parliamentary virtue. Would it not be
more just for people to be excluded from office for having demonstrated
their disaffection to 'common Freedom', or taken arms to destroy it, rather
than simply '*for refusing out of Conscience to take the* Nationall Covenant?'
There was a sustained critique of the hypocrisy of Covenant-takers, giving
specific examples of individuals who had done poor service to the cause
and yet were on the right side of the Covenant—Manchester, King, Sir
Henry Vane the elder, Hunscott the beadle who was also an excise man, and
Mayor Gurney—as well as of Lenthall's treason and Bastwick's machinations to cover it up. Lilburne's sufferings were rehearsed around the now
familiar set of grievances.[82]

There was a new organizing concept to make sense of all this—the
dangers of monopolies, increasingly a term used to signify the opposite of
common right and freedom.[83] The clergy, the Merchant Adventurers and
the Stationers all enjoyed powers which infringed on the legal rights of the
freeborn Englishmen. They were also vested interests, and to prevent the
development of such corrupt interests the self-denying ordinance ought to
be fully implemented, and annual elections instituted. Self-denial, the refusal
to benefit from the war effort by taking office, had been a corollary of the
creation of the New Model Army. It was not, however, a marked feature of
the behaviour of many prominent parliamentarians. As Lilburne put it elsewhere, Parliament men seemed unable to find time to do justice to the well
affected, but could nonetheless 'find time enough to settle great and rich
places vpon some of themselves, and to enjoy them, for all their own
Ordinance to the contrary'.[84]

Publication of *England's birthright justified* finally spelt the end for Overton's
press, which was now successfully tracked down and seized by Hunscott.[85]
The alliance among Lilburne, Overton, and Walwyn had developed as they
converged on a number of concrete issues as the focus of their political
campaigns. They shared a practical diagnosis of what was wrong, although
they seem to have arrived at it from rather different directions. For Lilburne,
monopolies were wrong primarily as specific infringements on common
right. For Overton and Walwyn, and John Wildman (who also seems to
have been interested in these campaigns by this point), monopoly signified

something more abstract: oligarchic corruption akin to that which had brought down the Roman republic, or infringements on the primitive freedoms of a Christian or of natural or divine rights.[86]

There were also mature means by which to fight these battles. By the late summer Lilburne had become a compelling figurehead for wider public campaigns, and the organization of petitions around partisan positions, for which his cause seemed to offer a meaningful symbol. His skills in this world had put him in demand, too:

> being here about *London*, [Lilburne] had discovered the perverse proceeding of the Parliament, & how hateful all sorts of conscientious people...were unto them; and thereupon invited others, and joyned with them by Petitions to induce them to a better temper. And this his forwardnesse for the publicke good, occasioned all men who had any publick greevances to discover, to come to him and to ask his advice.[87]

As we have seen, this made him many enemies 'for all that had any guilt upon them new or old were greatly affraid of him'.[88] In the ten months since his engagement with Prynne he had become a significant figure in London's polemical battles and an important figurehead for opposition to Presbyterian mobilization, able to get support on the streets which helped pressure Parliament into releasing him without ever bringing his case to Quarter Sessions.

It is not clear how he supported his family prior to the grant of £100 to his maintenance while awaiting trial, but it is clear that he had found a public role as the figurehead in the battle for what was becoming defined as the Englishman's birthright. Lilburne continued to present himself as a martyr— an unjustly persecuted man whose steadfastness was the guarantee of the truth of his beliefs. Martyrs provide a focus for solidarity, helping to bring together a community of shared belief. The community Lilburne sought to unite in the coming years was not defined as the religious Independents but as those who had fallen foul of the corrupted parliamentary regime, or who might do in the future. Just as bishops had corrupted the civil state under Charles I, so were the Presbyterian faction a corrupting influence now. The response to his combat with Prynne, and his embroilments in the world of unlicensed printing, was to lead him to denounce the House of Lords as the paramount threat to the rights of Englishmen. In retrospect he was to see this as his second great battle, following that with the bishops in the 1630s.

Confrontation with the House of Lords, 1646

Released from prison in October 1645, Lilburne seemed at last to find parliamentary process running in his favour. On 10 November the House of Commons confirmed the quashing of his Star Chamber conviction and awarded reparations to be paid, at a level to be set by the House of Lords. The vote may have been related to proceedings against Denzil Holles, the leading Presbyterian and peace party politician, whose loyalties were then in doubt: Samuel Browne was also to report on Lilburne 'touching the Businesse of Mr Holles'. Ten days later the Lords voted on taking off the Star Chamber fine, although the result was not recorded.[89] In January 1646 *Innocency and Truth Justified* appeared, laying out the full case for his reparations and arrears, his service to the cause, the hard usage he had suffered, and what it implied about the integrity of Parliament. This was still a highly political issue, though, requiring him to navigate Parliament's committees and interest groups. The letter of support written by Cromwell on the eve of the battle of Langport had been republished twice, but on the other hand, he had to attend the Committee of Accounts, chaired by Prynne, to verify his claims about arrears. There was neither 'Justice nor honesty in him, and who is my deadly and implacable enemy', and Lilburne had faced a close cross-examination.[90]

Printed accounts of his treatment by the Star Chamber seem to have been timed to increase the pressure on those considering his case for reparations. The Commons examination of the case was reported to the Lords on 26 January 1646, and Lilburne himself petitioned the Lords on 2 February. After three postponements the Lords eventually discussed the matter on 13 February. An account of the hearing was published, recounting Lilburne's punishment with named witnesses to vouch for the details. He was represented by John Bradshaw, a rising parliamentary lawyer, who concluded with a stirring peroration:

> there was never more indignity and greater dishonour to the justice of the Kingdom, then by this wicked sentence, and the cruel execution thereof, thereby proclaiming it to all the world that an English Gentleman must be made a slave to satisfie the malicious and verulant humors of a tyranicall Court of Iustice.

Lilburne's sufferings, he might have said, were potentially those of all Englishmen. In the light of the full testimony about the arbitrary action of the court, and the cruelty of his punishment by the court and harsh treatment in the Fleet, the Lords confirmed the quashing of the sentence.[91]

The issue of his reparations, however, was held over for another day. He was eventually awarded £2,000 compensation three weeks later, on 6 March, and a committee was appointed to find assets against which this sum could be charged—it included Viscount Saye, who could have been presumed to be one of his sympathizers in 1638, and Lord Willoughby, who like Lilburne had tangled with Colonel King over events at Newark the previous year. Bradshaw called for the reparations to come from the estates of the principal architects of Lilburne's sufferings: Coventry, Laud, the earl of Arundel, and Cottington. Lilburne had himself suggested this earlier— he did not want to take money from seized estates, since the title to such estates was not secure, and they had been seized for public purposes which were possibly a higher priority. He too favoured Arundel's estate, and those of the Bishop of London, both of whom continued in possession of their lands and rents, despite their opposition to Parliament. However, the committee decided instead to impose one-third of this sum each on the estates of Cottington, Windebank, and James Ingram, the warden of the Fleet, which had all been sequestered (seized) as a result of their delinquency. Lilburne petitioned the Lords on 24 March, noting the liabilities already imposed on these estates and proposing the terms on which the settlement might be made. An ordinance formalizing these arrangements passed its first and second readings, was passed to a new committee with a different membership, and was finally agreed in the Lords and sent to the Commons for approval on 27 April. Such a lengthy and painstaking process was uncertain, however, and at this point settlement of his claims stalled. The parliamentary record peters out and Lilburne later claimed that it was the hostility of Sir Henry Vane, senior, in particular that frustrated the ordinance: a man with whom his father and (especially) his uncle were now in increasingly open conflict.[92]

Signs of progress in pursuit of his arrears had also to be placed against a generally hostile political background. The Stationers had been spurred to action by the publication of *The last warning To all the inhabitants Of London*, in March 1646. Two days after its publication they searched Larner's house and shop, finding fourteen copies of the pamphlet. Larner was arrested and with the help of the constable brought before the Lord Mayor, where he demanded the 'liberty of a Free-man of England' not to answer interrogatories. He refused to pay the fee demanded of him and when he was brought before the House of Lords on 3 April, appealed to the Commons in terms very similar to those later used by Lilburne. The press was Overton's and was spirited away, continuing to work until later in the year. Overton himself, meanwhile, began to publish in support of Larner.[93]

Moreover, by the time of the Commons order for compensation Colonel King had got Lilburne arrested on a charge of trespass, on 14 April. Lilburne was sure it was retaliation for the charge of high treason that Lilburne had brought before the House of Commons, and a way to gag him, but it undoubtedly complicated his quest for compensation: Lilburne was worried that the ordinance for his reparations might 'stick' in the Commons if he was 'diverted from following it, and I did not know but this arest might do it'. Lilburne's response was that there were formal charges of high treason against King, and that as a witness he was debarred from speaking: this case would be heard before the Court of Common Pleas, and was essentially delaying the Commons, the superior court, from hearing its business. This was, he said, a breach of Commons privilege, and a measure to stop him making that case, since the procedure in Common Pleas was that he would have to plead either guilty or not guilty to the charge before him: he would not be able to open up the whole case.[94]

There was hostile press too. In January Thomas Edwards had begun work on *Gangraena*, his sprawling, repellent catalogue of the heresies and religious errors that disfigured the parliamentary cause: documenting in great detail the need to re-establish religious discipline. It was eventually published in three parts, each coinciding with key phases of Presbyterian mobilization. The first part had been published as the military alliance with the Presbyterian Scots was being renewed. Lilburne had enough public profile to figure in the catalogue, and as a name the reader is apparently assumed likely to have known. The claims of *England's birthright* about the origins of political power figured as error number 151 in the list, while works by Overton and Walwyn were also denounced. Conversations in bookshops about liberty of conscience and the sale of unorthodox books in Westminster Hall itself figured among the signs of how dangerous these times now were. A major theme was the political ambition of the Independents: that, for example, they took advantage of the defeat at Leicester to promote their partisan aims, or that there was a plan to get Lilburne elected to Parliament, representing Southwark. Their opposition to ecclesiastical authority was sure to lead them to oppose civil authority too.[95]

That first part had invited readers to submit more material about religious excess. The second part now appeared, alongside the promotion of a Remonstrance in London which was very hostile to the sects, and strongly in favour of the Solemn League and Covenant and a rapid peace settlement. It also took on those who had denounced the first part, including Walwyn, who was discussed at length. Walwyn had defended religious nonconformity against the Presbyterian threat in *Toleration Justified*, published in late January, and his argument was close to that of Overton's *Divine Observations*, which appeared the same week. Through the rest of 1646 he published a series of pamphlets against Edwards, expressing amazement that men such as he should be presented as dangers to the state: 'it is my extream wonder that any well-affected person should affirm me to be a man dangerous'. Overton and Lilburne again appeared, and the case was made more plainly that 'Independencie now is no religious conscientious businesse, but a politick State Faction'. Hugh Peter, Edwards said, was now trying to get Walwyn and Lilburne elected for Cornwall.[96] Rather than suffering saints, these men formed a political faction, an interest that was destablizing government, and were in fact giving better than they received by way of suffering. The increasing profile of Lilburne, then Walwyn and Overton, reflected the extent to which they were emerging as key threats from the chaos of error and schism Edwards was so diligently denouncing. Opponents such as these seemed capable of doing Lilburne harm, and certainly of barring access to his reparations and arrears.

★   ★   ★

As his suit with King rumbled on, and against this heated polemical background, Lilburne spoke about these broader issues too, and quite destructively. In the *Just man's justification*, published on 6 June, he repeated many of the charges against Colonel King, and reproduced the twenty-two articles exhibited against King the previous August. But he also wondered out loud why Manchester had not dealt with King's misconduct, speculating that it was because King's chaplains had prevailed with Manchester's chaplains to '*cast a cleargy mist, over their Lords eyes*, that he should not be able to see any deformity in Colonell *King*'. There was a more general insinuation that this should have been dealt with by martial law, as Lilburne had urged.[97] This aspersion triggered an instant response from the earl. Hauled from his bed at 6.00 a.m. five days later, Lilburne was called by warrant to appear at the Lords.

Over the previous year, Lilburne had come to see that the war was not between Crown and Parliament, but between defenders of an Englishman's legal freedoms and monopoly powers. Chief among those monopoly powers was the House of Lords, and he now chose to escalate this dispute dramatically.

He refused the warrant, saying that the Lords could not summon a commoner and while en route to the Lords, wrote (without help, he claimed) a 'protestation and appeal'. He circulated the paper, which sought to explain to the Lords that by proceeding against him they were, in effect, seeking 'to destroy *Magna Charta* and to tread, it under their feet'. As a result, if they did so 'I would draw my sword against them every man as freely as I would doe against the King, and the desperatest Cavalier with him'. Called to the bar, he demanded a written copy of the charge, and to be allowed to submit his protestation, which was refused. Having refused to plead he was committed for contempt and sent to Newgate at the pleasure of the House.[98]

His dispute with Colonel King might have got him into the kind of trouble he was used to, but he had chosen to pick an altogether bigger and more fundamental fight: about the jurisdiction of the House of Lords. Ironically, this might have owed something to King's own example from the previous year, when he had refused to accept the Lords' judgement against him in the dispute with Willoughby while the case was being heard in the Commons.

This escalation might well have been premeditated: Lilburne's protestation came from his pen suspiciously quickly, and it seems that he was well prepared for this fight.[99] He certainly did not retreat, once he had picked the fight. From Newgate he published *The Free-Mans Freedome Vindicated*, in which he was yet more outspoken about Manchester: '*his Lordships Head hath stood it seemes too long upon his shoulders*' for protecting King, and for failing to pursue those who handed over Lincoln without a fight. He repeated his general case, that the Lords had no jurisdiction over him, but elaborated a more startling claim. The Lords had been created merely by prerogative power 'and never intrusted or impowred by the Commons of England, the originall and fountaine of Power'. Power came from the people who 'betrusted' their representatives; those betrusted powers should be exercised for the good of those who trusted them. Having fought for liberty, Lilburne was committed to resist this encroachment on his rights, and the powers of the Commons: '*I . . . am resolved . . . to the last drop of my blood, against all opposers whatsoever, having so often in the field &c. adven[t]ured my life*'. His appeal then was from the bar of the Lords to 'my competent, proper and legall triers and Judges, the Commons of England assembled in Parliament'.[100]

He had petitioned the House of Commons on 16 June, calling on them to resist this assault on their jurisdiction, and in a postscript to the published version made an even more bracing declaration about the original freedom of Adam and Eve, all of whose descendants 'are, and were by nature all equall and alike in power, dignity, authority, and majesty, none of them having (by nature) any authority dominion or majesteriall power, one over or above another, neither have they, or can they exercise any, but meerely by institution, or donation, that is to say, by mutuall agreement or consent'.[101]

Many historians have seen in this kind of rhetoric a decisive shift—away from appeals to established rights and the restoration of a past state of affairs, towards appeals to fundamental, abstract principles. Lilburne seems to appeal here not to his version of the constitution—as set out in Magna Carta, the Petition of Right, and other key texts—but to political principles beyond them. It is hard though to see this as a consistent position—in the same texts, and certainly in the coming years, he appealed indiscriminately, and a little confusingly, to both established liberties and divine or natural rights. In fact his critics accused him of having it both ways—disregarding those laws that inconvenienced him on the grounds that they interfered with natural rights, but insisting that other established legal rights were his both by inheritance and according to natural law. In truth, he was an activist, drawing on those arguments that would work at particular moments, while collaborating with people who shared his political goals, but not necessarily his ideological grounds.[102] Walwyn seems clearer, for example, that Magna Carta offered insufficient protections for the individual conscience, and that the argument should rest instead on natural law claims. It was Walwyn who famously told Lilburne that he put too much faith in Magna Carta, a 'beggarly thing'.[103]

In any case, Lilburne was now as outspoken about the Lords as he had been about the bishops nine years earlier, and he developed an equally effective public theatre to dramatize the fight. Called before the Lords a week later, he told the keeper of Newgate that he could not as a freeman 'dance attendance' at the Lords without betraying his birthright. This point of principle became the basis for a theatrical display, as he refused to plead, or to kneel.[104]

These were finely judged and deeply offensive insults. Seventeenth-century England was a highly unequal society, in which social status delivered political power. Fitness for office depended on social standing, and social standing was normally reflected in political office. The need to recognize and acknowledge social distinctions was taken very seriously: to deny social respect to an officeholder was to undercut their political authority. Before the war, in fact, the Court of Chivalry had heard many cases brought by men who felt a public insult was a threat to their political authority or even to royal government. There was in everyday life an acute consciousness of whether social proprieties were being observed—hats removed, eyes lowered, respectful demeanour adopted. By the same token, there was a highly charged game of sailing close to the wind in these things, of making small but deniable gestures of disrespect—perceptible to the audience but difficult to challenge. During the 1640s, stories about the breakdown of social order were often illustrated with examples of very gross disrespect that seemed to demonstrate that chaos was engulfing the country. All this, of course, was particularly important in formal settings—showing appropriate respect for place and occasion, and the dignity, for example, of a courtroom. Lilburne himself was very aware of these things—noting in 1638 for a public audience how he had respected hat decorum with Attorney General Banks, for example.[105] There is no doubt that this refusal of the physical gestures of deference to the Lords was a calculated demonstration of his refusal of their authority, and one he gleefully reported to a print audience that had not been able to see it at first hand.

In the face of this escalation the Lords ordered a further hearing at which both his protestation and his pamphlet would be considered.[106] As a result he was quickly back in Newgate where he was kept in close confinement: over the next three weeks he was not allowed pen, ink, and paper and was strictly searched, while his wife, friends, and counsellors were kept from him: 'my wife was forced to speak with me out of the window of a neighbouring house, at about fourty yards distance'. In fact his oppressors' 'cruelty and malice was so enraged, that they often threatned to boord and naile up the poore mans windows', while the clerk of the jail threatened to board up Lilburne's windows too, if he did not desist. No allowance was made for his maintenance. In the meantime four lawyers were working on a charge against him, about which he could discover nothing: it was utterly impossible in such circumstances to know what they intended to do with him.[107] The hostile public campaign against him continued too. Rumours spread by Prynne and 'other of my bitter Presbyterian Adversaries' claimed '*that I had conspired with other Separates & Anabaptists to root out the Members of this Parliament by degrees, beginning with Mr.* Speaker; *whom if we could cut off . . . all the rest would follow*'. They hoped, he claimed, that he would not get his fair trial, and that 'we might by the rude multitude, be either stoned to death, or pulled in pieces'.[108]

Formal charges were laid against him in the Lords on 10 July. The Lords wanted him to answer for four specific libels against Manchester in *The Just Mans Justification* and *The Free-mans Freedome*, and another against the earl of Stamford in the latter. 'But I told them, they had no judicature at all over me, neither would I in the least doe any thing that should declare my subjection to their power, although I should presently be destroyed for my refusall.' He refused to plead three times, and once again this refusal was accompanied by a theatrical display, repeated again in print for those who were not present: he would not kneel or remove his hat. Somewhat comically, but extremely offensively, he actually put his fingers in his ears so that he literally could not hear the charge: he claimed in fact that he could only tell that the reading of the charge had finished because the man's lips had stopped moving (not because he had heard any of it).[109] To have listened to the charge would have been a betrayal of England's birthright.

The initial charges were serious, but this was confrontation of a different order, which lost him, the Lords said, 'what favour he might have had'. He was fined £2,000, perhaps not coincidentally the amount he had been awarded in reparations for his contempt for the Star Chamber. He was also barred from military and civil office for life and imprisoned in the Tower, initially at the pleasure of the House. In September this was formalized as a sentence of seven years in the Tower. According to Lilburne the sentence was that he be kept in safe custody, but Wetton, the lieutenant, interpreted that to mean close confinement. Challenged by Lilburne, Wetton went back to the Lords, securing an order that bore out his interpretation of his order: no one was to visit Lilburne except in the presence and hearing of his keeper, who would also accompany him if he took the air, and if his wife wanted to see him she must live with him, not come to and fro. As a result Lilburne was separated from his wife until 16 September, and the sentence was confirmed the following day. In the meantime, the names of those who visited him were recorded, presumably as a means of intimidation. In all, he said, he had not experienced this kind of tyranny in jail since Oxford. He was not allowed out on bail until 9 November and was not freed until 2 August 1648.[110]

It is tempting to draw the parallel here with his refusal of the Star Chamber oath. There no charge had been read because he refused to swear to answer it; now he refused the jurisdiction and had to stop his ears in order to avoid hearing the charge. In both cases, without hearing a charge he was imprisoned for contempt. He was now defending his legal rights against the Lords, as he had done against the bishops nearly a decade earlier.

★   ★   ★

This was a principled position, but this dramatic and disastrous escalation is hard to interpret as anything other than the action of an impulsive, intemperate man blind to the virtues of prudence. He seems to have more or less invited repression in order to demonstrate his point. During 1645 he had taken the part of those opposed to the Covenant and fell foul of what he saw as the partisan use of Parliament's committees against him and his friends. That had led him into a series of confrontations and into prison, but early in 1646 parliamentary committees had seemed to begin to work more in his favour, offering the promise of fairly generous compensation for his sufferings. By April things were set reasonably fairly, but at that point Colonel King's intervention had threatened the outcome. This prompted him to denounce his political enemies, not least the earl of Manchester, and he was landed again in the kind of trouble he had faced in 1645. What then happened, however, was of a different order: he denounced not the partisan use of parliamentary power, but the jurisdiction of the House of Lords, and did so in highly theatrical, even comically confrontational ways. And it did not stop there. Following his arrest he published work that was bound to increase the temperature—*The Free-Mans Freedome*, *The Just Mans Justication*, and his *Letter to Mr Wollaston*. The result was a spectacularly arbitrary sentence, which made his point perhaps, but at an enormous personal cost, not least to the cause of his reparations.

Behind this escalation lay an increasingly explicit analysis of what was wrong with English politics, but his behaviour also illustrated that bullishness which has been such a part of Lilburne's posthumous reputation. It is tempting to see it as part of a temperamental Lilburne inheritance. Like his father, who sought trial by battle to break a deadlocked property dispute, or his uncle George, who was strongly assertive about his rights, Lilburne's honour was engaged in the political principles he had laid out, and he could not step down, however prudent that might have been at this particular juncture. This image of masculine honour, strongly associated with gentry values, was important to Lilburne—he often noted how he had sword in hand or by his side, and pledged commitments by his heart's blood. It is the other side of his punctilious and targeted discourtesies—profound respect and commitment to observing the honour code of gentility.[111]

This combination of principle, a stiff-necked temperament, and a gift for political theatre had by 1646 brought Lilburne to the attention of senior politicians on all sides. Over the summer the earl of Warwick had written urging Fairfax 'to be sensible of that fellows caridge John Lilborne, who Called him and Liftenant Generall Cromwell . . . at the Comons dore Traitors in the highest degree'. Charles I, in correspondence with key advisers about the current peace negotiations in 1646, suspected the Scots of harbouring anti-monarchical ambitions based on a belief that the supreme power derived from the will of the people. One of the two pieces of evidence he cited was that he could not get anyone to answer 'a railing Libel . . . written in defence of Lilborne'. Sir Edward Hyde, the future earl of Clarendon and a key royalist figure, had an annotated copy of the *Letter to Wollaston*, and the following spring he was asking Secretary Nicholas for more books by 'your freind Lilburne'. Reading him, along with Prynne and Milton, was educational, although not in the way those authors intended: 'for though they want Judgem[en]t and Logique to prove what they promise, yet they bring good materially to prove somewhat els they doe not thinke off'.[112]

It had also brought him allies. Overton had been publishing in support of Larner since the latter's arrest in March, and from July was active in publicizing Lilburne's cause. He was himself arrested in dramatic circumstances in August. Robert Eeles, working on behalf of the Stationers, had finally tracked down Overton's press, prompted by the publication of the *Last Warning*, as well as *An alarum To the House of lords, A remonstrance of many thousand citizens*, and several of Lilburne's pamphlets. On 11 August, with Abraham Eveling, he broke into Overton's bedroom with swords drawn, and arrested Overton as the printer, publisher, and distributor of Lilburne's pamphlets, as well as the author of the Marpriest pamphlets. Amid the ransacking of his house Overton demanded to see the warrant, and as he was dragged away before a gathering crowd, he protested that he was being arrested unlawfully. Before a committee of the Lords he was referred to as one of '*Lilburns Bastards*'. He refused to plead and was committed to Newgate. Again, in close parallel to Lilburne's tactics, he subsequently resorted to print: *A defiance against all arbitrary usurpations.*[113]

As he himself intended, Lilburne's troubles were represented as symptoms of something deeper. In October Overton wrote: 'By naturall birth, all men are equally and alike borne to like propriety, liberty and freedome'. This issue of propriety is not so much one of material equality as of political equality, 'Every man by nature being a King, Priest and Prophet in his owne

naturall circuite and compasse, whereof no second may partake, but by depu-
tation, commission, and free consent from him, whose naturall right and
freedome it is'.[114] For a wider coalition, Lilburne's travails were of interest
not just in themselves, and not as a matter of religious confessional identity,
but as an illustration of the tyranny currently threatened, and sometimes
exercised, over the birthright of Englishmen.

Walwyn had taken up Lilburne's cause some time before, in *England's
Lamentable Slaverie*, published in October 1645. He noted there that 'there is
some difference between you and mee in matters of Religion': it was not a
religious alliance. What united them was that Lilburne's treatment demonstrated a fundamental betrayal: 'a Parliamentary authority is a power intrusted
by the people (that chose them) for their good, safetie, and freedome; and
therefore...a Parliament cannot justlie do any thing, to make the people
lesse safe or lesse free then they found them'. It was this which united them,
'your constant zealous affection to the Common Wealth, and...your
undaunted resolution in defence of the common freedome of the People'.[115]

Vox Plebis (the voice of the commons), published in November, also took
Lilburne's cause but put it at the heart of an account that drew heavily on
classical Roman example—of the betrayal of the values of the republic, and
its citizens, by a corrupt oligarchy. The examples included the committees
that had been spawned by the parliamentary war effort: this was all territory
familiar to Lilburne, but the classical history was not part of his repertoire.
Its language was more abstract and reflected an emerging 'Leveller' idiom—
of representatives as the betrusted and of citizens as those who entrusted
them, for example. But a key immediate concern was to secure the release
of Lilburne and others. The author may have been Wildman, with whom
Lilburne was to be closely associated over the next five years.[116]

Practical support for Lilburne therefore helped to create an increasingly
close political alliance during 1646: his sufferings were a focal point for a
larger political analysis of the shortcomings of the parliamentary regime.
As a result, Lilburne's self-presentation began to take on a slightly different
gloss—for example, the new emphasis on monopolies which ran together
the authority of the clergy, Lords, and Merchant Adventurers. There was a
turn away from specific legal rights under Magna Carta and the Petition of
Right, or the claims made in the parliamentary *Book of Declarations*, towards
more abstract reflections on the basis of political freedom, and of authority:
natural law, Christian egalitarianism, and Roman history. This reflects a collaborative and clandestine publishing effort: exactly who wrote the pamphlets

produced from this milieu is often difficult to say. Given the work of the Committee of Examinations it is no surprise that much of the published work was anonymous, and in any case a number of these publications seem to have been penned by more than one hand. As a body of texts this reflects the coalescence of a group sharing the same concerns about what was wrong with the kingdom, albeit analysed from a variety of perspectives. It was this political affinity that had brought them together: they were a somewhat heterogeneous group ideologically and even religiously, but were united in their conviction that good people were being abused by the government.[117]

For his part, Lilburne's various confrontations grew out of essentially personal battles for what he regarded as his due: protection from the corrupt and potentially tyrannous behaviour of King and Manchester and reparations for his sufferings at the hands of Charles I's Star Chamber, due reward for his fidelity to Parliament, access to the presses on the same terms as his opponents, and freedom of religious conscience. Much of his self-presentation in these years was reactive—he claimed to be responding to attacks arising from a powerful Presbyterian mobilization which put the Solemn League and Covenant, not the rhetoric of 1642, at the heart of the proposed settlement. His experiences in 1646 had seemed to confirm the dangers of this new persecuting spirit: further prosecutions driven by his political enemies and a confrontation with the Lords which, in an odd symmetry, had led to a substantial fine and imprisonment following a charge he had never answered.

By late 1646, in increasingly close collaboration with these other men, Lilburne's distrust of those managing the war and dominating Parliament's committees had crystallized into arguments rather different from those of the 1630s. He was no longer disputing the nature of a true church, or the biblical basis of ecclesiastical office—he was arguing about the injustice of monopoly powers, or artificial creations like the nobility, powers that infringed the secular rights of the freeborn Englishman. As in the later 1630s, though, his tribulations could be seen as manifestations of much more general issues. The postscript to Lilburne's *Free-mans freedome vindicated* married claims for religious freedom with his case for government by consent as the only way to secure Englishmen's freedom. *Liberty Vindicated* had used Lilburne's case as an emblem for the larger threat of tyranny, and *A defiance* had spoken of a 'Nationall Disease' which prevented Englishmen from knowing their own rights.[118] The remedy for his sufferings had been generalized: it rested in firmer guarantees of the Englishman's legal

freedoms.[119] This came at considerable personal cost: his theatrical enact-
ment of these values had landed him a heavy prison sentence and fine, and
his wife could only see him by joining him in prison. Their next child was
to be christened Tower.

★   ★   ★

In July, *A remonstrance of many thousand citizens* had tried to mobilize
Londoners around this emerging political analysis. The persecution of
Overton and Lilburne was presented as an example of the threat posed to
all freeborn Englishmen by tyranny in church and state, and the engraving
of Lilburne from 1641 was reused as the frontispiece, but this time with bars
superimposed so that he looked out at the reader from his captivity.
Addressed to the Commons, front and centre was a claim about the origins
of political power, and the limits of the executive:

> We are your principals, and you our agents; it is a truth which you cannot but
> acknowledge. For if you or any other shall assume or exercise any power that
> is not derived from our trust and choice thereunto, that power is no less than
> usurpation and an oppression from which we expect to be freed, in whomsoever
> we find it—it being altogether inconsistent with the nature of just freedom,
> which ye also very well understand.[120]

This was a radical claim, of course, but also a radical practice. In 1641,
Parliament had issued what became known as the Grand Remonstrance
against the king, which complained about his policies and caused anxiety
and outrage by doing so in print for a public audience. Parliament, it was
argued, should not address criticism to the king in public, or appeal to that
public to agree. What was now happening, however, was far more radical—
a group of citizens were calling the executive back to the origins of its own
power, turning the arguments made by Parliament against the king in 1642
against the Parliament itself, as a restraint on its own actions. Not all his old
friends approved—John Goodwin and members of his congregation, for
example, did not support these petitioning campaigns.[121]

Lilburne's bull-headed challenge to authority lent itself to broader interpretation, and that interpretation reflected in part the ideas of those who
now stood alongside him. This political style emerged from the experience
of practical political action. Out of their opposition to the Covenant had
crystallized the view that the power of Parliament was held in trust, and that
its members were chosen to bear that trust. The war had been fought not to
rebalance the constitution between king, Parliament, and bishops, but to call

government back to answer the needs of those who entrusted it, to heed the *Vox Plebis*. Lilburne and his allies were reacting to an equally effective group of activists, notable among them Prynne and Edwards. Military victory would soon raise the stakes in these arguments among the winners. By late 1646 royalists were also watching Lilburne and his allies, and their treatment, seeing in attitudes towards them an index of what the king's opponents really thought, and how the parliamentarians really regarded 'the seditious demeanour of some leading men and the doctrine of the Levellers'.[122] These intertwining arguments shaped political debate in the coming year, and gave rise to some of the more remarkable episodes in English political history.

4

Leveller, 1647–9

Presbyterian mobilization and the emergence of the Levellers, 1646–7

While Lilburne had become embroiled in his battle with the Lords, Parliament's armies had been winning the war. The great victory at Naseby had been followed by a devastating campaign against the royalist field army in the south-west, and by 1646 the war was effectively over. A number of strongholds held out, but the king surrendered in late April. Negotiating the peace settlement, though, proved to be frustrating work and, breaking a deadlock, supporters of a Presbyterian settlement moved aggressively to mobilize support during 1647. What became the Leveller movement crystallized in response to this Presbyterian mobilization, itself a response to deadlocked peace negotiations.

Post-war negotiations were framed by the Newcastle propositions, which sought to restore a constitutional balance between king and Parliament in ways similar to all previous peace negotiations. They were no more than a modulation of what had been rejected in 1642 and at every formal negotiation since.[1] This continuity in the formal negotiating positions was superimposed over an increasingly chaotic public debate, in which many new and more radical opinions about what the war had really been about had developed, not least those of Lilburne and his fellow travellers. For this reason, among others, Charles rightly felt that he still had options. His English enemies were openly divided, and many of them were no friends of his Scottish enemies either. This, and the possibility that he might get foreign help, encouraged him to think that he might still win, as his enemies fell out. He was unlikely to submit to them as long as he thought something better might turn up and, in the absence of a unified parliamentary front, he had considerable negotiating power, since he was seen as essential to any future settlement.

Faced with this impasse it was Presbyterian activists who took the initiative during 1647, trying to shape parliamentary debate, take control of government in London, and demobilize the army. How they went about demobilization, however, set them on a collision course not just with their ideological opponents in the army, but at least potentially with all soldiers: they wanted to demobilize them without giving guarantees about arrears of pay and indemnity from prosecution for actions taken during their active service.

These were very serious issues, not least indemnity. Soldiers who had requisitioned supplies might face prosecution for theft or trespass, and if they had taken a horse, for example, might be liable to the death penalty since that was the punishment for horse theft. As one pamphlet put it in May 1647: 'Can we be satisfied… when our fellow Souldiers suffer at every Assize for acts meerly relating to the Warre? Is not our lives we seeke? For where shall we be secured, when the meere envie of a malicious person is sufficient to destroy us?' The pamphlet pointed out how many of the current assize judges had been unfaithful to the parliamentary cause during the war.[2] Unsurprisingly, many soldiers did not want to run the risk of hostile local courts following the war, but on the other hand, it is equally easy to understand the reluctance to give every demobilized soldier a 'get out of jail free' card.

The army politicized in response to this threat. The rank and file were increasingly incensed about the terms on which the Presbyterians were seeking to demobilize them, and the army began to organize its own political lobby, to put pressure on Parliament and London, in an increasingly tense confrontation. This offered potentially common ground with civilian opponents of the Presbyterians: in the battle against tyranny or injustice, or in favour of just reward for service to the cause of 1642. One of the signatories of the pamphlet quoted earlier, for example, was Edward Sexby, a serving soldier with whom Lilburne became closely associated over the next few years. More generally, this conjunction created for Lilburne, Walwyn, Overton, Wildman, and others the political opening on which their posthumous fame depends. They came together around the mobilization for an alternative peace settlement based on an *Agreement of the People*, which built on a wide alliance in the City and army: the Leveller movement.

In the past, some historians have been tempted to see this as the work of a 'party', organized and successfully infiltrating the army and promoting a coherent ideology.[3] As we have seen, though, the key figures were an ideologically heterogeneous group, drawing on different kinds of argument to

support their emerging campaign, sometimes in ways that seem contradictory.[4] It is better to see them as a movement coming together to thwart
a Presbyterian settlement while proposing a remarkable alternative. Each of
them arrived at this point from their own direction and were later to follow
divergent paths, but in these years were united behind this proposed peace
settlement. They were a more mixed group than the term 'party' suggests:
their campaign depended on wider circles of sympathizers—people who
shared these ambitions for the peace but were not pursuing a 'Leveller'
programme and were not part of a coherent party organization.[5]

This campaign was united by the call for a *just* peace. From October 1647
it was identified with the campaign for an *Agreement of the People*, of which
several drafts were produced; but it also depended on a sense of shared
sufferings which illustrated the danger of looming injustice. Lilburne's key
role was as a figurehead for this campaign: his sufferings illustrated what was
wrong with government, and what was therefore essential to any lasting
peace. He spent almost the whole of the period of Leveller mobilization
in prison, but seems to have been influential as a publicist—his writings
from prison, and his activism when free, were central to how a remarkable
proposed peace settlement took shape in opposition both to the formal process
continued at Newcastle and to the Presbyterian mobilization. Lilburne's *ideas*,
as far as they can be distinguished from those with whom he was cooperating,
seem to be less important to the development of what is thought of as
Leveller ideology.[6] It was Walwyn, Overton, and Wildman who brought
more abstract ideas to bear on the problem of a just peace.

The opportunity this group were now trying to seize grew out of two
dynamics: resistance to a Presbyterian settlement among religious Independents
and political radicals, and opposition to the unjust treatment of the soldiery,
those who had made the greatest sacrifices for the parliamentary victory.
In this complex political scene the Levellers achieved at times significant
political influence and an important voice: what they said has resonated
with subsequent generations.

★   ★   ★

In late 1646 London became the focus of this struggle. The third part of
Edwards' *Gangraena* appeared in December, directed much more than the
previous instalments against political enemies in the army: an expensive
and unpopular body and a potential obstacle to rapid settlement which also
harboured opponents of the Scots and of a Presbyterian settlement, and

which had now done its job. Edwards also drew his sights on the army's civilian friends, including Lilburne, Walwyn, and Overton. Publication coincided with the promotion of a petition calling for a Presbyterian settlement and disbandment of the army, which was condemned by the Commons but accepted in the City.[7]

Captivity did not prevent Lilburne participating in this battle. In anticipation of the next round of City elections in December, *Londons Liberty In Chains discovered* appeared under his name. It was really an argument that all citizens, not just the members of the Livery Companies, should vote for the Lord Mayor, prompted by the attempt to get Henry Wansey elected.[8] It was expressed, though, in more abstract terms, which were by now familiar: resisting the monopoly powers of the Livery Companies, which derived from the prerogative and clearly infringed on the rights of the citizens. It was another example to add to that of the Lords, the Merchant Adventurers, and the clergy: vested interests successfully sustained their place in power despite their lack of virtue or commitment to the good of the Commonwealth. Such 'prerogative men' had allowed the tyranny of Charles I, but were still in place, despite all the blood and treasure expended in opposing that tyranny. In *An Anatomy of the Lords Tyranny*, Lilburne had said that this had been his struggle from the start, and cited the Protestation as its justification. In the *Charters of London*, published in December, the core claim was stated very clearly:

> because the only and sole legislative Law-making power, *is originally inherent in the people and derivatively in their Commissions chosen by themselves by common consent, and no other.* In which the poorest that lives, hath as true a right to give a vote, as well as the richest and greatest.

The programme for the City, then, was not just free elections but also free trade: the restoration of a primitive liberty. The powers of the representatives were held in trust—they were the betrusted, not a caste apart. The rights of the poorest were shortly to be championed in national elections too, on similar grounds, in the famous debates at Putney.[9]

This was not simply an anti-Presbyterian position, therefore, but a more fundamental case about the rights of citizens. It was not obviously an Independent tract either, except that the power of the clergy was denounced as one of the monopolies that infringed on freedom. *The Charters of London* supported the arguments of *London's Liberty In Chains* by reproducing medieval charters to show that 'barons' (defined here as free men) had fundamental rights to participate in the choice of their government. The scholarship mattered in this respect—the charters were reprinted in full with annotations attesting to the authenticity of the transcription. It is clear that Lilburne expected to be challenged on these matters.[10]

The Independents lost this particular battle, however. At Common Council elections on 21 December many Presbyterians were returned, while those who had opposed the programme in the petition fared badly. The new Common Council called for the disbandment of the New Model, free elections, and reform of the committees which had underpinned the war effort but which were now regarded as unhealthy or even tyrannous innovations. These last issues resonated on the streets: there was a major riot at Smithfield in February against the excise, which probably reflected a wider hostility to the financial burden and administrative innovations of the war effort. But these issues did not necessarily belong to the Presbyterians. *Englands Birth-Right*, for example, had identified the excise on hats as an instance of parliamentary tyranny—collecting that duty was the kind of office that appealed to petty tyrants like the Stationers' beadle, Hunscott. The Presbyterians, by contrast, tried to connect such grievances with their attempt to disband the army and to restore elements of pre-civil war life. Other aspects of the Presbyterian programme were less easy to sell as a restoration of normality, however: their reform of the ritual calendar of the Anglican Church, for example, had effectively abolished many holy days and saints' days, and that was potentially very unpopular. In January and April there were demonstrations by apprentices, who now wanted recognized 'play days' to replace their lost holy days.[11] Nonetheless, while theirs was not necessarily the voice of a return to normality, the Smithfield riot, along with other disturbances, may have encouraged Presbyterians to get on with the demobilization. In March this became connected with raising an army for service in Ireland, where Protestant authority had still to be re-established following the rising in 1641. A plan was launched to disband the English armies immediately and to then conscript men for service in Ireland.

The injustice of these measures prompted the politicization of the army, particularly regarding arrears of pay and indemnity, but also the subsequent intended conscription for Ireland. It was easy to connect these relatively mundane concerns with a broader rhetoric about justice and recognition for service to the cause, as Lilburne habitually did. He had after all made much of the treatment he had suffered in the Eastern Association army. The difficulty the soldiers faced in securing justice could easily be seen as a symptom of the more general corruption of good government and one in which their honour was engaged. *An Apollogie of the Souldiers* published in late March, arguing the case of the ordinary soldier and worried about a possible betrayal by the officers, made exactly this connection. It made common cause with 'those honest people who have shown themselves with us, and for us in these our sad calamities', arguing it was entirely unjust that such people should be held in prison without trial or legal redress—a reference presumably to the sufferings of Lilburne, Overton, and Larner. Crucially, then, the pamphlet was arguing that the soldiers' experience was an example of the wider issue: the authors protested that their liberties as Englishmen were 10,000 times more important to them than their arrears as soldiers.[12]

That larger cause had been expressed particularly clearly in the '*Large Petition*' of March 1647, which became a manifesto for the alliance. Written clearly, in generalities and without a clutter of citations, it summarized much of what Lilburne and others had been arguing through 1646. Parliament was the most just executive power because it reflected the free choice of the people and was therefore the best guarantor of the safety and freedom of the governed. It had done essential work in overthrowing the tyranny of the 1630s, and abolishing key instruments of that tyranny—the Star Chamber and High Commission—and key symptoms of that misgovernment: the power of the bishops and ship money. However, 'after the expence of so much precious time, blood and treasure, and the ruine of so many thousands of honest Families, in recovering our Liberty. Wee still find the Nation oppressed with grievances of the same destructive nature'. The judicial power of the Lords; the new religious persecution, no less vigorous than that of the bishops; the monopoly of the Merchant Adventurers; the difficulty and expense of the law; the imposition of tithes; the oppressions of jail keepers; the castigation of the godly: these were all signs that the battle was not won, as was the failure to set the poor to work, but to suffer them to continue in idleness and wickedness. It claimed that anyone showing any sympathy for these grievances now met hostility: 'all the reproaches, evills, and mischiefs that can be devised, are thought too few, or too little to be layd upon them, as Round-heads, Sectaries, Independents, Hereticks, Schismaticks, factious, seditious, Rebellious, disturbers of the publike peace: destroyers of all civill relations, and subordinations'. Nonconformity had become a reason to be excluded from offices of trust, while 'Neuters, malignant and disaffected, are admitted and countenanced'.[13] The refusal to hear the army's concerns could easily be cast in the same way.

As conflict escalated, this potential alliance between civilian and army radicals strengthened. In the last week of April the rank and file of the army had begun to elect 'agitators' to represent their political demands, and there is evidence of connections between them and radicals in the City. This created a system of representation within the army, alongside, and perhaps potentially in tension with, the chain of command. Historians disagree about the relationship between these agitators and political activism, and their relationship with activists outside the army: the term is to an extent misleading, since the seventeenth-century term was closer to adjutator, a kind of representative or delegate more than an agitator in the modern sense.[14] Nonetheless, it is hard to think of this as anything other than a conscious politicization.

The General Council of the Army, established later in the year, brought the agitators and the officers together for a common purpose: the definitive study of that body argues that it successfully maintained unity in the face of the army's common enemies. Finding a way to speak for its immediate political demands, the agitators and General Council began to present their case in broader terms, scaling up 'bread and butter' grievances to seem like instances of more general or abstract issues of justice and honour.[15] They also, though, wanted to restore effective parliamentary government—this was a reaction against the growing paralysis and factionalism at Westminster.[16] In that sense it was a more conservative and consensual intervention than has often been allowed. Overall, it has been argued, it was attempts to use the General Council as a vehicle for a radical settlement that created divisions, weakening the army and condemning the body to oblivion.[17] Of course, those taking the Leveller side would have said the opposite.

While the politicization of the army did not occur at the direction or by design of civilian radicals, there was clearly an important dialogue between them and army activists. Lilburne certainly had connections with activists in the army and his ideas were important to its politicization. For example, as early as 1645, Richard Baxter visited the New Model and was alarmed by the religious and political ideas some soldiers were voicing. Those whose teaching did most damage, he thought, did so partly through the pamphlets of Lilburne and Overton, 'which they abundantly dispersed'.[18]

By the end of 1646, Lilburne had made a composition for his keep at the Tower in return for being allowed visitors, and pen and ink. As a consequence he was able to continue to develop this influence, through his writing but also through regular meetings with Edward Sexby, now one of the agitators, and others. Sexby also distributed Lilburne's pamphlets through the army. One contemporary, in fact, claimed that an agitator was a 'Monster of John Lilburne's generation...begotten of Lilburne with Overton's helpe', and Lilburne himself was lavish in his praise of their work. Sir Lewis Dyve, a royalist prisoner in the Tower at the same time, kept a close eye on Lilburne, and was convinced that he was well connected: Dyve's surviving notebook places great faith in Lilburne's knowledge of army affairs.[19] Lilburne's own writings make it clear that he was indeed keeping a close eye on the development of the army's petitioning in March. He was evidently suspicious that the more cautious officers were being manipulated, or were in fact actively betraying the people: that Cromwell, for example, was being gulled by Henry Vane and Oliver St John. As he put it in a letter to Sir Thomas Fairfax, the Lord General, in July, those chief officers sitting in the House of Commons he had found to be 'quivering spirited, overwise, prudentiall men'.[20] Looking out for allies in the army and staying informed is not the same, of course, as directing events: such evidence does not show that the politicization was being directed by civilian radicals such as Lilburne.

In fact, what Lilburne wrote suggests that he saw an opportunity and tried to use it. He had consciously turned to the army for support against the corrupted Parliament, placing his faith in the rank and file, not the officers, and he suffered no doubts about his importance: seeing 'that all my importunity and all the faire meanes I could use, would doe me no good... I made a vigorus and strong attempt upon the private Soldiery of your Army...not daring to meddle with the Officers, having had so large experience of the selfeishnesse, and timerousness of the chiefest of them, sitting in the House of Commons'. By contrast, among the common soldiers: 'with abundance of study and paines, and the expence of some scores of pounds, I brought my just, honest, and lawfull intentions, by my agents, instruments, and interest to a good ripenesse'.[21] This was a tricky tactical question: it has often been remarked that earlier in the spring Richard Overton had consulted the astrologer John Booker 'Whether by joyning with the Agents of the private soldjery of the Army for the redemption of com[m]on right and freedome to the Land and removall of oppressions from the people any endeavours shalbe prosperous or no?'[22] This was the very time the agitators were being appointed, but has most often been discussed in relation to how Overton thought, to his supposed 'rationalism'; it has less often been seen as evidence that this was indeed an alliance between Levellers and an autonomous army mobilization, and one attended by a degree of tactical uncertainty. Goodwin's congregation, or at least some members of it, clearly took a different view and acted to block some of this activity.[23]

Nonetheless, the emergence of the agitators, the turn to petitioning, vigorous discussion, and communication within the army, and perhaps equally vigorous discussion between the army and civilians in the City, depended on networks of connection and print in which Lilburne was a well-established player. They also involved the army in the world of manipulative publicity so familiar to Lilburne and others. So, for example, in early April, it was claimed, a petition hostile to the army's campaign for arrears and indemnity had been drawn up in London and then sent down to Essex, so that it could be circulated by the ministers and sent up as the voice of the county. In fact, though, it was no such thing, having had no public discussion: it was the view not of the county of Essex, but of 'a private party'. The petition had been printed before it had been made known or discussed. Such dark arts reflected wider conspiracy in the City and Parliament 'to inthrall & inslave us'. To succeed, and to escape shame and justice, they had to get rid of the army, and this was how they went about it. On this view, then, the army was the main bulwark against a tyranny posing a much more general threat than simply to the army's own interests.[24]

★   ★   ★

By the late spring of 1647 the battle lines were drawn between a Presbyterian mobilization and the army, and there was a strengthening coalition of interests between elements in the City and the army. As the civilian petitioning and army organization had proceeded, the Presbyterians were putting together a new army under the reliable command of Phillip Skippon and Sir Edward Massey, while their leaders in Parliament, Denzil Holles and Sir Philip Stapleton, continued to press on with the disbandment of the old army. Meanwhile, in London, the control of the militia passed into the hands of reliably Presbyterian householders. Through May the Presbyterian leaders were negotiating disbandment and promising an indemnity ordinance, but as they felt their prospects of securing a peace settlement with the king increase they pressed ahead with disbandment without first granting indemnity. Publications from within the army became increasingly strident, but the deal on offer remained disbandment now and indemnity later.

The *Large Petition*, drawn up in March, had become a manifesto for an alternative settlement based on justice and common right. In May, after weeks of discussion, it was burned by the public hangman at the order of the House of Commons. In the meantime two supporters of the petition, Major Tulidah and Nicholas Tew, who had fought for the right to petition, had been imprisoned. Tew was an ally of Lilburne's: he had been a collaborator with Overton's secret press during 1645, and following an arrest had managed to protect both Overton and, to some extent, Lilburne.[25] Lilburne now took up his cause along with Tulidah's, reprinting the petition, as well as details of the proceedings against the two men, and the resulting campaign for the right to petition. This case was used to illustrate how far Parliament's behaviour now diverged from the promises of its oaths—the Protestation, the Vow and Covenant, *and* the Solemn League and Covenant. It was a familiar roll call of Parliament's backsliding, picking away at the inconsistencies between word and action.[26] As Walwyn put it, rather more pithily, 'there is little good to be hoped for from such Parliaments, as need to be Petitioned; so there is none at all to be expected from those that burn such Petitions as these'.[27]

In such circumstances the army was clearly the best hope of influential support for a more generous vision of English freedoms. *Plaine Truth without Fear or Flattery* set out a familiar case about parliamentary betrayal linking it to the current treatment of the army. In such circumstances

> Wee the free Commons of England, the reall and essentiall body politicke…
> may order and dispose our own Armes and strength, for our owne preservation
> and safety; and the Army in particular (without question) may lawfully retaine,
> order and dispose of their armes and strength, to and for the preservation and
> safety of the King and Kingdome, the principall end for which they were raised.

This dangerous-sounding doctrine, that the people and the army could act independently in defence of their freedom, was justified with reference to the Parliament's own *Book of Declarations*, a point of reference throughout.[28]

Early in June drastic action transformed the army's political position. The king was captive at Holdenby, Northamptonshire, in Parliament's custody. In the late spring rumours spread of a plot to remove him from there, and to use control of his person to force a Presbyterian settlement. A counter-plot was floated in response, reported in a letter written either by Sexby or by Edmund Chillenden, someone Lilburne had known well since the 1630s.[29] On 2 June a Cornet Joyce, almost certainly with Cromwell's foreknowledge and perhaps with his consent, went to Holdenby House with a company of soldiers and took custody of the king the following day.[30]

At the same time, the army began to advance on London, offering a very real threat that they would simply take over the situation. At a general rendezvous at Newmarket on 4 and 5 June the army adopted a *Solemn Engagement*. This became another key text, a manifesto for the army, and what its political organization was intended to promote. It said that the army would not disband piecemeal, but as a whole, and only once its grievances had been met. An army document, centrally concerned with immediate grievances, it nonetheless made a connection with the rhetoric of Lilburne and his fellows: 'that we ourselves, when disbanded and in the condition of private men, or other the free-born people of England (to whom the consequence of our case doth equally extend), shall not remain subject to the like oppression, injury or abuse'.[31] It was now that the General Council of the Army was created, and it was this body that would agree to disbandment, once satisfied that these conditions were met. It also produced a new peace settlement to present to the king—the *Heads of the Proposals*. Clearly the army was now negotiating independently with the king, who was in their custody, and this offered a major threat to the initiative taken by the Presbyterians.

Not the least threatening aspect of this was that the *Heads* opened up genuinely new ground, dropping the demand for the abolition of bishops and the establishment of a Presbyterian Church. The bishops could remain, but would lose their coercive powers—there was in effect to be toleration around an established national church. The *Heads* also relaxed the demands about the nomination of officers of state, those who could not be pardoned, and who would be excluded from office. On these issues, central to all the negotiations since 1642, the army was offering significant concessions to the king. As the army moved closer to London the pressure was increased by the demand to impeach eleven members who had been central to the Presbyterian campaign. The whole confrontation culminated in August with an army occupation of London and the flight of many prominent Presbyterians.

While this mobilization and occupation of London was a decisive challenge to the Presbyterian peace plan, it did not in itself meet the aspirations of radicals in the army and the City, and suspicion of the officers persisted. Thomas Rainsborough, one of the more radical figures among the army leadership, had kept Lilburne informed about the *Heads of the Proposals* as they took shape, and the danger that the officers would betray the aspirations of the ordinary soldiers as expressed in the *Solemn Engagement*. In August Lilburne had republished *The just mans justification*, with an appendix calling on the agitators and soldiers to defend to the death the principles of the *Solemn Engagement*. The same month new agitators were appointed and Lilburne took a close interest from the Tower in how this was being done, and what it might mean for the cause of a just peace.[32]

The army, the king, and the people's rights, 1647–8

Despite his imprisonment, then, Lilburne had remained politically active, partly through direct connections with those leading the action, and partly by publication. However, there is some doubt about quite how much influence he had. Two days after the rendezvous at Newmarket, the Lords had noted that 'the Distempers in the Army and the City were fomented by some prisoners in The Tower of London, and company did come to them'. They named Lilburne but also David Jenkins (Fig. 4.1), a royalist judge whose reading of common law was increasingly embarrassing for Parliament. Having opposed ship money and other royal innovations, he was now telling the

Fig. 4.1. David Jenkins (1582–1663)

soldiers that their indemnity would be much more secure if granted in an Act signed by the king than an ordinance of the two houses. The lieutenant was ordered to restrict their freedom to read, write, and receive visitors. In July, directions to commissioners from the army negotiating with the House of Lords included the demand (also present in the earlier *Engagement*) that prisoners who were not delinquents or criminals should be released. Lilburne and Overton were among those named.[33] There were other connections too, through John Rushworth, a signatory of this paper and secretary to Sir Thomas Fairfax: his sister married John's younger brother, Henry, during 1647.[34] Robert, his elder brother, was a rising military officer, and also active in the army's political campaign.

On the other hand, John White, the lieutenant of the Tower, had been keen to emphasize the previous autumn how comfortable Lilburne was, and how many people came to see him, but had been dismissive of their importance, including the 'stragling Souldiers'. It has also been pointed out that there was no code for 'Lilburne' in the system of cyphers used by Henry Marten in sensitive correspondence during 1647, suggesting perhaps that we should not take Lilburne at his own estimation. The newsbooks were more convinced of Lilburne's influence with the agitators, but they may have had a malign intent in saying that the soldiers were under his spell.[35] There is a better case, in other words, that Lilburne kept himself informed than that he had significant influence over the direction of events. At the time of the army's occupation of London, Nehemiah Wallington, a London wood-turner and avid consumer of news, anxiously recorded rumours about the intentions of the army. As he did so, he took it for granted that Lilburne, in the Tower, 'well knew the intents of the Army'.[36]

If his practical importance *has* been overstated, however, it is nonetheless clear that from his prison cell he had become an important voice calling for the army to act to preserve the liberties of all Englishmen. In doing so he had become associated with championing the role of the Agitators, even when in conflict with their superior officers. In this confluence of interests the key text for civilian radicals was perhaps the *Large Petition* from March, publicly burned in May; for their army allies it was the *Solemn Engagement* made in June. The politicization of the army was certainly in good part self-generating and was not the product of infiltration by a distinct and well-organized 'party'. Nonetheless, there was clearly a dialogue between the army and fellow travellers in the City, and Lilburne was important at least as a figurehead in this dialogue. He had also published frequently throughout the year: *The Oppressed Mans Oppressions declared* (January); *The out-cryes of Oppressed Commons* (with Overton, February); *The resolved mans Resolution* (April); and *Rash Oaths unwarrantable* (May). This represented a distinctive publishing presence—we might even say brand—recognizable from the alliterative titles, the design, and the presses from which they came.[37] These works concentrated on a by-now familiar range of injustices—his imprisonments, the tyranny of jailers, the illegality of the Lords' proceedings, the Covenant, and Presbyterian malice in print. And those injustices continued to occur: he had been called before the Committee of Examinations again in February, to be questioned about the publication of *The Oppressed Mans Oppressions declared*, and a by-now almost ritualistic set of exchanges ensued.[38]

These publications, converging with the writings of his allies, had cumulatively cemented his new alliances around some more abstract principles. Thus, *Regal Tyranny* (sometimes attributed to Lilburne but by him attributed to the author of *Vox Plebis*) contained a clear statement about Christian egalitarianism: 'amongst the *Sons* of *Men,* that live in mutuall society one amongst another in *nature and reason*, there is none above, or over another, against mutuall consent and agreement'. Sovereign power can only be created by consent, and in accordance with the Law of God, Nature, and Reason. '[I]t is not lawfull for any man to subject himself, to be a slave'. Given Lilburne's own insistence on his social status, and his later disavowals of any intention to level men's estates, it is difficult to imagine that he would have read this as socially levelling; it was surely a statement about equality before the law, and the political equality of all citizens:

> Power is originally inherent in the People, and it is nothing else but that might and vigour, which such and such a Society of men contains in it self, and when by such and such a Law of common consent and agreement, it is derived into such and such hands, God confirmes the Law: And so man is the free and voluntary author, the Law is the instrument, and God is the establisher of both.

The constitutional history of England was the history of charters designed to negotiate these powers.[39]

Lilburne and his Independent allies were not engaged in a battle for the rights of a religious minority, therefore, but rather for the freedoms of all Englishmen: the *Resolved Mans Resolution* was 'to maintain with the last drop of his heart blood, his civill Liberties and freedomes, granted unto him by the good, just, and honest declared lawes of England, (his native country)'.[40] These claims remained grounded in concrete issues, however. *Regall Tyrannie*

discovered decried the corruption of the current House of Commons, which
had fallen away from its reforming purity, not least in its financial operations,
'which to the Common-wealth they are not able to give an account of'.[41]
The Resolved Man's Resolution detailed the hardships visited on Elizabeth, and
the long record of duplicitous and half-hearted behaviour of Sir Henry Vane
senior.[42] So recognizable was this repertoire, and store of examples, that it
was in fact easily satirized. *The Recantation of Lieutenant Collonel John Lilburne*
sets out a very familiar-sounding narrative of his sufferings, before arguing for
submission to royal and ecclesiastical authority.[43] Part of the joke, of course,
was that he was now a very high-profile opponent of the parliamentary
leadership and its preferred religious settlement.

By the summer of 1647, Lilburne was presenting his own hardships as
exemplars of a tyranny which could be opposed by the army, particularly
the common soldiers, and their Independent friends. A noticeable element
of this case was the profiteering and sharp financial practice of some parliamentarians, although opposition to this clearly sat uneasily with a campaign
to get arrears of pay for the army or Lilburne. Perhaps, though, it was an
attempt to take this ground from the Presbyterians by presenting it as a larger
manifestation of the corruption of the parliamentary regime.[44] Lilburne
illustrated his own case by publishing letters detailing how prominent men,
particularly Henry Marten and Oliver Cromwell, had fallen away from their
support for his pursuit of reparations and arrears.[45] Their pragmatic
behaviour was part of the malaise; and for the rank and file of the army,
similar behaviour among the officers threatened a similar betrayal. Lilburne's
sufferings, he argued, were emblematic of the threat posed to the common
soldiery and all Englishmen. His own business was not narrow and particular,
he wrote to Fairfax, 'I am confident that [the Commons] have not a businesse
of greater weight and consequence before them, then mine in the latitude
of it is, *for it is concerning the essentiall and fundamentall liberties of themselves, of
me, and of all and every individuall Commoner of England*'.[46]

★   ★   ★

The Presbyterian campaign had failed as a result of the direct action
of the army, not because of a successful counter-initiative in Parliament,
London, and the presses. As Lilburne put it, the army now realized and
believed 'that the wicked and swaying Faction in both Houses, would
destroy them, and inslave the whole Kingdome'. As a result, they 'doe not
onely dispute the two Houses orders and commands, but also positively

disobey them, as unjust, tyrannicall, and unrighteous: And being now thereby dissolved into the originall law of Nature, hold their swords in their hands for their own preservation and safety.' This they had been taught by Nature, and by the Houses' own declarations and practices.[47] Much of the army's own rhetoric was consensual—an attempt to restore proper conduct to a Parliament currently riven by factional hostility—but this does not conceal the revolutionary potential of this situation.[48] The army had emerged as a key and autonomous player in any settlement, although there was clearly internal division within the army about its political pro- gramme. John Lambert and Henry Ireton, who are usually credited with authoring the *Heads of the Proposals*, had taken account of the views of the radicals in the rank and file, but the proposals still seemed to many of them and their City friends to have been too easy on Charles. The result was an ongoing debate within the army and in print about what to do next.

Following the occupation of London in June it had been widely expected that Lilburne would be freed, but he was not. A petition in his favour was referred to a committee chaired by Henry Marten on 23 August, and three days later Lilburne wrote to Fairfax asking for his case to be heard before a committee to be chosen by Cromwell and others.[49] His appeal to the Commons against the Lords was due to be heard on 7 September, and the day before that Cromwell visited him, on the pretext of inspecting the ordnance at the Tower. His real purpose was to try to get Lilburne to be more amenable, saying that he regretted that their friendship had not pros- pered. He was frank about his main worry, though: whether Lilburne would be 'quiet' if he was freed. Lilburne was equally frank in response, claiming that he had not wavered in his friendship, but his old friends had fallen away from their commitment to the cause. He would be quiet if he saw justice being done. He pressed for payment of his reparations, about which Cromwell urged patience, offering an army position in the meantime. Lilburne, though, said he could not serve Parliament or the army as they currently behaved (although he does in fact seem to have received payments from the army that autumn). Instead he offered to go abroad for a year, if he was paid his reparations and arrears. The meeting in the Tower ended without a peace being declared, but Cromwell did apparently promise to use his influence to get Lilburne released.[50]

Cromwell did not deliver, though. Lilburne's business was postponed on 7, 8, and 9 September, and when it was finally heard, on 14 September, 'upon long debate thereof' it was put off. He had been imprisoned the previous year for contempt of the House of Lords, claiming that it had no jurisdiction over him, and for slander of two of its members: his case was sent back to the committee so that the precedents for the Lords' jurisdiction over commoners could be examined.[51] In the meantime he was not being a particularly obliging prisoner. Offered leave to go out of the Tower on condition that he gave bail to the committee, he instead offered bail to the lieutenant of the Tower, saying that if he would not take it then he would force his way out. As a result it was ordered that he could not be visited by more than two people at a time, and that no more could arrive until those two had left. Nonetheless, early in October, it was reported that 'those of Lilborns faction in the Tower' were planning a number of impeachments.[52] Cromwell's visit to the Tower shows that Lilburne was sufficiently influential to be worth conciliating, and that if not conciliated, that he was worth keeping in jail.

This disappointment, which can only have confirmed his gathering view that Cromwell's pragmatism amounted to a lack of principle, may have encouraged Lilburne to dabble in direct negotiation with the king. Since January 1647 he had been in contact with royalist prisoners in the Tower, including Lewis Dyve, whose notebook records these contacts, and Judge Jenkins, who helped Lilburne to pursue his legal education in prison.[53] A part of this was expert tuition on Coke's *Institutes*, which had been an important text for Lilburne since 1645. Written during the 1620s, Coke's reading of the common law tradition had been inconvenient for the Charles I, and the final three volumes of his *Institutes*, including his commentaries on Magna Carta, had been seized in 1632. As a result, at Coke's death in 1634 much of his great work existed only in manuscript form. In the very different circumstances prevailing a decade later, however, Parliament had ordered publication of the final three volumes. The commentaries on Magna Carta (volume 2 of the *Institutes*) appeared in 1642, and the last two volumes in 1644.[54] These texts, closely associated with the development of the Parliament's cause in 1642, had been important to Lilburne's publications during the previous two years. Now, armed with Jenkins' advice on how to read them, they became an even more crucial resource for him, not least in the public trials which awaited him.

The view that the current, corrupt Parliament had to be brought to account, and restored to purity in its service of the Commonwealth, was therefore the basis for some unlikely alliances. While in the Tower, Lilburne also struck up a friendship with Sir John Maynard, an influential Presbyterian MP and prominent critic of the army, imprisoned in September 1647 in the

wake of the army occupation of London. When Maynard appeared before
the Lords in February 1648 he refused to hear the charges, drawing direct
comparison with Lilburne's own appearance in 1646, and Overton and
Lilburne both published in support of his case.[55]

This focus on legal freedoms created very different coalitions than the
arguments about church government. That too supported new alliances:
Lilburne's old friend William Kiffin, who had felt the lash of Presbyterian
intolerance, had also been in contact with the king, floating the possibility
of a more tolerant settlement with the king at its head, and Lilburne showed
some interest in that possibility. For Lilburne, though, what was really at stake
was legal rights. Anglicans, Presbyterians, and others might have been fellow
sufferers as much as political opponents—they had all, potentially, fallen foul
of the abuse of legal rights. The key to his politics was his calculation of who
offered the best means of securing liberties, and he could be equally suspicious of the leadership of the House of Commons and of the army, equally
alert to the potential of apparently strange bedfellows in opposing tyranny.
For him the key issue was not the future of the monarchy, but securing the
rights of the freeborn Englishman. If the latter could be done under a
monarchy, then he had no objection to that; by the same token, he was not an
unquestioning supporter of the army leadership. From his prison cell, John
Lilburne was a participant in the attempt to defeat the Presbyterian mobilization,
and on terms which had the potential to shift the political map considerably;
but the key to getting them acted upon was the attitude of the army.

★   ★   ★

As negotiations between the king and the army leaders proceeded, frustrations
with the army officers increased and this helped precipitate a showdown
in October. *The Case of the Armie Truly Stated*, drawn up on 9 October
(probably by Wildman) and published on 15 October, amalgamated the
emerging constitutional proposals of the Levellers with the soldiers' grievances. The main thrust was that nothing effectual had been done for the
army or the people of England, because Parliament and the army officers
had obstructed the will of both. Arguing that the people were the only
and original source of political authority, it was clearly pushing the army
leadership to use its political influence for a much more radical purpose
than the *Heads of the Proposals*.[56]

It was presented to Fairfax on 18 October and a General Council of the
Army was summoned to discuss it on 21 October. The first meeting took

place a week later, at Putney, resulting in the famous debates. This fame derives, however, not from *The Case of the Armie*, which is in truth a difficult read, but from the *Agreement of the People*, which seems to have been tabled at Putney. This has been seen as a key moment when the Levellers intervened—the *Agreement* is usually interpreted as a document produced outside the army, and the Putney Debates as a response to that lobbying. In fact, it seems clear that Putney was one of a series of meetings at which the General Council tried to find a consensual political platform, and that the tabling the *Agreement* was a surprise. It may not have been in any obvious way a specifically *Leveller* document either, having been generated by a distinct, though related, group of Independent radicals.[57] The interpretation of the ensuing debates is also controversial, as is the precise meaning of the text of the *Agreement*, but it had two features which are undisputed, and remarkable. It argued that the source of political power was the people (although scholars find it hard to agree about exactly who 'the people' were); and it reserved certain rights to individuals which could not be legitimately infringed by the state (seen by many as important to the later human rights tradition).[58]

In practice, it was a statement about the peace settlement: the signatories felt themselves bound 'to take the best care we can for the future, to avoid both the danger of returning into a slavish condition, and the chargeable remedy of another war'. A firm peace should be based on 'the grounds of Common-Right and Freedom', offering a fair reward for the sacrifices of the war. If people had understood their rights correctly they would not have opposed the cause, and if the peace was properly established there would be no return to slavery. All this is quite familiar from 1645 and 1646, but what was new was the remedy by way of parliamentary reform. Parliaments should know when they would meet, but also be of limited duration. To avoid 'the long continuance of the same persons in authority', with the attendant dangers, the Parliament had to be regularly recalled to the basis of its authority in the will of the people. But by the same token elected parliaments would be supreme, their power 'inferior only to theirs who choose them' and extending to all issues except for those matters 'expressly or implicitly reserved by the represented unto themselves'. Those reserved powers were: 'matters of religion' (which were a matter for the individual conscience before God, although there could be some prescribed but not compulsory form of public worship); conscription; there should be no questioning of what was done in the past after the dissolution of the current Parliament; laws should apply to all equally; and all laws 'must be good, and not evidently destructive to the safety and well-being of the people'.[59]

At the core of this was the belief that the Commons was the representative of the will of the people: it should be the supreme power in the land, treating everyone equally, but it should also be answerable to the will of the people. In order to achieve this latter goal the *Agreement* called for a redistribution of parliamentary seats to make it more evenly representative; the dissolution of the current Parliament; the election of a new Parliament from April, by means to be decided by the end of the current Parliament; and that future parliaments be chosen every two years. Hopes were high among its supporters, encouraged by the apparent support of Oliver Cromwell.[60]

The first day at Putney was taken up with a discussion about whether the council ought to consider the *Agreement* at all. It was not clear who it spoke for or why it should be the particular focus of discussion. Cromwell also raised the issue of whether it was consistent with previous declarations and engagements made by the army—not an unreasonable question given the way that Lilburne and others habitually argued. A committee was therefore appointed to consider all the army's statements since June. The second day opened with a prayer meeting, designed to promote unity, but a debate on the *Agreement* seems to have been forced on the meeting which went straight to the heart of the matter: what did more equal representation mean, and who would choose the representative? This debate has often been at the heart of discussion about what the Levellers meant by 'the people', and the real ideological basis of their campaign: whether everyone should vote in elections to Parliament, or only those with a stake in the property of the kingdom. On the third day the *Agreement* was considered alongside its previous engagements.[61] The Putney Debates concluded without the General Council adopting the *Agreement of the People* as its political platform.

This was not an episode in the history of the Levellers so much as a struggle over the army's political programme in which the Levellers participated. Nonetheless, the language and argument of the *Agreement* is clearly close to that of the pamphlets of Lilburne, Overton, and Walwyn, and there are many direct connections between these City radicals and the army. On the second day of the debates, Wildman had published *A call to all the soldiers*, intended to put additional pressure on the officers to adopt a radical platform, and although essentially an army debate, it was not confined to its ranks. Cromwell was threatened with impeachment in the House of Commons, and Henry Marten and Thomas Rainsborough, both sympathizers with those pushing for an *Agreement*, claimed that the move would have had the support of 20,000 citizens. There were five more meetings before 8 November, and discussions of similar *Agreements* and Engagements continued throughout the following year.[62]

Ultimately, therefore, the Levellers were influencing, or trying to influence, an argument within the army: the Putney Debates were primarily internal to the army and centred on what the General Council was going to do with its political power. The struggle to make it use that power to secure a peace based on an *Agreement* continued, and the term 'Leveller' gained currency as a term of abuse in the propaganda battle around this campaign. It had apparently been familiar in royalist circles the previous December, but reference was now made to the 'new party of Levellers *in the Army*'. Lilburne himself referred to the term reluctantly, and always as a 'nick-name', and he was consistently anxious to distance himself from the implied desire for social levelling—the abolition of social distinctions.[63] Nonetheless, a number of the contributions to the debate reflected this belief that a democratic representative would necessarily be an enemy of property.

The *Agreement* was not based on a return to some version of previously agreed constitutional principles, but instead on an abstract sense of justice. The nature and origin of these underpinning ideals has been much debated. Did this radical departure come from natural law theories, precedents from classical history, or Christian egalitarianism, for example? The debate about the *Agreement* at Putney in particular has been closely examined for clues about what lay behind it, and what different groups might see in it. Historians have not been able to agree, partly because the *Agreement* itself was a peace proposal, largely concerned with practical proposals and intended to unite people of diverse political views: it was not a text in political theory. A key argument, though, has been that by abandoning the attempt to restore established rights and instead insisting on practical measures to enshrine an abstract political principle—the sovereignty of the people—the *Agreement* abandoned the common law arguments to which Lilburne was so attached, and instead turned to natural law.[64]

For Lilburne, however, this seems much too neat. He did resort to natural and divine law, or to reason, when he found existing laws not to his liking; but he continued to assert that he was restoring something that previously existed, and was reflected in the law, and such landmarks as Magna Carta and the Petition of Right. He seems not to have understood the conventional distinction contemporaries made between divine law (eternal, unchanging, and known unto God) and natural law (imprinted in the hearts of all men through their natural reason). He also went beyond a conventional view that the human laws should be congruent with natural law, seeming to take abstract principles as tests of validity of the common law, and yet at the same time insisting on rights granted to him by the common law, not by abstract right. He appealed to natural law and medieval charters and oaths inconsistently, promiscuously, and even perhaps instrumentally, when it suited him.[65] Before and after the Leveller campaigns he seems to argue more for what he saw as existing legal rights which protected him from government tyranny, using appeal to divine or natural law when the precedents were against him. In doing so he was arguing for what modern scholars call a 'negative liberty', a freedom from interference. In modern thought this is distinguished quite sharply from a more positive sense of liberty—a freedom to have or become something, which is underpinned by natural and timeless rights that are intrinsic to our humanity. That latter 'Leveller' position, if such it was, drew more from the other leaders than from Lilburne.[66] Of course, his theoretical inconsistency did not mean that he was not on to something.

Lilburne had in any case been involved in this gathering campaign only from the sidelines, and being in prison of course had no direct role at Putney. As far as we can tell he had no direct role in drafting the *Agreement* either. He was, however, freed on bail shortly after the Putney meetings and given a hearing before a Commons committee on 2 October, although was unwell and unable to complete his plea.[67] Not long after that he petitioned the Lords and attended a Commons committee the same day. In this context his claims were very definitely grounded in existing rights and a notion of negative liberty: he claimed to the Committee that the Lords' proceedings against him were illegal 'and gave in many Precedents, which he undertakes to prove. His Expressions were in Law very high'. A week later a petition from the East India Company which also involved the jurisdiction of the Lords was referred to the committee considering Lilburne's business, which was growing in size.[68] The proceedings were adjourned until 26 October, but never completed. He seems by that point to have been given freedom to leave the Tower, because on 5 November the Lords asked the Lieutenant why Lilburne had been allowed out without their authority, and four days later, perhaps in a spirit of compromise, the Commons ordered that he could be given liberty to attend their committee, a formulation which did not directly challenge the Lords' power to imprison him but did allow him freedom to prepare his case.[69]

His example had been important to the genesis of the campaign for an *Agreement*, although it clearly rested in part on arguments that were not his. He also had close connections to some of the people close to the radical cause. Rainsborough visited Lilburne on 30 October and one of his first acts when bailed, on 9 November, was to meet one of the agitators, Tobias Box.[70] Soon after, he got closer to the action, but it was a disappointment. At Putney the agitators had asked for, among other things, a general rendezvous of the army, under the joint command of the General Council and the Lord General, presumably to get signatures to the *Agreement*. This was refused and instead the commanders called separate rendezvous. On 15 November two regiments assembled at Corkbush Field, in Ware, Hertfordshire, with Leveller slogans and papers. This was a breach of discipline in itself, but one of the regiments should not even have been there and attended in defiance of all but one of its officers. Fairfax and Cromwell confronted the mutineers, condemning three to death (of whom one was executed following the drawing of lots) and arresting three officers (one of whom was an MP and sent immediately to Parliament to be dealt with there).

Lilburne had been keen to join the action. As one hostile commentator jeered: 'big with hope Legislative John was got as far as Ware, to behold the Lords worke (as he tearmed it) effected, and himselfe made a great man, being pitched upon by some wretched ones in the Army for their Generall, to go before them out of the Land of Egypt'. He had ridden from London to be present, suggesting something of the importance attached to these events, but never got to the field, and returned to London that day.[71] His brother's regiment was one of those that mutinied, although Robert himself was not present. These events subsequently assumed tremendous symbolic importance in accounts of the revolution—a key moment at which the opportunity for radical political change was lost and the conservative views of the officers were imposed. It did not loom so large in contemporary perception, but it clearly made direct action by the rank and file in the future seem far less likely.[72]

The irruption on to the political scene of the Leveller/army alliance seemed politically significant to royalist observers. One of Clarendon's informers claimed in early November that 'The Lords have been soe scared by the new party of Levellers in the Army as they have shewen a willingnes to conferre in this p[re]sent exigency w[i]th some of the Kings party'. This campaign for a settlement based on quite different and very radical proposals drove deep wedges into an already fractured parliamentary coalition, and offered the royalists further hope of winning the peace. A few days later it was claimed that 'such is the good Kings ill fortune as if they had continued in the feare they were in of the Levellers but one day longer knowe it for certaine that the King had bin on Wednesday night last at St James upon allmost as good tearmes as you and I could wishe; but that conjuncture is almost, but not quite, past'. When, on 25 November, 'Lilbourne with many others went to the Parl[iamen]t to demande justice there for the death of the innocent Agitator (shott by ord[er] of Fairfax & his Councell) . . . five them were imprisoned'. The royalist hope was clear: 'if they differ heatedly we shall find a way to rise'.[73]

Events continued to move against the Leveller campaign, however, from the winter of 1647 onwards. In November a plot to assassinate the king was revealed, and John may have been instrumental in warning him. The revelation apparently came from Henry Lilburne, shortly to fight for the king in the second civil war, who John claimed had been alienated from the parliamentary cause by the experience of serving under Sir Arthur Hesilrige. While it seems highly improbable that Lilburne himself had any serious interest in the royalist cause at that point, he and his friends were clearly very critical of elements of the army command and parliamentary leadership. Wildman had published *Putney Projects* in December, under the pseudonym John Lawmind, and it seemed a homage to Lilburne in other ways, demonstrating in painstaking detail the gap between the undertakings given by the army leadership and their actual behaviour. It revealed 'The Old Serpent in new Forme', and set out '1. To spread abroad the cloak of promises, wherewith they have covered themselves 2. To present them naked in their actions.'[74]

★ ★ ★

Meanwhile, the search for settlement between king and Parliament had broken down completely, and in early January exasperation with the king reached a new pitch. He had escaped from his captivity in Hampton Court claiming that his life was in danger, and fled to the Isle of Wight, where he was taken into custody and incarcerated at Carisbrooke Castle. From Carisbrooke he launched a new initiative, responding to a peace negotiation that became the Four Bills. In some ways the most favourable offer he had received from Parliament, it separated out four pieces of legislation essential to the settlement. The bills gave control of the militia to Parliament for twenty years and limited royal power thereafter; allowed the Houses of

Parliament to adjourn to any place of their choosing, on their own authority;
imposed parliamentary approval on elevations to the peerage, thus limiting
royal power over the composition of the Lords; and gave safeguards against
retribution for actions taken during the wars. This legislation would be
the framework within which other proposals would be considered, including
the abolition of episcopacy. They did not insist on a Presbyterian settlement in its place, though—this was in one way a deal which made common
cause with the Independents against the defeated Presbyterians, in something of the way Lilburne seems to have suggested to Jenkins, or Kiffin to
the king.[75]

While Charles was stringing out this negotiation, however, he was
finalizing a deal with the Scots. This became the Engagement—an offer to
establish a settlement in England based on the Solemn League and Covenant
(although no one would be forced to swear against their conscience), and
with a Presbyterian Church. Charles gave guarantees about the settlement
achieved in Scotland after the Prayer Book rebellion a decade earlier, and in
return the Scots promised to use peaceful means to get Charles to London
to enter into direct, personal treaty negotiations with Parliament. However,
if that was not successful, then 'an army shall be sent from Scotland into
England'. The army would be there 'for preservation and establishment of
religion, for defence of His Majesty's person and authority, and restoring
him to his government, to the just rights of the Crown and his full revenues',
as well as the privileges of Parliament, the rights of the subject, and a firm
union of the kingdoms.[76]

These were clearly incompatible settlements, and there is no doubt
that Charles was simply exploiting the divisions among his enemies. He
rejected the Four Bills on 28 December, two days after secretly agreeing the
Engagement.[77] On 4 January the Commons passed a Vote of No Addresses,
'having received an absolute negative' they held 'themselves obliged to use
their utmost endeavours speedily to settle the present government in such a
way as may bring the greatest security to this kingdom in the enjoyment of
the laws and liberties thereof'. To ensure that they received 'no delays nor
interruptions in so great and necessary a work', they agreed that neither
House would make any further approaches, that no one else could make an
approach without the approval of both Houses, that infringements of this
order would be construed as treason, and that they would receive no more
messages from the king.[78] The Lords approved the measure on 17 January,
and their exasperation with Charles was presumably complete when the

contents of the Engagement became public in February. For the time being, clearly, the talking was over.

Having missed the action at Putney and Ware, Lilburne used his new-found freedom to participate very actively in these tense politics. The Commons had agreed in December to hear a report about his imprisonment, and on 7 January ordered Marten's committee to report the following week.[79] By then Lilburne and others were organizing a petition in Southwark as part of a much wider campaign to shape the peace. Its aim was to avoid a new war by persuading Parliament to deliver on the promise of reform, calling on people to 'propound each to other the chief Principles of your Freedoms, and the foundation of Justice and Common Right'. If that were done, 'questionless... you shall understand the Desires each of other, [and] you will unite together inviolably to pursue them'. Lilburne, with Wildman and two others, wrote to sympathizers on 7 January with guidance on how to organize the petitioning. 'Active men' had been appointed in every ward and division in London and its suburbs, several of whom were to form a committee to promote it. They were to hold meetings to read the petition and collect signatures, and to get as many people as possible to agree to accompany the petition when it was eventually presented. It was also being promoted in Hertfordshire, Buckinghamshire, Oxford, Rutland, '&c.' The letter from Lilburne and the others asked that it be passed on to 'the most active men in every Town, to unite the Town in those Desires of Common Right', and to take their signatures. There would be a general meeting at Dartford for supporters from Kent on 23 January.[80]

Lilburne had contributed to the costs of printing that lay behind this campaign,[81] and ten days later he chaired a meeting at the house of Mr Williams, a gardener, in Ratcliffe Highway, near East Smithfield. It was one of a more regular series of meetings held at the Whalebone Inn behind the Exchange, or at the Nag's Head in Blackwall: the 'commissioners' for the petition were apparently meeting at the Whalebone every Monday, Wednesday, and Friday. The business of this particular meeting was to discuss tactical concerns. It was attended, though, by George Masterson and Robert Malbon, who turned out to be opponents of the petition, and after the meeting Masterson reported proceedings to the House of Lords, claiming he had uncovered a plot. He testified that the petition was directed to the Houses merely 'as a Colour and Cloak': 30,000 copies were to be printed, given to the newsbook publishers and 'put into the Hands of all that could read'. It was clearly intended to be a manifesto rather than a petition to

Parliament. Worse, some of those present, he said, had been worried that the general temper of the country was against them, and that petitioning Parliament would be a damaging distraction in the current circumstances. In response Lilburne reported rumours that Cromwell and Ireton were playing a double game—securing concessions on the promise of an earldom and the lieutenancy of Ireland respectively, and that because of this duplicity several men were willing to kill Cromwell. In particular there was a second 'Felton', willing to assassinate this enemy of the Commonwealth, a reference to the man who had killed the Duke of Buckingham in 1628.[82]

The most damaging allegation, however, was that there was an actual plot. A 'plain man of the Company' had objected that mobilizing this petition might put power in the hands of the '*generality of the people [who] are wicked*', and that they would then '*cut the throats of all those that are called Roundheads, that is, the honest, godly, faithful men in the Land.*' Lilburne had been reassuring: 'he that hath this Petition in his hand, and a blue Ribband in his Hat, need not fear his throat cutting: Or, this Petition in your hand, will be as good as a blue Ribband in your Hat, to preserve your throat from cutting'. To Masterson this was evidence of a plot to cut throats: as Lilburne summarized the charge, 'That there was a designe … contrived by me &c. to destroy or cut of both houses of Parliament, and that we could not be far [from] the intention of executing it, in regard I had appointed blew ribons to be worne in the hats of all those that should be saved alive'. In this case then it was the Levellers who wore the 'Cloak'—the petition was but a cover for a plot to raise the people and to destroy the Parliament.[83]

Lilburne's response to these accusations seems plausible on the basis even of Masterson's account of what was said—that the petition and the blue ribbons would be a defence against the hostility of the people, not that they would be badges marking those to be spared in the case of an uprising against parliamentarians. Lilburne and Wildman were both reported to have claimed that the petition would appeal to many royalists, and that a number of them had said that only the personal obligation they had entered to the king prevented them from joining the campaign. Commitment to the principles set out in the petition would have created a new political solidarity against corrupt political leaders. Before Parliament, however, Lilburne passed over what he had said about Cromwell, Ireton, and the second Felton.[84]

When all this was reported to the Lords the next day they took the threat of political disorder very seriously, declaring Lilburne's conduct 'of dangerous Consequence and moving of sedition'. They also sought a conference with the Commons 'concerning the present safety of the Kingdom'. When they asked the Deputy Lieutenant of the Tower why Lilburne was out and about, it turned out that Lilburne had been using the order of the House of Commons to 'permit him to go about upon his Occasions; and that very seldom he rendered himself to the *Tower*'. The Commons heard Masterson's testimony and the Lords' views the same day, and immediately revoked their order that he should be allowed out to prepare his case. Lilburne, Wildman. and Masterson were called to the bar for the following morning, at 9.00 a.m.[85] The alarm triggered hurried attempts to mobilize the militia.[86]

When they appeared, Masterson repeated his testimony, and Lilburne answered. He gave a long narrative of events 'after some Salvo premised by him of his right as an Englishman', denied absolutely that the petition was simply a colour or cloak, and then 'with some Expressions and Desires concerning himself, concluded his Discourse'. In the meantime he had told the deputy lieutenant that he would only go back to the Tower by force, and that he had many friends present. The deputy therefore asked for the appropriate powers, should he need them. Lilburne declared that he 'could not submit to that Authority that had committed him; [and] that, rather than return, he would chuse to have his Head cleft by one of the Halbardeers'.[87] He need not have worried—he was now imprisoned by the authority of the Commons, not the Lords, to face trial before the King's Bench 'for treasonous and seditious practices against the State'. To his enemies this performance was further evidence of his lack of 'meekness', that his sufferings were not those of a truly persecuted man. Wildman, who had put on a similar show, was committed with him, and Masterson was ordered to put his testimony into writing.[88] Lilburne remained in prison until early August, forced to sit out what became the second civil war.

This petition was an extension of the campaign for an *Agreement of the People*, seeking to establish a new basis for peace, beyond the terms of the formal negotiations since 1642, distinct from the claims of the Solemn League and Covenant, and alive to the new tyrannies to which the war had given rise. The sentiment it was trying to tap into was potent: in January, as the petition was being mobilized, it was reported that the recent quartering of several regiments in London had galvanized discontent about the 'decay of Trade, skarcyty, & dearnes of provysion, not bringinge in of Bullion, and all other causes of povertie'. Everything was blamed on the army and there had been active plans 'to rayse a tumult'. Fortunately prompt action by the city's magistrates had summoned the militia and order had been maintained.[89]

By promoting new grounds for political settlement, its proponents claimed, a new alliance became possible cutting across the divisions of 1642 and which also addressed the grievances fostered by the war: as Lilburne had told the meeting in January, by propounding 'the chief Principles of your Freedoms, and the foundation of Justice and Common Right', a new and broadly embracing alliance would emerge, united 'together inviolably to pursue them'.[90] It was this new solidarity that would protect its partisans from the fury of the people.

In the coming months there were contacts between Levellers, other proponents of an *Agreement*, and royalists, although there was in reality little hope of a settlement with Charles I on these terms. In the short term the royalists thought, like the parliamentary leadership, that disunity was the real threat to Parliament's position. As one of Clarendon's correspondents put it, 'The intent at present is to take Lilborne out of the way, & in this I know they will goe as farr as they dare, Cromwell his old friend is his adversary, & if Cromwell doe not ruine him, I really beleeve that he will in the end by ruined by him'.[91]

This campaign offered a remarkably creative solution to the problem of establishing a peace, illustrating how these uncertain political conditions fostered new thinking. It was also remarkable for the means by which it was being promoted. Much of Masterson's testimony was contested, but not his claims about the sophistication of this mobilization.[92] Petitioning was a well-established political practice, and Lilburne and others presented inter-ference with petitioning as an infringement of an Englishman's liberties. But the practice had been transformed over the previous few years. When counties and towns had petitioned on partisan grounds between 1640 and 1642—in favour of the Prayer Book, for example—it had caused local pol-itical battles, as there were over the raising of the militia.[93] The *New Found Stratagem* had claimed that similarly manipulative means were being used to make the county of Essex speak for a sharply partisan point of view. The underlying logic, however, was that such petitions spoke for established political communities, and to successfully present a case in that form carried some weight. These latter tussles reflected a further development: how peti-tions could now be the voice of an ideologically partisan interest, rather than an established corporate interest such as a town, county, or trade. By the later 1640s, Lilburne and others could identify the supporters of particular petitions as distinct partisan communities, and the promotion of petitions could even be the means towards the creation of such communities—those at the meetings at the Whalebone and at Mr Williams's house were using the petition to foster, not simply to reflect, a view of how to strengthen Parliament's resolve.[94]

More than this, a printed petition supporting a partisan point of view could now be a way to state a position rather than a way to seek redress or satisfaction: to a hostile observer, in fact, it might simply be a seditious paper. Over the previous four years Parliament had taken this view, refusing to hear, denouncing, or even publicly burning petitions, but there were political costs in doing that: there was, to some extent, a game of bluff and counter-bluff in such campaigns. This new mode of petitioning did not simply reflect the development of partisan mobilization and solidarity, therefore, but also the increasingly sophisticated ways in which print could be used to make political interventions—scattered in the streets or distributed at the door of the House to those members willing to take a copy. It was one of the instruments by which a much more intimate connection could be made between an active citizen and the business of Parliament, a Parliament that was now in permanent session with an elaborate system of committees.[95]

The Leveller campaign was a product of this emergent political world—in that respect it reflects a more general, but no less remarkable, phenomenon. Spontaneous organization of like-minded citizens in London's taverns, private homes, or around army campfires was a prelude to sophisticated lobbying in close and knowledgeable dialogue with parliamentary business. It is easy to see why those trying to settle a peace felt they needed to exercise control over this citizen activism. At the same time that Lilburne and Wildman were jailed, the General Council of the Army was reformed, apparently consensually, to limit membership to commissioned officers: clearly this would make it more difficult for those outside the army to harness its political leverage. Leveller publication continued, partly through the friendly pages of the *Moderate*, launched in June and active until September 1648, which is often described as the Leveller newsbook. That seems an exaggeration, but the *Moderate* did editorialize in support of the Levellers, reprinted petitions (which continued to be presented), and drew on a network of correspondents that seems to have overlapped with circles of Leveller sympathizers.[96] Nonetheless, the Levellers had in the end been demonstrably marginalized following Ware and the arrests of Lilburne and Wildman, while army unity had been secured by restoring the command of the senior officers.

The second civil war and the regicide, 1648–9

Royalist hopes of a military victory in the new war proved hopelessly opti-
mistic. The Scots did not cross into England until early July, and when they
did it was with only 9,000 of the promised 30,000 men. There were risings
in Wales, leading to the battle of St Fagan's and a siege of Pembroke Castle,
brought to an end by Cromwell. Help from Ireland was not forthcoming
and royalist sympathizers in the English provinces were not able to convert
an amalgam of discontents into coherent or concerted armed support for
Charles I. In fact, the only substantial rising in England was in Kent, which
was easily faced down by Fairfax, from where the royalists were chased to
Colchester and besieged. Risings in Wales were also put down quickly, and
so a unified force could be sent north to meet the Scots, who were led by
the Duke of Hamilton. Parliament won a great victory against superior
numbers at Preston and, trying to regroup, Hamilton led his army south the
following day, pursued by Cromwell. The Scots met a further, and decisive,
defeat near Warrington after two night marches. One thousand of Hamilton's
men were killed, another 2,000 taken prisoner, and the remnants of his cavalry finally surrendered at Uttoxeter on 22 August.

By this time conditions at Colchester had become terrible. Part of the
logic of a siege was that the pressure on the town created suffering among
the civilian population, which was the responsibility of the defenders.
The defenders were, in other words, under pressure from within as well as
outside: by August the inhabitants of Colchester were suffering appalling
privations, and had begun to eat the dogs. The royalist command continued
to hold out, though. Contemporaries thought it was dishonourable to prolong resistance beyond the point where there was a reasonable chance of
victory—forcing a besieging army to storm a doomed defence was simply
a waste of lives. By the time Colchester fell there was no sympathy for those
in command of the defence, who had inflicted futile sufferings on the
inhabitants and unnecessary loss of life on both sides. They did eventually
surrender, partly in the light of the news of Hamilton's fate, but two key
commanders were court-martialled and executed. These were the first of
a number of vengeful executions: Colonel John Poyer, who had put his
troops behind the rising in Wales, was publicly executed in Covent Garden
six months later, while the Duke of Hamilton, the earl of Holland (who had
raised troops in south-east England), and Lord Capel (one of the commanders

at Colchester), were tried and executed during 1649.[97] There was a legacy of bitterness arising from the second war which, although on a much smaller scale than the first war, had been marked by greater ferocity, and all to no effect. This was a war deliberately fomented by a defeated king.

Lilburne had been no more than a spectator in all this. In April the Tower was becoming crowded, since 400 troops were stationed there by a government worried about reports of risings and disorders from around the country. Special order was made that Lilburne and the others were not to be moved, but the Commons also ordered that he should be brought to trial and in the meantime awarded him 40s a week for maintenance. He published accounts of his appearances and legal broils, and on 8 May he appeared before the King's Bench in his case with Colonel King, having sued a writ of habeas corpus.[98] His plea was not a good case in law, perhaps characteristically; in fact it was to some extent incoherent—he sought the judges' opinion in his favour while rejecting the precedents set by their predecessors. But it was also a hopeless case—the King's Bench, entirely predictably, dismissed the suit on the grounds that the Lords was the higher court, and thus not subject to review by the King's Bench. He was seeking to use habeas corpus as an instrument of universal liberty, when in fact it was a product of common law, used for particular purposes and regulated by common law practice.[99]

Although not a strong case in law, it clearly had resonance on the streets, and by late summer national politics seemed once more to be moving in his direction. On 23 July, at the crisis point in this second war, a petition with 8,000 or 9,000 signatures was presented to the House calling for Lilburne's release, and Maynard, his friend from the Tower, spoke at length in the Commons in his favour. On 1 August the Commons received another petition on his behalf and resolved that he should be freed from restraint, asking the Lords to discharge him. A Committee was established to consider how he could 'have such Satisfaction and Allowance for his Sufferings and losses as was formerly intended by this House', while his accounts were resubmitted to the Committee of Accounts for audit. The issue of his release was to be discussed directly with the Lords the following morning.[100]

The Commons committee met on 4 September, but it was clear that the settlement of Lilburne's claims proposed in 1645 was no longer viable. Cottington's estate had in the meantime gone to Say and Sele, and Windebank's son had compounded with the parliamentary authorities and thus secured his father's lands. The committee agreed to assign the reparations instead from the estate of Lord Coventry—he had been Lord Keeper at the time of the Lilburne's Star Chamber conviction and so could be seen as one of the key figures in the injustice done to him. The progress of the ordinance stopped on 5 September, however. Sir John Clotworthy, one of those appointed to count the votes against the measure, was himself seeking payment from sequestered lands, but Lilburne blamed the earl of Manchester, whose son and brother were both in the House of Commons. The Speaker, too, opposed the settlement on principle, saying that taking the lands of the son to pay for the sins of the father was unjust, and a principle that threatened them all. He proposed instead that Lilburne be paid from public revenues. Lilburne petitioned again, setting out the whole issue, but was thwarted by Vane, the Speaker, and the Montagues who then, in a 'thin House', saw through a vote to award him £300 in ready money from the composition made by Sir Charles Keymish for his part in the second war the previous summer, and £3,000 from lands newly seized following those risings.[101]

Lilburne accepted this as the best he was likely to get after the 'manie baffles' and setbacks over the years. The estate of Sir Henry Gibb, in Jarrow, County Durham, was suggested to him, and this seemed attractive, since his father and uncle were both committee men in the county. On 9 September the Durham County Committee asked the local Sequestration Committee to settle lands to the value of £3,000 on him from Gibb's estate, but at this point John got cold feet. The possibility of a personal treaty between Parliament and the king was in the air, and that might make the title of lands recently seized from royalists very insecure, and he was in any case resentful of his treatment at the hands of his political enemies in the Commons. He had, he claimed, 'no stomack to his, or any other Delinquents Lands' and asked instead for £3,000 in cash, to be raised from seized assets on the estates of Sir Henry Gibb, Sir Henry Bellingham, and Sir Henry Bowes— wood that had been felled on the estates, and the impropriations of church revenues belonging to the estate. Although approved by the committee it was resisted in the House of Commons, notably by John Blakiston, MP for Newcastle and a powerful figure in the north. Although he was an Independent and hostile to the Scots, he was an ally of Hesilrige's in the north-east: an opponent of George Lilburne's and a political opponent of the other Lilburnes too.[102]

Lilburne had thereafter given up on the process again, concentrating instead, he said, on trying to prevent another 'cheat' by the army.[103] Nonetheless, it is striking how quickly and completely his fortunes had changed. By the time the second war was over, Lilburne was free, and at last getting a sympathetic hearing at Westminster.

*   *   *

Having won the second civil war so decisively, the army was now the dominant player in the search for a settlement, and had potential allies among those alarmed by any suggestion of easy peace terms for this reckless king. Lilburne's prospects and those for a revived campaign for an *Agreement* rose at the same time, but Parliament had little option other than to renew negotiations with the king. One week after the victory at Preston, on 24 August, Parliament repealed the Vote of No Addresses, and formal negotiations opened on 18 September. There was a familiar air about these negotiations—the Treaty of Newport—both in the substance of the conversation and Charles's approach. On 9 October he wrote to a friend that he had made concessions in that day's negotiations, 'merely in order to my escape, of which if I had not hope, I would not have done'. His plan was to appear unable to deny them any demand, so that they would relax their guard.[104]

There had been no very visible change in Charles and there was a concerted reaction to these negotiations: it was quite reasonable to fear that if they produced anything it would be a sell-out, offering no just reward for the sufferings of the people, particularly in the renewed and futile second war. Lilburne in fact began to use 'Personal Treaty man' as a term of abuse, a kind of counter to the slur implied by the term Leveller: someone who was so casual of the good of the Commonwealth that he would have embraced a personal negotiation with the king at the expense of the campaign for an *Agreement of the People*.[105] This anxiety about a potential sell-out fed a new willingness in the army leadership to work with the civilian radicals. The failure to get the General Council to adopt of the *Agreement* at Putney had not ended political discussion in the army, and throughout 1648 the development of new 'Engagements' went alongside petitioning that kept alive the issues debated at Putney.[106]

Nonetheless, the second civil war, and the threat that Parliament would simply carry on negotiating in the same vein, galvanized the campaign for a new departure. Prior to the opening of the Newport Treaty a new petition had been presented to the Commons, *To the Commons of England in Parliament Assembled*, the '11 September petition'. It is usually attributed to Lilburne and Walwyn, and set out the many things that the people had not yet obtained, despite their sacrifices and their victory, and restated many of the familiar Leveller claims. It was claimed that 40,000 people signed. Whereas previous petitions of this kind had been met with a strong rebuff, this time the Commons promised to listen, and over the following months thirty similar petitions came in from army regiments.[107]

The army leadership, and particularly Sir Thomas Fairfax, were at the sharp end of this, since it was they who could broker a settlement. They were, as a result, under pressure not to agree to the Newport Treaty. A leading figure in promoting the alternative settlement was Henry Ireton, who advocated bringing the king to trial and electing a new Parliament. This pressure culminated in the *Remonstrance* of the army, drafted by Ireton and discussed in the Council of Officers between 9 and 15 November. It called for an end to the negotiations at Newport, and 'capital punishment upon the principal author and some prime instruments in our late wars'. This was a clear statement of intent, and a bracing departure from the desire to talk to the king, but it did leave some room for 'pity, mercy and pardon' if there was a 'full and free yielding on his part'. Ireton wanted the army to say publicly that they were willing to execute the king, but were also willing to see him escape with his life if he could be persuaded to some genuine contrition, and a submission to the will of the people.[108]

On the final day of the army's discussions, however, the Commons voted that the king should be settled 'in a condition of honour, freedom and safety, agreeable to the laws of the land'.[109] The choice before the army could hardly have been more stark. Oliver Cromwell, still in the north and therefore not directly involved, was clear about the prospects of Newport: 'this ruining, hypocritical agreement'.[110] Over the next few days negotiations between key army figures and civilian radicals and Independents produced an amended *Remonstrance* that was accepted by the Council of the Army on 18 November. There was now an agreed platform for settlement in opposition to the Newport Treaty. The *Remonstrance*, including the demand for capital justice on the principal author of the recent troubles, was presented to Parliament on 20 November.

While Parliament prevaricated, Thomas Rainsborough, a senior officer who had been sympathetic to the *Agreement* both at Putney and since, was killed at Pontefract, where royalists continued to hold the castle despite the defeat of the Scots and the fall of Colchester. Rainsborough had been captured and was killed trying to escape, a death which secured for him the status of a martyr, and his funeral was attended by crowds wearing the green colours now recognized to be a badge of affiliation to the Levellers. The army had advanced to Windsor, where there were further discussions at which Lilburne was present, about what to do.[111] It was against this background that Parliament rejected the *Remonstrance* on 1 December and ordered Fairfax to come no nearer to London than he already was: the Parliament's support of treaty discussions at Newport had led once more to direct confrontation with the army. This time, however, it was resolved conclusively in favour of a less inhibited army leadership.

Five days later, Colonel Thomas Pride arrived at the Palace of Westminster before 7.00 a.m., along with several regiments and a list. Those on the list were denied entry to the Houses, while others, seeing what was going on, absented themselves. Over the next six days the army kept watch on the entry to the House, eventually arresting forty-five members and excluding many others, while many chose to stay away. These events, known to posterity as Pride's Purge, had a dramatic effect: prior to the purge there had been 471 members of the House; in the course of its life only around 200 ever took their seats in the 'Rump' Parliament, and attendances were sometimes very low. Through December 1648 the House was short of a quorum several times.[112] Nonetheless, the deadlock had been decisively broken. On 15 December the Council of Officers had called for the king to be brought speedily to trial, and on 28 December the purged House acceded to the pressure: a first reading was given to a bill to establish a High Court of Justice to try the king.

This had been a decisive intervention by the army against the Treaty of Newport and in favour of putting the king on trial. Meanwhile the campaign for an *Agreement of the People* took flight again, and Lilburne, now at large and apparently enjoying some political favour, was directly involved. In November, prior to the presentation of the *Remonstrance*, there had been a meeting at the Nag's Head, at which a mixed group of Independents, soldiers, and Levellers had tried to make common cause. Ireton had conceded the formation of a committee to discuss a new draft *Agreement of the People*.[113] It consisted of sixteen people—four MPs, four Independents, four Levellers, and four soldiers, and Lilburne was one of them. Only one MP, Henry Marten, took part, and the other key players were Ireton, Lilburne, and Robert Tichborne.[114] In the first week of December, as the army occupied London, this group met and produced a new draft *Agreement*, which was presented to the Council of Officers on 11 December.

The document was actually titled '*Foundations of Freedom*', proposed as a 'Rule for future Government in the Establishment of a firm and lasting

PEACE'. It makes no mention of the king or Lords, discussing only the people's representative, the supreme power, and how it was to be kept answerable to the people it represented. It can clearly be seen as a revision of earlier drafts, and reflects the fact that there had been continuous discussion of the first draft throughout 1648.[115] It set out a new distribution of 400 seats and specified who might vote: those who had subscribed to the *Agreement* and were independent (not receiving alms, usually contributing to the relief of the poor, not servants or paid wages by a particular person, over twenty-one, and keeping their own house). There were exclusions on political grounds reflecting the immediate past, but this was to be a Commonwealth of independent Englishmen, equal in their political rights, and self-governing through their representatives. The limits on the membership of that Commonwealth were tighter than some had hoped at Putney—they reflected a view that in order to participate in the affairs of the Commonwealth, people had to be independent of any possible pressure—from employers or masters, for example.[116] The powers of the representative body were, though, supreme, except in some reserved areas—religion and conscription—and there was provision for a Council of State to act in some strictly limited circumstances, and for short periods of time only.

An appendix, added by Lilburne, seems a little miscellaneous by comparison with the clarity of the body of the text. It ensured there could be no self-incrimination in legal proceedings, that such proceedings would be concluded within three to four months, that there would be no abridgement of trade, the excise would be abolished, and there would be no imprisonment for debt. Trials would have the benefit of witnesses, both for and against the accused, the death penalty was restricted to murder, tithes were to be replaced in short order by something non-compulsory, and the interest rate would be limited to 6 per cent. These measures bear the clear imprint of Lilburne's own experiences and also his concern to see in the detail of individual sufferings the battle for individual rights, but it is also a document that reflects his legalistic approach, rather less bracing than the ringing theoretical declarations of many of the related documents. Even here, at the high point of the Leveller campaign for a settlement based on popular sovereignty, Lilburne was perhaps as interested in particular liberties as in generalized accounts of liberty.

What followed was a lengthy discussion—the Whitehall Debates. The Putney Debates are better known because they seem to hold the key to understanding Leveller political thought, but these debates at Whitehall were actually of greater political significance since they were practical discussions about what the army should do with undeniably real power. And Lilburne was actually there, and a central player, at this key point in the revolution. As co-author of the current draft of the *Agreement* he had considerable potential influence, perhaps the closest he got to real power in the course of his political life, but in the event he was to leave the debates in disgust, preferring to attend to his own business.

By one of those miracles of historical survival we have a record of these debates too, from the shorthand notes taken by William Clarke, although it records little of Lilburne's contribution. As the measures to put the king on trial were presented and enforced, there was a parallel discussion about an *Agreement*. This may reflect a subtle strategy—Ireton has been accused of using discussion of the *Agreement* to distract attention from the trial, something which Lilburne and others opposed. It seems more likely that he took these debates seriously, though, and it is certainly the case that the debates as a whole were very serious, ranging in particular over the issue of religious toleration. There was a profound disagreement about whether or not secular authorities had any religious responsibilities at all—private conscience determined such matters. For men such as Ireton, however, it was clear that God had demonstrated displeasure providentially throughout history—to allow idolatry, for example, would be to ignore God's manifest will.[117] These were issues of the utmost seriousness, and continuing significance, and it seems plain that they were sincerely conducted.

These meetings continued through December and into January, effectively discussing how the army would settle the kingdom. Another draft *Agreement* was produced on 22 December, by John Jubbes, with the encouragement of William Rainsborough, who had spoken in favour of a very broad franchise at the Putney Debates. Jubbes had also been at Putney, but left the army in April, although he had been at Colchester. His revision of the *Agreement*, apparently trying to bridge the gap between the Levellers and the Officers, can be read as a way of keeping the king on the throne, or the king's head on his shoulders, by setting the monarchy within a constitution based on popular sovereignty. The king could be restored but only with the *Agreement* as a kind of coronation oath, and any future king who challenged the authority of the Commons would be legally deposed. It extended freedom of conscience to Catholics and Episcopalians, effectively making common cause between them and Independents against Presbyterian intolerance. It also made provision for the end of complicated and restrictive feudal tenures, and for the reclamation of common lands and marshes that would be used to support the poor and demobilized soldiers.[118]

It is a sign of how finely balanced these debates were that a key element of this *Agreement* was that the king could retain his crown, while in another strand of discussion preparations were being made to put him on trial for treason. Lilburne himself had withdrawn, however, frustrated by the direction the debates. He later claimed that he had thought that the *Agreement* would either be accepted or rejected. When he discovered that the officers intended to discuss the draft he published it anonymously.[119] Certainly, he had not got what he wanted and did not stay to negotiate. Leading supporters of the army had approached him to make his peace with the impending army settlement, but he had refused and had also declined to take a seat on the High Court of Justice established to try the king. He did not think the trial of the king was legal and in any case wanted to establish the Representative of the People, before removing any checks to the current corrupt House. Reform of the Commons should have preceded discussion about what was to be done about the king and the Lords. Having lost patience with the Whitehall discussions he had gone north about his own private business, taking the best offer of reparations he was likely to get. On 21 December 1648 he had been granted his £3,000 from the sequestered assets in Durham he had proposed and it was to this that he now turned his attention.[120]

The resolution to try the king had won out over attempts to secure a settlement based on an *Agreement*, but the bill to establish the High Court of Justice to try the king did not have an easy ride. It passed the Commons on 1 January but was unanimously thrown out by the Lords the following day, and a week-long adjournment followed. The Commons proceeded without the Lords, using language that reflected some of the aspirations of those promoting the *Agreement*. Since 'the people are, under God, the original of all just power' and the Commons, as their representative, was the supreme power in the land, the consent of the Lords was not necessary. 'Whatsoever is enacted or declared for law by the Commons . . . hath the force of law, and all the people of this nation are concluded thereby'.[121] The principle seems admirable, but it was not widely appealing at the time—it proved difficult to get people to serve as commissioners, and men of convinced republican views regarded these proceedings as illegitimate.

On 20 January, the day the trial opened, the debates at Whitehall had produced a new *Agreement*, known subsequently as the *Officer's Agreement*. Comparing it with an interim draft produced in mid-December seems to confirm Lilburne's account—that the document he had published had been the one produced by the committee, and revised by mid-December in the direction of what eventually became the *Officer's Agreement*.[122] This latest version had much common ground with earlier versions, although it was clearly more conservative in some ways, giving stronger powers to the Council of State, and the reserved powers were more limited in crucial respects. They did not include religion, for example, and did stipulate that the representative could not take measures that would result in the levelling of men's estates. There would be a public profession of religion, although it would not be compulsory, and Catholics and Episcopalians were excluded from toleration.[123] Although a more conservative document than the December 1648 *Agreement*, it was remarkable enough. It enshrined popular sovereignty as the basis of government, represented in an elected legislature which was supreme in the constitution, and made answerable to those who elected it. Much of what Lilburne now identified as the struggle of his life was expressed in this document, even though it had retreated somewhat from the draft in which he had had a direct hand.

Lilburne thought that the discussions of a possible *Agreement* at Whitehall were a sham, but modern historians have emphasized the earnestness and seriousness of the meetings. Ireton's behaviour is consistent with someone trying to find common ground and being gradually pulled towards the position he had originally opposed; it is not clear that he was simply stringing the radicals along while he imposed his preferred settlement.[124] That Lilburne had a key role in the drafting of a new *Agreement*, but almost no role in discussions about how to revise or act on it, reflects his own political failings, his impetuosity, as much as it does the malign intention of his political opponents. Wildman and Walwyn had not left the debates when Lilburne did, although Overton had; neither did they sign a petition later in the month complaining to Lord General Fairfax about the way the debates had been conducted.[125] Perhaps divided among themselves over tactics, those promoting the *Agreement* seem to have failed to make the most of whatever opportunity was on offer here, Lilburne chief among them, and it is hard to credit him with great political craft for abandoning the field in this way; particularly since it was to secure his £3,000.[126]

There was indeed a revolution in the following weeks, but not one based on an *Agreement of the People*. Charles was charged with treason, having been present at the deaths of his subjects, and being therefore personally guilty of waging war on them. He had renewed the war, compounding his guilt, and had sought a foreign invasion, from Ireland. He had thus betrayed his trust as a monarch limited by the laws of the land, required to secure the rights of the people and to govern for their good. In response Charles simply refused to plead, denying the authority of the court. He appeared three times over the ensuing days, each time demanding to know by what right he was being tried, and refusing to acknowledge the authority of the prosecution. This also prevented witnesses against him being heard in court but they were eventually heard in committee on 24 January. On 27 January he was brought to court to hear the sentence where once again he called for a trial before the full Houses of Parliament. His plea was ignored and the sentence passed.

In the course of the following day there was also some toing and froing, as signatories to the death warrant were sought, and there was perhaps a final approach to the king. The fact that he was given so many opportunities to accept the authority of the court and to plead, and that there was evident hesitation even after the sentence was passed, has encouraged the suggestion that his death was not a foregone conclusion until very late in this process. Had he entered a plea, and thereby accepted that the people were the source of political power and their representative the supreme constitutional authority, he might have saved his life. In that case he could have lived to see a revolution, setting the monarchy within a constitution based on popular sovereignty. Nonetheless, throughout these months there were clearly powerful people who thought that the only Charles helpful to a settlement was a dead one, and were working purposefully to achieve that.[127]

Charles was executed on 30 January, dying bravely, and a kingless government was brought falteringly to life. After a pause, the Rump Parliament, that remnant that had survived Pride's Purge of two months earlier, legislated on its own authority. The monarchy and House of Lords were abolished in March, by acts which had only passed one House. The established Church followed.

The new regime claimed that this was the 'first year of England's freedom by God's blessing restored'; but it was quite possible to think that this was a military coup, and the action of a small group of men acting well beyond the law. Although these were dramatic changes to the constitution they were not directly based on the various revisions of the *Agreement of the People*: they seemed to be arrived at more pragmatically than programmatically. Since 1646, the grand question had been how to achieve a lasting peace. The Levellers had answered that question by asking first what a just government would look like; more pragmatic politicians had sought to answer it by removing what seemed to be the main obstacle to peace, their stubborn king whose responsibility for all the blood shed also called for punishment. They had tried the king, with some hesitation and appealing to Providence for guidance, and then haltingly settled a new constitution. The *Agreements* would have set about the problem quite differently, by suggesting how to reform the Commons so as to represent the people: they had not made any mention of the monarchy or the Lords and had in one draft explicitly entertained the possibility of putting the king back on his throne. Certainly, killing the king had not been the main point. What had happened, by contrast, was that the monarchy and Lords had been abolished but the Commons remained unchanged. Reform was to be the work not of a new representative but of the Rump of the Long Parliament, first elected eight years earlier and newly purged. Similarly, the Church of England had been abolished, but it was not clear what would replace it, and what would be the limits of toleration.

Lilburne had withdrawn long before, denouncing the backsliding and dishonest officers: 'and so absolutely discharged myself for medling or making any more with so perfidious a generation of men as the great ones of the Army were, but especially the cunningest of Machiavelians Commissary Henry Ireton'. He now saw the future of the people's rights in the hands of 'an everlasting Parliament purged twice by force of arms'.[128] This was not what the campaigns for an *Agreement of the People* had promised.

5

Traitor, 1649

England's new chains discovered, 1649

In its first few months the regime continued to act pragmatically, and with an eye on survival. On 7 February, following the abolition of the monarchy, a Council of State was established—essentially a powerful committee, governing in the place of a head of state, which was reappointed each year by the Rump Parliament. This was a dubious solution to the problem of executive authority, and the measures taken to establish the judiciary were no less so. About half of the country's judges agreed to continue to serve, six of them on the condition that the regime pledged to maintain the fundamental laws: hardly a vote of confidence. Over the coming year no progress was made on parliamentary reform, and as a result no new elections were held. Meanwhile, discussions about law reform also proceeded at a glacial pace. Slow progress in reform reflected the fact that the new regime was embattled—enjoying dubious legitimacy and beset not just by enemies in England, Scotland, and Ireland, but also by the more or less unanimous hostility of the main European powers. And while it was clear who many of its enemies were, it was not clear who its friends would be.[1]

The alliances of the 1630s had launched people on very different trajectories. For example, both Gerrard Winstanley and Thomas Totney might once have been thought to be natural allies of the nation's new governors, as hot Protestants opposed to the church policies of the 1630s, but their religiosity had taken them in quite different directions. Winstanley, a few years older than Lilburne, had been apprenticed to a godly woman, and like Lilburne had immersed himself in improving reading. He had pursued a respectable puritan path through the early 1640s, even taking the Solemn League and Covenant. Thereafter, however, he had a spiritual crisis, related perhaps to financial problems, and between 1647 and 1648 published tracts arguing that godliness rested on an inner understanding, not on established tradition or scripture. He expounded a new law of freedom and led an experiment in practical social renewal, settling on common fields at St George's Hill, in Surrey. Winstanley had a similar background and sympathies to Lilburne, and was perhaps connected through mutual acquaintances, including John Fielder, who Lilburne was later to represent in a dispute with parliamentary committees. By 1649, though, they had taken very different paths. Totney, like Winstanley, was a little older than Lilburne, and as an apprentice was also exposed to hot Protestant preaching in early Stuart London. He too had a relatively conventional path through the 1640s until a personal crisis in 1648, which led him to believe that he had been called, like Moses, to assemble the children of Israel—144,000 of them. He took to print, as Theaurau John Tany, supported by associates of Kiffin and Giles Calvert, again connections that had taken him close to Lilburne.[2]

Before the regicide Lilburne had professed a dislike for the direction of events and of leading figures, but others with apparently similar backgrounds made their peace with the new regime. John Hewson, for example, son of Lilburne's former master, had been a regicide and was soon reported to be taking a very strong line on the need to suppress Levellerism in the army. Oliver Cromwell, once Lilburne's champion, was now close to the heart of the new regime. Some of Lilburne's allies in more recent times were also to take different paths through the 1650s. Wildman, for example, had not denounced the trial and execution, and was now dealing in lands and pursuing a career in advocacy. For a while he was reconciled to the regime, although he was to return to more covert political agitation later in the decade. Over the coming years William Walwyn was increasingly withdrawn from political life.[3]

Where, among these former fellow travellers, could reliable alliances now be built? The declaration that this was the 'first year of England's freedom by God's blessing restored' seemed more to invite a discussion than to state a conclusion. Over the previous decade there had been a vituperative, cacophonous, and inconclusive debate about what the war was about. As a result England's freedom was now a subject of much deliberation, and quite what God had restored was not clear to everyone: killing the king certainly did not settle that question, whatever virtues it had as a measure to prevent a further war.

★ ★ ★

In these early days, the new regime was in fact much more active in dealing with its professed enemies than in making friends, but the vengeance taken on royalist captives exacerbated fears about what kind of regime it might prove to be. As the royalist historian Clarendon put it: 'Whilst those perfidious wretches had their hands still reeking in the precious blood of their sovereign, they were put to a new piece of butchery, as necessary to the establishment of their new tyranny'. Five royalist prisoners from the second civil war were brought to trial despite having surrendered—the earl of Holland, the Duke of Hamilton, Lord Capel, and the earl of Norwich along with Sir John Owen, who had killed a high sheriff during fighting in Wales.[4]

The captives could have been tried before the Upper Bench (the retitled King's Bench), but that might not have secured their executions. They might also have been subject to attainder (like Strafford), but that might not have given a sufficient gloss of legality to the proceedings. Instead they were brought before a newly convened High Court of Justice. Owen was a man of some obscurity, even to Clarendon ('one Sir John Owen'). The motive for trying a plain colonel alongside these great lords was clear to Clarendon: 'there should hereafter be no more distinction in quality in trials for life, but that the greatest lord and the meanest peasant should undergo the same judicatory and form of trial'.[5]

Proceedings opened on 10 February but the legal arguments were few. Clarendon was clear about the illegitimacy of the charges, as well as of the proceedings: Hamilton 'could not well be thought other than a prisoner of war, and so not liable for his life'.[6] All five of the prisoners had been granted quarter, and so might have expected to have been allowed their lives. This argument was dismissed, however, on the grounds that no promise made by military authorities could tie the hands of a civil court. S. R. Gardiner, the great Victorian historian and a man not given to hyperbole, thought that 'the result of the trials was a foregone conclusion'.[7] Hamilton's plea that as a Scot he was a foreigner and could not be tried was not accepted. On hearing his sentence Owen 'made a low reverence, and gave them humble thanks'. Asked by a bystander what he meant he replied that 'it was a very great honour to a poor gentleman of Wales to lose his head with such noble lords, and swore a great oath, that he was afraid that they would have hanged him'.[8]

All five were sentenced to death on 6 March and petitions for mercy followed. Those for Hamilton and Capel were dismissed without a vote.

Holland was condemned by a single vote, but Norwich was saved by the casting vote of the Speaker, who claimed to be grateful for past favours from him, although Clarendon suspected he was simply grateful for the opportunity to be able to pardon someone. Owen was saved by Ireton, who noted that they had heard many fine words on behalf of the aristocrats, but not a single word in favour of saving the commoner, not even from Owen himself. Clarendon was unimpressed, unsure if this clemency arose 'because they were satiated with blood, or that they were willing, by this instance, that the nobility should see that any commoner should be preferred above them'.[9]

Hamilton, Holland, and Capel were beheaded on 9 March outside Westminster Hall, only Capel attracting any real sympathy. As with the execution of Strafford in 1641, doubts attended the means rather than the end: as a statement about the nature and intentions of the new regime these proceedings have often been harshly judged. For Clarendon they marked the end of 'a year of reproach and infamy above all years which had passed before it; a year of the highest dissimulation and hypocrisy, of the deepest villainy and most bloody treasons, that any nation was ever cursed with or under'.[10] Some distance, then, from England's freedom by God's blessing restored.

It was this hypocrisy, so manifest to him as the royalist trials came to a head, that drew Lilburne back into public affairs. He had followed the prosecution of the prisoners closely, and had even been asked to serve as counsel for them. Although he could not defend their actions (he said), he was clear that the regime was indeed acting tyrannously. This knowledge drew him out of a short-lived period of withdrawal from public life, during which he had been 'in a kinde of deep muse with myself, what to do with myself, being like an old weather-beaten ship, that would fain be in some harbour of ease and rest'. Having resolved after the regicide not to 'ingage in any public contests again' he concentrated instead on looking after his family. He had, though, been watching events, to see if the new regime would set the nation free from tyranny, or whether it was 'but a meer changing of persons, but not of things'.[11] He now seemed to have his answer.

England's new chains, published at the end of February, made a powerful case about the hypocrisy of the new regime. It claimed to reflect the views of those who had supported the petition of 11 September 1648 (a touchstone for Leveller sympathizers), although pressure of time had prevented the gathering of signatures. It argued that Parliament had previously accepted that an *Agreement of the People* was the way to settle the country, although it had not approved a particular draft. But there was now a real fear that no *Agreement* would ever be adopted, and that the sufferings and hopes of all those who had supported the parliamentary cause would be betrayed. This fear was grounded in the actual behaviour of the Rump: the use of the Court of Justice, which breached the right of trial by jury; pressing sea men; regulating the press with greater ferocity than the Presbyterian leaders had done during 1647 and censuring John Frye, a member of the Rump, who had expressed doubts about the Trinity. Against this unpromising record, there was no sign of reform: no change to court proceedings or their costs; no greater freedom to petition (in fact further burnings of petitions); and a Council of State had been erected which had no standing in law and, therefore, no apparent limits on its power. The pamphlet demanded that the current assembly should not be dissolved until a properly reformed one could replace it, that MPs should live by the principles of self-denial, that the differences between the officers and the rank and file of the army should be mediated, and that long continuance in military command should be prevented. It also argued that other pressing matters should be resolved: press regulation should end, there should be action on legal reform, tithes should be abolished, and the Council of State dissolved.[12]

Later in 1649, Lilburne was to see this as the latest phase in his continuing struggle: he had first confronted the bishops, then the House of Lords, thirdly the Lords and Commons together, and this, his fourth battle, was with the Council of State.[13] Behind all these battles lay the threat to liberties posed by the tyrannous potential of each of these bodies. The Rump was not a representative of the people, but the creation of the army officers; they had departed from their agreements to represent the good of the people and were corrupt placeholders, now posing a serious threat to their own men and to the liberty of the people; the Council of State was simply the means by which this group would keep themselves in power, creating a self-perpetuating oligarchy. This was the outcome of a conspiracy by a small group to secure power:

> guarded by the strength of an army . . . to their ends inclined, and the captivation of [the] House . . . they may now take off the veil and cloak of the designs as dreadless of whatever can be done against them. By this Council of State, all power is got into their own hands—a project which has been long and industriously laboured for.[14]

Fig. 5.1. Sir Arthur Hesilrige (1601–61)

Over the next few months he put this case with increasing ferocity, identifying Cromwell, Ireton, and Sir Arthur Hesilrige as key players, and continuing to hope that Sir Thomas Fairfax would recall the army to its duty. In this battle, he declared himself 'As much an Englishman, as ever'.[15] It was a battle for absolutely fundamental freedoms: 'posterity we doubt not shall reap the benefit of our endeavours, whatever shall become of us'.[16]

There was, as ever, an element of personal experience behind all this, particularly in Lilburne's identification of the key individuals guilty of corrupting the government: he saw this tyranny at work in his more every-day dealings with the regime. Payment of his reparations had been blocked in September 1648 by John Blakiston, a local rival to John's father and uncle, who was an ally of Sir Arthur Hesilrige's (Fig. 5.1). Having fixed on assets on estates in County Durham seized from Sir Henry Gibbs, Sir Henry Bellingham, and Sir Thomas Bowes that would pay his £3,000 reparations, he found his title to them disputed by Sir Henry Vane, another enemy of the broader Lilburne interest in the north-east, while Hesilrige used his position on the sequestration committee, so Lilburne said, to delay payment.[17]

During 1649, in fact, Hesilrige came to occupy a central position in
Lilburne's case against the regime. He was descended from a major gentry
family, and had been a convinced opponent of the Laudian Church. Elected
to the Long Parliament, he was one of the five members who Charles
had tried to arrest in January 1642, and in the wars had fought bravely
(wounded twice, and suffering life-threatening injuries) and successfully.
His credentials as a servant of Parliament were very good, as good perhaps
as Lilburne's, and he was, like Lilburne, to be very suspicious of Cromwell's
ambitions. He was an Independent too. But his rise to power in the north-
east had allowed him to amass a large personal fortune and was attended
by accusations of corruption, and he had a reputation for fearsome anger
when crossed.[18] It really does seem to have been the resulting tussles with
the wider Lilburne family, busy trying to do the same, that led to the feud,
rather than any partisan differences. Lilburne's rhetoric about Hesilrige's
supposed abuse of power was often very high.

Throughout 1649 there were clear connections between arguments made
against the regime by London radicals, and potentially mutinous soldiers in
the rank and file who felt betrayed by their officers. In the late winter and
early spring there was lobbying within the army to re-establish the agitators,
and on 22 February a petition from Fairfax's regiment was presented to the
council, which echoed Leveller language. The council was anxious about
this, and it was now that John Hewson commended the use of martial law
to suppress it: those courts 'could hang twenty ere the magistrate one'.[19]
A petition of 1 March claimed that eight soldiers had been co-authors of
England's new chains, cementing the connection between Lilburne and agitation in the City and army. By refusing the right to petition, they claimed, the
army grandees were pursuing exactly the same path as the Presbyterians in
1646 and 1647, policies those same army leaders had strenuously denounced.[20]

Nonetheless, the eight soldiers were summoned and the five who stuck
to their guns were cashiered from the army on 6 March, the same day that
sentence was passed on the five royalists. The cashiered men were greeted by
cheering supporters and taken to London by carriage, publishing an account
of their wrongs shortly after: *The Hunting of the Foxes*. In it they contrasted
the Engagements made by the army at Newmarket and Triploe Heath in
1647 with the actual conduct of the grandees. The current conduct had
declined catastrophically from these first principles as a result of the private
interest of some individuals—a direct and conscious parallel between the
betrayal of the rank and file by their officers and the betrayal of the English

people at large by the people now in political control. Documents were reproduced to illustrate the argument and the narrative echoed Leveller language at many points. For example, Lilburne's earlier use of Parliament's distinction between the letter and the equity of the law was clearly stated: 'If the equity of the Law be superiour (as they say) to the letter, and if the letter should controll and overthrow the equity, it is to be control'd and overthrown it self, and the equity is to be preserved'. The argument was applied in a way that carried a clear threat of mutiny: 'the Officer is but the form or letter of the Army; and therefore inferiour to the equitable or essentiall part, *the Souldiery*, and to be controlled and overthrown themselves, when they controll and overthrow the Souldiery in the essentials of their being, life, liberty and freedom, as the Souldiery are'.[21]

Cromwell and Ireton were identified as the chief villains, acting in the name of the General Council but actually following their own interest; in fact, since the agitators had been excluded it was not a real General Council. The tyrannies of the new regime—the executions, the creation of the Council of State, the stopping of the presses—were not therefore 'to be esteemed as actions of the Army, they are not to be set upon the score of the soldiery, for the soldiery hath no mouth in their Councels'. In fact 'the Parliament indeed and in truth is no Parliament, but a Representative Glass of the Councel of War; and the Councel of War but the Representative of *Cromwel, Ireton*, and *Harrison*.' The hypocrisy was tangible: 'Was there ever a generation of men so Apostate so false and perjur'd as these? ... You shall scarce speak to *Crumwell* about any thing, but he will lay his hand on his breast elevate his eyes, and call God to record, he will weep, howl and repent, even while he doth smite you under the first rib.'[22]

In sum, the new regime had simply assumed the character of the old. The form of the conspiracy laid out here was very like the one the parliamentary opposition had discerned in the behaviour of Laud and Strafford. The parallels were quite closely drawn in these months, between the punishments inflicted on the prime movers in Caroline tyranny, and that deserved by the architects of the new tyranny. As *The Hunting of the Foxes* put it, 'We have not the change of a Kingdom to a Commonwealth; we are onely under the old cheat, the transmutation of Names'. In fact, the new tyrannies and new unclean spirits that intruded into the government were more 'wicked than the former ... and the last state of this Common wealth is worse then the first'.[23]

If this kind of talk took hold in the army at large it would pose a serious threat to the regime, but what got Lilburne personally into trouble was publication of the second part of *England's new chains* on 25 March. '[F]inding no redress at all [from the publication of the first part] we had prepared and were getting subscriptions to a second part, full of mettle & gallantry, but before we could present it to the Parliament, they haveing knowledge of it, voted it treasonable'.[24] In the second part Lilburne and his co-authors allied themselves directly with the opponents of the officers, denouncing the way that the army counsels now worked, and the ends to which the army's influence was being put. Tracing a narrative from the previous autumn, they showed the influence of officers in taking control of the army, and betraying the cause for which it had entered politics in 1647. They had discredited their opponents with name-calling, Leveller being a term applied to 'all those in the Army (or elsewhere) who are against any kind of Tyrannie, whether in King, Parliament, Army, [or] Councel of State'. The army leaders had new-modelled the City, sent Rainsborough to his death at Pontefract, and subjugated the Commons. It was exactly like the Presbyterian mobilization of 1647, except that it had succeeded. In the process an historic opportunity had been lost,

> thus the most hopefull opportunity that ever *England* had for the recovery of our Freedom, was spent and consumed, in such their uncertain, staggering motions, and arbitrary, irrationall Proceedings, whereby all parties became extreamly exasperated, as People that had been meerly mocked and cheated by fair promises.

The pamphlet ended with a call for the kind of open debate that would not be possible so long as the army and its friends in the Rump remained politically unassailable. It called therefore for a new representative elected by the principles of the *Agreements*, and for a similar representative of the army to be chosen by election from each regiment; the two of them to establish a proper and legal government.[25] It was, in other words, a direct appeal to the Rump to resist the army leadership and to resurrect the General Council of the Army.

This criticism was clearly placed in a wider context of royalist plotting and foreign hostility,[26] but if Lilburne is to be believed the regime was in two minds as to what to do with him. He claimed that on the morning of 27 March he had been offered a post in government. That afternoon, however, following his refusal, warrants were issued for his arrest, along with Prince, Walwyn, and Overton.[27] Between four and five the next morning around a hundred soldiers went to Lilburne's house, a large number of them seizing him from his bedroom. From there he was marched through the streets to St Paul's, where Walwyn, Prince, and Overton had also been brought, accused of having had a hand in publishing the pamphlet. Once in custody all four of them refused to incriminate themselves.[28]

They were brought before a hastily established committee which had explicit instructions to make clear that it was not a trial, perhaps in the hope of forestalling the refusal to answer that often met such examinations.[29] Brought before Bradshaw at Derby House, Lilburne for once did not recount his record of service to the cause, but instead argued from first principles that the Council of State had no jurisdiction: 'I now stand before you, upon the bare, naked, and single account of an Englishman, as though I had never said, done, or acted any thing, that tended to the preservation of the Liberties thereof'. He did not acknowledge the authority of the Rump. The votes, order, and 'Enacts' were, he said, 'nothing to me', however many members of the House repeated them to him: if the Parliament had originally been legally constituted, it was no longer.

> [The] Faction of a trayterous party of Officers of the Army, hath twice rebelled against the Parliament, and broke them to pieces, and by force of Armes culled out whom they please, and imprisoned divers of them and laid nothing to their charge, and have left only in a manner a few men . . . of their own Faction behind them that will like Spaniel-doggs serve their lusts and wills.

Here he really did seem to call for rebellion: should not the free people of England, '*soldiers and others*',

> as one man rise up against them as so many professed traytors, theives, robbers and high way men, and apprehend and bring them to justice in a new Representative, chosen by vertue of a just Agreement among the People, there being no other way in the world to preserue the Nation but that alone.

Overton and Prince made similar arguments.[30]

Once again he had named Cromwell, Ireton, and Harrison, claiming that Fairfax was simply their 'Stalking horse, and a cifer'. In the course of the day, he later claimed, he had heard Cromwell shouting from an adjacent room, 'if you do not breake them, they will break you'. Although Bradshaw had denied it was a trial, saying it was simply an enquiry as to who was the author of *England's new chains*, Lilburne nonetheless set off on a history of his sufferings against this kind of self-incrimination. He also denounced the use of martial law against a civilian in times of peace. The council, however, was implacable. The proceedings ended with all four of them being committed to the Tower on suspicion of high treason for their role in the publication of the second part of *England's new chains*. Parliament declared the pamphlet treasonous: seditious and destructive of the present government; tending to promote mutiny in the army; and a hindrance to the impending conquest of Ireland, since it threatened a new war in England. The declaration was to be published in all market towns and advice was taken about the best way to publicize it.[31]

There was significant support in the City for the four men and for the army: a petition for Lilburne's release on 2 April claimed 80,000 signatures, and there were further attempts to petition on his behalf on 18 and 28 April. The latter was presented by women who declared they were supporters of the 11 September 1648 petition, and seems to have drawn on some of the same forms of organization revealed by Masterson in his revelations about Lilburne in January 1648. The women were not allowed to enter the House and according to one account were sent away to do their dishes. They had, though, gathered 10,000 signatures and they returned on 5 May, expressing their dissatisfaction with the response to them (and their husbands).[32] Despite the potential embarrassment, or worse, the regime was intent on punishing Lilburne, and moved to get on with it quickly. On 11 April a resolution was passed to try him and the others before the Upper Bench. Less than a week later *A Manifestation* defended the four of them against 'Common Calumnies' that they were Levellers who wanted to abolish social distinctions, that they were agents of the king or queen, Jesuits (intent on undermining English Protestantism), atheists, or separatists. 'We know very well that in all Ages those men that engage themselves against Tyranny, unjust and Arbitrary proceedings in Magistrats, have suffered under such appellations, the People being purposely frighted from that wich is good by insinuations of imaginary evill'. Their anxiety on this point may have reflected the fact that the Diggers had broken ground two weeks earlier.[33]

The public defence of the regime was becoming more effective. Earlier in the year John Milton had been commissioned to respond to *England's new chains*, although he never actually did. However, a lengthy defence of the regime had been published earlier in March and there was now a more concerted effort to respond to these enemies within, led by John Canne, who had been Lilburne's first publisher. He now came to the defence of the regime though, in two works called *The Discoverer*, one of them a direct answer to *England's new chains*, the other a revelation of the machinations of the leading Levellers.[34] The issue of social levelling was clearly an important one in this propaganda tussle, and the Levellers were at some pains to refute it. 'We profess . . . that we never had it in our thoughts to Level mens esttates, it being the utmost of our aime that the Common-wealth be reduced to such a passe that every man may with as much security as may be enjoy his propriety.' Social hierarchy, they claimed, was important to political order: 'For distinctions of Orders and Dignities, We think them so far needfull, as they are animosities [*sic*: animators?] of vertue, or requisite for the mainten-ance of the Magistracy and Government'. But these social distinctions were not created 'for the nourishment of Ambition, or subjugation of the People but only to preserve the due respect and obedience in the People which is necessary for the better execution of the laws'. They were proponents of good government, not of social chaos: 'That we are for Government and against Popular Confusion we conceive all our actions declare . . . Tis somewhat a strange consequence to infer that because we have laboured so earnestly for a good Government, therefore we would have none at all'.[35]

Writing a little later, Clement Walker, who was not entirely a friend of the Levellers, agreed that the name was earned 'onely for endeavouring to Level the exorbitant usurpations of the Councel of Officers and Councel of State', not to level property.[36] This put clear distance between them and the Diggers at St George's Hill led by Gerrard Winstanley: Lilburne was later to decry the attempt to father on him the '*erronious tenents of the poor Diggers*' set out on the *True Levellers Standard* and the *New Law of Righteousness*.[37] On their own account the Levellers sought good government, achieved through a sound and legal constitution. They were not seeking power for themselves, but for the principles of an *Agreement of the People*, which was once again set forth as the solution to the Nation's ills.

The army, mutiny, and the campaign for an *Agreement of the People*

In these months, then, the new government was faced not just by royalists, the need to take military control in Ireland and Scotland, and the more or less universal hostility of other European powers, but also with the embar-rassment (or active hostility) of religious radicals and (they feared) groups such as the Diggers. The remorseless campaign by Lilburne and others to draw attention to the resulting hypocrisies in its behaviour was unlikely to lead to a change in behaviour, but it was certainly a further headache. To the extent that it might encourage mutiny in the army, it was potentially much more than that.

During April, soldiers had been chosen for service in Ireland by lot but some, including 300 in Hewson's regiment, refused to go until Leveller demands for the English settlement had been met. Between 24 and 26 April there was a mutiny in Whalley's regiment, which had been ordered from quarters in Bishopsgate Street to a rendezvous at Mile End Green. They refused to leave, and it was the direct intervention of Cromwell and Fairfax that brought it to an end—fifteen soldiers were court-martialled, five of them condemned to death and six to be cashiered after the public shaming punishment of riding the wooden horse. All were pardoned, however, except the man believed to the ringleader, Robert Lockyer.[38]

Lockyer had an honourable military record and had been at Corkbush Field, where he stood up for the *Agreement* against the officers. He clearly viewed himself as a martyr to these political principles, and forgave the members of the firing squad on Ludgate Hill for their complicity in murder.[39] Lilburne and Overton had written in his defence, citing the army engagements as well Sir Edward Coke, condemning the use of martial law against soldiers who claimed their civil rights when the courts were open for business. The connection between army mutiny and the campaign for an *Agreement* could hardly be plainer.[40] Public sympathy did not save Lockyer's life, but his claim to martyrdom did resonate in London where he was accorded a hero's funeral. On 29 April a procession of some thousands accompanied his coffin to Westminster. His horse was led before the coffin, an honour usually reserved for high-ranking officers. The black of mourning was mixed in the procession with Leveller sea-green ribbons. A group of women brought up the rear, the whole thing carried off in dignified silence, aside from the trumpets that signalled the funeral of a soldier.[41]

On 1 May, from the Tower, Lilburne and the others produced a further draft *Agreement of the People* which was, as the title had it, 'a *Peace-Offering* to this distressed *Nation*'. Signed by Walwyn, Lilburne, Overton, and Prince, it was a fulfilment of a promise made in the *Manifestation*, and the preamble hoped that the *Agreement* would show that they were 'not such wilde, irrationall, dangerous Creatures as we have been aspersed to be'. The essentials were familiar—it called for 400 seats, for example, and annual elections—but there were firmer safeguards against oligarchy. Representatives would not serve two successive terms and would have to renounce remunerative positions while serving. Only religion and conscription were listed as reserved powers, but a number of other necessary measures essential to the peace were enumerated, and a number of Lilburne's specific concerns were included (for example, protection from self-incrimination). Given the sad experience that if there were insufficient safeguards government tended to 'Arbitrary, and Tyrannical power', it was declared that the representative could not take away or give up any part of the *Agreement*. And for the avoidance of doubt, it specified in this section about future tyranny that no future representative could 'level mens Estates, destroy Propriety, or make all things Common'. The penalty for a representative suggesting these things was a charge of high treason.[42]

Later the same month discontent in the army resulted in direct confrontation. On 6 May, soldiers in Banbury rallied around the manifesto set out in *England's standard advanced*. It reprinted the new *Agreement* and declared the soldiers were acting to promote that cause, along with the Engagements made during 1647. Denouncing tyranny in terms very similar to those of *England's new chains*, it argued that the soldiers were now acting simply as Englishmen in terms reminiscent of Lilburne's declaration following his arrest:

> Be it therefore known to all the free people of *England*, and to the whole world, That (chusing rather to die for Freedom, than to live as slaves) we are gathered and associated together upon the bare accompt of Englishmen, with our swords in our hands, to redeem our selves, and the Land of our Nativity, from slavery and oppression.[43]

This rising lasted less than a day: Colonel Reynolds brought three troops of loyal men from his own regiment to restore discipline. In the course of the confrontation, William Thompson, one of the mutineers, killed a lieutenant. Thompson had once been a corporal, but had been cashiered following a brawl in a tavern. He now rode off while other men went to Salisbury, where a significant part of two full regiments were in mutiny. There were hopes too of a mutiny in Buckinghamshire, although it failed to materialize. The Salisbury mutineers moved north, and although they failed to make contact with Thompson's group, or the hoped-for mutiny in Buckinghamshire, they followed the River Windrush to Burford.

Fairfax and Cromwell hurried to the scene, arriving on 14 May. Storming the town during the night they took 400 prisoners, several hundred other mutineers having made their escape. All those captured were liable to the death penalty for mutiny, but in the event only four men were condemned, including William Denne and Thompson's brother. Denne was pardoned, apparently having shown some regret, but Thompson and two corporals were shot. Colonel Eyre, another veteran of Corkbush Field, had also been taken. Being now a civilian, he was sent to London for trial by a regular court. William Thompson, meanwhile, was pursued into Northamptonshire by Colonel Reynolds, who eventually caught up with him in woods near Wellingborough. Thompson refused quarter and was shot dead having himself killed two men. Army discipline had been restored.

This turned out to be a crucial victory for the regime. With the Leveller leaders in prison and the army mutiny crushed, the Leveller mobilization was defeated, and with it the hopes for an *Agreement of the People*. A nervous government passed a new Treason Act in May.[44] The hopes expressed in the *Agreements* lived on, of course, not just in the 1650s but in the centuries that followed, and also, in one of the more remarkable episodes of English history, in the attempt led by Edward Sexby to export an *Agreement of the People* to French rebels. Between 1651 and 1653, with the support of the English government, Sexby was in Guyenne, supporting rebels against the Crown (the Frondeurs). Interestingly, it was a shorter version of the third *Agreement* that he was promoting, rather than the more conservative 'Officers' *Agreement* from December 1648.[45]

Unsurprisingly, given the apparent link between his writings and the mutineers, there was no sign of release for Lilburne. Petitioners on his behalf appeared at the door of the House at the beginning of May, at least one of the petitions apparently reflecting a quite systematic citizen organization: the well-affected citizens of Cripple-gate called for the appointment of agitators in every ward to work on behalf of the imprisoned men. Their petition was countered by 'resolved' apprentices, presumably mobilized by similar means. The only concession from the Commons was an order to the lieutenant of the Tower ensure that he, Walwyn, and Prince had sufficient provision.[46] Imprisonment did not silence Lilburne, of course. *Legall and fundamentall liberties* was published on 8 June, giving the now familiar narrative of his life as clear evidence of the tyranny of the governments under which he lived. He told how he had tried to set up as a Soap Boiler, but been thwarted by the effects of the excise, and as a coal merchant, but been thwarted by unjust imprisonment. The Merchant Adventurers had prevented him from investing in the Low Countries' cloth trade: the same obstacles of prerogative, monopoly powers, and arbitrary government that had plagued him throughout his life. He also claimed that he had been offered money and government office to keep quiet. His conclusion was predictable, and dripping with damaging sarcasm: '*The first yeer of* England's declared Freedom, *by the lying and false pretended Conservators thereof, that never intended it*'.[47]

A briefer version was published in mid-July which included a call to impeach Cromwell, citing many precedents. It was directed explicitly at all those who had approved of the petition of 11 September 1648, who were said now to be meeting regularly at the Whalebone Tavern and routinely and unjustly described as 'Levellers'. Above all, though, it was an exhortation to press for an *Agreement*: 'which I hope and desire you will make the final Center, & unwavering Standard of all your desires, hazards and indeavours, as to the future settlement of the peace and government of this distracted, wasted, and divided Nation'. However, he did acknowledge the danger of doing so: an *Agreement* was 'detestable and abominable to the present ruling men, as that which they know will put a full end to their tyranny and usurpation, and really ease and free the people from oppression and bondage'. The civil threat was closely linked to the denial of the voice of the soldiery—the army's betrayal of its Engagements under the leadership of the Grandees now underpinned the government of those same men. An *Agreement* was the only defence against self-perpetuating interests, supported by the 'everlasting army', which the free people could now see would keep them in bondage and slavery, under the '*new erected robbing government*'.[48]

Lilburne's indignation, and provocation, reached a new pitch in the late summer, although he was distracted by personal tragedy. In late July he had been allowed out of the Tower to visit his family, who were afflicted by smallpox. He lost his two sons, and Elizabeth and their daughter were gravely ill for a time. He claimed that he had delayed print for fear of losing this freedom to be with his family,[49] but on 10 August *An impeachment of high treason* appeared over his name, consisting of a rather rambling and loosely connected series of documents. The essential thrust, though, was clear, and inflammatory: as the title page put it, Lilburne set out to prove by principles of law, parliamentary precedent, and reason that '*Oliver Cromwel* [is] guilty of the highest Treason that ever was acted in England, and more deserving of punishment and death Then the 44 Judges hanged for injustice by *King Alfred* before the Conquest'. Such justice, though, would only be possible 'before a legal Magistracy, when there shal be one again in England (*which now in the least there is not*)'.[50]

This was perhaps a conscious reaction to the recently passed Treason Acts, of 14 May (in the days after the suppression of the Burford mutiny) and 17 July.[51] It was certainly a more outspoken, or at least more detailed, statement of the arguments of the previous months, reproducing in fact *To all the affectors*. The case against Cromwell was elaborated partly around a rejection of the trial and execution of the king—this, said Lilburne, had been an act of spite and vengeance. He claimed that Cromwell had offered to put the king back on the throne and had reacted spitefully only when Charles 'had forsaken them, and accepted a better bargaine from the *Scots*'. It retold the rumours about Cromwell and Ireton selling out to the king, and the appetite for an assassination of Cromwell which Masterson had reported from the meeting in East Smithfield in early 1648. Cromwell, it was claimed, was driven on by a thirst for power, and the people had received no benefit from the regicide and subsequent settlement: trade had decayed, a new war was threatened with Scotland, there was popular discontent, and the only clear fruit of all this was to put Cromwell and his cronies in power. As specific evidence of the corruption of the regime Lilburne reproduced a letter he had sent to Cornelius Holland narrating his own experience of suffering and injustice, and a statement from Colonel Robert Huntington explaining how the betrayal of the army's Engagements had led Huntington to lay down his commission.[52]

The government was also anxious about the potential of a Leveller-royalist alliance in these months,[53] but there is little reason, despite contemporary suspicions, to think that Lilburne had any actual involvement in such plots. He had been rumoured to have been in Paris in early March, not long before his arrest, sent by 'Rogues' in England to deliver a message of some kind, although the rumour at the time was that he had been taken by the Prince of Condé and hanged.[54] Lilburne himself claimed that Thomas Verney, son of the king's standard bearer killed at Edgehill, had tried to draw him into correspondence about a plot to put Prince Charles on the throne, but that it was a trap to lay him open to a treason charge. Behind this he claimed to see the hand of Hesilrige and others.[55] It was not completely implausible to accuse him of involvement in royalist conspiracy, since he had been an opponent of the regicide and was quite explicit in *An Impeachment* that the new regime was not simply a disappointment, but actually looked much worse than anything that had come before. He had also said in print that he would prefer to restore the Prince on the basis of an *Agreement* than to see it happen by conquest with the help of foreign arms. Done that way 'the people will easily see ... this transcendent benefit' of the disbandment of all armies and garrisons, since the Prince would enjoy foreign peace and be free of domestic competitors. As a result they would be able to say 'they injoy something they can in good earnest call their own'.[56]

However, the most effective rebuttal of the claim that the four Levellers were simply royalist stooges was Walwyn's:

> For those weak suppositions of some of us being agents for the king or queen, we think it needful to say no more but this: that though we have not been any way violent against the persons of them or their party (as having aimed at the conversion of all, and the destruction of none), yet do we verily believe that those principles and maxims of government which are most fundamentally opposite to the prerogative and king's interest take their first rise and original from us—many whereof though at first startled at and disowned by those that professed greatest opposition to him, have yet since been taken up by them and put in practice. And this we think is sufficient, though much more might be said to clear us from any agency for that party.[57]

In fact, the more hopeful sign, according to one royalist observer, was 'the Encreasing the Devision betweene the Levellers and Crumwellists'. On this view, forceful suppression or indulgence were equally promising for the royalist cause: 'twilbe well either way, for by theire suppression ... more will grow, and by theire letting them alone I hope they will Encrease to such a number as may obstruct [the conquest of] Ireland (if not doe something of better consequence here) to w[hi]ch I hope you have a regardfull eye'.[58] Rather than actively adding to royalist strength, in other words, their actions were dividing and weakening the Rump.

Certainly the change in tone in Lilburne's attitude to Cromwell was dramatic and symptomatic of a profound rift—he had, after all, at one time credited him as the man primarily responsible for his release from prison in 1640, and had seen him as a powerful ally against Manchester and Colonel King, and in getting reparations paid in 1645 and 1646. However, to Lilburne the regicidal regime was not simply a pragmatic compromise, it was a treasonous betrayal behind which lay Cromwell's naked ambition despite his 'late seeming changes'.[59] But not all of his erstwhile friends agreed. *Walwins Wiles*, denounced the Leveller leaders in resounding terms, and included an endorsement from Lilburne's long-term friend William Kiffin, as well as Edmund Rosier, one of his earliest contacts in the puritan underground. A number of independent churches expressed their support for the regime.[60]

Despite these anxieties and Lilburne's provocative writing, it seems that the regime was in two minds about how to handle him. On 4 July a search had been ordered of his rooms 'for scandalous and seditious books, papers, and writings', and on 20 August a warrant had issued against him for publication of *An Impeachment*.[61] There are signs, though, even in Lilburne's own writings, that the regime was open to reconciliation with him. An associate of Cromwell's called Hunt had apparently tried to dissuade Elizabeth from delivering the letter from Lilburne to Cornelius Holland which was eventually published in *An Impeachment*. It seemed to be part of a potential deal: Hunt wanted to know how much Lilburne was owed so that he could tell some Parliament men, 'who were resolved to help me speedily to all my money down, and my liberty too'. Elizabeth had been persuaded, and did 'rejoyce', but for Lilburne it was a plain subterfuge, playing on her 'facile credulity'.[62] In mid-August his father received £200 from the sequestered estate of Thomas Bowes, to pay to John, whose family was 'sick and in want of maintenance'.[63] He even claimed that in February that Henry Mildmay *'had Commission (as he said) to proffer Me and my Comrades large places and preferments; so we would sit still and let* the Grandees goe on with their work'. He had of course, 'with detestation refused'.[64]

Later in the year Mr Richardson and Hugh Peter, both religious men close to the regime, visited Lilburne in prison, apparently hoping to find common ground with him. Richardson, in fact, had visited all four Levellers, and 'prest very hard for union and peace ... telling us, men cryed mightily out upon us abroad for grand disturbers, that sought *Crom*. blood for al his good service to the Nation, and that would center nowhere, *but meerly labored to pul down all those in power, to set up ourselves'*.[65] In May, however, Lilburne said in print that he had told Peter

> if it were possible for me now to chuse, I had rather chuse to live seven years
> under old King *Charls* his government, (notwithstanding their beheading him
> as a Tyrant for it) when it was at the worst before this Parliament, than live one
> year under their present Government that now rule.

He went on to say that if they carried on as they were, Prince Charles would 'have friends enow, not only to cry him up, but also really to fight for him, to bring him into his Father's Throne'.[66]

While the regime explored ways of conciliating him, his intransigence and appeal in the army made him seem dangerous, and this surely weighed in the balance. Although mutiny was limited, Lilburne's writings did resonate with a wider public.[67] What tipped the balance was publication of *An outcry of the youngmen and apprentices of London,* appealing directly to the soldiery, particularly those who had cooperated in the suppression of the Burford mutiny. It spoke in defence of the *Agreement* and a vindication of the Burford mutineers which had appeared the previous week. The familiar case that the officers had led the common soldiers to renege on their Engagements, and the necessity of a settlement based on an *Agreement,* was easily read as an incitement to further mutiny. In fact the question was put directly:

> whether you justify all those actions done in the name of the Army upon your account, and under pretext of that Engagement since the Engagement it selfe was broken, and your Councell of Agitators dissolved? And whether you will hold up your Swords to maintaine the totall abolition of the peoples choicest interest of freedom, viz, frequent and successive Parliaments, by an Agreement of the People, or obstruct the annuall succession?

Could the suffering people expect their help and assistance in removing 'those *iron bands and yoaks* of oppression'? The soldiers were invited to think as Englishman: 'our fellow-Countrymen (the private Souldiers of the Army)... being the *instrumentall authors* of your own slavery and ours'. The implication was clear: a mutinous army might deliver the kingdom from bondage.[68]

Of course, there was more to this than Lilburne, but the vindication of the Burford mutineers had cited *An Impeachment* and *Legall Fundamentall liberties* directly.[69] Soldiers garrisoned in Oxford, on 8 September, called on their officers to join with them in demanding a free Parliament in line with the demands of the *Agreement* and the restitution of the General Council of the Army, as well as the abolition of tithes and payment of arrears without deductions for food consumed. When this was refused, they took control of New College, where the arms were stored, and placed their officers under arrest. Little came of it—order was restored two days later by the governor of Oxford, and the ringleaders were in prison—but Fairfax wrote to the Council of State pointing out that while martial law was sufficient to deal with mutinous soldiers, there was no similar way to deal with their civilian friends. On 11 September the council was ordered to give direction to the Attorney General about people to be prosecuted under the new Treason Act. Lilburne, in prison for publishing *England's new chains*, and with a warrant against him for *An Impeachment,* was now to be examined, along with witnesses, about his role in the publication of *An outcry*. A week later the lieutenant was ordered to receive him at the Tower on a charge of high treason. On the same day a number of warrants were issued to apprehend those associated with the publication of *An outcry*.[70]

There is a minor scholarly industry in unpicking exactly who wrote what in these closely related pamphlets: each was no doubt part of a relatively coordinated and collaborative publishing effort. Lilburne's own voice is clearest in those pamphlets dealing directly with his own sufferings, and a growing hostility to the people behind them—Cromwell, Hesilrige, Ireton, and Vane. But as ever, these were for Lilburne instances of a more a general threat, in this case all too obvious, that entrenched vested interests would corrupt the government. It was this which supported the claim that Cromwell was not just corrupt, but treasonous, a leading player in a conspiracy no less harmful than that of Laud and Strafford under Charles I. An *Agreement* would make this kind of behaviour impossible, safeguarding the people's interests by providing a permanent defence against tyranny. In those more abstract documents Lilburne's voice is harder to discern. His conviction shines forth more clearly in his burning indignation at actual instances of injustice, rather than in the theorization of liberty. His was a pragmatic, particular, but forensically effective critique.

By September the Rump's achievements were limited, or at least defensive rather than constructive. Royalists had been executed and two Treason Acts passed. On 20 September legislation sought to beef up the regulation of printing.[71] Attempts were being made to establish a Presbyterian church, albeit one without powers to compel attendance, reflecting the fact that many people, whatever their misgivings, thought some form of national church preferable to complete toleration. There had been no parliamentary elections, and no progress on parliamentary reform which would have been the preliminary to fresh elections. Lilburne's writings, and his contribution to the wider campaign for an *Agreement*, were a response to the dubious and pragmatic origins of this regime and to its weak record of reform. They were clearly wounding. Moreover, what seemed like a call to open resistance was very hard to ignore: Lilburne was certainly making enemies for whom the stakes were very high. He likened the illegality of the charge against the four men in the Tower to the trials of the king and prominent royalists earlier in the year; *Mercurius Pragmaticus* reported that Lilburne's bootmaker would not take an order for new boots since he would not live long enough to use them.[72]

Treason trial, October 1649

On 14 September, Lilburne was summoned to a hearing at the Inner Temple before the Solicitor General, Prideaux. There was some irony in this, since Prideaux had been involved in Parliament's life-saving threat of retaliation in 1643 if Lilburne and other prisoners of war were executed for treason. His purpose now was to 'pursue some things that doth concern you... having taken some evidences of consequence about high matters that you are and will be charged with'. Prideaux wanted to inform Lilburne about them before a trial, and to see what he had to say about them. The first question was about *An Impeachment*, and Prideaux invited him to acknowledge his authorship and make good on the charges it laid. Rather than answer that question, Lilburne produced from his glove a copy of a new and equally inflammatory pamphlet, *A preparative to an hue and cry after Sir Arthur Haslerig*.

It claimed that Hesilrige had used his position in the committees governing the north-east to thwart Lilburne in getting his reparations, and had stopped his rents once Lilburne was in jail. This caused his wife and children considerable suffering, at the time when his family was afflicted by smallpox. Hesilrige had been one of the men who had committed him to prison and close confinement, actions tantamount to attempted murder. He had also played a central role in the alleged plot with Thomas Verney to entrap Lilburne in royalist conspiracy, confessing that 'unlesse *Lilburn* and *Walwin* were taken off, they could not bring about their design: for... they are great Politicians, and if they live we cannot carry on our design; for they are Obstacles in our way'. This was the behaviour of a tyrant.[73]

Lilburne said (in an exchange later at issue in the trial) that he certainly was the author of the *Hue and cry*, save for the many printer's errors. About the *Impeachment*, though, he remained coy. Setting out his battle for freedom, peace, and justice through the tortured negotiations of the previous autumn, he once again juxtaposed his position with those who had been willing to enter a personal treaty with Charles I. This led to a full discussion about the status of the Parliament: whether the Rump was still a Parliament after the purge and after the death of the king who had summoned it. It was by this power that Prideaux was asking questions, and Lilburne was consistent in denying the Rump the status of a Parliament. But he refused to answer the question about authorship on the very familiar ground that 'it is against the Law of England *to compel a man to answer to a question against himself*; and your House did so adjudge it in the daies of their Primitive purity, in mine own Case'. Prideaux pointed out that this was not the same as saying that it was illegal for the Attorney General to ask questions, but Lilburne would not admit his authorship, or that he sent a copy to the garrison at Warwick Castle. He repeated his view that Cromwell was a traitor, but refused to acknowledge his role in printing and disseminating the books in question.[74]

In *Salva Libertate*, published a little later, while awaiting trial, Lilburne had threatened to withhold gestures of respect, since Prideaux was not a proper Attorney General, but certainly throughout these initial exchanges Lilburne was keen to emphasize his respectability: he was bare headed when he first spoke and did not put his hat back on until Prideaux had. He promised, as he did in court, that he would be civil 'in word and jesture', reflecting the fact that had known Prideaux for 'many yeares as a gentleman of note'. Here again, his sense of theatre was nicely judged, an acute way of distinguishing between what he was opposed to (Prideaux's office) and what he accepted (social order): as often in such confrontations, Lilburne's courtesy was a way of more clearly defining the object of his attack. As he noted, his fellow opponents of the personal treaty with the king, had been '*commonly* (but most *unjustly*) *called Levellers*'. Clearly he was not, and could show respect for social distinctions; but he could chastise Prideaux:

> I WONDER WITH WHAT FACE YOV CAN CALL THIS A PARLIAMENT, who indeed and in truth are nothing else but the PRINCES OF THE ARMYS SLAVES AND VASSALS . . . *they would purge you, and purge you, again and again, to* SUCH LOATHSOME DREGS THAT YOVR VERY SELVES SHOVLD ABHOR YOVRSELVES; But Sir, it seems, you judge it better to go hand in hand with them . . . then to contest with them.[75]

Not so freeborn John. It was the principles of peace, freedom, and the liberties of the nation that he sought and whose enemies he abhorred; and it was this battle that he was now going to fight in court. He would remove his hat to a gentleman, but not bow to tyranny.

Five days later Henry Marten, Saye, Cornelius Holland, and Bartholomew Hall were ordered by the Council of State to help Prideaux in preparations for a trial and witnesses were summoned. Thomas Newcombe, a printer, was to be re-examined about the publication of *An outcry*. On the same day a Leveller plot to take Windsor Castle was reported to the council, along with rumours of malignant and Cavalier plots: it is not surprising that the regime felt embattled.[76] The trial was to be conducted not in a normal court, but by a special commission of oyer and terminer to 'hear and determine' the case. Thomas Dafthorne (or Daffern) had been taken at Warwick Castle with a book of John Lilburne's. Believed to be one of his 'emmissaries', a local Justice of the Peace had been ordered to examine him in late August. On 22 September, two days after the new legislation regulating the press, a large number of printers were rounded up and entered £300 bonds for good behaviour. Among them was Thomas Newcombe, who was now bound to appear for his role in printing *An outcry*, and to give evidence against Lilburne.[77]

By early October the Council of State was confident of its case. Colonel Purefoy, the governor of Warwick, was ordered to attend (he didn't) along with other witnesses who could testify about Dafthorne, 'so that the ... book sent abroad by [Lilburne] may be charged upon him, and proved to be his'. George Poole was put in the Gatehouse for receiving books from Lilburne. Judges Jermyn and Puleston were particularly urged to attend, as members of the commission of oyer and terminer, as were others who had not been named to the commission, but who might nonetheless lend assistance. On 13 October the Council of State reported to Parliament that the Attorney General had sufficient evidence against Lilburne and that the trial would take place the following Thursday, 18 October.[78] Not long before, a lengthy justification of the actions of the Commonwealth had been published, which had given a prominent place to the Leveller leaders among the current threats to the regime.[79]

Despite these preparations, however, Lilburne seems to have been involved in some ongoing negotiation with the regime. On 20 October he wrote to William Heveningham, a member of the Rump, claiming that the commission of oyer and terminer was illegal. Instead he proposed that he should choose one judge and his opponents eleven, and that there should be a public hearing and final determination of all their differences based on legal principles. The determination should be published and Lilburne should have two friends present to keep a record without any danger to their own freedom. Before he received a reply, however, the trial date was set for 24 October, leaving Lilburne no choice (he said) but to publish this 'proffer'.[80]

Publication of Lilburne's proffer became part of a propaganda battle in advance of the hearing. Lilburne complained that 'abundance of my own and ancient acquaintance were set upon me to callumniate, bespatter, and reproach me', so that they might become 'instruments to take away my life'. A parliamentary declaration of 27 September denounced Lilburne as an atheist given up to licentiousness, and a confederate of the royalists. Lilburne blamed this on Thomas May, a well-known writer now in the pay of the Rump.[81] While these 'base and wicked petitions, papers and books... were hugged and imbraced',[82] he said, those on his behalf had fallen on deaf ears.

Lilburne was in fact becoming a test case for loyalty to an increasingly embattled regime. On 11 October, in response to a fairly public debate about whether people were obliged to obey its authority, the House of Commons had agreed that all its members should subscribe to an Engagement: 'I do declare and promise, That I will be true and faithful to the Commonwealth of *England*, as the same is now established, without a King, or House of Lords'. The following day it was extended to the armies, navy, lawyers, universities and other places of learning, and local officeholders throughout England, including the City of London.[83] Lilburne's publications put him more or less directly at odds with this.

He was certainly characterized as one of the key contributors to a very unhealthy public culture, notably in Cuthbert Sydenham's *An anatomy of Lievt. Colonel John Lilburn's spirit and pamphlets*. Sydenham, an Independent minister in Newcastle, deplored the polemical culture, which of all the outrages of recent years was the greatest stain on the glory of the nation. The press, he complained, 'is made a common Strumpet' so that books, which were previously 'monuments of industry and seriousness of mens spirits, and records of the vertues and noble acts of brave men, adorned with Reason and Judgement' had now 'Pasquils and Libels, stuft with the rancor and rage'. The authors could only restore their own reputation in this world by 'defacing the names of their betters'. Perhaps hypocritically, though, the title page promised to prove Lilburne to be 'a common Lyar and unworthy of civil Converse'. Lilburne's charges against Cromwell and Hesilrige were rebutted with a mixture of lofty disdain and detail, suggesting perhaps that the great men themselves were above responding. But it also hinted at Lilburne's treasonous sympathies: 'It's well known, besides his trading in *Cooks Institutes*, what malignant converse he & Judg *Jenkins* have had together, some fruits of it we see in his Pamphlets'. Thomas May probably had a hand in this publication too, and Lilburne later denounced Sydenham as one of Hesilrige's favourites.[84] Again, it seems, the regime and its friends were becoming more proficient in the dark arts of publicity at which Lilburne excelled.[85]

This seems to have been published about a week before the trial opened, and it was against this unpromising background that Lilburne's family sought to head off the confrontation. On 22 October, Robert and Elizabeth petitioned the Rump, asking for financial support to allow him to go abroad with his family and anyone else who wanted to join him. Despite the actions that had got him into trouble, which they regretted, they claimed that he had been a consistent servant of the public good and had never let material considerations interfere with that. His current circumstances, however, meant that he could not afford to go overseas without help. The petition was fruitless, so Robert made the offer directly, and John published it as his second 'proffer': to '*transplant my self into some part of the West-Indies*', if the government would help him to do it.[86] Further petitions from Robert and from the supporters of the petition of 11 September 1648 (his 'Whalebone friends') met with rejection—indeed the latter was not heard and members of the House literally refused to touch it.[87] In the meantime, more witnesses were called and the sheriffs were ordered to prepare the Guildhall for the trial.[88]

Mercurius Pragmaticus claimed that this show of intent was in part a bluff—that 'severall persons Eminent for Power and Trust in the House' had visited Lilburne in the Tower to warn him of the danger he was in, and to encourage him to escape. The lieutenant had been instructed to allow him to walk in the streets to facilitate an escape, but this had failed, 'hee intending nothing lesse, fearelessely continued to see the result of their malice'. This then redoubled the determination of the regime to see him dead.[89]

His position was certainly less than fully yielding. He published a letter from him to the lieutenant of the Tower about his summons to Prideaux, under the title *A Salva Libertate*. The letter denounced the 'Mock power sitting at *Westminster*', claiming that 'the intruding Generall *Fairfax* and his forces had broak and annihilated all the formall and Legall Magestracy, of *England*, yea the very parliament it self'. Prideaux, he said, was 'no Atturney Generall either in Law, or Reason'.[90] During the first hearing he had refused to answer Prideaux's potentially incriminating questions, but he had done much to incriminate himself subsequently, publishing an account of that hearing, with its very clear statements about the illegitimacy of the Parliament

and Cromwell's tyranny, for example, and bringing his charges against
Hesilrige directly to Prideaux's attention. He seemed intent on confrontation.
At the end of *Strength out of Weaknesse*, he wrote:

> ALL *The Petitions to the pretended House, for their Courtesie or Favour towards mee,*
> *by any Persons whatsoever, though never so nigh to me; I totally disavow, disclaime, and*
> *disowne, as altogether done against my Consent, Will and Mind, being absolutely*
> *Resolved, by the strength of God, to lay down the last drop of my blood, in Defence of*
> *my foregoing Discourse.*[91]

During the trial, in fact, the Attorney General cited Lilburne's refusal to
petition on his own behalf as evidence of his attitude to the regime and the
authority of the court.[92]

By the eve of the trial Elizabeth, 'perceiving that nothing would serve
[the government's] turn, but absolutely her husbands life', had 'besought
her husband to stoop as low as possibly he could for the safety of his life'.
Moved by her anguish of spirit Lilburne had weakened, writing to Lenthall
on 24 October asking for more time to prepare for the trial. This, too, was to
no avail: by now the regime seems to have been set on a determined course.[93]

The regime was also a little anxious, however, and with good reason as
events were to show. On 23 October the militia committee for London,
Westminster, and Southwark was ordered to be ready 'lest any disturbance
might grow by the tumultuating of those of his faction whom he has misled'.
The men disposed should be 'true to the interest of the commonwealth, and
under faithful commanders'. Meanwhile General Skippon was ordered to
set a guard in the light of 'certain and secret information that some of that
desperate party are resolved to put themselves into Guildhall with swords
and pistols, and when Lilburne comes to trial, to make some bloody disturbance': he was to 'use the best means you can to prevent that mischief'.
Fairfax was ordered to have 'such forces as you judge sufficient to be in arms
and readiness to prevent mischief'.[94]

★   ★   ★

The trial opened at Guildhall on 24 October and provided enthralling
theatre. The Great Hall was built in the fifteenth century and was in
Lilburne's time much as it is today. Over 150 feet long and fifty feet wide,
under a high ceiling, it is now said to accommodate 900 people for a
reception and 750 for a meeting. It had been the scene of a number of
high-profile trials in the past, including those of Thomas Cranmer and

of two of the Gunpowder plotters. North of Cheapside, not far from Soper Lane, the scene of Lilburne's first arrest, and a short walk from St Paul's, it was a major landmark in the city and central to its political life. Over the next two days, before what seems to have been a full house, Lilburne used this stage very effectively to dramatize the fundamental political debate, to an appreciative audience within the court and attentive crowds on the streets outside.

The commission consisted of forty-one men: the mayor, nine judges, the City's recorder (chief legal officer), nine aldermen, and twenty-one others. Alexander Rigby, another judge, was on the commission but did not attend.[95] The key figures in the proceedings were to be Richard Keble, who presided, and Philip Jermyn, a judge in the Upper Bench, who was clearly hostile to Lilburne at many points in the trial.

First the Grand Jury was empanelled, to hear whether the indictment against Lilburne was 'true', that is worthy of hearing. Twenty men were summoned, and another called from the Hall to make twenty-one. Captain Sweeting, a pewterer in Cornhill, appeared in answer to the summons but was put out of the jury, perhaps because he was thought to be '*too much of Mr. Lilburnes principles*'.[96] Keble then read the charge to the jury, which a number of commentators subsequently condemned as partial and leading. He underlined the importance of their task, the basis of the law of treason, and assured them that their task was not to decide on the principles of treason but only the facts of the case.[97] The crier then read the indictment: enrolled on parchment, it was nearly two yards long and half an ell (about twenty inches) wide. The jury then insisted on hearing witnesses to the bill, without interference from the Attorney General. In the end, after four hours' consideration, not all of the articles in the bill were found worthy of an answer.[98]

Lilburne was brought into court by the lieutenant of the Tower and handed over to the custody of the sheriffs of London, and one of his principal tactics immediately became clear. Asked by the crier to raise his hand he launched instead into some preliminary skirmishes about the legality of the proceedings. In a lengthy opening statement he recounted his previous trials at the hands of successive tyrannous regimes, concluding that even the royalists in Oxford had tried him in an open court. When he had finished Keble rather wearily replied, '*Mr. Lilburn, look behind you and see whether the Dore stands open or no*'.[99] Lilburne pronounced himself satisfied with that and moved on.

His next target was the legality of the special commission of oyer and terminer. This was a special warrant to a named group of people to 'hear and determine' cases, and such powers had been crucial to the development of royal jurisdiction during the Middle Ages. During the thirteenth century this had been routinized in the powers of assize courts, which had begun to meet regularly in each county and, by the fourteenth century, in sessions of the peace.[100] Lilburne's argument was that the use of special commissions was now only allowed in the face of insurrection and rebellion, when assizes or quarter sessions (the normal courts exercising a regular power to hear and determine) could not be used. Clearly Lilburne was not in open rebellion, and the normal courts were available: the procedure therefore infringed his rights under Magna Carta and the Petition of Right, to a hearing by the known laws. Moreover, although he had not resisted arrest he had been taken by soldiers, which was an illegal use of military power. The legal disadvantages he suffered as a result of being denied access to the regular courts were significant—the pretended crimes were committed in Surrey and yet were being heard in London, the proceedings were unfamiliar to him and the legal documents he had seen were on parchment in an obscure hand and were in an even more obscure Latin.[101]

All this was met with patience but without much interest. Keble's response was 'you are fully heard', while Prideaux, discounted the legal concerns. The court had heard the commission before Lilburne had been brought up and was fully satisfied, '*as for M. Lilburns Crimes committed in Surry, his own Conscience best know what they are; but M. Lilburn at most can but yet guesse at what we intend to Try him here for*'. If he would put himself to trial, by raising his hand and acknowledging his identity, he would get the benefit of the law. Only when a further series of exchanges had been concluded—about whether Prideaux, as a member of the Rump and therefore *parti pris*, could reasonably participate in the proceedings, and what exactly was signified by raising his hand—did Lilburne finally allow himself to say that he was John Lilburne, son of Richard Lilburne.[102]

This trench warfare had dragged out proceedings dramatically—the fullest contemporary record reaches the twenty-sixth page before we finally get to this point, the reading of the indictment. That was itself a lengthy document— over 4,000 words, to which were added lengthy readings from five pamphlets. Lilburne was charged with treason under the acts passed on 14 May and 17 July 1649, and the final summation was very clear: through the words cited, and many other 'trayterous, poysonous and malicious expressions . . . published and openly declared' Lilburne had intended 'to stir up, and raise forces against the Government', he had tried 'to stir up mutiny in the Army', 'to set them in mutiny and rebellion against the publick peace, and to manifest contempt of the Lawes of this Common-wealth and free State'.[103] The five pamphlets named were *An Impeachment, Salva Libertate, The Legall Fundamentall liberties, An outcry*, and the *Hue and Cry*. All of them had been published from prison where he had been sent for his role in publishing *England's new chains*, and two of them had been published after the process had started to try to pin responsibility for *An outcry* on him.

Lilburne initially refused to plead without taking legal advice, saying that he feared a disadvantage if he had not understood the niceties of the law. Reassured that there could be no disadvantage to pleading not guilty, but also pressed for an answer, his plea was conditional: 'I am not guilty of any of the Treasons in manner and form, as they are there laid down in that indictment'. Having pleaded he immediately returned to his request for counsel, recounting how in his previous treason trial (at Oxford in 1642) this had been allowed. The court's position was clear—that counsel could advise on matters of law, but he first had to answer the matter of fact: whether or not he was the author of the words read out in the indictment. No counsel could help him with that. Once the matter of fact had been established then legal issues might arise, in which case counsel would be appointed. Lilburne repeatedly asserted his disadvantage in not understand-ing the law or the process, and that his life might hang on such details; the judges countered that they were under oath to do justice, and so their souls were at stake in treating him fairly. He also, and again it seems rea-sonably, objected that he had not had time to digest the long and detailed indictment, but again Keble was unsympathetic—the court needed to prove that he was the author of the five books mentioned. Lilburne's memory should serve for that, even if he had not committed the whole indictment to memory.[104]

A whole day of court time had been taken up by this skirmishing. Lilburne's strategy seems a knowing, and effective, means to try the patience of his judges: the reading of the indictment, and Lilburne's questions about whether the court was open, whether its commission was legal, what was signified by raising his hand and by pleading, and whether he should have legal counsel. In the final lines of the record there are signs that his judges had been needled by his refusal to acknowledge titles granted by the Rump, by his assertion that they were denying him justice, or were even in con-spiracy against him, and by his attempts to draw them into legal argument: Keble closed by admonishing him that he had '*trifled away his time*' and asserted that the court was bending over backwards to be fair to him by allowing a second day for the trial, with the doors wide open so that all might see justice done.[105]

The second day of the trial opened with some controversy about the finding of the Grand Jury the previous day. Jermyn claimed that Lilburne was accused of treason by the jury, causing discussion among the jurymen, who asked their foreman, Manwaring, to 'tell Iudge *Iermin* of the wrong he did the Iurors in so saying'. The court was adjourned while members of the jury made it clear that it was the witnesses who were accusing Lilburne of treason; the jury had simply found some of the matters in the indictment worthy of answer on the basis of the witnesses's evidence. *Mercurius Elencticus* claimed that this 'so astonied the Judges that they looked as if they would have eaten the Jury', and that they had threatened them. But the jurors were particularly clear that they had not found it treason. The atmosphere was clearly tense: other members of the jury had apparently been reluctant to have the issue discussed openly in court, for fear of tumult.[106]

Once this was cleared the business of the court resumed with further skirmishes about who Lilburne could talk to and whether he would have counsel (it was not allowed), after which the trial jury was sworn in. Lilburne identified himself as John Lilburne, son of Richard Lilburne and formerly lieutenant colonel, but did not hold up his hand. It was evidently a lively crowd: 'the noise of the people in the Hall great, the Prisoner said he could not heare, and had some few lines before read over to him'. He had earlier interrupted the reading of the indictment when he saw Prideaux whispering to the judges and was now rebuked for addressing the people in the court directly: '*Quiet you your self, we will quiet them for you*' said Keble.[107]

There was a further delay as Lilburne objected against the court's statement that he had pleaded not guilty, saying that he had entered a plea against the errors in the indictment, not to the charges. Finally, however, Prideaux began to make the prosecution case: that Lilburne had denied the legitimacy of the present government, and had tried to stir up rebellion against it and to stir up mutiny in the army. He produced witnesses to prove Lilburne's authorship and circulation of *An outcry*, *Salva Libertate*, and *An Impeachment*, and cited evidence about the authorship of *The Legall Fundamentall liberties* from other writings where Lilburne himself claimed authorship. The prosecution case was in that sense limited—to prove that he was the author of words which self-evidently proved the charge.

The testimony, however, did not prove Lilburne's authorship. Thomas Newcombe, the printer, had handled proofs of *An outcry* with Lilburne and Captain Jones, but as Lilburne pointed out, he only testified that Lilburne alone had handled one page of uncorrected proofs—this was far from establishing that Lilburne was the author. Four soldiers were called—John Tooke, Thomas Lewis, John Hawkins, and John Merriman—who testified about an encounter with Lilburne following a chance meeting on the street. Lewis knew him well and they fell into conversation, Lilburne suggesting that they have a beer at a nearby tavern. There he asked them if they knew about *An outcry*, and gave them a copy, which he said was available from many booksellers in the city. He had also asked them about their pay, which Prideaux wanted the jury to think was an incitement to discontent. Merriman had signed the copy of the book that he had given them, and that very copy was produced in court. But as Lilburne said, showing that he had a hand, apparently a rather minor one, in the printing, and that he had given a copy to some soldiers, who could have bought it from a number of booksellers, hardly demonstrated that he was the author and was inciting mutiny.

Thomas Dafthorne had testified that the previous August he had gone to Lilburne's house in Southwark, having bumped into him on the bridge. There he was given a copy of *An impeachment* to deliver to Colonel Ayres at Warwick Castle, something confirmed by other witnesses. Ayres, or Eyre, had been one of the mutineers at Burford, initially imprisoned in Oxford but moved to Warwick where he could do less mischief. This then was a critical claim—that Lilburne's incitement had been put before someone previously actively in arms against the regime.[108] Lilburne refused to say whether he was the author, even though his name was on the cover; pointed out that this was not testimony about authorship and was pretty limited evidence of incitement; and that it had taken place in Surrey, not London, and so should have been heard by a court in that county.

The other two matters of fact ought to have been easy to prove, since *Salva Libertate* was the printed version of a letter he had handed directly to the lieutenant of the Tower, and Lilburne had himself given a copy of *A preparative to an hue and cry* to Prideaux, in front of witnesses, at the 14 September hearing, saying that it was his. The proof of authorship of the *Salva Libertate*, however, depended on proving that the manuscript now produced in court was in Lilburne's handwriting, something he refused to acknowledge ('you may see the valiantnesse of this Champion for the peoples liberties, that will not owne his own hand', said Prideaux). There was also a question of whether the place in the Tower where Lilburne handed over the letter was in London or not, since not all the precincts were.

As for *A preparative to an hue and cry*, Lilburne claimed that he had said the text was his apart from the printer's errors 'which are many', a phrase which does appear in Lilburne's printed account of the hearing. Prideaux's two clerks, called as witnesses, claimed not to be able to remember him saying that, but the lieutenant of the Tower, who had taken him there, did confirm it. Was this enough to cast doubt on the claim that Lilburne was the author of the words as they appeared in the indictment? With his life at stake, perhaps so.

Lilburne then refused to own authorship of any of the books in question, even though *An impeachment* had his name on the cover and other publications with his name on claimed that he was the author of *Legall Fundamentall liberties*. This denial of authorship infuriated Prideaux, who began to use the denial to attack Lilburne's character: '*that is not the true principle of a true Christian, nor an* Englishman, *nor a Gentleman*'. Lilburne responded that he had denied nothing, merely pointed out that the prosecution had not proved its case—it was not up to him to incriminate himself, after all.[109] Prideaux concluded with readings from the treason acts and, despite interruptions from Lilburne, summarized the charges: he clearly denied the legitimacy of the current government, incited resistance and mutiny, and was obviously the author of these texts, despite his disreputable refusal to own up to that.

The hearing had taken four or five hours by that point. Since the indictment was very long, too long to be committed to memory in one reading, Lilburne asked for respite before making his response—first for a week and then for an hour—but was denied. Famously, he was also refused permission to go and relieve himself, and so called for a chamber pot, which he used in the open court. Summoning his strength, he stood with a copy of Coke's *Institutes* in his hand (an image immortalized in a contemporary engraving, and readily recognizable, see Fig. 5.2) and delivered what proved to be a life-saving performance. There was immediate excitement when the scaffolding in the hall fell down, 'which occasioned a great noise and some confusion by reason of the peoples tumbling'. According to one account this 'amazed and terrifyed the unjust Judges', creating a long delay, so 'that for almost the space of an houre, they did nothing but stare one upon another'. Lilburne used the time to 'prepare himself... that when he came to speake, he did confute them with good *Law* and honest Reason'.[110] There was further excitement when he outraged the judges by claiming 'you that call your selves Judges of the Law, are no more but norman intruders, and

The names of the Jury of life and death

Fig. 5.2. John Lilburne in court, with Sir Edward Coke's *Institutes* in hand (1649)

indeed and in truth, if the Jury please, are no more but Cifers, to pronounce their Verdict'. Judge Jermyn was outraged by this '*damnable, blasphemous heresie*', which was '*enough to destroy all the Law in the Land; there was never such a damnable heresie broached in this Nation before*'. Keble refused to let him read to the jury from Coke's *Institutes*, worried that he might 'puzzle' them with his erroneous reading, making much of Lilburne's miscitation of a precedent.

The exchange caused a buzz and the crier had to call the crowd to order to hear the court.[111]

This part of Lilburne's strategy—to cast doubt on the legality of the court and the detail of its proceedings, and to play up the role of the jury—was clearly understood by Prideaux and the judges. Keble even seemed to suggest that it had affected the choice of a special commission, the fear being that before an ordinary court he would have been malapert and out-talked them. Certainly, retorted Lilburne, 'I am not daunted at the multitude of my Judges, neither at the glittering of your scarlet Robes, nor the Majesty of your presence and harsh, austere deportment towards me, I blesse my good God...who gives me courage and boldness'.[112]

The meat of his defence, though, rested on detail—there was no proof that he was the author of the books. He had held the proofs in his hand and given away copies of the book but that did not prove his authorship. Some of the allegations related to events in Surrey and perhaps in precincts of the Tower that were in Middlesex, and so a London jury had no power to hear him on those charges. The acts on which he was being tried were passed after his arrest—in fact he had been in prison prior to their passage—and it had not been shown that the pamphlets in question had actually been published after the date of the legislation. Was it not possible that they had been published earlier, and post-dated?

Having cast doubt on the matter of fact he started on a narrative of his life intended to demonstrate that he was a champion of England's constitution, although Keble cut him off—the court wanted to hear the matter of fact, 'not to hear the story of your life'. He ended with a direct appeal to the jury, 'my sole Judges, the keepers of my life':

> know your power, and consider your duty, both to God, to Me, to your own Selves, and to your Country; and the gracious assisting Spirit, and presence of the Lord God omnipotent, the Governour of Heaven and Earth, and all things therein contained, go along with you, give counsell, and direct you, to do that which is just and for his glory.

This was received with loud cries of amen and an '*extraordinary great hum*', alarming the judges and leading Major General Skippon to summon three more companies of foot soldiers.[113]

Prideaux attempted to sum up despite interruptions from Lilburne, who continued to try to cast doubt on the legality of the proceedings, in this case by claiming that two witnesses were needed to establish the truth of any fact. Both Prideaux and Keble contested this, and Keble directed the jury to disregard it. For Keble the issue was plain—there were three charges, the evidence for them was in the books, and the question was whether Lilburne was the author or not. Yet it was clear that Lilburne's performance had them rattled. Prideaux complained in his summing up that Lilburne had by 'glossing speeches or insinuations, [sought] to wind into the affections of the Jury, as he cunningly and smoothly hath done, by calling them his fellow Citizens and the like'.[114]

It worked. Returning an hour later, the jury declared that he was not guilty of any of the treasons charged against him. The verdict was greeted with elation: 'immediatly the whole multitude of People in the *Hall*, for joy at the Prisoner's acquittall gave such a loud and unanimous shout, as is believed, was never heard in *Yeeld-Hall*, which lasted for about halfe an hour without intermission: which made the Iudges for fear, turne pale, and hange down their heads'. At the moment of his acquittal Lilburne seems to have been an exception to the general mood: our chief witness says he 'stood silent at the Barre, rather more sad in his countenance than he was before'. Lilburne himself says that 'my countenance fell and changed, as being rapt up with Spirituall singing praises unto God, even at the very Barr'.[115] A man of generous spirit, as he left court he gave money to his guards to have a drink on him.[116]

He was taken back to the Tower, accompanied by cheering crowds. That night bonfires were lit in celebration. Lilburne later claimed that despite the presence of troops in the court and the surrounding streets, the verdict had been greeted 'with the greatest acclamations and shoutings for joy by the people … that I believe have bin heard in London for some ages past'. The bonfires and celebrations 'terrified, amazed and affrighted the guilty Consciences of my corrupt Judges' so that they went back to their homes under guard.[117] This does not seem to have been a hollow boast. '[E]xtraordinary were the acclamations for the Prisoners deliverance, as the like hath not been seen in *England*, which acclamations, and loud reioycing expressions, went quite through the Streets, with him to the very gates of the *Tower*, and for joy the People caused that night abundance of Bonfires to be made all up and down the Streets'.[118] '[T]hat worthy Champion and Patriot of his COUNTRY [was accompanied] … not onely with the Joy and acclamation of his friends, but of all sorts of PEOPLE', it was said. The bonfires, and the bells that rang out that night, showed that 'all the Tyrants that ever exerciz'd power here were not half so hatefull to the PEOPLE' as the current regime. The newsbook *Mercurius Pragmaticus* agreed that those celebrating included those who only two days earlier were Lilburne's 'deadly Enemies' but who now 'Commended the Resolution and Gallantry of the Man, and in a manner acknoledging the justnesse of his Cause, and the vilenesse of his adversaries'.[119]

In the short term, however, Lilburne was returned to his captivity, on the basis of the other charges for which the Lords had committed him.[120] When he and the other three Levellers were eventually released, on 8 November, they were marched in great companies to a feast at the King's Head Tavern in Fish Street. A commemorative medal recorded that he had been 'saved by the power of the Lord and the integrity of his Jury, who are juge of law as wel as fact'.[121]

★ ★ ★

This has been celebrated as a triumph of the people against a regime acting tyrannously, and that is surely right. He had been imprisoned for publishing *England's new chains*, but tried for other publications under legislation passed while he was in custody—if his defence had a certain DIY flavour the regime seemed to be acting just as experimentally. His fearlessness and tenacity in court, in defence of his rights, was an inspiration to a later generation of writers caught in the toils of censorship in the long shadow of the French revolution.[122] Many contemporary commentators agreed that the trial jury, and the audience in the court, were representative of a broader public opinion; indeed, that is what made the judgment so galling, perhaps alarming, for the regime. It seems clear that they had lost not just the case, but the battle for public opinion too.

The two juries—of Grand Inquest to hear if the indictment was 'true' and the trial jury—had been empanelled by Rowland Wilson, the Sheriff of London. He was a sitting MP and a member of the Council of State, a man 'who had not a dram of affection or compassion towards [Lilburne] in the least'. Keble's charge to the Grand Jury, it was said, had 'remarkable things in it' which, like the two days of the trial itself, 'might make ingenuous men blush'. Theodorus Verax, the author of the fullest transcript of the trial, said the jurors were most, if not all, 'engaged persons', that is people who had taken the Engagement, promising to support the new regime. The newsbook *Mercurius Elencticus* was in no doubt that both juries had been packed in order to secure a conviction.[123] The Grand Jury consisted of men of relatively high status: at least twelve and possibly fourteen Common Council men, and three aldermen, with a lot of other experience of civic office represented too. It also reflected a mix of Presbyterian and Independent opinion, and as far as we know therefore represented a reasonabie cross-section of the views among London's civic leaders. The trial jury consisted of men of lower social status, and Lilburne did object to at least nine potential members including men from St Pancras, Soper Lane, and St Antholin, both parishes known to him. Their relatively low status makes it more difficult to assess their likely attitudes, and Lilburne's objections tended to exclude the higher-status men, with the result that half the jury came from the unfashionable parish of St Sepulchre, outside the City walls.[124] Lilburne himself said he did not know any of the jurors, recognizing only two faces among the trial jury. There is no reason, therefore, to think that Lilburne (or anyone on his behalf) had successfully manipulated the membership of the juries: if anything the opposite was likely to be true. It was therefore very significant for the government that the Grand Jury was not fully compliant, and the trial jury completely undermined the government's position: as the medal said, with great integrity, perhaps with courage. That they acquitted Lilburne seems to have been in spite of efforts not to empanel men sympathetic to his views.

The most detailed accounts of these events come from opponents of the regime. That by Verax has been used ever since as the authoritative record, incorporated into the State Trials, and cited by lawyers subsequently. It was not a perfect record, 'Being as exactly pen'd and taken in shorthand, as it was possible to be done in such a croud and noise, and transcribed with an indifferent and even hand, both in reference to the Court, and the Prisoner; that so matter of Fact, as it was there declared, might truly come to publick view'. But Verax assured his readers '*I have been as upright, and indifferent in writing and transcribing of the foresaid discourse, as possibly I could, without maliciously, designedly, or wilfully, wronging either the Court, or Mr. Lilburne the Prisoner, as possibly a man could be, at least in my apprehension, and if any thing be amisse, the second Edition may peradventure mend it, if more exacter Copies can be got*'.[125] The author of *Truths victory* claimed that only two private shorthand records were made—his own and that of Mr Hinde. The government was not planning to publish any version, since the event was 'so rediculous on their part, that they cannot endure so much as to hear of it'.[126] Neither did the government publish the indictment, which it ought to have done.[127]

In early November the Council of State was collating copies of all materials relating to the trial for presentation to Parliament. According to *Mercurius*

Pragmaticus the regime was mired in recriminations: some leading figures blamed the judges, others the jury, all of them regretted not having tried Lilburne by council of war, under martial law. Some even suggested that the jury should be called to account for their verdict, and that new charges and witnesses should be brought. *Mercurius Pragmaticus* claimed that at a meeting in Whitehall Mr Scott had said that the judges deserved to hang for not having prepared the trial better, and another, perhaps Mr Ermin, '*That unless this fellow (meaning* Lilburn) *were removed, & that for opposing their Authority, the People would never submit to it*'.[128] On 6 December the Council of State ordered Edward Dendy to search for and seize all books purporting to be a narrative of the trial, and to search named ships for a sea chest and box containing scandalous pamphlets by John Lilburne.[129] Unsure perhaps what to do next, and embarrassed by the verdict, the regime seems to have left public discussion to be dominated by its critics, although *A brief discourse Of the present power of Magistracy and Iustice* did put the government line in response to the arguments Lilburne had made in court.[130]

Verax, the author of what became the main record, was certainly not neutral. It was the pen name of Clement Walker, a West Country Presbyterian who had been active in the war, and had, for example, publicly criticized Nathaniel Fiennes for surrendering Bristol too easily in 1643. After the war, he was a scourge of radicals and Independents—no natural ally of Lilburne's, certainly, although he was also critical of Presbyterian factionalism. It was the purge and the regicide that really put him on Lilburne's side: an MP, he had wanted to accept the king's answers to the Treaty of Newport and was imprisoned at Pride's Purge. He was the author of *The History of Independency*, which denounced the radicals in the army and Parliament, blaming them for the new tyranny: his enemies were Lilburne's too, and the case was made in comparable terms. On the opening day of Lilburne's trial his papers were seized and he was committed to the Tower shortly after. He was never brought to trial, and died in the Tower two years later.[131] The tone of two shorter accounts of the trial, *Truths Victory* and *Certaine observations upon the Tryall*, was also strongly against the government.

The press controls introduced in July had been effective in reducing the number of newsbooks, and the regime was clearly committed to controlling the news. At the time of the trial, though, none of the pro-government titles mentioned it at all: no pro-government message was systematically promoted.[132] As a result, those titles hostile to the regime which were still in business had a field day: the front pages of *The Man in the Moon, Mercurius*

Elencticus and *Mercurius Politicus* were all taken up with verses celebrating the embarrassment of the regime. *Pragmaticus* in fact claimed that the trial had silenced all other news that week and devoted almost the whole issue to an account of Lilburne's dealings with the regime before and during the trial. *Elencticus* agreed that it was the greatest news of the week, and those who had tried to cut him off had '*become the Kingdomes scoff*'. For the *Man in the Moon* the moral was that 'W[h]en *Theeves* fall out *true Folks* come by their Goods'. The '*Juncto*' and Lilburne, falling out, had delivered the precious knowledge that they were both knaves, although, to be truthful, Lilburne was the more honest of the two.[133]

In the absence of a strong counter-case, these accounts have dominated— from the surviving record it seems unquestionable that Lilburne had exposed a capacity for tyranny and abuse by the new regime. Those who acquitted him seem to have spoken for a broader range of opinion than simply his own close political allies and the most implacable enemies of the regime.

6

Citizen, 1649–52

Faithful to the Commonwealth, 1649–51

Rather remarkably, Lilburne stood for election as a member of the London Common Council less than two months after his acquittal, and was in fact elected on 21 December. Not the least surprising thing about this was that to take up the office he would have to take the Engagement. It had been imposed on officeholders in the weeks before Lilburne's treason trial—a symptom of the same crisis of legitimacy that had led the regime to bring the charges against him. It was soon to be extended to all adult males, a necessity (it was claimed) in the light of the efforts of 'dis-affected persons' who were undermining the settlement of the nation under the present government. The aim was to foster unity

> as well against all Invasions from abroad, as the Common Enemy at home; and to the end that those which receive benefit and protection from this present Government, may give assurance of their living quietly and peaceably under the same, and that they will neither directly nor indirectly contrive or practice any thing to the disturbance thereof.

In standing for, and accepting, election Lilburne was engaging with the most fundamental political argument of the day: could he give these commitments in order to take up office?[1] On 8 November Walwyn, Overton, and Prince were all released from the Tower having taken the Engagement, although Lilburne had not.[2] Taking the Engagement was not necessarily a sell-out, therefore: Winstanley, the Digger, took it on the grounds that it offered the best hope of social change.[3] What would Lilburne do?

For him the trial of the king and the subsequent settlement had been a pragmatic political manoeuvre which did nothing to establish the legal rights for which he had gone to war in 1642. It was pushed through by the army leadership and was sustained by the army and a Council of State which was composed of men who had a direct vested interest in this regime and which lacked constitutional authority. This was the kind of oligarchic interest which the *Agreements of the People* had sought to prevent: people who had become entrenched in power, and were not executing their trust on behalf of the people in a reliable way. A settlement based on an *Agreement* would have secured the nation from that danger by preventing tyranny, and ensuring rights—enforcing the principle of self-denial. Lilburne had no confidence that the current regime would be less prey to self-interest and arbitrary will than the king had been, or that it would act less tyrannously. He had not supported the regicide, at least not before a just settlement had been reached about what should follow the monarchy, and had said in print that for him a king who accepted an *Agreement* was preferable to the army leadership and its creatures, the Rump and the Council of State.[4] The Engagement bound the nation to the present order; an *Agreement* would have bound them to a just settlement based explicitly on abstract principles of political right: the contrast could hardly be more stark.

Following his election, however, he did take the Engagement, apparently therefore declaring and promising that he would be '*true and faithfull to the Common-wealth of England, as the same is now established without a King or House of Lords*'. He then asked to be allowed to speak, but Alderman Tichbourne, who was presiding, at first refused. Tichbourne relented, however, when those present cried out 'hear him', but quickly cut him off when he heard what Lilburne wanted to say. As he would no doubt have done even if he had been allowed to speak, Lilburne instead published his explanation of his position on the Engagement.[5]

It centred on his understanding of the term 'Commonwealth'. This was not, as the clear intention of the government had been, simply the title of the current regime, or 'the present parliament, Council of State, or Council of the Army'. For him, it was two things: 'all the good & legall people of England'; and the 'essentiall and fundamental Government of *England, as it is now established*'. That essential and fundamental government consisted of three elements: free annual parliaments; trial by jury; and that no one could be dispossessed of 'life, limb, liberty or estate' except by due process of law. By Commonwealth, then, 'I do not in the least vnderstand it to be meant abstract, or individually of the present *Parl*. Counsel of STATE, or Councel of the ARMY, or all of them conjoyned'. He then went on to denounce the Engagement makers—they were not the Commonwealth named in the

Engagement, they were subordinate, or trustees, not the supreme power, and he would oppose all those who invented titles in order to create a prerogative power by which to oppress the people. In this printed version he signed himself to Tichbourne 'yours, so farre as you are truly the COMMONWEALTHS'.[6] In truth, this was another statement of his commitment to the principles of the *Agreement*; its burden is pretty much the inverse of what the Engagement was inviting him to promise, while his election bore testimony to his popularity in the City.

He had been silenced on the day, and his election clearly caused alarm to the Rump—it is the only business recorded in the Journals for 26 December, prompted by a petition from the Lord Mayor and Court of Aldermen. This was taken very seriously, 'as a matter much concerning the publick Safety', and on their petition the election was quashed. For his role in the election Philip Chetwin was disabled from being a freeman and imprisoned in Warwick Castle. Edmond Caverly was also committed and John Fenton was dismissed as a common council man. The grounds on which all this was done are obscure.[7]

Securing election may well not have been the primary purpose, however: there is more than a suspicion of contrived political theatre about this. As was often the case, the detail Lilburne offered seemed to point to the objections being raised against him. He explained that his family home was in Southwark, but he had taken lodgings in the City while looking for a suitable place for him and his family. Having eaten, drunk, and lodged there (satisfying the requirements for political participation in the City), he went with the other inhabitants of the ward to Blue Coats Hall in Christ Church ward mote, for the Common Council election. There, 'by the affection of diverse Inhabitants', he was nominated, and elected by a majority on a clear show of hands. Although he didn't say it, he was in effect one of the betrusted of the inhabitants; he had not sought office, but had been nominated by those among whom he happened now to be living.[8] This seems to be a defence against the charge that he had lodged in the City and sought election simply to force a confrontation of this kind over the Engagement. Alderman Tichbourne had been one of the special commissioners in his treason trial two months earlier which, although Lilburne does not mention it, must have added to the frisson. Unusually for Lilburne's writings, the pamphlet gave full details of the publisher and claimed to have been licensed by the Stationers' Company.[9] His appetite for theatre, and to embarrass those in power, was apparently undiminished.

Nonetheless, he also had a life to lead. By this time, he later said, he had become wearied 'with tossings & tumblings' in the world, and he had been reassured by Cromwell that there would be no need for 'more strugleings in England by us for our Liberties' once Scotland (which had proclaimed Charles's son their king) was subdued. As a result he had withdrawn from politics having also received 'many entreaties to sit still, from my faithfull and endeared wife', who felt that all her support through his troubles had brought them nothing.[10]

Tracing the course of his public life, it is sometimes easy to forget that he had a family, and perhaps (or at least intermittently) the normal concerns of a family man. He set out in a number of places how his public concernments occupied his conscience and therefore commanded him more urgently than the welfare of his family: '*although I love my wife as deerely as any Man in the world loves his*', God had given him the strength to see such concerns 'but as subordinate things to his Will and Pleasure'.[11] He never mentions the birth of any of his children, or speaks of them by name in any of his publications.[12] This despite the fact that Elizabeth eventually gave birth ten times: something only possible because she and the children followed him so loyally throughout his troubles. Elizabeth and their first child had accompanied him to quarters in Boston when he was on active service in the autumn of 1643. When he left the army the family moved to Half Moon Alley in Petty France, where they still lived in February 1646.[13] During 1645, however, Elizabeth had moved into Newgate with John, and had given birth to a daughter, Elizabeth, there.[14] In 1649 they had three children, but had lost both their sons to smallpox, Elizabeth and their daughter surviving serious illness. During that illness he had spoken movingly of the suffering of his son, calling out in the night for his father, who was then imprisoned in the Tower, but it is a rare expression of emotion about his children, made in the context of an attempt to get parole to visit them. On 12 October 1650 Elizabeth gave birth to a son, John, the second son to bear that name.[15]

In general this family and emotional hinterland is invisible in the life of the public Lilburne. Following his acquittal and his intervention in the Engagement controversy, though, he does seem to have settled into his family concerns. Two years later he wrote in a public letter to Elizabeth, 'when by a cleare & faire vote, I was legally chosen by the people a common-counsel-man in London; did *I* not take it patiently & sit downe in silence, al though the Parliament arbitrarily voted me out of it'.[16] In 1655 Elizabeth petitioned Cromwell for help, asserting among other things, 'that none could ever bear themselves with greater caution and reservednes than he did after his trial at Guildhall, as may be testified by credible persons'.[17] If she thought Cromwell (of all people) would believe it then it must have been a plausible claim. It does seem that Lilburne now made a genuine attempt to live a settled life: as he put it to pursue 'the tranquility of this Common-wealth in my little sphere'.[18] He now enjoyed the longest period of liberty of his adult life, although a simmering feud with Sir Arthur Hesilrige was soon to precipitate another crisis.

★   ★   ★

How then was Lilburne to feed his family? An apprenticeship in wool, a desire perhaps to work in print, and a period in brewing had all, for one reason or another, not worked out, and his long-term campaign for reparations, damages, and arrears of pay from the army had still to bear full fruit. He continued to attribute the last of these frustrations to the machinations of his factional enemies. He had settled for cash to be raised from the estates of three men in trouble following the second civil war: Gibb, Bellingham, and Bowes. Following Lilburne's arrest in 1649, Hesilrige had allowed Bellingham and Bowes to compound (meaning that Lilburne could no longer secure ready cash from assets on their estates) and had stopped the rents being paid to him from Gibb's lands. As a result, one way or another, by the end of 1649 Lilburne had only received £600 of the promised £2,400. He asked Lenthall to help him get Hesilrige to pay the rest 'upon the nayl', or to get it paid from the estate of Lord Keeper Coventry, 'upon whom it was once ... fixed upon'.[19] Meeting Hesilrige's clerk shortly after his release, Lilburne told him to tell Hesilrige that he would have his arrears if it cost him his heart's blood, and that although there was no point in going to law against such a powerful man, he carried a rapier and dagger and would seek satisfaction if he did not receive his payment within eight days. The message seems to have worked, and he received £800 arrears from Hesilrige.[20]

Rather surprisingly, Cromwell now intervened to help him. In 1649 Cromwell had led the long-delayed effort to reconquer Ireland. Following the rising of 1641, the Irish Confederacy had established a large degree of political and military control. It was on the whole pro-Stuart as well as Catholic, since the English Parliament was so virulently anti-Catholic, and following the execution of Charles I the Irish had, like the Scots, declared his son to be their king. There were therefore numerous reasons why the new regime wanted to see the Confederates crushed, and in 1649 a major, and devastatingly effective, campaign had been launched under Cromwell's command. Arriving home, Cromwell had presented Lilburne's petition to Parliament for the unpaid balance of his reparations. He also asked his friends on the Council of State to take special care that the monies were paid while he went on campaign in Scotland, the next most serious security problem. He invited Lilburne to join him as he made his way north from London, a rather signal complement given the pressures he was facing.[21]

Lilburne had petitioned the House in January, and in February nearly £500 had been paid to Richard Lilburne for his son. Parliament ordered a committee chaired by Marten to consider the rest of the claim, recommending in July that the remaining money, around £1,600, should be paid from the estates of Bellingham and Bowes, or the lands of the Deans and Chapters. The Deans and Chapters had been abolished in April 1649 and their lands put at the disposal of the state: while Lilburne had been dubious in 1648 about accepting the land of delinquents, worried that the title might prove insecure, there is no reason to think that land taken from the episcopacy would trouble his conscience or that they were particularly insecure. An Act was introduced on 19 July and had passed its third reading eleven days later, awarding him the balance of his reparations from lands sequestered from the Dean and Chapter of Durham.[22]

While the pursuit of his reparations seemed finally to be nearing its conclusion, Lilburne moved back to the City from Southwark, and sought a settled profession. Rather than return to wool, books, or beer, he took up the trade of a soap boiler. This was an unglamorous profession, but one that required a substantial capital outlay and therefore one that attracted relatively rich investors. It also seems that William Kiffin, a long-term associate, was involved in the trade and Lilburne had apparently tried to establish himself in it in 1649.[23] In November 1650 Lilburne signed a petition to get the excise on soap removed, on the grounds that excise had already been paid on all the ingredients for its manufacture—in effect the tax was being raised on the labour necessary to make it and that was a heavy burden since the production process was unreliable. The high levy also fell unevenly, since much production was done privately without paying any duty, and offered an incentive to that kind of production, and to theft. It was also a burden on the poor, since they had to use soap, however much it cost. Instead the soap boilers suggested that it should be replaced by a tax on imports of the materials from which it was made. The twenty signatories of the petition offered to collect this money, in return for a commission, and to match the revenue of the current excise on soap.[24]

This kind of arrangement between those involved in a trade and the expanding tax administration was very common, and part of the normal politics of seventeenth-century England.[25] Lilburne was only one of the twenty of course, but the fact that he put his name to a petition which referred to the Rump as 'the supreme authority the Parliament of the Commonwealth of England' reinforces the sense that he had decided to make his peace with the regime, if not quite on the terms required by the Engagement. It was also a phrase that appears at the head of a further intervention authored by Lilburne himself in a 'humble address' responding to objections to the proposed scheme. This was addressed to MPs individually, rather than to the House, and was presumably intended for circulation at the door of the House as part of a lobbying effort.[26]

In fact, his abilities as an advocate and lobbyist, rather than his talents as a soap maker, seem to have offered him the best hope of making a living in the 1650s. He had tried to get a more formal training in the law in the Temple, claiming in a letter to Lenthall that he needed this to protect himself, since he had so many enemies and had been denied counsel in his trial. Lenthall, and others learned in the law, had assured him that no freeman could be denied admission if he wished to learn the law. To get admission, however, he was sent to the treasurer of the Temple, none other than the Attorney General, Prideaux. Having paid a sizeable fee to his servant he was given an appointment with Prideaux but found him, perhaps unsurprisingly, *something waspish*, and he was denied admittance to the Bar. Lilburne may have been trying to embarrass Prideaux as much as to enter the Temple—he asked Lenthall to protect him from Prideaux, but also to forward an offer to drop his attempt to enter the Temple if Prideaux would *be an effectuall instrument, speedily to help me to my money*, currently detained by Hesilrige. Failing that, he hoped he might be able to find lodgings nearby and study more informally.[27] If it was an attempt to embarrass the government he dropped it quickly: in the same open letter to Elizabeth published two years later, he emphasized how he had acquiesced in this rebuff as he had with the quashing of his election to Common Council: when denied by the Attorney General 'to be admitted unto that common *English right*, did *I* not sit downe without Struggleing for satisfaction for that *Injurie* done?'[28]

Even without a formal legal training, however, Lilburne was a valuable advocate. It seems clear that people came to him for advice and support when entering this world of lobbying and print, and it was not just a metropolitan phenomenon either. As early as 1648 a newsbook had claimed

NIL ADMIRARI

Fig. 6.1. Sir John Wildman (1622/3–93)

that Lilburne had been willing to plead cases against the committee for plundered ministers for a penny fee. Now, unable to settle on another trade, and constantly asked for counsel by his friends, he 'resolved to undertake men's honest causes and to manage them either as Solicitor of Pleader, as I saw cause'.[29] Wildman (Fig. 6.1) had taken this path into advocacy in 1649, and in November 1650 both Lilburne and Wildman were engaged as counsel by John Poyntz, who had fallen foul of the regime for unauthorized printing of a Parliamentary Act in 1647, something he had done in the course of a land dispute.[30] Now, again with Wildman, Lilburne was engaged as an advocate for inhabitants of the Lincolnshire manor of Epworth, who were embroiled in a decades-long dispute over drainage schemes in the Fens. In the course of this work he finally seemed set to establish himself in a competent estate. In doing so, he presented himself as doing no more than trying to secure Englishmen their rights under the Commonwealth as he had defined it—the essential and fundamental government of the nation, which ensured that life, limb, property, and liberty could only be taken by due process of law.

Advocate in the Lincolnshire Fens, 1650–1

The Lincolnshire Great Fen stretched over 400,000 acres, providing local people with a living through their customary rights to fish and fowl, and to cut reeds: such common rights allowed a subsistence to people who did not have large amounts of land. Following the Dutch example, however, entrepreneurs had wanted to drain the Fens in order to reveal land of rich agricultural potential, and in 1626 Charles I had licensed Cornelius Vermuyden to drain land in Hatfield Chase, to which the Isle of Axholme was later added. Work could start within three months of securing agreement from the commoners, but could not start without their agreement.[31]

Fourteen manors had been drained at a cost of £100,000, but it could only be effective if a drain was also cut through the manor of Epworth, and the drainers were awarded 7,400 acres in Epworth as reward for the benefit that they had brought.[32] However, the whole scheme had been dogged by resistance from the start, and inhabitants of Axholme, the people from Epworth among them, were closely involved. In 1627 and during the following two years those doing the work were subject to physical intimidation while their works and equipment were destroyed. Those among the leaders of the resistance who came from Epworth were closely related by birth, and included women, suggesting a fair degree of communal support. It was also clear, though, that some of the local inhabitants were tempted by the opportunities the drainage presented. The rector of Wroot, one of the settlements within the manor, became a supporter of the drainage, recognizing that it would increase the value of his living. John Newland, a substantial local inhabitant, and probably a relative of the rector, also saw benefits, and became a supporter of the improvement. He was in turn able to influence a wider circle, not least the considerable number of people who were in debt to him. Over time it became clear that there was greater solidarity and involvement in resistance to the change in two of the settlements in the manor (Belton and Haxey) than in others, reflecting their different economic interests and social solidarity.[33]

These divisions allowed successive attempts to negotiate a settlement, but each attempted settlement was in turn disputed, a process that was to last into the 1690s. Those resisting the drainage in these early years had let their cattle graze on the newly enclosed land, hoping to prompt trespass prosecutions which would then test the legal title—forcing the court to rule whether this was indeed trespass or instead that these were in fact common lands. All these suits had been stopped by injunction in 1634, and those who had trespassed or damaged property were subject to swingeing fines, which would be remitted if they acquiesced in the deal. This pressure, Lilburne claimed, had made possible an apparent agreement in 1636 that divided the common lands. Whatever the truth of the accusation of duress, the deal did not stick and attempts to force a legal hearing of the title continued. It does seem that more local people were coming to see the advantages of the drainage, although Lilburne later claimed that their numbers were overstated, signatures were forged and duplicated, and so on. And if the number of genuine supporters of the drainage was increasing so too were disputes in the manor: the Church Courts and Quarter Sessions dealt with an increasing number of conflicts in these years, perhaps reflecting rising internal tensions.[34]

Those opposed to the current agreement were able to cite a fourteenth-century deed, which had insisted that no change could be made to the use of the commons without the agreement of all the commoners, something the improvers had clearly not achieved. This gave legal grounds to nullify the current agreement, therefore, but the deed proved difficult actually to view. Meanwhile, from the mid-1630s there was an influx of settlers on to the land allocated to the proprietors (those who had invested in the drainage in return for land). Many of these incomers were Dutch or French Huguenots, and they settled especially in Wroot and Sandtoft.[35]

As things stood in 1642, then, there had been a complex local conflict—a series of contested agreements reflecting differing views of the communal interest and of existing legal rights. There was a broad division between, on the one hand, the proprietors and their tenants, and on the other, the commoners, many of whom felt they were being given a poor deal in return for the loss of their common rights. This was made more obvious by the fact that many of the tenants were Dutch or French incomers, particularly in the settlement of Sandtoft. But it was not quite this simple—there were local inhabitants attracted by the profits to be made from the drainage, and a number of people had been willing to sign agreements dividing up the drained land. There was plenty of contemporary testimony about the increased value of the land but also about the collapse of daily wages for labourers—presumably partly as land was turned over to animal husbandry and the demand for labour fell.[36] Attempts at legal settlement had run alongside episodes of violence and accusations of forced agreements.

The civil war created new opportunities to pursue these battles, and concerted efforts were made to reclaim all the land, turning the proprietors and
their tenants out. In 1642 some sluices were opened, ostensibly as a military
measure in support of Parliament, but partly also to make farmland unwork-
able. There seems to have been very strong support for the Protestation in
Epworth in 1642 and so the military claim was not completely incredible,
but exactly what was done targeted the interests of the proprietors, causing
considerable damage, and preventing the sowing of crops the following year.
It has even been suggested that support for Parliament in the Isle was tactical,
and actually motivated by a desire to reopen this local battle. Lilburne was
more circumspect in his own account: 'Tis true indeed, the Commoners
being in Armes for the Parliament in 1643. did take advantage of the Time;
and as they had been put out of possession by force, and could not through
the Tyranny of those Times have any Legall Remedy; so by force they put
Themselves into possession again of above 3000 acres'.[37] There were further
riots in 1645 and, in November, the minister of Sandtoft petitioned the
House of Lords about the damages suffered, 'on the behalfe of themselves as
other the french and dutch inhabitants of the newe improved groundes' in
the Level. The damage was enumerated as 'destroying of rape and grasses, in
cutting of ploughs and other instruments of husbandry, filling of rivers and
ditches. In spoyling of the Church, in breaking all the seats, and burning
them; breaking all the glasse windows, pulling down the lead of the Church
and steeple'.[38]

The immediate result was an order from the Lords on 10 December,
seeking to restrain further disorder,[39] and in February 1646 the issue was
taken up. The opponents of the drainage petitioned that they had been
trying to get a legal hearing for fifteen years. In response, the Lords ordered
that the proprietors' tenants pay their rent to the committee at Lincoln, to
be paid out to the winner when the legal title was finally tried. If there was
no trial or parliamentary ordinance confirming the proprietors' title within
a year then the tenants, having harvested that year's crop, should leave.
Meanwhile the commoners were reassured that the order restraining further
disturbances did not prevent them from using the land they currently had
access to. All this seems like a victory for the commoners, but the history of
violence continued to colour the dispute, and in March a counter-petition
to the Lords from the proprietors recounted that history once more.[40]

The following year there were more attacks on the drainage works and a
new legal claim from the commoners to regain all 7,400 acres: 'the Warr

being over, the Commoners intended to recover their Right legally, or els legally to have been evicted'.[41] Daniel Nodell, a gentleman recently settled in nearby Owston, and a former parliamentary officer, became the full-time solicitor for this claim and this may have been a source of some of the impetus.[42] It is clear, though, that this legal campaign went in tandem with continuing direct action, and that some local officeholders were complicit. In June 1647 there was a major confrontation, involving considerable physical intimidation and subsequent attacks on individuals and property. Nodell had played a leading part, gathering a large body of men to meet with the proprietors ostensibly to parley, although witnesses suggested that the purpose was primarily to intimidate, or even to murder. Nodell and two justices of the peace were ordered to appear at the Lords.[43] It was perhaps the cumulative pressure of this campaign that led some of the signatories of the 1636 agreement to try to back out, while many of the others had since died.[44] In November the inhabitants petitioned once again to allow the matter to come to a speedy trial—that having been delayed apparently by the intervention of the Lords.[45]

Matters seem to have rested there, a few minor incidents aside, until 1650 when a concerted attempt was made to clear the proprietors and their tenants out of the manor, reclaiming the 3,400 acres allocated to them. Attacks on the houses and outbuildings of the tenants were apparently intended simply to drive them from the land. Again Nodell appears to have been closely involved in this physical intimidation, and the commoners had the more or less open and active support of a local Justice of the Peace, Michael Monckton, who later became a Quaker, suggesting radical sympathies.[46]

It was at this point that Lilburne and Wildman became advocates for the commoners alongside Nodell. Lilburne had connections with Wildman already of course, and there may have been other connections arising from his military service—Epworth is only twelve miles from Tickhill, the castle which Lilburne had seized in defiance of the earl of Manchester, and Manchester had described it as defending access to the Isle of Axholme. Much of Lilburne's military service had been done between Newark and York, and troops in Manchester's army had been in the Isle in October 1644 during Lilburne's service. Nodell had also served in the Eastern Association army and it is not impossible that he had met Lilburne during that time.[47]

Then and since there has been controversy about how to interpret Lilburne's role in these disputes, in which physical violence featured so prominently. The turn to Wildman and Lilburne certainly coincided with renewed attempts to reach a legal settlement, as a number of commoners grouped together in test cases against the tenants of the proprietors. The proprietors responded once more by securing injunctions in the exchequer and, according to Lilburne, planned to drag out the legal process, some of them boasting 'That the Commoners should never have a Tryall at Law'.[48] In February 1651 an exchequer decree confirmed instead the division of the commons, but it was clear in advance that some of the commoners would not accept the adjudication, and when it was read out a number left before the reading was complete. Direct action continued, and it is here that opinions differed, and continue to differ, about the role of Nodell, Lilburne, and Wildman.[49]

Much of the anger centred again on the settlement at Sandtoft. John Mylner claimed that the previous October eight or nine men with clubs, staves, shovels, and spades had struck some men dead and 'beate [him] almost dead in his owne garden soe that hee hath never beene his owne man to this day'. In May he was taken prisoner and carried twenty-six miles to a Justice of the Peace. In June 1651 more than eighty houses were pulled down, including that of the minister, along with barns and stables. Mylner and his family were left homeless, forced to sleep for much of the summer on a dry dike with his own three children and four others. This did not end the harassment, however: 'they came by in the morneing & evening with fire in theire hands and flung the fire amongst them & said wee will roote you out, you shall stay noe longer there'. Others testified that they had been offered the chance to stay in their houses if they would agree to pay rent to the commoners. There was plenty of testimony that Wildman, Lilburne, and Nodell had been involved in organizing this violence, but no concrete evidence was offered, and all three denied leading it.[50]

In his published account of the commoners' cause Lilburne was apologetic, and unsympathetic to this violence:

> it must be confessed that some of the Inhabitants..., especially of the poorer sort,...were impatient and took their possession of the whole by force of multitudes, as they lost it by force, and in their rage...did foolishly throw down many poor houses, that the Drainers had built for their Tenants upon the inclosed ground.

This 'folly of the multitude none of the most discreet Commoners and tenants of the Isle do justifie'. They, having found the grounds now vacant, had peaceably entered them, and 'desire nothing but a legal trial'.[51] While this may reflect Lilburne's view of the importance of legal resolution, however, contemporaries and modern historians have detected a much broader basis for the use of club law than simply the poorer sort.[52]

At last there was an exchequer order to hear the case, and a jury was empanelled in Lincolnshire[53] and this seems to have reinvigorated the commoners' faith in their representatives. The same month Lilburne and Wildman received a 999-year lease of 2,000 acres of common land in return for 'a settling of a peace and to p[ro]tect them from suites in regard of a great Charge that they had heretofore'. Nodell received 200 acres for services already rendered and to take on a trial of title, after which Lilburne and Wildman were to seek an Act of Parliament recognizing the commoners' title. Following the attacks on Sandtoft in June, and despite his claimed disapproval of the violence, Lilburne had taken possession of the damaged minister's house.[54]

Wildman now went to London to lobby there, leaving Lilburne to organize the 2,000 acres. On 19 October 1651 Lilburne, Nodell, and others went to the church in Sandtoft where Nodell spoke to the minister in Latin, perhaps because the minister was French and this was their shared tongue. Lilburne said to the minister and congregation 'this is our Comon, you shall come here noe more unles you be stronger than wee'. The witness, John Amory (one of the French settlers), claimed that Lilburne had 'lads' and men with him, with swords at their sides. They stood at the door of the church in order to 'awe' those who came in. Having prevented the minister from preaching Lilburne then prayed and preached in his place. Later, they 'made a Cowhouse of the Church and spoyled it, hewed downe the pulpit, tooke downe the windowes and totally defaced the church'. From that point it was used to store hay. This was attested by a number of witnesses, but not his claim that an ox had been slaughtered there, and hung up in the church on the orders of Nodell and Lilburne, which was asserted by only one witness.[55]

Much of this was contested and the testimony is hard to evaluate: there were accusations of partisan political bias (Nodell was a committed parliamentarian, who had taken the Engagement, Gibbon, the chief figure on the other side, was said to be sympathetic to royalism and to the Scots); and it was also said that some witnesses would change their testimony for cash.[56] It is hard to see Lilburne's behaviour as particularly edifying, or high-minded, but it may have been that in this very tense situation he was a moderating influence. One of the tenants of the Drainers said that

Nodell was passionate on behalf of the tenants and the February decree, but that Lilburne had told him 'hee should not bee passionate for they would have the more advantage against us'. He had identified himself with the commoners on the basis of his newly awarded lease ('our commons'), and demonstrated that they had force at their disposal, but he had perhaps restrained Nodell. The violence with which he was directly associated was against the fabric of the church, and the disruption of communion—a symbolic attack on the Sandtoft community, rather than the violence against persons and property more generally earlier in the year. It may also have had a more precise legal purpose too: the plan for the 2,000 acres included division into four parishes—the opponents of the drainage were here wiping Sandtoft off the map in order to establish a new pattern of settlement based on their title. The strategy seems in fact to have been to deny the proprietors and their tenants 'quiet possession', and to establish their own: Lilburne and others tried to secure rent payments to the commoners, and the rioters also destroyed leases held by the tenants. This use of 'club law' in the course of a property dispute was rather like that suffered by Richard Lilburne in the long-running dispute at the family seat in Thickley Punchardon, in which both sides aimed ultimately at a legal settlement.[57]

In the past this has been seen as an extension of Lilburne's Leveller activity and, according to his detractors, a product of his ambitions for social levelling. Lilburne's public advocacy was eminently conventional and respectable, however, even if he may not have been blameless in the violence on the Isle. *The case of the tenants* sets out a history of the dispute which emphasizes throughout the desire for a legal settlement. There is no socially levelling language, and in fact as we have seen Lilburne equated impatience and disorder with the poorer sort in a way that was utterly conventional among seventeenth-century gentlemen. There is no rhetorical escalation of the kind he indulged in with respect to his own disputes over reparations, and instead there is straightforward advocacy. He contested the claim that the drainage benefitted the commoners, setting out how local farming practice had been affected, and discounted the argument that the drainers should be recompensed for the cut they had made through Epworth—that had been essential to their works elsewhere, and had not been intended for the benefit of the manor. He admitted that the commoners had gone beyond the law in the past, but insisted that they 'shall be ready and willing to submit to the judgement of the law in the Case'.[58]

By the summer of 1651 Lilburne was apparently quite active as an advocate, securing plaintiffs their legal rights and offering his family the hope of a secure living. By this time he was representing his uncle George in a dispute over sequestered lands before the parliamentary committee at Haberdashers Hall, and earlier in the summer he had represented John Fielder who had fallen foul of Parliament's Indemnity Committee in Surrey. That committee had powers to intervene in legal disputes to protect servants of the state from malicious prosecutions, enforcing the kind of protections that the army had been seeking in 1647 at the point where its campaign had overlapped with the mobilization for an *Agreement of the People*. He had been helped by Gerrard Winstanley in an earlier round of the dispute. Now though, Fielder, or Lilburne on his behalf, claimed that the committee had intervened in a private matter, overturning a verdict reached before a jury at the Surrey Assizes. Lilburne's speech to the committee on the subject of the 'People's Freedom' was published in October.[59] Despite the violence in Epworth then, there is every sign that respectable advocacy, drawing on his skills in the world of parliamentary committees, lobbying, and print, was at least one part of his plans for the future.

It has to be said, however, that the respectable tone adopted in Epworth stands in some contrast to two petitions written the previous year on behalf of commoners in nearby Holland and Kesteven, which are also attributed to Lilburne. Those petitions are suffused with familiar rhetoric about fundamental rights, tyranny, and oppression. They cite Magna Carta and Parliament's *Book of Declarations* in a characteristic way, inverting the accusation of social levelling by claiming that it was the projectors (those behind the plans for the drainage scheme), not their opponents, who were destroying property. This later added to suspicions that his advocacy posed a threat to social and political order.[60] Nodell had certainly been interested in a wider campaign, telling commoners that 'he would have Colonel Lilburne to go into Yorkshire Hatfield and Thorne, and to do there as they had done in Lincolnshire and they should give the Attorney General work enough'. The fact that the legal case was weaker there did not matter: 'we will make something of it'. In particular, Lilburne was being tempted into the dispute over property rights in the manor of Crowle by Jasper Margrave, and again he was accused of being willing to use coercion to get people to pay rents to Margrave and others. Nodell was reported to have been more ambitious too: 'they would obey no order that should come but try it att Lawe and would try it as oft they would and saith theire Case would bee a leading Case for all the fennes in England'.[61]

There has therefore been a persistent suspicion that Lilburne was up to more than he was admitting. One strand of the promises to the tenants was that the law was not settled, that there might soon be another Parliament, and one in which Lilburne would be influential. This shaded into denials of the legitimacy of the current authorities, at least if some of the witnesses were to be believed. The Council of State, clearly suspicious, wrote to the sheriff in July, noting that there had been 'riotous and tumultuous gatherings' about the Epworth commons. Such meetings should not be allowed, and the law invoked so that 'by the punishment of some, others may be deterred'. Diligent care was needed 'in such times as these' to prevent 'meetings of the multitude'. The worry was that such pretences might be a prompt 'to begin insurrections, and carry on designs to the interruption of the public peace'. If the local forces could not be relied upon the sheriff was given the power to bring in forces from elsewhere.[62]

Given his history, Lilburne's actions were now inevitably going to carry a political charge. Sir John Maynard, who had spoken in favour Lilburne's release from the Tower in 1648, was involved in opposition to the drainage, a cause later taken over by his son.[63] In representing Fielder before the Indemnity Committee, Lilburne had inflated claims about the specific case to the more abstract issues about the rights of freeborn Englishmen which had informed his interpretation of the Engagement. He was shortly to do the same in his advocacy for his uncle George, with catastrophic personal consequences. Even in Epworth it is not completely clear whether he, Nodell, and Wildman could not or simply would not restrain the violence. It is perhaps significant that much of the evidence about Lilburne's involvement in 1651 comes from an enquiry in 1653, when Lilburne was on trial for his life once more. In that trial a central issue was whether he was simply seeking his legal rights as a freeborn Englishman, or was a turbulent and subversive spirit who posed a permanent threat to the stability of the government. That seems to have inflected what people wanted to know, or say, about his involvement in Epworth: one witness deposed that Lilburne had written to Nodell claiming that he could raise 30,000 men if, as Parliament intended at the end of 1651, he was to be banished from England.[64]

What we can say with certainty is that Lilburne's name is not on the more radical and confrontational petitions from Hatfield: his *public* advocacy in the Fens was much more limited in its claims, as befits a man aiming to secure a 1,000-acre estate through a legal settlement of the disputed titles in the manor. While commoners elsewhere took advantage of the rhetoric of the times to present themselves in new ways, the Epworth case is made in thoroughly conventional, and respectable, terms. He signed himself a free holder of the manor and denounced the folly of the multitude: he presented himself as a champion of the due process of law against prerogative right and in preference to club law.[65]

If Lilburne did not present this as a revolutionary movement behind a Leveller programme, however, it was nonetheless a distinctive product of the crisis of the 1640s. The leadership of the local middling sort was crucial in Epworth and rested on a legal knowledge that did not come from Lilburne, Nodell, and Wildman. What those three offered instead was knowledge about lobbying the rapidly growing parliamentary bureaucracy. Nodell was clear that changes of regime offered new legal opportunities, while one commoner revealed that Lilburne had been attractive to them as an advocate because he 'was a powerful man, & hee having freinds would give a sooner end to the business which would take off the Clamour of the Inhabitants'. Part of the menace detected by the government was the power to affect Parliament that Nodell apparently boasted: 'there is none I hope in the house but friends John Lilburne, Wyldeman & my selfe have made our Case knowne to the Parliam[en]t & they looke but lightly of us but wee will have it printed and nayle it upp uppon the Parliament doors & make an outcry and if they will not heare us over will pull them out by the eares'.[66] It would not have been possible for the commoners' fathers or grandfathers to talk or act in quite this way, and these forms of active citizenship reveal something of the transformations of the relationship between central and local government in the revolutionary decades.

For Lilburne's part, the legal defence of particular interests in this new world of parliamentary committees was easily reconciled to his view of the Commonwealth as consisting of the legal people of the nation and their established legal rights. This kind of advocacy on behalf freeborn Englishmen, in their personal legal battles, might have been the grounds for a new career consistent with his political principles, even if he had not managed to secure his 1,000 acres in the Fens.[67]

The Lilburnes and Sir Arthur Hesilrige, 1645–51

Lilburne took credit for quietly accepting the quashing of his election to the Common Council and the refusal to admit him to the Temple, while his rhetoric (and probably also his actions) in Epworth had not been inflammatory. However, his ability to see issues of fundamental political significance in the detail of his own sufferings was to get him into really deep trouble once more, in disputes that took him away from the Isle of Axholme and, in fact, into exile.

Lilburne was assertive about the dignity of his background, and had a family to provide for, and there was no necessary conflict between pursuing his own interests and his broader concern for the rights of the freeborn Englishman. His position was now much improved—he had possession of an estate in Durham, taken from the lands of the Dean and Chapter, and had hopes of securing another 1,000 acres in the Fens. But he blamed the many obstacles he had faced in achieving this position on influential men—notably Sir Henry Vane senior and, latterly, Sir Arthur Hesilrige—and he continued to experience frustrations at their hands.

At the same time his uncle was also meeting obstructions in building his business interests, from many of the same people. George Lilburne seems to have been an abrasive businessman, whose interests were persistently found to be suspect. One of his religious opponents had accused him of hypocrisy, contrasting a case of alleged horse theft and a record of excessive drinking with George's strictures about the Sabbath. His enemies also found the variety of his business interests disreputable: 'His trades are Infinite, chandler, grocer, mercer, linnen Draper…fermer of Coliary, fermour of Land, Keelman, Brewer & which is the calling that he stands to I wonder? Or whether do all these make up but one calling?'[68] John owed a lot to his uncle, of course. In 1641, when John had been at odds with his father (whose own land disputes were threatened by his son's trouble with the regime), it was George who had set him up as a brewer. By the late 1640s they were not in close political agreement: George helped organize a petition calling for the king's trial, something about which John was more hesitant, and there are signs throughout the 1640s that he remained a supporter of a strict Presbyterian settlement, although his sympathies with the Scots seem to have evaporated in 1648 when renewed warfare brought another Scottish invasion of the north.[69]

Whatever their differences about politics, however, they had enemies in common. George, like John, contrasted his own convictions and sacrifices with the behaviour of others, and in particular he carried a grudge about the alleged lukewarmness of Sir Henry Vane, senior (Fig. 6.2), which had cost Parliament control of the north in 1642. John had his own grievances with Vane, not least that he had been a member of the Star Chamber court that punished him in 1638. When Lilburne had first become embroiled in conflict with Colonel King and with Bastwick and Prynne, however, Vane

Fig. 6.2. Sir Henry Vane the elder (1589–1655)

had supported Lilburne. For Vane, he was an ally in parliamentary attacks on Denzil Holles, the prominent Presbyterian, and he had probably been help-ful in getting Lilburne released from prison in June 1645, following his committal by the Committee of Examinations for his letter to Prynne. It is clear, though, that it had been an alliance of convenience. When Lilburne's attempts to secure payment of his reparations stalled in April he blamed Vane.[70] Payment of his reparations then 'lay asleep'[71] until September 1648, and he again thought Vane had a significant hand in that.

This hostility to Vane was shared by John's father Richard and his brother Robert too. Vane was Parliament's Lord Lieutenant in Durham and both John and George thought he and his son, Henry junior, were opportunists.[72] Following the Scottish invasion of 1643, parliamentary control of the north-east had offered local supporters the chance to recover or establish their influence. Both George and Richard appeared regularly on Durham committees and commissions from the mid-1640s onwards, and they evidently used their position on the County Committee to challenge

Sir William Armyne, the principal commissioner in the north and an ally of Vane's, suggesting that they themselves were not averse to the accumulation of local power and influence.[73] By 1645, they saw Henry Vane as an obstruction to their interests in the north-east, and in that year were apparently gathering evidence about his political reliability.[74]

An important route to financial recovery after the war was through the profits from sequestered royalist estates, and the local coal mines were very tempting in this respect. George had been building up interests in the coal mines in the early 1640s and was involved in a number of suits in relation to Lambton where, his tenants claimed, he had demanded what turned out to be unrealistic rents. At least one of them said that this was because production was disrupted by the war, particularly in 1644 when the Scottish and royalist armies were both present.[75] In July 1644 George had been among those awarded control of delinquents' collieries, and this created further frictions. In fact, by the mid-1640s a number of local gentlemen, seeking to benefit from the parliamentary victory, were showing that they had sharp elbows. For example, George had ruled against a local gentleman, John Blakiston, in a property dispute in 1647. Blakiston had then taken revenge by publicly accusing George of using his position to accumulate land. In the event the committee accepted George's honesty in the matter, and further confrontation was delayed by John's imprisonment and trial, following the publication of *England's new chains discovered*.[76] Nonetheless, it was symptomatic of the tensions among the victors in County Durham, and John's own obstruction at the hands of Vane clearly intersected with these local political battles.

These overlapping conflicts had also begun to create open conflict between George and Hesilrige, and again this seemed to be connected with John's frustrations. Early in 1649 his frustration with Hesilrige had led to a threat of violence.[77] For his part, George traced Hesilrige's hostility back to his refusal to follow Hesilrige's will in his office as surveyor of bishops' lands, relating to a dispute with Edward Colston over the falsification of records. The battle lines among the various parties were similar in that dispute to those in a dispute between John Musgrave and John Barwis, also in the mid-1640s. Musgrave had produced a series of pamphlets which escalated into attacks on parliamentary privilege and accusations of treason. John Lilburne seems to have had a hand in those disputes, offering advice on the use of print and, seemingly, offering something of a model for their political vocabulary. The list of Musgrave's enemies contains some familiar names too: Sir Thomas Widdrington and John Blakiston, for example.[78] Behind these men, it seemed increasingly clear, stood Hesilrige.

For his part, Hesilrige seems to have decided early on that the Lilburnes were 'stiff obstinate men, and opposed old Sir *Henry Vane*, and Sir *William Armin*, and in time will oppose me'. John's defence of his father and uncle suggests something of what Hesilrige might have disliked: he claimed that Hesilrige could not accept their 'old honest blunt way...in doing their duty without favour or affection'.[79] There had been several flashpoints during the 1640s. George claimed, for example, that Hesilrige had imposed an excise on coals exported from Newcastle without parliamentary sanction. George refused to impose a similar duty on exports from Sunderland, but was for his part accused of seeking an obvious commercial advantage for his coal interests in the rival port. When George accused Blakiston of protecting his dubious allies from sequestration, the issue was heard before Hesilrige's Committee, and John directly accused Hesilrige of partiality in Blakiston's favour. As we have seen, when John was granted reparations in 1648 it had been resisted by Blakiston, and following his arrest in 1649 Hesilrige allowed two men to compound with the authorities, thereby regaining possession of their lands and denying John his cash. He had also stopped John's rents from the other estate. Lilburne's brother Henry fought for the royalists in 1648, a defection John blamed on his experience of serving Parliament under Hesilrige; and his other brother, Robert, had been ousted from his place as governor of Newcastle by the rapacious Hesilrige.[80]

★ ★ ★

Increasingly central to these battles was possession of the coal seams at Harraton, which were quite a prize: Harraton was the richest colliery on the Wear. In February 1645, Sir Lionel Madison had written to Henry Vane noting that Thomas Wray, 'a grand papist and delinquent had gone away'. As a Catholic, Wray was barred from making a composition and regaining possession, so this opened the prospect of a struggle for control of the pits. Madison flagged not only his own preliminary interest, but also the ambitions of George Lilburne and others in that respect. He recommended to Vane that he offer £100 to £200 per pit in order to secure Harraton 'from others' and also to prevent the sequestration committee taking all the profits meanwhile.[81]

Since Wray no longer had possession, the land was held for the benefit of the state. Some people claimed, however, that Wray's title to the colliery was dubious and so not all the colliery was now in the hands of the state. In particular, Josiah Primatt, described as a leather seller and citizen of London, claimed that he held a forty-one-year lease on a significant part of the colliery, agreed in 1629, and that Wray had only held one-quarter of the colliery. The issue was genuinely complicated, as differing claims were made about different seams, and there was even some difference of opinion about how many seams there were. But George Lilburne and George Grey had entered possession of the colliery as tenants of Primatt, and their landlord claimed that they had rescued the mine from ruin following disastrous floods in 1640 in which fifty men had died. This was in 1647, and the following year they had suffered further losses to fire and flood. Their investment had made the pits workable and also established some claim to the profits. Their opponents, by contrast, claimed that they had simply taken property for their own use that should have been sequestered from Wray for the benefit of the state. The difficulty of proving the title rested in part on the differences over the number and names of the seams, and the title for each of them.

A new round of conflict apparently opened at least partly as an element of the recriminations over the second civil war. Thomas Shadforth, who had appeared on Durham committees alongside Richard and George Lilburne throughout the 1640s, was suddenly suspect, having been accused of prudently staying out of the conflict until after the parliamentary victory at Preston. In response he resurrected accusations of delinquency against George Lilburne, on grounds that appear very dubious and which George had answered on previous occasions. In the subsequent dispute, though, accusations of corruption against George were also repeated: that he and his allies on the Sequestration Committee 'had procured many leases to himself and others . . . at low rates, giving in no accounts, or unjust ones, and buying their goods at very low values, to the gain of £10,000'. Some of the accusations related to Ford Manor[82] but, presumably in the light of all this, the colliery was seized from Lilburne and Grey by Hesilrige and his son-in-law Colonel George Fenwick in 1649. They also rehearsed the accusations of corruption against Lilburne and Grey.[83]

On 20 October 1649, Thomas Midford and Richard Lilburne had dissented from the Durham sequestration committee's decision to lease out the whole colliery because part of it should not have been under sequestration. They did so on behalf of John Levitt and Josiah Primatt. At the same time, John Hedworth, George Grey's son-in-law, claimed that part of the colliery had been entailed to him, and so that part could not be sequestered either. In response to the complexity of the disputes about title, and the connections between the parties and men prominent in the local parliamentary administration, the County Committee gave three months to Hedworth to prove his title and, in response to Primatt, to certify who had been in possession of the colliery at the time it was seized. In the meantime, it was difficult to find any takers for the lease, so the committee let the colliery to Francis Hacker and others for five years at an easy rate.

A key figure in deciding these issues was Hesilrige, who chaired the sequestration committee in Durham and also the national committee at Haberdasher's Hall. By 1649, John Lilburne had been so appalled by Hesilrige that, on the eve of his trial, he had denounced him as a traitor. He said that Hesilrige held an arbitrary power, the consequence of having established himself as lord paramount, not least by chairing both the sequestration and militia committees without parliamentary warrant. Through that arbitrary power he was keeping Durham in slavery: something manifest in the injustices suffered by all the Lilburnes.[84] Having reached this view he challenged George and his father to denounce Hesilrige publicly, hoping thereby to flush him out and remove the obstacles to his own interests.[85] John protested to his uncle that

> his crimes should not be my ruine; and therefore if he would not endeavor to bring his business to a final trial,...I would become prosecutor in the States behalf, to bring him to his deserts; but if he knew himself clear, and would endeavor his justification by a final Tryal, I would venter my life and estate with him, and become his Agent to mannage his business for him.[86]

By settling the disputes between Hesilrige and George Lilburne one way or the other, he would clear the way for the pursuit of his own interests in Hesilrige's fiefdom. With this aim in mind he now became directly involved in this battle, particularly over the title to Harraton.

Although his religious and political commitments were not irrelevant to all this, and it seems clear that Lilburne was the victim of injustice, there is an element of these conflicts that was more routine—at root, it was a dispute over assets seized from the enemy and rewards for service, we might almost say a tussle over the spoils of war. That view fits George Lilburne very well, who was later accused of gouging his tenants at Harraton. John was also, in these years (and again quite reasonably), protecting his business interests.

★   ★   ★

In early 1651 this seems to have remained a matter of gentry squabbling rather than anything more dangerous, and John's reconciliation with Cromwell seems to have continued. During 1650 Cromwell had helped him secure payment of his reparations and had invited him to dinner as he led his army north to Scotland. Lilburne wrote to Cromwell in January 1651, thanking him for his 'late signall & most remarkabell freindly carradge' towards him in Parliament and the Council of State, on Cromwell's last day in London before leaving for Scotland. Lilburne said his conscience was clear of 'either directly or indirectly ploting, contriving or acting any thing to the ruine of the publique' or of any man 'intrusted with the mannadgment of its affairs'. He ended with a considerable flourish, announcing his personal loyalty, but it is clear that rumours circulating about his intentions had made Lilburne anxious.[87] There are signs in fact that Lilburne was being actively helpful to the regime—in May 1651 he exhibited two informations against delinquents to the Committee for the Advance of Money, on behalf of his brother. One of them was against Philip Jermyn, who had been a judge in the 1649 treason trial, so perhaps this work brought some personal pleasure as well as a sense of public service.[88]

Whatever service he was doing the Commonwealth in the summer of 1651, however, John was soon to run out friends and protectors, as his confrontation with Hesilrige, in alliance with George, came to a head. In February 1651, a hearing about Harraton had been ordered at which Hesilrige was to be present. The matter continued to drag out between April and July, finally reaching an impasse when the Committee for Compounding was equally divided, and therefore unable to give a decision.[89] George, meanwhile, had petitioned Parliament, setting out his record of loyal service and complaining about the malicious accusations of delinquency that had dogged him for four years. He begged a speedy judgement and seems to have found favour: the House referred the petition, saying that if nothing else could be charged against him then the accusation of delinquency should be dismissed. Henry Marten, a long-term ally of Lilburne's, counted the votes in George's favour.[90]

Lilburne, acting as his uncle's advocate, seems to have lost patience, however, and went into print. *A just reproof to Haberdashers-Hall*, published on 2 August 1651, denounced the committee in resounding terms, charging that it had been subject to undue influence. He set out the history of the dispute over Harraton along with the many other ways in which Hesilrige had sought the destruction of the Lilburne family. The pamphlet reproduced numerous committee papers, petitions, statements, and administrative orders relating to Harraton, but concluded with extravagant denunciations of Hesilrige personally. Along with his associates he had 'exercised an arbitrary and tyrannicall power over us, against and without law'. In doing this without any parliamentary order he threatened 'their ruine and destruction, by alienating (as much as in him lyes) the peoples hearts and affections from them'. He likened Hesilrige's crimes to those charged against Cardinal Wolsey and repeated the charge several times that Hesilrige was worse than the earl of Strafford—one of the more inflammatory claims of the *Preparative to an hue and cry*. Hesilrige had encouraged Lilburne's tenants to resist him and thereby rendered his lands potentially not 'worth unto me one groat, the tenants rebelling both against the State and me'. By these means Hesilrige had reduced them to something near the status of French peasants 'that can call nothing they buy or work for their own, longer then their Lords and Master please to let them injoy it'.[91] Local feelings were evidently also running high by this point, and Hedworth, Grey, and Ralph Rokesby cut the ropes of the water pits, flooding the mine workings at Harraton—presumably to prevent others profiting from what they regarded as their property.[92]

Despite the strength of his language, there were no immediate consequences for Lilburne, and publication of the *Just reproof* might have been treated as an irritation, but not one worth escalating. Robert Lilburne was an increasingly influential army officer, and during these summer months there was an escalating security problem. In August 1651 the Scots had invaded England and Robert was involved in the action in Lancashire, against the forces raised by the earl of Derby. Robert won a total victory in August which did his reputation further good, and although he never seems to have mentioned it (which is uncharacteristic), it is possible that John saw service with his brother that summer.[93] In any case, following what looked like the final defeat of the Scots and of Charles II at the battle of Worcester on 3 September 1651, Cromwell had again entertained Lilburne at his house in the Cockpit.[94] There was no love lost between Cromwell and Hesilrige, in fact.

For his part, Hesilrige seems to have pursued the grudge with Lilburne by relatively low-key means, having a hand in an escalation of Lilburne's dispute with his tenants. This was, perhaps, an attempt to embarrass him into silence, or at least to become more circumspect about casting the first stone. Lilburne had apparently been pursuing his family and business interests with some single-mindedness. He had raised the rents on his newly acquired estates and as a result became embroiled in conflict with recalcitrant tenants. Two of them were out of lease and Lilburne wanted to acquire their farms for his own family. One tenant, William Huntington, was particularly obdurate in defence of his own interests. He claimed that his tenancy was his wife's tenant right, unaffected by sequestration. It also seems that they had had a better offer lined up before lands were awarded to Lilburne—another potential beneficiary had agreed to let them have part of their tenancy back on very favourable terms—and so Lilburne's stewardship of their lease offered them far less than they had hoped for.[95] Huntington proved very effective at using print and parliamentary committees to fight for his rights in the autumn of 1651—in exactly the way that Lilburne was at that moment encouraging the inhabitants of Epworth to do. Huntington in fact succeeded in causing Lilburne no little embarrassment, perhaps with some help from Hesilrige.

In order to persuade Huntington to leave the farm Lilburne offered him £5 for the corn that was sown, and to take one of Huntington's stepsons into his own care until he was twenty, in order to relieve pressure on the Huntington household. Alternatively, he suggested that they might stay as tenants, at the old rent, so long as they would actually pay it. They continued to resist, however, and in June 1651 the Committee for Removing Obstructions in the Sale of Deans and Chapters Lands ordered Huntington to pay all arrears of rent and to quit possession. Despite further attempts at mediation Lilburne was, on his own account, reduced to forcing Huntington from the land.[96]

In November, Huntington delivered a printed petition to the House of Commons—using the tactics of public shaming against one of the masters of the technique. His rhetoric was nicely tuned, again turning tables on a master of this kind of publicity:

> May it...move your godly Hearts to pity the sad and deplorable Condition of your Petitioner, who now stands deprived of all his Livelyhood and Subsistence, the said M. *Lilborn* leaving him nothing but a poor sickly Woman and five small children, and not a Cows milk to stay their hungry hearts.

Lilburne had been ferocious, he said. No sooner had he perfected his conveyance of the lands he 'immediately thrusts' Huntington's family out, and most 'barbarously and tyrannically, against Law and Equity' took possession of corn, cows, hay, and other stock.[97]

Huntington had gone to Hesilrige for protection, and Lilburne saw Hesilrige's hand in this canny lobbying in London, including perhaps writing the petition for him. Lilburne later called Huntington Hesilrige's 'gross Knave'.[98] It is of a piece, perhaps, with Hesilrige's apparent silence in 1649, when he seems to have allowed Cuthbert Sydenham to do his talking for him.[99] The timing was acutely judged too, or at least fortuitous: it was the same week that Lilburne published the case for the tenants of the manor of Epworth, a cause in which he had a 1,000-acre stake.

Lilburne, clearly getting a dose of his own medicine, was robust in reply to Huntington's 'false and lying petition'. He asked for a hearing before Parliament, claiming that Huntington had been made poor not by Lilburne but 'by his own letcherous baseness in conversing with Whores, and getting of Bastards'. He had tried all fair ways before going to legal extremity, as any man would who 'would maintain his right'. Local sympathies seem to have been against him though and Lilburne had tried to court local public opinion. Finding himself there one Sunday he opened the church (which had been shut up and sequestered), preached a sermon, and then gave his version of the dispute from the pulpit. In response to rumours that there was 'hard dealing by me to some of my Tenants' he had offered to arbitrate the disputes before witnesses.[100] The dispute rumbled on for several more years.

In the meantime, there were further delays in getting a resolution to the Harraton dispute. At one hearing Arthur Hesilrige had questioned John about the *Preparative to an hue and cry*, and a long exchange had resulted in the now familiar challenge for an open hearing and arbitration. Delays settling the dispute over Harraton had been caused in October by the County Committee's slowness in assessing the damage done by Hedworth and his fellows when they drowned the pit, and proceedings clearly dragged on after that. New parties registered their interest on 12 November, but on 26 November Lilburne was expecting a final judgement the following Tuesday (2 December).[101] When the judgement was eventually given it supported Hesilrige's action, perhaps rather predictably, and it was at this point that the dispute finally escalated to a pitch that caused outrage in Parliament.

In these years, then, Lilburne seems to have been preoccupied with the relatively mundane stuff of gentry rivalry and battles for land and preeminence. Reparations and compensation had been an essential feature of Lilburne's family well-being, and in fact continued to be so after his death. It was also inevitable that, given the circumstances, pursuing these interests would entail engaging with the parliamentary administration, and therefore embroilment in its politics. He had never been able to enter the wool trade, and his time as a brewer had been cut short by his war service. Without an estate, or trade, he and his family depended on recompense for the sufferings that had prevented him from acquiring either. His wider family had also suffered losses in the war and had sought to repair them by profiting from the victory. That embroiled them too in the world of parliamentary committees, with their extensive powers over property and publicly held assets. However, the men who had frustrated the Lilburne family could be seen as prime examples of the dangers of oligarchy—rather than self-denying representatives, the betrusted, they were men entrenched in Parliament, its committees, and the army. It was not completely outlandish to claim that his sufferings were a local example of the very general threat posed by men with entrenched political power, such as Hesilrige. Nonetheless, there is some irony in his wrangles with his own tenants and, of course, the charge of profiteering was equally easy to direct against the Lilburnes.

Confrontation and banishment, 1651–2

Despite the insecurities of the regime, not least renewed military conflict with the Scots, Lilburne's increasingly strident denunciation of Hesilrige had not forced a confrontation. In fact, during 1651 Lilburne seems to have been actively helpful to the regime in minor ways, and to have been on cordial terms with Cromwell. However, the feud with Hesilrige escalated, with spectacular consequences, when Josiah Primatt presented a petition to Parliament on 23 December complaining about the corruption of justice in his case.

The petition briefly set out his case, and claimed that it was simply being ignored: he could get no justice because of 'the Power and Influence of the said Sir *Arthur*'. A proper hearing had been delayed and the ordinary course of justice through the courts denied to him. When it did finally come to a hearing Sir Arthur had attended every day, pleading against Primatt, 'which is humbly conceived to be contrary to Law, he being a Member of the supreme Authority'. He also prejudged the case, directing 'the said Commissioners what to judge therein'. As a consequence, he had 'over-awed most of them'. Following the full hearing he had 'kept private Correspondence with some of the said Commissioners' to the detriment of Primatt's case. Under this pressure, the majority of the commissioners 'not daring . . . to oppose the Will and Pleasure of the said Sir *Arthur*, have, contrary to clear Evidence before them . . . refused to relieve him'. In fact they had done what Hesilrige told them to, and Primatt's only possible remedy now lay with Parliament. Accordingly, he asked them 'to provide for your Petitioner's Relief from the Oppression and Tyranny of the said Sir *Arthur Heslerigg*, and for the Dispensation of Justice, without Fear or Favour; as to your Wisdoms shall seem most just'.[102]

The House was immediately concerned. Primatt was called in and asked if he admitted that he was the author, and questioned further about its printing. He named Newcombe, the printer who had testified in Lilburne's trial two years earlier. Asked who had helped him draw up the petition he named Wildman among others, and affirmed that those who had advised him had all agreed that he should present it. Lilburne was called in to answer whether he had had a hand in distributing the petition. Lilburne admitted that he had distributed it to members of the House, including Hesilrige and Fenwick. Pressed to answer if he had distributed it to people who were not members, he said he had delivered it to 'divers who desired to read it'. This was crucial to assessing the legitimacy of a petition, as we have seen: in this instance it distinguished a request to the House to hear a grievance from a public denunciation of one of its more eminent members. Lilburne also confessed that he had been employed by Primatt and George Lilburne 'from the beginning in managing this Business', and had directed the printing. Although he had not written it, he had been there when it was written, and 'liked it well'. A committee was appointed to consider the charges made in the petition.[103] A little over two weeks later the House asked the committee to consider the 'plotting, contriving, printing, and publishing' of the petition. The motion was passed comfortably.[104]

On 15 January the whole matter was considered, with startling results. First the House heard and dismissed all the charges made against Hesilrige, agreeing that the petition was not just false, but malicious. As a consequence, the 'Printing, Publishing and Dispersing of this Petition, both before and since it was preferred to the Parliament, is an high Breach of Privilege'. As the January gloom descended, candles were brought in and the House turned its attention to the punishment for this scandal. Primatt was fined a total of £7,000 (£3,000 to the use of the Commonwealth and £4,000 in damages to various parties, including £2,000 to Hesilrige). He was committed to the Fleet until it was paid.[105]

Lilburne's punishment was still more dramatic. He was fined the same amounts but was banished from England, Scotland, and Ireland, and the islands and territories belonging to them, 'and not to return into any of them, upon pain of being proceeded against as a Felon, and in case of such Return, shall suffer Death, accordingly'. He was given thirty days to leave.[106] As Lilburne later pointed out this was in itself unjust—he was merely Primatt's accessory and yet had been punished more severely.[107]

Neither Primatt nor Lilburne had been formally charged, they had not been allowed to answer, and had not been heard in their own defence. They were simply called to attend to hear their sentences the following Tuesday. More was to come though. On the following day, 16 January, the House heard a committee report about *A just reproof*, a book that Lilburne had admitted before the committee was his. Several passages were read, which the House agreed contained 'Matter false, scandalous and malicious'. It was to be burned by the common hangman, along with Primatt's petition. George Lilburne and George Grey were called in to account for their profits from Harraton colliery, and further enquiries ordered into the authorship of Primatt's petition, along with petitions from commoners in Hatfield Chase in the Fens, and from 'well affected Citizens'.[108] This interest in the fenland petition suggests very clearly that Lilburne was suspected of agitating more widely—the report that resulted from the parliamentary order included testimony about Nodell and Lilburne's willingness to escalate the dispute in Axholme, as well as their comments about the legitimacy of the current Parliament and the expectation of a new one. It also paid close attention to their role in the violence. Lilburne's speech in favour of Fielder had also been published in October, with its ringing assertion that the people's rights were in play in the conduct of the Indemnity Committee.[109]

When Lilburne attended to hear his sentence 'he was commanded to kneel, but he obstinately denied'. As a result he was ordered to withdraw, and the time he had to leave the country was reduced by ten days. Having knelt and heard his sentence Primatt was committed to the Fleet.[110] On 20 January a petition was presented on Lilburne's behalf, calling for the sentence to be quashed and for a full legal hearing of the cause that lay behind it. On 28 January Lilburne published a remonstrance reporting the petition and claiming that 'his affection to the Parliament, and zeal to the publick freedom, renders all forrein Nations so unsafe to him as that (in effect) he is banished into a wilderness and exposed naked to the fury of Bears and Lyons'. It also laid out all the legal objections to this latest injustice.[111] But it was to no avail. After some further discussion and a little redrafting, the Act banishing Lilburne was passed on 30 January.[112]

Lilburne thought Cromwell had been crucial to this and had intervened to ensure that the Act of Banishment had been passed. An insider had told him that Cromwell had 'decreed' the sentence before a cabal of seven or eight MPs in his own chamber several days before it was actually passed. Following the presentation of the petition on 20 January, spirits had been flagging, but Cromwell, speaking on another issue, had pronounced the sentence 'as righteous … as ever was passed by this house'. Perhaps then, and certainly later, there were MPs who doubted it was a legitimate piece of legislation.[113] Lilburne claimed that Cromwell had told Elizabeth that the sentence appeared disproportionate because it reflected the fact that other things were feared from him:[114] rumours had apparently circulated earlier in the year that he, Wildman, and Henry Marten were conspiring against the regime and he had been anxious to reassure Cromwell in the letter he sent in January.[115] The interest in the petitions from Hatfield Chase and the 'well-affected citizens' also suggests that Lilburne was suspected of covert agitation, of which he may not have been innocent. On the other hand, Lilburne also reported that Cromwell had said his banishment might only have lasted three months, if he stayed quiet.[116] Avoiding a public trial and martyrdom, but getting Lilburne out of the country, was clearly an attractive solution.

In the end, though, it is hard to explain the savagery of this response. For the first two years of its life the Commonwealth had been embattled, but with decisive victories in Ireland and, most recently, in Scotland, it was far more secure. In that context there was something of a contest to define the regime's future, in which Cromwell held the ring between, broadly speaking, those with high hopes of fundamental change, often with strong army links, and moderates more interested in stability and settlement, often from more respectable gentry backgrounds and more influential in Parliament. In deciding what to do about Primatt's petition, MPs may have been eager to assert their right to consider the matter themselves, and not to leave it to the courts as the army preferred. Hesilrige was particularly prominent as a defender of the Rump against army influence, and this may have added something to the desire to assert the Rump's power to govern its own affairs.[117]

Whatever the political dynamics of the situation, the hostile spirit was maintained, and Lilburne's passage from the country was handled with equal malevolence. The reduction of the time given him to leave was perhaps a means to trap him. There were delays in granting him a passport to leave the country, and petitions in his favour were read and set aside, or simply ignored. At the end of January he left London, taking a horse at Finsbury stables by Moor-fields, and *being accompanied with great store of my freinds on horse-back, who brought me divers miles on my yourney*. Following the tearful intercession of the wife of the Mayor of Dover he was eventually allowed on board a ship at Dover bound for Ostend without a passport. He claimed that he had actually been denied a pass by the Speaker, something that could, he noted, have cost him his life, since he would have been unable to leave the country before his time was up.[118]

★　★　★

Lilburne had a genius for seeing issues of fundamental importance in the detail of social and political life. As a soap boiler he spoke out once again for the small businessman. In County Durham he saw in legal disputes, and in particular in the way they were handled, evidence of tyranny and a threat to all. It is not completely clear that he was sincere in saying that he just wanted to 'sit still' in these years, since his election to the Common Council looks rather like a staged challenge to the Engagement, and his flirtation with admission to the Temple to study law seems similarly barbed. But he did really seem to be pursuing his immediate family and business interests through 1650 and into 1651, without any very direct or at least open involvement in national political controversies.

There is certainly something less than heroic about these causes: it is not easy, for example, to take his side against his tenant William Huntington. George Lilburne's dispute with Arthur Hesilrige over the Harraton colliery clearly lacked the partisan frisson of the earlier round of combats with King, Manchester, and Prynne, and might appear like standard gentry wrangling. And yet Lilburne elevated them to the same status and underwent an extraordinary punishment in the latter cause. Having helped to invent the sovereign English people, or at least to give the notion very wide circulation in the campaign for an *Agreement*, he saw in the mundane and even slightly disreputable aspirations of everyman the stuff of practical liberty. This lacked the polemical intensity of the Leveller-led campaign for a peace based on an *Agreement of the People*, but it was consistent with the ideals which had drawn him into those campaigns, and the public demonstration of their value seemed to have a similarly debilitating effect on the legitimacy of the regime.

His pursuit of his financial interests in these months had not been as high-minded as his pursuit of religious and political freedoms in the previous decade, but it had revealed just as clearly the potential for parliamentary tyranny. The difficulties of getting commitments honoured and awards paid were a significant theme of Lilburne's account of his mistreatment through the previous decade, revealing the machinations and corruption of his political enemies. Given his personal debts to his uncle and his own failure to get reparations from Parliament, it is easy to understand how Lilburne might perceive in this evidence of Parliament's capacity to act unjustly, blind to the rights of ordinary Englishmen. The breathtaking malice of his fine and banishment, and the manifest injustice of the means by which it was imposed, were out of all proportion to whatever human weaknesses Lilburne had betrayed in pursuit of his family interests: it was an arbitrary action by a regime that feared more of him.

7

Exile, 1653–7

Amsterdam and Bruges, 1652–3

For Lilburne exile was another staging post in his sufferings: '*I . . . have aboundantly tasted of Gods tossing and tumbling dealings with me in this World, which to me as a mere man hath bin nothing but a vale of teares*'.[1] In a published letter to Elizabeth in March he reassured her that his sufferings (and therefore her own and those of their children) were worthwhile: 'if it be his pleasure to let this cross I am under to lie upon me, for the tryall of my faith & patience & sonne-like dependance upon him, his Good will & pleasure be done'.[2]

For an English audience he presented this as the latest chapter in his persecution as a champion of English liberties. The sentence, though 'dreadful', was 'not in the least terrifying to a good conscience'. Writing in late January, before he went into exile, he sounded defiant:

> I am resolved, that as in heart I defie all injustice, cruelty, tyranny, and oppression, all arbytrary Usurpation and Usurpers whatsoever, so in person (come life, come death) I will not be so treacherous to my self, to my wife and children, and especially to this Nation (the Land of my Nativity) in general, as personally to yield my active submission for exilement.[3]

Quoting Overton, he promised that he would not allow his body to be a servant of tyranny by active compliance.[4] He was fortified in this defiance by his record of sufferings and the model of Christ, who had suffered but also offered strength to his suffering followers: that 'we might go on cheerfully in bearing the yoak of our master, he hath ingaged himself to bear part of it with us'.[5]

If he had been seeking the welfare of his family since 1649 it had ended in disaster. The £7,000 fine spelt ruin and his exile of course made it hard for him to earn a living. Elizabeth was clearly very worried about the welfare of the family and had approached both Hesilrige and the Council of State for mercy. In conversation with Hesilrige it turned out that he intended to treat this as caution money—not to be collected unless Lilburne caused further trouble. In a printed defence of Hesilrige it was said that he had taken the lands seized from the Deans and Chapters into his own name, instructing the tenants to pay their rent to Richard Lilburne for the use of Elizabeth and her children. As John put it, Hesilrige 'would keepe the power in his owne hands & thou shouldst fare, thereafter as I behaved my selfe'. John, of course, refused to accept such conditions, saying it would make a '*Schoolboy* of me', and would not allow Elizabeth to receive help from Hesilrige.[6]

In a number of letters at this time he noted Elizabeth's concern, and his own sufferings at the sickness and death of his baby daughter, but would not give in to Elizabeth's womanly weakness, drawing instead on his masculine strength. '[Oppressed] with sicknes, and the death of my litle Babe,... my most intire affection to her compelled me to deale with her is she had been a Suckinge Babe'. He could not, though, conceal his impatience that she was willing to see him to return to England 'upon such sneaking terms as my Soul abhors'. For him his exile was his 'wedding day' to a godly cause, and he broadcast to the world his irritation at Elizabeth's backsliding. Although they had agreed on a 'Mode or Methode' for managing his case, on her return to England she took other advice, 'falles off from all... and enters into new paper skirmishes with me, something filled with womanish passion and anger'. In his own mind he had responded patiently to her weakness: 'by reason of the sicknesse of my children (which I knew might not a little trouble her afflicted minde) I bore with her'. To be silent about the injustice of his banishment, though, would 'not only forfeit my good name as a man, but as a Christian', and thereby jeopardize the life, liberty, and property of all Englishmen.[7] This reveals not only his expectations of his wife, but also the importance he attached to his own masculine honour: if he gave in he would have undermined all those causes he had promised to defend with his sword in his hand or with the last drop of heart's blood. The egotism and misogyny do not sit easily with modern readers.

★   ★   ★

In 1649, Lilburne had offered to leave England for the West Indies, taking those of a like mind with him. His financial position would have ruled this out in 1652, but in any case so too did the terms of his banishment, which excluded him from the territories, dependencies, and islands of England, Scotland, and Ireland. Catholic Europe was clearly not safe for him, but neither was much of Protestant Europe.

He chose Amsterdam, a place with which he had some familiarity and some connections. His first arrest had come following a visit there in 1637, and thereafter the press of the English congregation had used his case to make targeted interventions in English politics. He now claimed, slightly at odds with his earlier accounts of that time, that in 1637 he had been 'forced to flie out of England into these parts for shelter, the usuall and most noble receptacle among all the parts of the earth of many a brave and gallant christian spirit'. The United Provinces offered 'the greatest freedome, that I have red or heard of any upon the whole Earth' and among all its cities he chose Amsterdam, 'more famous for freedome, and flourishing thereby, more then all the rest'.[8] His lodgings were in Heiligeweg (Fig. 7.1),[9] in the heart of the English exile community, close to the English church, in the house of Elizabeth Bezar. Elizabeth probably had West Country roots: migrants to Amsterdam with that name living in and around Heiligeweg came from Wiltshire and the name appears frequently in the parish registers there, a county where the cloth trade was very important.[10] Lilburne himself, of course, had cloth connections which in the 1630s at least had intersected with networks of puritan fellowship and publishing.

Amsterdam, though, was not a comfortable place for Lilburne. It was a haven for religious dissenters of all sorts, but as a consequence was also a divided city. The English-speaking Protestant community had been prey to the same divisions as that in England and John Canne, for example, who had coordinated Lilburne's campaign in the 1630s had, like Bastwick and Prynne, come to see Lilburne as a danger. Canne had published a pamphlet very hostile to him on the eve of his trial in 1649, and Matthew Simmons, who had been involved in the print trade with Amsterdam in the 1630s, had published pamphlets both for and against him.[11] His religious allies from the 1630s, in other words, were not more likely to see him as their friend than any of his erstwhile allies in England. There were also rising tensions between England and United Provinces, as an attempt to negotiate a Protestant union between the two governments gave way to commercial and diplomatic rivalry. In May 1652 war broke out, and in the meantime Lilburne was clearly suspect. A magistrate in Middlebourg, where Lilburne stopped en route to Amsterdam, was frank in his suspicions: '*a verie good pretence for the Parliament to send over a man of braines at this time, to spie out our*

Fig. 7.1. Lilburne's Amsterdam: the area around Heiligeweg and the English Reformed Church

doeings, and thereby the less to be discerned, in giveing them intelligence'. In Amsterdam he had been reported to be '*a meane, base and unworthy fellow, as if I were a rogue and had bin whipt therefore'*.[12]

At the same time there were royalist exiles in the city who suspected Lilburne of spying on them, or who might simply want revenge on him. In May 1649, Isaac Dorislaus had been murdered by royalist exiles while in The Hague trying to negotiate the Union, revenge for his part in drawing up the charges against Charles I. On his first night in Amsterdam, Lilburne stayed at an English inn on the harbour, and the following day the inn was visited by '*two or three English Gentlemen, supposed to be some of the Kings party, and diligently enquired, calling aloud and demanding where is that rogue and traitor* Lilburne, *uttering many other unhandsome speeches concerning me'*.[13]

Lilburne was also being watched by the Commonwealth regime. The surveillance was in the hands of Thomas Scot, who had risen from obscurity through the parliamentary committees in Buckinghamshire. In the late 1640s he had been a convinced opponent of the Presbyterians, and a strong supporter of the army's resistance to them. He had supported the trial and execution of the king, even urging that those Lords who did not support the regicide should be impeached. But he had also turned down an invitation to join in finalizing the *Agreement of the People* in December 1648. Around midsummer the following year he had been put in charge of all the regime's intelligence gathering, both domestic and foreign, and we know something about this work due to the survival of his own retrospective account of it. When Charles II was restored to the throne key supporters of his father's execution were captured and brought back to England. Scot had fled to Amsterdam and then to Brussels, where he was recognized in April 1660 despite his disguise. He was sent to the Tower on 12 July, found guilty of treason on 12 October, and executed five days later. At some time between arriving and his trial he had revealed something of his work for the Cromwellian regime, apparently in the belief that it would save his life: it is possible that he had surrendered, hoping to secure clemency.[14]

Keeping an eye on the Levellers had been one of his first concerns. At the time of his appointment, in 1649, they were reported to be trying to raise mutiny in the army in order to hinder the mobilization for Ireland. He had paid a weekly salary to some young men and apprentices to keep company with key figures who were at liberty (Lilburne, Overton, Walwyn, and Prince were in prison).[15] Scot's interest in Lilburne figures reasonably prominently in his account of his surveillance activities across the whole

decade, and when Lilburne was sent into exile Scot had employed Hugh
Riley to keep tabs on him. Riley had been on the same ship from Dover but
he had proved ineffective: 'John's genius was too mighty for him'. More
useful to him was Captain Wendy Oxford, who was on the same boat, and
sent correspondence to Scot voluntarily.[16]

Given his unusual name it seems very likely that he was the man in
trouble for refusing to pay tithes, burial dues, and the Easter offering due
from his holdings at Potton, Bedfordshire, in the summer of 1639, and also
the Cambridge gentleman who denounced another man to the parliamentary authorities for scandalous words in July 1642. This might suggest an
uneasy relationship with Charles I's church, and reasonably strong parliamentary sympathies in the early stages of the crisis. It might also suggest an
anxiety about his fortune, and a willingness to cement it through influence
gained at the expense of denouncing others. He had served at Edgehill in
St John's regiment (alongside Lilburne's), in the Eastern Association army,
and was later a captain at the Newport Pagnell garrison.[17] He was evidently
keen to get on, petitioning for a commission in January 1649 having 'formerly done good service in the discovery of divers disaffected persons, and
[being] now employed upon some such service'.[18] By the early 1650s he
was involved in sequestration business, but was accused of corruption and
had been convicted of perjury in relation to proceedings against Lord
Howard on 25 June 1651. The sentence was carried out on 21 January 1652,
the week of Lilburne's banishment, when he was pilloried and exiled.[19] His
subsequent publications were quite clearly hostile to the regicides, but in
supplying Scot with intelligence he was perhaps trying to secure his own
return. His information about Lilburne revolved around 'his printing there
and practizeing in England'.[20]

It seems that no one was quite sure what to make of Lilburne—his own
career showed that he followed his own mind, not his political alliances—
and he was regarded with suspicion on all sides. In passing sentence the
Speaker, in the name of the whole House, had cast Lilburne as a perennial
troublemaker. The sentence had taken into account, so it was said, 'the parliaments former favour and clemency', in remitting his past 'errours and
transgressions'. His current relapse not only tried their patience, however: it
seemed of 'so sad and dangerous consequence, that it extended to a high
breach of the priviledges of Parliament'.[21] Lilburne claimed that exile was
execution by another means, and that the Parliament had hoped his reputation as a former zealot for the Parliament would get him '*by some desperate*

Roialist or other in some base way to be murthered.[22] By some of the Dutch
magistrates he was 'imagined to be one of the Parliaments spies & by some
of the mad or ranting crue of the Cavaliers (for being formerly a zelot for
the Parliament) I have bin really sought for, & enquired after by them as a
traitor & rogue'.[23] He was not alone and perhaps not idle in his sufferings:
in February 'Lilburne the Leveller' was reported to have been in Bruges
with 'some of his tribe', before leaving for Rotterdam.[24] Meanwhile, back in
England rumours soon circulated that he was plotting against the English
government with both the Dutch authorities and the royalists.

In order to try to clear his name with each of these hostile constituencies,
Lilburne published a long text, his own *Apologetical Narration*, which set out
the reasons for his exile, and its injustice. He told Elizabeth that he had
particularly wanted to clear his name to the suspicious local authorities.
Published in parallel Dutch and English, it ran to seventy-two pages, offering a detailed account of his public embroilments, and reproducing official
orders and declarations from the Star Chamber and Parliament. The account
of his sufferings under Charles I was very full, and reproduced the *True
Relation*, with its witness statements about his wounds and the cruelty with
which the Star Chamber sentence had been imposed. It also contains a
fairly detailed account of the dispute over Harraton, and reproduced the
petition in support of his cause presented to Parliament on 20 January.
There were less detailed accounts of other parts of his autobiography—his
stalwart commitment to Parliament between 1640 and 1642, and his vigorous parliamentary service, rewarded by prosecution by backsliders after
1645. It set out, in other words, a fairly consistent account of a man committed to Parliament, who wanted a just settlement, and who had not
supported the regicide. His current banishment was unjust, and the narrative placed some emphasis on Cromwell's personal betrayal and now active
hostility to Lilburne. He took the increasingly common view that Cromwell
was a hypocrite, whose personal ambition was cloaked in godliness, and
set out his opposition to Cromwell becoming king, something that was
already, apparently, rumoured to be his plan. The clear implication was that
nothing should be read into Lilburne's banishment except that he was
the victim of injustice, and he once again disavowed any ambition to level
property or magistracy.[25]

Such a very thorough history of his troubles was no doubt therapeutic,
but to produce it in Dutch suggests that he did, in fact, have a local audience
and some reason to court it. The sale of the pamphlet was stopped in

Amsterdam, when the magistrates seized copies, 10,000 sheets of paper in all, at some cost and (it seems) threat to his livelihood. That forced him, he said, to 'travell and looke out for my selfe, where Safely to abide and print without offence'. The magistrates' motive is suggested, perhaps, by his plan to publish the *Manifestation* and the third *Agreement*, from May 1649, in Dutch[26]—had the magistracy of Amsterdam now got an agitator among them?

At the beginning of April he was still in Elizabeth Bezar's house, but by May had moved to Vianen, on the river Lek just south of Utrecht. The town was known as a place of refuge since it enjoyed jurisdictional independence—as a result fugitives of all sorts congregated there, beyond the reach of the magistrates of Amsterdam and elsewhere. Lilburne likened it to Zoar, the city where Lot took refuge, and which was spared the wrath that engulfed Sodom and Gomorrah.[27] Not long after, though, he was in Bruges: if the tensions around his presence in Amsterdam had driven him to Vianen, it may have been the coming of war that drove him out of the United Provinces altogether. In late May the refusal of a Dutch fleet to lower its flags on meeting the English navy had increased tensions, and a last minute embassy from Holland failed to avert war. Lilburne had apparently intervened, publishing a statement about the disputes between the two countries in Amsterdam. War was formally declared on 10 July, by which time Lilburne was living in Bruges, in Mary Brugh, in what he later described as his 'delightsome palace in my little Garden-house'.[28]

Lilburne had, by May, realized that Wendy Oxford was spying on him on behalf of Scot. He also suspected Scot of trying to draw him into trouble, either by trapping him in conspiracy, or by convincing the royalists that Lilburne was his agent.[29] Scot's later confession says nothing about that, saying only that Oxford was keeping him informed about Lilburne's publishing activity. He was very aware that Lilburne's works were being smuggled into England,[30] and this was certainly of interest to the English regime. Copies of his *Apologeticall Narration* being imported to England had been seized, while in April 1652 a book that Lilburne had sent to Samuel Moyer was passed on to the Lord President, and referred to the Committee of Examinations.[31] Moyer was an Independent, but more importantly a member of the Council of State, who had supported the *Agreement of the People*, and Lilburne credited him with having stood up for the truth against Hesilrige over Harraton. In the next year, Moyer fell out with the regime, when the Rump was dissolved and replaced by a Protectorate with Cromwell at its head.[32] A potential friend, then, but apparently not one who was comfortable with Lilburne's current stance. In June more of Lilburne's books were seized, 'being sent over from foreign parts', and in December he was reported to be attracting 'a great concourse of people' having published a declaration touching the 'Liberty of the People, and the Freedom of Nations, which gives ample satisfaction to the States'.[33] Earlier in the year, rather incredibly, he had been reported to be in command of a Dutch man of war.[34]

Clearly Lilburne was no friend to the English regime, but many of the royalist exiles remained very suspicious of him. Sir Edward Nicholas wrote that 'It is more evident to all men that the rogue Lilburne was banish'd...merely to gain him credit and trust on this side'.[35] After he moved to Bruges, though, he seems to have developed cordial relations with some of the royalist exiles, notably the Duke of Buckingham. Scot thought this correspondence was simply intended to 'fish' Lilburne, to see if he could be of service to the king. He did hear, however, that Lilburne thought the king could be restored for £10,000 (another source says £100,000), by first preparing the minds of the soldiers 'by such bookes as hee could write and send amongst them' and then by distributing appropriate amounts of money among them.[36] Buckingham took Lilburne's advice about to how to get permission to return to England, but a pass was eventually offered only on condition that the duke reveal all of his dealings with Lilburne. This deal the duke refused as a matter of honour and Lilburne was clearly attracted to Buckingham as a man of integrity, who had done a lot to preserve him from ·the wrath of the Cavalier exiles.[37]

Nonetheless, despite these contacts, his oft-reported presence among other Cavaliers seems to have been an ambiguous pleasure for them. While some recognized he was 'more able to set the Crown on the King's head than ever Scotland was', others referred to him as 'infamous John Lilburne'. Secretary Nicholas thought him a 'rogue' and clearly found his boasts of friendship with the Duke of Buckingham distasteful. Clarendon believed him a better man than the earl of Roxburgh, for whom he had no time, and noted that 'Lilburne is not without reputation with some greate persons heare'. He was himself sceptical, though: 'I am thought an obstinate foole, for not understandinge that he will ever be able or willinge to do good'. It was for this reason that the Duke of Buckingham was a better man to deal with him.[38]

What he was up to was a matter of speculation in the gossipy royalist community:

> Here a parsel of strange people come to towne mixt as we thinke of the Presbyterian & Levelling partie. Lilburne & some other of them have close consultations with [the Duke of Buckingham] and that they have some designe in hand I have for certaine from one of the packe that pretends to be very honest, & will contract acquaintance w[i]th me at least as much as I will let him. What it is they meane to attempt I can not yet discover.[39]

In August, one correspondent reported the duke's comings and goings, noting that they had tried to involve Lord Hopton in whatever scheme they had in mind, but to no effect. He reported speculation that they had a plot to take advantage of 'Lamberts discontent and [planned] to distroy Crumwell's person on whom L. will be revenged'.[40] In September, Lilburne seemed to have been in contact with the earl of Crawford, who was briefly in Bruges before going to Holland, and the correspondent noted that 'I found him the night before in [Culpeper's] chamber where we had a short silent rencounter, for as soon as I stept in he went out. [Culpeper] told me his businesse there was onelie to bring the English newes booke w[hi]ch he had not before seen y[ou] may believe this & no more if y[ou] please'.[41] Many royalists continued to believe Lilburne was simply a double agent, or even an agent provocateur, and although he subsequently denied involvement in royalist plots, his denials were so precisely worded as to remain ambiguous. The parliamentary regime, on the other hand, received regular reports of his dinners with local exiles and weekly trips to Ostend to send and receive letters from England, rather surprisingly carried by William Prynne's man.[42]

Quite what Lilburne was up to in this world of double-dealing and intrigue (if indeed he was up to anything) is hard to say. It is on the face of it unlikely that Lilburne was serious about serving as an informer or becoming actively involved in royalist conspiracy. In his *Apologetical Narration* he expressed his habitual pride that he had fought openly for the Parliament, in the field with his sword in his hand, with good grounds in law and equity, and not by any underhand means. There is a strong ring of truth in his protestation that 'to be a spie upon any termes in the world, is so contrary to my disposision and frame of spirit, that I had rather be hanged then give reall cause to be judged so absolute a knave & dissembler as a spie must be'.[43] Throughout his many broils he had been willing to suffer punishment, and so it seems unlikely that this banishment would break him. He had also, throughout his political career, wanted to thrash out his political differences with people in open disputation.

As to royalist conspiracy, it is hard to believe that he would simply have supported a restoration of the monarchy, any more than he would simply go along with the imposition of the Commonwealth. *As You Were*, published in May, included a letter to William Kiffin, an old ally who sided against Lilburne in 1649, but with whom he was quickly back on good terms. He told Kiffin that even if he had been interested in putting Charles II on the throne he would not have gone about it their way. Charles seemed unwilling to trust his own judgement and depended instead on a multitude of councillors. As a result, Scot would know from tavern talk anything they planned before it was 'a quarter ripe for execution'. Lilburne's reputation was extremely important to him, and would certainly have been at stake in any such plan:

> I have professed to be a *man of Conscience* and one that could *die* for his *principles* and never could be threatned from them, *nor courted out of them, by anie persons in the World what soever.* And it hath bin one of my maine principles, and so declared by the *constant series* of my practise, *that evil must not be done by any, that good may come thereby.*

Above all, had he cooperated in the conquest of the people and the imposition of a king, 'or any else might rule over them by his will and pleasure: I should not only account my selfe, *one of the greatest murtherers in the World*, but also one of the *basest fellowes* that ever breathed upon the face of the earth'.[44]

His broader political position was clear in the *Apologetical Narration*, and stated very fully in *As You Were*. He supported no party, but only those who would support an *Agreement* and the principle of self-denial—the two safeguards against the kinds of corruption that had led to Parliament falling off from its commitments of 1642, and the army grandees to fall away from the army's Engagements in 1647.[45] He continued to cite Parliament's *Book of Declarations* in support of his position, alongside scripture, and to advocate an *Agreement of the People* as the bulwark against tyranny. He was willing to put such principles above family and friendship, and it is difficult to believe that he could seriously have participated in a royalist reconquest unless confident that a restored monarch would safeguard these principles.

On balance, then, it seems likely that Lilburne was, as ever, following his conscience, while hopeful of a return. There is certainly no hint in Scot's account that Lilburne was actually playing a double game or informing on the royalists; nor in the papers of John Thurloe, a secretary of state at the

heart of a network of spies during the 1650. At the same time, if Lilburne
was up to anything very ambitious by way of subverting the Commonwealth,
Scot was sceptical about its significance: 'his mountains did not bring forth
suitable births', and the principal fruit of his printing was against Cromwell
and Hesilrige 'vpon personal quarrels, & my self in scandalous reports'.[46]

★ ★ ★

The *Apologeticall Narration* and *As You Were* made no secret of his hostility to
Cromwell, but it seems that Lilburne was hopeful of making other friends
in the regime. He tried to make himself useful to his long-time ally Henry
Marten, now a member of the Council of State, writing to suggest that
the English provide a convoy for ships to Ostend.[47] He wrote again on
8 September reporting an encounter with Edward Brooks, a master's mate
on one of the frigates recently taken, which was 'misarabelly plundered and
desperaitely burnt'. He set out the sufferings of the survivors, making a case
for reward and reparations to them, but also that the Commonwealth should
look after its mariners, since they were its principal bulwark. Lilburne was
anxious to disavow any ulterior motive in this: he wrote not 'to cury fauour
with you or the rest of your brethren'. He wrote only to manifest 'that
English sperit that is in me'. If keeping close to right and truth would not
'bring me backe againe to England, I never desire againe to see it'. He
signed off as 'An honest Englishman at the hart'.[48]

Return was clearly on his mind then, but he was not willing simply to
abandon the public position that had got him into trouble. In March 1653,
against a background of increasing discontent with the Rump Parliament,
he published *John Lilburne Revived*, which denounced the Rump in strong,
and familiar terms. This was partly a refutation of a report, attributed to
Wendy Oxford, that he was dead. More substantively, though, he implicitly
wanted to make good his case against Cromwell and to act on the 'indeared
affection, that I justly beare to the Land of my nativitie above all nations in
the world' and the same affection he had for the 'multitudes of the honest
in habitants thereof, for their former tender affection in the day of my great
adversitie'. In practice he was not demanding an *Agreement of the People*, but
did insist that there should be a two-year limit on public office, and clear
ban on nepotism—this to prevent the kind of power accumulated by
Cromwell and his son-in-law Henry Ireton, and following Ireton's death
and his widow's remarriage, by Cromwell and his new son-in-law Charles
Fleetwood. He also entered into dispute with Oxford, who had been stung
by Lilburne's personal attacks and made claims about Lilburne's role in the

regicide. This had forced Lilburne into print with the result, he said, that he could not enter into public disputation in a more measured way. In light of what had happened to Dorislaus, Lilburne thought these rumours were life-threatening.[49]

The third part of the pamphlet was a letter to Henry Marten from the previous November, written in similar terms to those that survive from the same time, offering helpful suggestions about the management of England's maritime interest: this time suggesting that the English fleet could take control of ships laden with valuable cargoes of silk currently lying in Ostend. He urged Marten to use English naval power to bring this trade within English protection and control: the excise on those cargoes would considerably aid the war effort. It seems clear that this correspondence with Marten, a part of which was now made public, was intended to demonstrate how helpful Lilburne could be to the public good in a properly ordered Commonwealth. He had found Marten 'by many years experience to be one of those amongst that great Assembly and Counsell in which you sit, that principally minde the real good of their Countrie and of the generalitie of the inhabitants thereof'. He again emphasized his disinterested patriotism: 'my End is no other then English in it, it being in no manner of respect a farthing advantage unto mee'.[50] Marten was himself reputed to have taken no profit at all from his public service, and was no friend of either Henry Vane or Cromwell.[51]

Clearly Lilburne continued to be a willing servant to the Commonwealth on his terms, and sought to demonstrate that in practical ways to a man of influence. This letter also reveals that Lilburne's reading had taken a new direction, taking in 'some store of Historie'. Much of the body of the letter recounts examples of political virtue (and vice) drawn from Polybius and Plutarch—a clear departure from a diet of citations from parliamentary directions, scriptural precept, biblical history, and Coke's *Institutes*. Lilburne had had a grammar school education, and claimed reasonable Latin (although not the technical Latin necessary to deal with the common law) and a little Greek. However, there is little sign before this that classical history had been one of the sources of his political thought, except indirectly.[52] That does seem to be because he had not read them seriously, rather than that he had only now seen their relevance to his situation. He noted that 'my old truehearted, plain and blunt friend Mr. Moyle of your house . . . often used to clap me on the back, & call me Noble Cato; which before I came to Flanders did not fully understand, what he meant by it. But haveing red so much of famous Plutarchs Lives lately, with so much delight and seriousnes as I have done . . . I now fully understand his meaning'.[53] Cato, the austere champion of the values of the Roman republic, in opposition to the incipient imperial ambitions of Caesar, would have been a familiar figure to anyone with more than a passing interest in Roman history: that Lilburne had not got the joke suggests he had not previously had such an interest. These classical histories were central to renaissance politics, though, and there are other signs that he was beginning to read in that literature. For example, he had previously used Machiavellian and Machiavel in their conventional, negative sense, but was now perhaps more aware of what Machiavelli had actually written. His letter to Kiffin had referred to Machiavelli and other politic authors, and in June 1653 he referred to *The Prince* as 'his most rememorable book'.[54] Exile, like earlier spells in prison, had afforded him the opportunity to pursue his political education.

Without much apparent warning, a revolution in affairs at home brought with it at least the hint of an opportunity for return. The Rump was increasingly at odds with the army. Conservative in religion and law reform, it was a source of frustration to the hopes of the godly. In late spring Cromwell lost patience with its conservatism and on 20 April 1653, having listened to some of its proceedings, sent its members on their way, with a denunciation ringing in their ears. John Lambert had suggested that Cromwell call elections for a new Parliament while Major General Harrison, who had played a role in the actual dissolution of the Rump, suggested instead a nominated assembly of the saints. Cromwell was drawn to the latter idea, and on 6 May congregational churches were invited to nominate men from whom the Council of State could select appropriate representatives.[55] The result was the body which, having given itself the title Parliament, became known as Barebone's Parliament after one if its leading figures, Praise-God Barebone.

This turn in affairs offered hope to the exile of course: if the body that had banished him was now dismissed, would its legislation stand? Cromwell's view, that its passing had not caused so much as 'the barking of a dog',[56] surely offered the prospect of a reprieve for the stranded patriot, England's noble Cato.

Return to England and trial, 1653

The regimes of the 1650s were caught between the hopes of reformers and the conservatism of those on whom they depended—the county gentry who still ran the localities. The Rump had passed some dramatic legislation—the blasphemy and adultery acts that imposed draconian punishments—which marked out the boundaries of a new religious order which was tolerant within these sharply drawn bounds. It had also passed a Navigation Act, tying the nascent colonial trades to English ships and the London market in a way that was to provide the foundations for empire. But on law reform and the promotion of the gospel it had disappointed radicals. Lilburne's desire to test the validity of his banishment was potentially at the core of this: his demand for the rights of an Englishman was couched in terms that were not exclusive to people who we might think of as his natural allies, and was therefore a potential embarrassment to the regime. Lilburne's return, and the government's response, became another moment when the nature of England's freedom was debated, and was again a very public spectacle.

Elizabeth had arrived in Bruges with news of the dissolution on 3 May, and returned to London with a letter asking for a pass for her husband to return: he was now 'weary of his exilement'.[57] It was to no avail, however, and in mid-May Lilburne wrote *A defensive declaration*, not published until 20 June, which set out the injustice of his banishment and the dangers posed by the plots against him by Scot and Oxford, which also poisoned minds against him in England.[58] He sent an address to the Council of State from Calais in mid-June, noting the encouragement given to Elizabeth that the time might be right for an end to his exile, and he wrote to Cromwell from Dunkirk.[59] He published a number of humble addresses to Cromwell, including one in Dutch and English, seeking to build bridges. Aside from a plea for mercy, a key claim was 'That the authority of the late Parliament being taken from them for misgovernment, your Petitioner hopes you will please to suspend at least the execution of any Acts made by them, which shall not clearly and evidently appear to your spirits and consciences to have such Justice in them, as God may truly be glorified in your execution of them'. His own intentions were entirely benign: unable to 'find the least cause why he should be rendred a person so abominable, that he is unfit to live or breath in this Commonwealth'.[60]

On 2 June, perhaps not coincidently, the council was finally presented with a report on the disturbances in Epworth in 1651, which had been commissioned in January 1652 as Lilburne had been sent into exile. It included accusations about Lilburne's complicity in the violence, his interest in escalating the dispute to include Crowle, in Hatfield Chase, and reports of the violent language used by him and others against the Rump. Certainly, Cromwell was said to be 'violent ag[ain]st him, so much as to the preiudice of his wisedome, since he may possibly bring his authority into the scale with so inconsiderable a Creature'. That does seem to be what Cromwell had done. Clarendon observed from exile, 'I shall judge much of Crumwells power and interest both in the Councell & Army as John ... [is] hanged or not hanged: and I see letters from no ill hands in England, that it is a measuringe cast betweene them, and infallably that one will hange the other'.[61]

It certainly seems that Lilburne's addresses to Cromwell went straight to press: the Lord General was not being engaged in a private correspondence here. By this time the *Defensive Declaration*, written the previous month, had appeared in print with an appendix setting out in more detail the plots and methods of Thomas Scot, and offering a lengthy defence of his dealings with the Duke of Buckingham. Lilburne had by then, he said, published defences in 'several languages' in order to protect himself.[62] Suspicion about his closeness to the royalists may not have been groundless, either. In June, Buckingham was said to believe 'he hath a notable interest in that Saint', and owed permission to travel to him. They had been closeted together in Calais that month, and Buckingham was reported to have arrived privately in London at the same time. Rumours of the plan to put the king back on his throne for £10,000 or £100,000 circulated, as did speculation that Lilburne was on some errand from the Dutch, was intent on prosecuting Hesilrige 'and the rest of his Ennemys', or that he came 'on the leveling account to imbroile the Nation'. Such was his reputation that 'it seems great changes and designes must attend the motion of that ... eminent Commonwealths-man'.[63] In any case, permission to return was not forthcoming and, impatient of delay, he crossed from Calais on 14 June, arriving in London shortly after.[64]

He claimed in his third address that he had returned only at the importunate pleading of his wife, but it seems possible that army impatience with the conservatism of the Rump Parliament had encouraged him to think there was a political opportunity for him.[65] It was certainly a very public campaign from the start. One observer wrote: 'It cannot be expressed what posting here is up and downe about John Lilburne in Citty, Country & Army; many thousands and some of them considerable Officers have subscribed a Petition on his behalf; Twenty eminent Citizens offred to be bound, body for body, or in [£20,000] bond a peece for his security'. By returning he had, of course, broken the law, but such was the public interest that the judges did not know how to proceed, or whether to use a council of war on the grounds that he had been sowing division in the army and the fleet. The Council of State was divided, 'and its thought it may make some alterations both in Army and Country, if any extremity should be used'.[66]

However, it did not go well for him. Four days earlier Henry Scobell had sent a parchment copy of the Act of Banishment to the Attorney General in response to a formal writ from Prideaux, presumably in preparation for a prosecution.[67] As soon as Lilburne arrived the mayor, John Fowke, secured him in Sheriff Underwood's house, who then took him before the Lord General and the council. They sent him that evening to Newgate, and charged the Attorney General to proceed against him according to the Act for his banishment.[68] According to one observer, 'it is verilly believed he will be hanged forthwith'.[69] Lilburne, though, petitioned Fowke, who Lilburne had heard was only cooperating in the prosecution for fear of his own life should he refuse. Prosecution by an unjust Act was a threat to everyone he said, including Fowke. Lilburne was clearly now more combative: he complained that his three humble addresses had no effect on 'those Gentlemen sitting at Whitehal, that have by their wills and pleasures assumed the present governing of the free Nation of *England* (after they have destroyed and rooted up by the roots, by their swords, wills, & pleasures, all the formal setled legal Power and Government of this ancient free Nation)'. He sought Fowke's permission to publish his case in London in order to save his neck.[70] The council passed on the petition from him to the Lord General and the Attorney General, along with his letters, 'to make such use of as he shall find necessary for the state'.[71] Lilburne in the meantime turned his attention to securing his rights in his own defence.[72]

It is possible that Cromwell intended to secure a guilty verdict but then to pardon Lilburne.[73] Whatever the truth of that, Lilburne's legal position looked very weak: Theodorus thought that 'Legislative John Lilburne has almost brought his neck into a noose'. He was now on a direct collision course with the government, which for its part was determined to carry on according to the terms of his banishment: if 'he be found within any of our dominions, he shall be apprehended, and die without mercy as a felon; so that there needs no further trial or legal proceedings'. Lilburne's character seemed to be the issue. A pamphlet was published defending Hesilrige's behaviour in relation to Lilburne's lands, a version of a letter sent by Hesilrige on 21 June. As one observer read the situation: 'truly my Lord

General's intended government of this commonwealth for the future, and Lilburne's turbulent restless spirit, seem to be altogether incompatable. Nay, I hear some of his letters written while in exile have been intercepted, which, if he were to come to another trial, would be highly urged against him.' Another observer repeated the thought that 'Free born John . . . will speedily be hanged'.[74]

Lilburne, for his part, had been using all his skills to affect public opinion: as he said to Fowke his three humble addresses 'are . . . publikely in Print, all up and down the streets'.[75] The trial had originally been fixed for 21 June, the day Hesilrige had written the letter published in his defence. The Dutch ambassadors observed mounting tension, reporting that the trial had been postponed until the new Parliament had met by the intercession of a popular petition.[76]

When Barebone's Parliament assembled on 4 July, it was greeted by Cromwell in lavish terms: 'Truly you are called by God to rule with Him, and for Him . . . I confess I never looked to see such a day as this . . . when Jesus Christ should be as owned as He is, at this day . . . this may be the door to usher in the things God has promised.' Fifth monarchists, radicals who expected the return of Christ, declared that these were 'Overturning, Overturning, Overturning dayes', urging the members to seek the 'erecting of the Kingdom of Jesus Christ to the uttermost parts of the earth'.[77] They were to find, however, as their predecessors had, that more immediate and secular business got in the way of these millennial aspirations.

Of more immediate significance for Lilburne, the new regime proved as determined as the old to proceed, and preparation of the case against him continued: on 13 July the Council of State ordered William Strickland to present to Parliament 'the informations, examinations, and other papers concerning Lieut.-Col. John Lilburne and his carriage in foreign parts'.[78] Parliament was not directly involved in proceedings, but there are signs that there was a divided attitude among its members, and that he had some potential supporters. Nonetheless, when a petition to suspend proceedings was put to the vote on 14 July it was denied.[79]

★   ★   ★

The trial opened at the Old Bailey on 13 July amid very obvious displays of support for Lilburne. He was accompanied in court by Richard Overton and a number of members of his wider family: his father, his son-in-law, and his two cousins, William and George, sons of his uncle George. Three regiments of horse were stationed in and around St James's and the case was clearly of some political significance. Troops that had been due to march for Scotland were kept in town for fear that there might be trouble.[80] The propaganda battle continued: on the day of the trial, government printers published testimonies about his relationship with exiled royalists and sympathies for the Dutch.[81]

Since the new assembly had confirmed the Act of Banishment the government apparently needed only to prove that Lilburne had returned to the country to secure his condemnation. Lilburne dug in, though. Asked to hold up his hand, he turned to Lord Chief Baron Wylde and asked what raising his hand would signify. After a lengthy disputation with the court he acknowledged his name and heard the indictment. He demanded counsel and sight of the indictment and, armed with Coke's *Institutes*, eventually got his way, despite some heated exchanges. He was allowed to go into the garden and prepare a list of his objections to the indictment while the court adjourned, but the court delayed letting him have a copy. On the following day he 'struggled very earnestly for some hours on this point' and at 2.00 p.m. managed to secure another adjournment so that he could study the indictment properly. At 5.00 p.m. that evening he still had not received the copy, and sent a number of supporters in search of it. He eventually received it at 10.00 a.m. on the morning of 15 July and was able to get more time, delaying the hearing again until 16 July. Further discussion of technicalities relating to his objections and to counsel dragged out the hearing until the evening, at which point he also demanded a formal hearing (oyer) of the Act of Banishment, to test whether the legislation was in fact sound. This latter demand was potentially very threatening, if he was to go beyond technical questions about the legality of the Act: this could easily be made a question about the legitimacy of the regime and he had, ominously, referred to it as the 'pretended Act' at several points.[82]

One observer thought that this was the core of his case: he had pleaded 'with as much Law as he could finde in the Volumes he brought to the Barr' and argued that there had not been a Parliament in England since the execution of Charles I. If the last assembly had in fact been a Parliament then Cromwell and the others who had dissolved it were themselves guilty of high treason under legislation 'made by themselves when a Parl[iamen]t': that is, in the previous decade.[83]

All this was attended with great theatre: 'whatever he said was much applauded by the rabble, and endeavours were not wanting to inflame them into a Muteny, but in the height of the sport a guard of horse dispersed them'. At that point he 'refused to answer while the Troope was there, saying that the Court was not free by reason of that force upon it'.[84] When he demanded the oyer he 'cried out again and again, My Lord, rob me not of my Birthright, the benefit of the law'. Behind this performance in court lay the threat of publicity. If, before this large audience, he was denied justice and a right to speak for his life, he threatened to 'cry out, and appeal to the People...that my Lord Mayor, and this Court by violence robs me of my Birthright by Law'. Proceedings descended into shambles, above which Lilburne was able to make himself heard: 'My Lord, will you murther me without right of Law'. Without the oyer, Lilburne and the people would have reason to believe 'that there never was such an Act of Parliament as you pretend, nor such a Judgment as it pretends to be executor of, nor no such crime...as any judgment of felony can be imagined to be grounded upon'. Instead, they would conclude, all the proceedings from first to last were simply 'a malicious packt conspiracy against me, to murder me'.[85] Petitions, and this publicity, made it even more imperative that the government win the case: 'I beleeve my next will tell you he is condemned & executed', wrote one observer, because 'the many seditious Libells and pamphlets scattered in his behalf, and the infinite appearances of people at his tryall, so that strong guards are appointed for feare of insurrection, will accelerate his ruine'.[86]

Proceedings had been tense and often heated. Lilburne had succeeded in raising a number of technical issues, seeking by 'many simple evasions to helpe himself'. First, was the Lieutenant Colonel John Lilburne named in the Act the same person as the John Lilburne named in the indictment? He had pride in his military record and habitually used his military rank in publications, but during the trial, very unusually, he published as Mr Lilburne. Second, the judgement against him had given him thirty days to leave, but the Act only twenty. He had left the country, in fact, without seeing the Act, so as a free man, not as a felon. Third, the indictment said that he had been found and was 'feloniously remaining' in the England: it did not claim that he had returned feloniously. And so on. This war of attrition before a lively crowd and reported freely in the press put increasing pressure on the court. Alderman Atkins 'was in a pitiful frighted condition, when the prisoner appealed to the people against their [the judges'] injustice', and called on Colonel Okey to send troops to keep him secure.[87] Eventually Lilburne agreed to hand in his objections to the indictment, and a hearing of the Act was promised so long as his counsel signed a request. Further process was postponed until 10 August.

Peter Richardson, writing in late July, said that in his five sessions in the previous week Lilburne had 'most courageously defended himself' with Magna Carta as his buckler. As a result 'they have left him alone, although he be not yeat quitted'. In particular, he thought that Lilburne had forced Prideaux to 'quit the field', having encountered him with 'many opprobrious termes'. Another observer noted that he had made so many exceptions that the proceedings had been deferred for a month, while public sympathy in the City and elsewhere was manifest in the petitions for his release: the trial 'serves the Towne for talke, severall petitions from severall places are dayly presented to the Parl[iamen]t Councel of State and Generall in his behalf, and infinite numbers of Pamphlets, and some very libellous are hourly printed and dispersed by his friends about the Towne'. Tension was palpable in the City, the stationing of troops confirming that the government thought 'this fellow soe considerable', while many printed tickets had been scattered on the streets asking '*And what, shall then honest* John Lilbourn *die?/Threescore thousand will know the reason why*'. Another observer noted, 'It is not to be imagined, how much esteeme he hath got onely for vindicating the ancient lawes and liberties of the people against the usurpations of this tyme'.[88]

The trial contributed to the sense that this was an embattled regime. Reporting that 'Honest John Lilburne' would soon come 'to his second tryal', a letter intercepted by Thurloe in late July, also reported concerns about the durability of peace with the Dutch and the ability to put more than one admiral at sea in the coming winter. At the same time, fearing an invasion from the Scots, 'Many of our horse are marched northward'. Meanwhile, 'Our general is no ways satisfied with this Parliament, nor the Parliament with him; and the people with neither of them. At this time men see the difference of the government of one, and the management of affairs by a multitude, who are still divided and fall into factions.'[89] It was rumoured that Parliament was divided about what to do about Lilburne, as on other issues, and Theodorus suspected that a 'purchased' sessions at the Guildhall might be the preferred means to deal with Lilburne expeditiously.[90]

Against this background, public sympathy for Lilburne clearly made the government jumpy. Petitions were presented on his behalf on 29 July by women led by Katherine Chidley, an eminent Leveller. The women refused to accept that the Parliament could not hear their petition because, as women (many of them married), they had no place in law. In fact, they threatened that if they were not heard then their husbands would come with swords in their hands 'to defend the Libertys of the People', admonishing the Parliament men to look to themselves and not persecute Lilburne, that man of God.[91]

On 2 August another petition was presented by 'divers well-affected and constant adherers to the interests of Parliaments, and their own native fundamental rights and freedoms therein concerned'. It came from 'young men and apprentices, of the Cities of London and Westminster, Borough of Southwark, and the parts adjacent', and was full of Lilburne's language and analysis. The current 'Assembly' had taken government on itself and the people expected 'from them the preservation of their Libertys, with the administration of Justice', particularly in Lilburne's case. Failing that 'they would do all they could for the vindication of their Rights and that Lilborne would prove a Sampson if nothing but his blood will satisfy'. The threat was palpable, and six of those responsible were examined at the bar of the House by the Speaker. Their spokesman, though, was silenced by his fellows, who commanded him 'not to answer any demands, but to demand an answer to this petition'. Parliament resolved that the petition was 'a most high breach of the privilege of Parliament' and 'scandalous and seditious'. The six who had presented it were taken into custody, and two weeks later committed to Bridewell and set to hard labour 'during the pleasure of the House'. The petition 'and this whole business' was referred to the Council of State. Lilburne, meanwhile, was to be kept a close prisoner in Newgate.[92] The same day the Council of State formed a committee to examine those who had presented the petition, while another committee set about examining 'such persons as they shall hear to be dangerous to the peace of the commonwealth'. That committee was to have power to detain them until the council decided what to do with them.[93] The results of the examination were due to be presented to Parliament on 15 August.[94]

The government had also been gathering material which purported to show how Lilburne had conspired with royalists during his exile, and Lilburne resorted to print to rebut the claims. As he complained, 'it is a stratagem of a new nature, and far unsutable to the way of true Christians, to print against the prisoner under Tryal, such particulars as are altogether forraign, and nothing relating to the way of his Indictment: I believe, it is a malice that can scarcely be parallel'd'. William Packer had been prominent among those denouncing Lilburne as 'an Atheist, a denyer of God and the Scripture... an hypocrite, an apostate, and a great combining enemy with the Nations enemies beyond the seas against its welfare, peace and freedom'.[95] Another report said that Lilburne had, on 5 August, 'printed a most horrid thing ag[ain]st the General; and sayes that since the publishing of the Act for his banishment, it hath received severall interlinings purposely to destroy him'.[96]

Lilburne had of course played his part in making it a trial of right between him and the government, and not just of his breach of the terms of the Act. The fact that the trial became so protracted increased the possibilities for public lobbying: accounts of the first few days of hearings, and of his exceptions to the indictment, circulated even as these preliminary skirmishes were still in train.[97] Lilburne eventually recorded twenty-three petitions and pamphlets published in his favour during the trial.[98] Speculation continued about the regime's plans—whether or not, for example, he would be allowed to rot in Newgate until the next law term. The Venetian ambassadors thought that it was his popularity and his connections in the army that prevented an immediate death sentence, although the presence of troops had not been enough to prevent some 'slight tumult'.[99] When the court met again it was said that there were 6,000 men gathered around 'who would never have suffered his condemnation to have passed without the loss of some of their lives'. The conduct of the regime was likened to the arbitrary proceedings which had brought the earl of Strafford to the scaffold. Two companies of men were posted near the Old Bailey and mounted soldiers patrolled the streets.[100]

When proceedings resumed on 10 August, Lilburne secured another day's delay on the grounds that he had in the meantime been a close prisoner in Newgate, without access to his friends, and with his legal counsel out of town. The following day he appeared and the court produced a copy of the Act, but he claimed it was an insufficient copy and a further delay ensued. A pamphlet published that day gave public advice to the jury and to the soldiers guarding the court. On 12 August he was finally induced to plead to the Act, which he did 'as a most sordid and illegal one', leading to further heated exchanges in the course of which Colonel Barkstead told him 'there was a necessity of taking away his life, for that he was a pestilent fellow, and a seducer of the people'. Lilburne 'tartely replyed that 'twas fitter for him to be selling his bodkins and thimbles, then to sitt there as Judge on a person so much his superior and that the Commonwealth could not expect happy dayes while such persons as he shar'd the Government'. Finally, on 13 August, the court agreed to hear his exceptions to the indictment, but not to the oyer of the Act. The hearing was set for the following Tuesday.[101]

In all this, according to the Venetian Ambassador, 'His arguments and subtle wit [drew] immense crowds and plentiful sympathy'.[102] Dragging the court through the technicalities had helped make a powerful case that big issues were at stake, that were relevant to everyone present. It

> was apparent to all honest Christians that he had...been a constant Sufferer for and Assertor of the Fundamental Rights and Liberties of the free-born people of England, and that he would seal the same with the price of his precious and innocent bloud; desiring, that what he died for, might be recorded to future Ages and posterities.[103]

Hearings resumed on 16 August. On that day a pamphlet appeared addressed to the jury, advising them that they could judge the legality of the Act, and that in doing so they would protect not just Lilburne, but themselves and their posterity:

> it is evident to every one of your consciences, that he is not charged with any thing that in the true Law of England is a fellonious crime; nor hath in the least deserved to die: you can do no less then pronounce him not guilty; and in so doing, not only preserve this most miserably afflicted man and his family, but in him, your selves, your wives, children, families, and posterities, in the preservation of our antient Laws and Liberties.[104]

Writing on 18 August, Peter Collinson said that Lilburne 'keeps us still in suspense, and wee cannot tell, what will become of him' and he 'comes to morrow to stake again'.[105] The Dutch ambassadors reported that an end was in sight and that the conclusion 'may be not to his advantage'. Tensions remained high: 'Many soldiers marched up and down the town to day, to prevent insurrections and disorders, which are very much feared every where'.[106]

On 19 August, Lilburne was still refusing to plead. The Recorder opened proceedings that day complaining that the business had been 'so long and tedious, and intending that this shall be the last day'. It was not, however. Lilburne continued to deny the legality of the Act, the discrepancies between the judgement and the Act, and to argue that his actions could not be considered felonious; the court continued to press on the particular issue, of whether he had violated the Act. He was pressed to accept trial by the jury, or to see the court proceed by some other means. Finally, the hearing was to go ahead, more than a month after the initial hearing, on the following morning, 20 August.[107] His life was in the hands of the jury, and Elizabeth, presumably in a state of some anxiety, now visited John Booker, the famous astrologer, to ask how the 'jewry [will] find him'.[108]

On 20 August the jury was empanelled, with just one or two objections, and then Lilburne 'made a Speech and Oration for several hours'. He repeated a number of the technical objections but concluded on the most general principles. If Parliament ordered an unlawful thing, the jury could still disobey, just as the midwives had refused to follow Herod's order to murder all male children. If the jurors went along with an unjust act, by contrast, they would have to answer for it before God. The Commonwealth counsel concentrated on the simple, but now controversial case that the Act was legal and that it had been made by a lawful power. As in 1649, Lilburne had taken the trial into essentially political territory, partly by dragging the court through technicalities. It had been a wearying process: the Dutch ambassadors reported that the trial 'hath been for these three days continually upon hearing, and after a pleading of twelve or sixteen hours long' the verdict had been sought.[109]

The verdict went Lilburne's way, and not on the grounds of the technicalities. The jury's verdict, after a long deliberation, was that he was '*Not guilty of any Crime worthy of death*'.[110] In the context this spoke to the larger arguments about the legality of the banishment, which had been upheld by Barebone's Parliament: it was at least partly a verdict on the regime.

As one account noted, 'the tryal hath been so remarkable that every one thirsteth to know what was said, and what was afterwards the result of all'.[111] There were celebrations in court: the 300 or 400 people present gave a shout of joy that was apparently picked up by the soldiers guarding the court. It lasted half an hour and was audible across the city. Soldiers sounded their drums and trumpets, cries of 'Long live Lilburne' rang out, and there were public thanks in Hertfordshire.[112] Lilburne's victory did not settle his conflict with the authorities, however: as the Venetian Ambassador wrote, '*what matters more is the discovery thus made of the unpopularity of the present government*'.[113]

★   ★   ★

The 'multitude', expecting to hear Lilburne's freedom proclaimed, were disappointed. Instead they saw the mayor produce 'an Order (as I take it, 'twas from the General [Cromwell] himself) for the continuance of his Imprisonment, which is looked upon by all people as an act contrary both to Law and Reason'.[114] The court had not issued the warrant for his arrest, and so had no power to release him. Lilburne, still a danger to the regime, was not therefore released from prison. Meanwhile the Council of State

moved quickly to try to understand what had gone wrong. On 22 August
they ordered key figures from the City and legal officials 'to attend Council
at 8 a.m. to-morrow, to give account of the proceedings'. The council
resolved to examine the business and its conduct, 'particularly the judges
and jury', and to report to Parliament promptly. One of the jurors admitted
that they had met to concert their verdict at the Windmill Tavern on the
morning of the 20th, and according to one report the blame for the government's embarrassment was placed squarely on their shoulders. Their
explanation that they had acted 'on the fundamentall Lawes of the Land and
the dictates of their owne Consciences' apparently cut little ice. According
to that report members of the jury were fined. At the same time the council
resolved to examine 'any scandalous or seditious papers dispersed, or words
spoken at the said trial, in derogation of the authority of Parliament', and
report on that too. The same day they set about revising the Treason Act, and
began to prepare a new Act the following day to supply its defects 'in reference to this present Parliament and Council of State'.[115] There were
rumours of suggestions that jury trial should be abolished altogether.[116]

This was presumably the context for the gossip reported by the Dutch
ambassadors that the government was not going to leave things there but
intended to 'bring him before a high court of Justice, and there accuse him
of treason and other crimes'. This was a personal hostility: 'it is very certain,
that many of the Parliament are very bitter against him, and irritated the
more by his book written in prison, wherein he doth grosly exclaim against
them and their government'. There was acute anxiety about his public
support, as there had been before the trial, and 'Out of fear of insurrections
and commotions, three regiments of foote and one of horse were sent for
to town, who marcht through the city on Saturday last'. The threat was
made clear, repeating that 'some libells [were] scattered up and down not
long since, that if Lilburne doe suffer death, there are twenty thousand, that
will die with him'.[117]

The enquiries continued on 23 August, when the sheriff or clerk of the
peace was ordered to give the council the names of the jurors, all of
whom were ordered to attend at 3.00 p.m. The Lord Mayor, Recorder, and
Attorney General, meanwhile, were ordered speedily to send the council
an accurate account of what had gone on. Those jurymen who did not
attend were ordered to appear at 8.00 a.m. the following morning.[118]
Further oral and written testimony about the proceedings was solicited the
following day and the reports for Parliament were still being prepared on

30 and 31 August.[119] Rather ominously the council, having considered a report from Colonel Tomlinson about 'the business of Hatfield Chase', added Tomlinson to the committee appointed to make an extract of the papers relating to the trial, and on 6 September 'The persons who gave testimony to Council concerning Lilburne's deportment in foreign parts' were summoned to the council 'to swear to the truth of what they delivered'. Clearly a case was being built.[120]

Meanwhile, Lilburne was taken under guard from Newgate to the Tower 'to be there secured for the peace of the nation', along with others rumoured to be suspected of conspiracy with him.[121] Lilburne published a lengthy narrative of his life, *The just defence*, which rebutted the charge of turbulency of spirit,[122] but the regime was clearly unconvinced. Against the background of renewed unrest in Scotland and fears of royalist plots, Lilburne was still rumoured to threaten the stability of the regime, and troops were detained in London for fear of unrest.[123]

The Dutch Ambassadors reported on 2 September that Lilburne would be moved from the Tower to 'the islands of Man, Guernsey, or Sorlings, there to evaporate his turbulent humours; whereof he is full, as they say here'. The jurors, they thought, would 'not escape unpunished either in bodies or estates'.[124] The propaganda battle continued: in late September *An hue- and cry after the fundamental lawes and liberties of England* had decried his continued imprisonment, connecting closely with denunciations of the regime.[125] In late November *Lieut. Colonel J. Lilburn tryed and cast* gave a detailed refutation of Lilburne's version of the Harraton dispute, and justified the Act of Banishment and the government response to his return from exile.[126] Meanwhile, the Council of State was evidently still worried about habeas corpus writs served by Lilburne in the Upper Bench, telling Barkstead, the lieutenant of the Tower, to respond 'that Lilburne is committed to him by warrant from the Council of State, in order to the preservation of the peace and safety of the nation, in pursuance of an order of Parliament'. Legal advice was sought.[127] A few days later Barkstead was instructed not to let Lilburne appear before the Upper Bench again without an order from Parliament or the council.[128] On 10 January, however, Barkstead was given permission to 'admit such persons as he thinks fit' to visit Lilburne,[129] and he remained in the Tower until March 1654.

In December 1653, Barebone's Parliament had voted for its own dissolution following protracted in-fighting. This spelt the end of the Commonwealth, and its replacement by the Protectorate. Oliver Cromwell was to govern as

Lord Protector under a written constitution, the Instrument of Government, drawn up mainly by army officers. Although the Lord Protector was bound to call parliaments every three years, this was rather like the settlement offered to Charles I in 1647, and Cromwell resembled a monarch in his place. In particular, it was not based on the principle of parliamentary sovereignty, a cornerstone of the parliamentary cause since 1642. Many people thought that this had been Cromwell's plan all along, and that this was the final stage of his betrayal of godliness and reform. That was surely unfair, but the origins of the Instrument betray considerable hesitation and perhaps unease at the new constitutional arrangement.[130]

Whatever the propriety of the new constitution, the change of regime seemed to offer another opportunity like the one Lilburne had seen in the dissolution of the Rump earlier in the year. John Streater, whose views were close to Lilburne's, had been imprisoned after publishing a pamphlet called *The Grand Politick Informer*. He now argued that his prosecution had lapsed with the dissolution of the Parliament that had convicted him: the finding in his favour came in January and he was freed on 11 February.[131] The precedent was a dangerous one for a government intent on keeping Lilburne off the streets, and this seems to have prompted them to move him to Jersey, which was done in early April. It was believed that only the Lord Protector could order his release from there: habeas corpus would not reach.[132] Another observer felt that he had been sent to Jersey so that Cromwell should be 'the lesse offended by the Levellers'. There Lilburne would 'be close prysoner, and kept from pen, Inke and paper'.[133] In contrast to 1649, then, the fact that he had been found innocent did not lead to freedom, and there were in any case doubts about the legality of the 1651 Act. Slingsby Bethel, writing a later hostile account of Oliver Cromwell, saw in this evidence that the Protectorate was a less just regime than the Commonwealth brought in by the regicide in 1649.[134] There is certainly something to that view.

Jersey was certainly a hard imprisonment. In the castle at Mount Orgeuil he had no easy access for visitors, or to the presses and their output. He was isolated and out of the public eye, remote from his family. Despite his victory in court this was another exile, and one imposed by apparently arbitrary means. There is perhaps finally a suggestion that this, the latest of his tribulations, was indeed a source of despond:

> Frailties and infirmities I have, and thick and threefold have been my provocations . . . I dare not say, Lord I am not as other men; but *Lord be merciful to me a sinner*, But I have been hunted like a Partridge upon the mountains: My words

and actions in the times of my trials and deepest distress and danger have been scanned with the spirit of *Jobs* comforters; but yet I know I have to do with a gracious God, *I know that my redeemer liveth*, and that he will bring light out of this darkness, and clear my innocency to all the world.[135]

Final imprisonment: Jersey and Dover, 1653–7

In exile and prison Lilburne receded from public view, although rumours continued to haunt him. The governor on Jersey, Colonel Robert Gibbon, was suspicious of him and his influence over the soldiers, and Lilburne's chief comfort seems to have been the care shown for him by Elizabeth Crome. His health and well-being were clearly suffering, and the governor eventually gave him more freedom to take the air, but Lilburne refused to do so with 'a dogge at his heels'. Chafing against this new exile, he seems to have been an angular and difficult prisoner, and there were difficulties about the payment of his allowance.[136] In May 1654 it was rumoured that following 'discovery of some manuscripts by him prejudicial to the Protectorate he has been put to death in prison, without further form of trial'. He was, the report said, 'a man of singular ability', but others were unsympathetic: a mock last will and testament was published in London, restating the case that he was a turbulent and fractious man.[137] The following month the Council of State issued an order that he should not be allowed to leave the island without special order.[138]

His father-in-law, Henry Dewell, visited in late June 1655, fifteen months into his latest captivity. He came with an offer—that Lilburne could be released from these frustrations if he promised to behave himself. Lilburne of course refused—that would be a form of slavery, since his freedom would be at the will of another, he would only be freed by the law.[139] His father-in-law urged him to desist from trying to have all things his own way; 'the law is my only way' he replied. Reflecting on this episode, Gibbon wrote that 'I cannot but report, that he is the very same man as formerly'. Lilburne was, though, willing to be moved to the Isle of Wight and Gibbon supported this, saying that if anything would work it might be this: on the Isle of Wight his friends could visit and try to talk him into some 'meek and quiet' spirit. Revealingly, though, Gibbon also acknowledged that Cromwell might think he was just trying to get rid of his most troublesome prisoner. Gibbon also passed on a characteristic offer of arbitration of the issues, which Lilburne had apparently promised to honour. Lilburne requested a visit from his own father, prompting further anxious correspondence between Gibbon and Cromwell—whether they should be allowed to converse in private and whether Lilburne simply intended to use it to send papers out.[140]

There was, however, gathering pressure to treat Lilburne better than he was willing to treat himself. Elizabeth petitioned for his relief at the end of July. Despite the 'solicitacions and a tedious Journey' by her father, 'his restraint is still most severe'. She said 'his senses, health, & life endangered, and all (as is humble conceived) because he is some way or other represented to your highness as a person of soe great as violence and rashnes, as not fit to be trusted with his owne liberty or any part thereof'. She resisted the temptation to set out his various sufferings and asked instead whether it was his current conditions that made him rebellious. Severe imprisonment, a trial for his life, and social isolation that had constituted 'such matter of continual provocation' that nothing could be expected of him, except the rash statements that had alarmed the government. If he was freed 'his demeanour and converse would not any way savour of violence, but that with all quitenes he would thanckfully receive and enioy the same'. She engaged her own life that he would not then disturb the state.[141]

Richard Lilburne, now in his seventy-third year, petitioned the same day, and in much the same terms. He was seeking a chance to talk to his son, as the man 'that may well know more of his disposicon, and more certainly, then any other'. John was, he admitted, 'conceived to be a person soe captivated & transported by his passions into rashness and violence, that nothing (were he at libertie) would withhold him from disturbing the peace of the Commonwealth'. He also admitted that the council might 'have grounds for such conceivings from some rash and unadvised expressions whereunto in his times of Restraint [to his father's grief] he hath been too much adicted'. He too, though, attributed this to the restraint, hard usage, and manifold afflictions of his current situation, and expressed confidence that if he 'could conveniently discourse his minde unto him, that he should persuade him into a peaceable behavior for all future time'.[142]

Something seems to have worked to soften the attitude of the regime. In September, Cromwell agreed to bring Lilburne back to the mainland, and in October he sailed to Dover via Weymouth, where he spent a few days with William Harding, the mayor, arriving in Dover on 11 October. Dover may have been chosen as another place where habeas corpus did not reach: one of the Cinque Ports, it had a particular relationship to the English Crown.[143] It was at least closer to his friends and family, however, and they continued to petition for his release. Lilburne himself remained committed to his position—his freedom could not depend on the indulgence of the powerful. A similar commitment led him to refuse generosity from Hesilrige. Elizabeth was living in some hardship with their new child Benomy near the Guildhall, and Hesilrige offered her access to lands in Durham. Lilburne refused.[144]

★   ★   ★

During a visit in November John had spoken to Elizabeth of his spiritual unrest, and in the next few months he underwent a profound religious experience, resulting in his conversion to Quakerism.[145] There may be a clue to his state of mind in the name of the child: Benomy is often said to mean 'child of my sorrows'. The name was often given to children whose mother died in childbirth or whose father had died, or who died young. In this case, perhaps, it speaks to the despondency which for the first time seems to inflect some of his writings.

Lilburne's converted to Quakerism in May that year. On arrival in Dover, having been in discussion with Mayor William Harding in Weymouth about Quakerism, he requested Quaker books from Giles Calvert, and was particularly impressed by the writing of William Dewsbury and James Nayler. After that he had a number of conversations with a shoemaker, Luke Howard, at Dover Castle, a man who had experience of some of the same circles as Lilburne, including William Kiffin's congregation. For the historian Pauline Gregg 'it was their emphasis on the witness within which made such a strong appeal to Lilburne', and she drew attention to the similarities between Howard's own conversion and some of Lilburne's experiences. But it was also a lesson in humility. In Dover Lilburne was allowed out on parole and attended Quaker meetings. Leaving one with without having experienced conversion he was followed by George Harrison, who told him 'Friend, though art too high for truth'.[146] That he was guilty of spiritual pride apparently came to Lilburne as a revelation, a decisive step in self-knowledge.

This conversion to Quakerism was regarded with suspicion at the time and since—was it sincere, and did it betoken a withdrawal from politics, or even an admission of defeat? In fact it was not an unnatural conclusion to his religious journey, although the detail of that journey is somewhat unclear. Christian rhetoric had of course suffused Lilburne's writings, but he had not defined his cause in religious terms. He had consistently claimed to suffer for the legal rights of the Englishman, a civic inheritance which restrained tyranny, and had never claimed to suffer for a particular theological or confessional position. Paradoxically, therefore, although he often referred to the strength he drew from his faith, and from Christ's example, for much of his life we have comparatively limited insight into the details of his faith.

However, he had lived through a crisis in English Calvinism, taking a path which led fairly naturally to this point. The challenge to Calvinism under Archbishop Laud had particularly involved a re-emphasis of the importance of clerical authority, the value of many traditions not explicitly licensed by scripture, and the edification of the congregation. The successful reaction against this had unleashed forces which also undermined Calvinism though: the attack on the bishops had been associated with a more general anti-clericalism and even opposition to the existence of national churches. Lilburne had been at the hard edge of this argument: he had for example argued not only that the Church of England was not a true church, but that Christians should avoid hearing any of its ministers preach, while his breach with the Presbyterians led him to say openly that he was opposed to the regulation of the church by the 'leaden' laws of men.[147]

This clear separation of the religious and secular spheres seems also to have been associated with a separation of his sometimes immediate sense of God's presence from the detail of his political life.[148] Cromwell, by contrast, was convinced that at times he could see God's direct purpose for the detail of human affairs. He was prone to periods of apparently agonized indecision, punctuated by energetic action fired by great religious certainty. To Lilburne this was a vanity, and one source of his hypocrisy. Lilburne referred disparagingly to the Independent 'party' after 1649—those who confused their religious conscience with their political life. As a consequence they acted in the same way as the Laudians or the Presbyterian party, albeit in the name of a different confessional position. A revealing term of abuse he used for those on the Council of State was Knipperdollings, a reference to one of the key figures in the regime of the Münster Anabaptists, led by John of Leyden. For many early modern Christians these people had brought the power of godliness into disrepute by using it to justify all sorts of sin and misgovernment. In the same way, in Lilburne's view, the Knipperdollings of the Independent party had made the power of godliness more reproachfull and contemptible, in the Eyes of the Sonnes of men than ever the foolish & ridiculous actions, Fathred upon and said to be committed, at Munster...by Iohon of Leyden & Knipperdolling: whom in folly, murder, madnes, & ridiculousness: you have, visibly in the face of all the world outstripped.[149]

This points to a sharp separation in Lilburne's mind between personal spiritual growth and the civic duties of a Christian. The charge against those who could see the hand of God at work in the detail of secular life was really one of vanity. His own faith had given him strength to oppose the corruption of the civil state, a corruption that was often driven by the secular ambitions of persecuting clerics (bishops and Presbyterians), but it was not expressed in a desire to reconfigure the state according to his own religious convictions.

The disintegration of the anti-Laudian reaction signalled a larger crisis in English Calvinism, and the emergence of further alternatives which, for example, laid still greater stress on the relationship between the individual and God, on the conscience rather than scripture as a guide to that relationship, and which rejected compulsory religious organization or national churches. That latter pole of argument related to the relationship between secular and religious orders, between 'erastians', who believed that the national community should also be a religious community, and separatists, who thought they were different orders of human life, governed by different laws. Lilburne, clearly, had been consistently anti-clerical and anti-erastian throughout his adult life, and although at times he had felt the immediate presence of God, this was in individual experience, not a blueprint to be imposed on society as a whole.[150]

In all this Lilburne had some fellow feeling with the early Quakers. In fact Quakerism was very much alive in many of the circles in and through which Lilburne had moved. Another prominent Quaker, John Farnworth, enjoyed great success on the Isle of Axholme, particularly in Haxey, in 1652 and 1653. Michael Monckton, a Justice of the Peace very sympathetic to the Epworth commoners, who Lilburne must have known, was to become a prominent Quaker.[151] That same summer he had represented John Fielder before the Indemnity Committee, and Fielder too had subsequently become a prominent Quaker.[152] Henry Clarke, who had supported Lilburne's cause at his 1653 trial, was a Quaker, and when he had stayed with Harding in Weymouth, en route from Jersey to Dover, they had discussed Quaker religion.[153] The rapid growth of Quakerism owed a lot to print as well as to evangelical work, and Lilburne's access to it was facilitated by what he read. Giles Calvert, whose press had sometimes been helpful to Lilburne, was very active in Quaker printing.[154]

He discusses his conversion at length in *The resurrection of John Lilburne*. The second edition of the pamphlet gathers letters to his wife, Harding, and Elizabeth Hunniwood, along with a declaration of his faith and a letter denouncing the beliefs of the Baptists, addressed to Robert Barrington, one of the 'meer outside, imitating without life or power, *Water-Baptists*' at Dover. Much of it is devoted to expressions of his new faith, and the comfort it has given him, and the sections dealing with his Quaker belief are heavily annotated with scriptural citation, far more heavily than any of his publications, even those in the late 1630s. There is much that is easily identifiable as a Quaker style—for example, he refers to Harding as the 'commonly called Mayor' of Weymouth, signifying his respect towards inward, Christian virtue over the trappings of human convention. He again published as plain John Lilburne, dropping his military rank.[155]

It is primarily a work of piety, expressing to people important to him (for a print audience) 'the measure of the light of the Lord now shining clearly within me' and '*the life and power of those divine and heavenly principles, professed by those spiritualized people called* Quakers'.[156] His letter to Elizabeth explains how this has led him to abandon an interest in his earthly, fleshly concerns, and he urges her too to see beyond the snares of these everyday worries. His recent isolation had forced him, 'whether I wil or no, in spite of my teeth, once again [to] give ear to the serious and plain voice, call or counsel of the Most High, speaking in, and unto my soul'. This was his most immediate experience of God, and he compared it more than once to the lesser exhilaration even of his experiences in the 'Bishops time'.[157]

In the light of this resurrection, Elizabeth should now feel released from her efforts on his behalf. But he also offered an example for her, entreating her: '*not to much cumber thy self in thy many toilings and journeyings for my outward liberty, but sit down a little, and behould the* great salvation *of the* Lord'. He was clear, though, that this renunciation was also a renunciation of family. He was called now to follow the heavenly and divine voice 'through the denyall of my own (or naturall reason) will, wit, wisdom, desires', to throw off worldly things, including family: 'yea, even to a final denyal of father, kindred, friends, my sweet and dearly beloved (by me) babes, or thy own self, who *viz*, thy self, for many yeers by-past hath been to me the greatest & dearest of all earthly delights and joyes'. Her evident money worries were no longer his:

'I am sorry thou art so straightly put to it for money, *but to live upon God by faith in the depth of straights, is the lively condition of a Christian*'. As he wrote to Harding, his intention now was to draw on the strength of this faith 'to redeem my lost, and mis-spent by-past precious time, and not now to consult with flesh and blood in my daily taking up the *Cross of Christ*'.[158]

This apparent withdrawal was regarded with suspicion by the authorities and disapproval by his former allies: 'all my old and familliar friends (in a manner) are so much troubled and offended with me..., and my great adversaries so jealous of the reall intentions of my heart'.[159] In *The chasing the young quaking harlot out of the City*, Thomas Winterton denounced Edward Burrough and James Nayler, both prominent Quakers, as 'false deceiving, jugling Prophets'. They were guilty of spiritual pride, of luring followers into a false belief, and of 'abundance of dissimulation' in relation to the 'Sword'. He took in Lilburne's *Resurrection* as further evidence that the claim to receive the spirit directly undermined the account of the Gospels, and the debt of Christians to Christ. He also pointed out that Lilburne had struggled against his national authority as Saul had done, and that Burrough encouraged his readers to 'Make Warre in righteousness... wound the head of your enemies, and manage Warre against *Gog* and *Magog*'. Who in the current context, were Gog and Magog?[160]

The implication of quietism was clearly present, then, but was not certain. These early Quakers were very capable of confrontational behaviour—challenging worldly authorities and in doing so demonstrating that they were committed to the spiritual kingdom.[161] Lilburne clearly shared some of this, in his grossly transgressive disrespect for the House of Lords, for example, or in his more general declarations that he was no respecter of persons.[162] *The selfe afflicter*, a hostile pamphlet, in fact attributed Quakerism's appeal for him to their heat and zeal, and hatred of the world.[163] While there was clearly potential for confrontation and transgression in Quaker spirituality, however, there was also an emerging debate on how engaged with the world Quakers should be. In 1655, George Fox, another prominent early Quaker, had very publicly withdrawn from political engagement, giving Cromwell a personal assurance that he would not disturb the powers that be.

The issue was very much alive at the point Lilburne converted. In October 1656, James Nayler rode into Bristol on a donkey, accompanied by bare-headed followers, seeming to demonstrate the grossly transgressive potential of Quakerism. Quakers usually refused to doff their hats except in the presence of the divine. His point was to dramatize the view that we all have the spark of Christ within us, but to many contemporaries this seemed simply blasphemous: were these bare-headed Quakers suggesting that Nayler was divine? His trial in December of that year was one of the key moments at which the limits of England's freedoms were tested, and his punishments were severe. They were also strikingly akin to those visited on Lilburne and the puritan martyrs nearly twenty years earlier. In fact, Lilburne's punishments at Parliament's hands were brought up in the debate about how to treat Nayler. The generosity of the support voted to Lilburne in prison (£2 per week) was thought to be relevant to the discussion about what to do with Nayler: some thought imprisonment on such terms was too soft an option.[164]

Lilburne publicly claimed in effect to have adopted Fox's position, although he refused to give any formal assurance on the matter. When Elizabeth showed his letter to Cromwell and to Charles Fleetwood, there was scepticism, but Lilburne declared himself incapable of deceit *'having then the very dreadful, and aweful, immediate, convincing, judging and burning up power of God upon my soul'*. He would not, though, give an undertaking like George Fox had done, despite Elizabeth's prompting. Lilburne thought any such declaration would have been made for his own human ends, 'to avoid further persecution, and the like'. To make it would have made him a 'pharisaical imitator'. While he admired Fox, his 'particular actions' were 'no rules for me to walk by'.[165]

For Lilburne it was no human undertaking that bound him—and here there is a connection with his earliest resistance to oaths. Instead, he renounced the temporal struggle altogether: 'I am already dead, or crucified, to the very occasions, and real grounds of all outward wars, and carnal sword-fightings & fleshly buslings and contests; and...therefore I confidently now believe, I shall never hereafter be an user of a temporal sword more, nor a joyner with those that so do'.[166] As a later, sympathetic, commentator put it, 'being not yet so far convinced as to believe the use of the sword was unlawful, nor perfectly approving that point of self-denial, he refused to purchase his liberty on this condition'. He was in time convinced of the principle, but would not use it to secure his freedom.[167]

This renunciation of a desire for earthly liberties seems sincere, although it is difficult to be sure, and of course there were at the time ample grounds for doubting its sincerity, or at least reliability. Since the 1630s he had distinguished between his duty in opposing civil tyranny and his personal religious faith, and in 1649 had seemed to turn away from the hurly burly of political life in order to pursue his family interests. He had not been able to avoid such embroilments then, however, and it is possible that he was reserving the right to take up the former cause again if his conscience provoked him: his record showed how a particular injustice might easily prompt him back into public controversies. Richard Hubberthorn, who knew Lilburne, wrote in his defence, admitting that 'God owned [Lilburne] in opposing many of the unjust powers of the Nation, is as plain, else had he not lived'. But he had lived to be converted, and Hubberthorn wanted his readers to believe that Lilburne was now a changed man.[168]

Nonetheless, Lilburne's name certainly continued to carry a political charge. The use of a special commission of oyer and terminer against fenland rioters in 1654 was thought to be risky, given Lilburne's experience, while defendants in a treason trial arising from a royalist rising in 1655 prepared a briefing paper for their address to the jury which drew directly and explicitly on the argument he put to his own jury, that they could throw out a bad law, or at least refuse to prosecute and thereby leave it on the conscience of the judges. In December of that year Edmund Chillenden, whose life had intersected with Lilburne's at many points over the previous two decades, had written to Thurloe assuring him that he, Chillenden, posed no threat to the regime. Part of his case was that 'when petitions formerly of Lilburne and the Levellers have brought their petitions to the several congregations where I have binn, I have caused them to be throwne by, and never yet where I was, were any signed'.[169]

There were other ways in which he had not quite left his past behind. In the spring of 1656 Lilburne wrote to Margaret Fell, a very influential Friend, asking for her help in resolving a conflict with Anthony Pearson, an associate of Hesilrige's, about Lilburne's lands, which were still in Hesilrige's name. He had called on many Friends to vouch for his honesty, and to try to resolve the difference, but he remained unwilling to regain the lands except on the grounds that Hesilrige had acted unlawfully in taking the title. At the end of a lengthy letter about it, suffused both with Quaker rhetoric and the more familiar detailed narrative, he complained that the dispute had 'set my wife, my father [?] to his vtmost power togeather by the eares with me in such atorminting [*sic*] contest as J neuer with any of my adversaries went through in all my life tyme'.[170]

Contemporaries can be forgiven their scepticism, therefore, but at this distance in time Lilburne sounds sincere in saying the statement of faith he now gave:

I do here solemnly declare, not in the least to avoid persecution, or for any politick ends of my own, or in the least, for the satisfaction of the fleshly wils of any of my great adversaries, or for the satisfying the carnal will of my poor weak, afflicted wife; but by the special movings and compulsions of God now upon my soul.[171]

His long confinement, according to later Quaker accounts, had 'changed the temper of his mind, from an active and bustling to a serious and contemplative cast'. By preventing him 'from conversing in the busy seenes of life, [confinement] had furnished him with opportunity to be more conversant with himself'.[172] Hubberthorn had written to George Fox in 1657 that having met Lilburne twice in Kent he was sure that he 'is zailus and forward for the truth: he hath a sight & comp[re]hention which his deepe he sees that the truth Comprehends all and hath a love unto it & desire to ataine [it]'.[173] It is tempting to think that in this extended exile, from England and then from family and friends, he had truly abandoned political struggles in favour of pursuing his own spiritual growth.

If true, it was timely. He was now being allowed out on parole, sometimes spending nights away from prison and preaching to Quaker meetings in Kent. Elizabeth was expecting another child, and she took a lodging at Eltham, nearer to John. In the summer of 1657 he was released to stay with her for the lying-in, but Elizabeth found her husband 'very sicke and weake': he was in bed when he received the order to return to prison. He died ten days later, on 29 August, the day he was due back in prison. Bethel thought he had been imprisoned 'until he was so far spent in a Consumption that [Cromwell] onely turned him out to dye'.[174]

Two days later his funeral took place at The Mouth at Aldersgate, London, a well-known Quaker meeting place. His burial was not without controversy. Some of the mourners, his old Leveller friends, and perhaps Elizabeth herself, had tried to cover the coffin with a velvet pall, but 'the Quakers would by no means admit of it, Alledging that the lesse there was of pomp, the more of piety'. His body was taken out to the street at 5.00 p.m. where an unnamed mourner again tried to give him this honour, but the Quakers again resisted. It was said that 4,000 people accompanied the coffin as it was taken on the shoulders of his Quaker Friends to the churchyard at Bethlem by Bishopsgate.[175]

★   ★   ★

Lilburne was in his early forties, not old even by seventeenth-century standards. His health had not been good from the time of his imprisonment on Jersey, however, and this may be one reason why the last four years of his life saw a much reduced public figure. The pace of his publication certainly slowed dramatically, and this final period of exile and enforced absence from the hurly burly of politics seems to have ended with a personal withdrawal.

Over the previous two decades, of course, he had been far from retired. He had participated in many forms of activism characteristic of the revolutionary decades—print, petitioning, crowd demonstrations, soldiering, and legal trials. He had also followed a religious journey through the crisis of Calvinism, and emerged it seems at a point of withdrawal from worldly concerns. He illustrates the complexity of the politics of the period—the difficulty of reducing the issues to simple binary choices. He was against tyranny, which led him into conflict with every government of his adult life. He opposed bishops and popery, and for a while identified in this the need for reformation of the church, which made him a fellow traveller with Prynne and Bastwick, but his commitment to the individual conscience had at another point made him a closer ally of the royalist divine Jeremy Taylor, and in the end led him to something close to political quietism. He went to prison in 1638 as an ally of Bastwick, the Presbyterian, and was published in England in 1641 with a preface by William Kiffin, who became a prominent Baptist. By the time of his death he thought them both deeply mistaken in their religious beliefs, but the settlement for which he campaigned, an *Agreement of the People*, would have protected their rights as securely as it would have his own. Lilburne's career reveals the fluidity, dynamism, and creative power of the revolutionary decades, but also the difficulty of reducing the conflicts and alliances to two sides. The divisions at his funeral about how to honour him reflect that. Opinion about what was really at stake in his serial struggles, and in the wider political crisis, continued to differ long after his death.

8

John Lilburne and the English Revolution

Freeborn John, 'the lovable egoist, lucid though garrulous, and sure of himself'

Lilburne's life seems to demonstrate the force of the Chinese curse—he abundantly tasted the 'tossings and tumblings' of the interesting times in which he lived.[1] He had been on trial for his life three times: in 1642 for treason against the king; in 1649 for treason against the Commonwealth; and in 1653 for returning from exile. In May 1641 he was hauled up before the House of Lords for allegedly treasonous words, perhaps at the insistence of the king himself. At that point he had already spent three years in prison having refused to promise to answer the questions about to be put to him. Captured at Brentford, he spent nine months in dreadful conditions in Oxford Castle. Taking up his pen in 1645, he was called to account by order of one or other of the Houses of Parliament on five occasions that year, three of them involving brief detentions, and the final one, in August, leading to three months in Newgate. He was arrested on a trespass action brought by his factional enemy Colonel King in April 1646 and appeared before Parliament again in June, spending three weeks in close confinement in Newgate. In July he was sentenced to seven years in the Tower by the House of Lords. Greater freedom to come and go, granted in November 1647, had ended in him being committed again, and with a new charge for his role in seditious petitioning (for which he was never tried), and he was not released until August 1648. He was free this time until March 1649, when he was arrested for the publication of *England's new chains discovered*, and was tried in October under the Treason Acts passed while he was in jail, for things he had published from captivity. He was freed on 8 November following his acquittal and remained at liberty for more than two years, something of a record. His banishment in December 1651 for his role in Josiah Primatt's petition, however, resulted in exile, the last of the trials for his life, and then further imprisonment.

In the period of just under twenty years covered by this book, then, he seems to have spent around twelve and a half years in prison or exile. He had also spent twenty months in the army. Between the summer of 1642 and the end of 1644, he had seen very active military service, being involved in life-threatening action at Edgehill, Marston Moor, and especially Brentford. He was wounded in action, captured a castle, and almost lost an eye in an accident involving a pike in 1646. Put the other way, after his initial arrest there were only six years when he was not in arms, prison, or exile: the longest periods of liberty being November 1640 to July 1642 and November 1649 to December 1651.

In the course of this life he fought some important legal battles, which have been of lasting significance, serving as an inspiration to subsequent generations. The parliamentary decision to overturn his imprisonment for refusing to plead before the Star Chamber has been assimilated to the interpretation of the 5th Amendment in the USA, and the decision in his favour was for example cited in the Supreme Court. His constant demand for an open trial has been cited in relation to the 6th Amendment, while his refusal to plead before the House of Lords in 1646, demanding instead a hearing before *his* peers, rested on a reading of Magna Carta, an enlargement of its interpretation that has continued. In all this he was 'the most public and persistent habeas corpus litigant of any age'.[2] His participation in the campaign for an *Agreement of the People* of course earned him a prominent place in the pantheon of heroes of libertarianism and the left alike.

He owed his life to two juries: that in 1649 which claimed that it was a judge of law as well as fact; and that in 1653 which found that he was not guilty of any crime worthy of death. Lilburne also therefore became a champion of the jury as a bulwark against political or tyrannical judges, and the argument that juries were judges of law as well as fact long outlived him.[3] His example was immediately important, as a caution against proceeding by special commission of oyer and terminer, and as a model for others accused of treason and thinking how to address their jury. Clement Walker thought that Lilburne's trial had taught the Cromwellian regime 'That is an easier Matter for them to pack a Butcher-row of confiding, partial Judges, then a Jury'. This was a persistent idea—that juries offered greater protections against the executive than judges do. As we will see, his example was important to late eighteenth-century radicals, and part of the hinterland for Fox's Libel Act of 1792. This legislation has been seen as another important defence of the power of juries to restrain executive abuse of the courts.[4]

Very little survives of him, though, beyond what he published and what was published about him, and this material gives very little direct insight into his internal life. For example, he shared his adult life with Elizabeth, who followed him to garrisons and, when allowed, into prison. It was a crucial relationship for him and one on which he was at times very dependent. It was Elizabeth who petitioned for his release from Oxford Castle, and who carried the threat of retaliation against royalist prisoners from London to Oxford through enemy lines. She was clearly an intermediary with Hesilrige and Cromwell, trying to secure his return from exile and release from prison, and can be glimpsed in some of his publications working the corridors at Westminster. It was a marriage marked by great hardships and sacrifice. One of their ten children was named Tower, having been born there, and another Benomy—child of my sorrows—and they had the time and misfortune to be able to name two children John, and two Elizabeth. Following his death Elizabeth was a petitioner for state support, living under the threat of the fine imposed on him, and dependent on his small prison pension.

Of this family life John says very little, however—he notes the death of his children, but not by name, and his references to Elizabeth are intermittent and often admonitory. He mentions the hardships his family endured, claiming at one point that the 'ruine and destruction of me, my wife and tender infants' might lead him to '*eate my owne flesh*', but he did so for immediate political purposes—in this case to press his claims for reparations.[5] Elizabeth was clearly a courageous and considerable figure, but she is really only visible as a footnote to John's autobiography, and in his last publications appears for example as a weak vessel, a temptation which might weaken him in his service of God, a burden rather more than a support. Dismissive of her money worries, he encouraged her to leave him alone and look to her own spiritual well-being.[6] This thoroughgoing subordination of the welfare of his wife and children to the pursuit of his conscience, honour, and reputation is striking, to say the least. Behind it lay the certainty that his battle was the battle of all Englishmen, and that he had been called by God to fight it.

For the same reason he appears to have kept few friends. It is tempting to see in his relationship with his father something of a model for his relationship with other powerful men. There was clearly a profound respect, manifest in his refusal to be styled 'yeoman' in court in 1642, or in his self-identification in court in 1649 and 1653—John Lilburne, son of Richard Lilburne, gent. He may have learned something too from his father's legal difficulties—the attempt to end a land dispute deadlocked by the absence of relevant documents by invoking a trial by battle. John frequently argued for the virtues of a quicker process, was acutely aware of the tactical importance of knowing the law, and also repeatedly called a single and decisive arbitration of his own disputes. When John's confrontation with the courts in 1637/8 exposed his father to potential ruin, however, it is clear that his son accepted the breach in the relationship and pressed on with his own battle. He seems to have been strongly drawn to other men he saw as protectors and patrons, but also capable of repudiating them completely when they disappointed him. Thus, his one-time hero, Bastwick, or his once darling friends the earl of Manchester and Oliver Cromwell, all became his enemies.

Drawn to such figures, he also expressed the strength of his convictions in a capacity to disavow or express his independence from them. As he wrote to Cromwell, he was a man that 'neither *loves Flattery*, nor fears *Greatnes or Threatning*'.[7] But he could, equally, be reconciled, as he was with his father, who was there to support him in court in 1653 and petitioned for his release in 1655, and with Cromwell on a number of occasions. It is a tempting view, but difficult to probe any further on the basis of what John has left us: it is frequently frustrating not to be able to draw the curtain back a little further.

John was proud to claim that he was a son of the leading house of the Lilburne family, which traced it roots back as far as the Norman Conquest. The image of him in court with Coke's *Institutes* in his hand is clearly that of a gentleman, and it is not perhaps an over-reading to see gentry pride in his signature to his examination before Sir John Banks and Sir Edward Littleton in 1638, which he promised to seal with his 'dearest blood' (Figs 1.4 and 5.2). The Lilburne family did not thrive in these interesting times, however. At his death John had three living children, and a fourth, Bethia, was on the way. By 1688 John, Elizabeth, and Benomy had all died without issue and Bethia, although still alive, was unmarried.[8] He had not established them in a competent estate, either. His failure to settle successfully in a trade was a subject of satire,[9] but it was a serious matter for his family.

Three months after his death Elizabeth petitioned for repeal of the Act of Banishment and associated fine of £7,000 imposed on him in 1653. This was finally done in August 1659,[10] but that only dealt with one of Elizabeth's problems. In the same petition she had also asked for the continuance of the

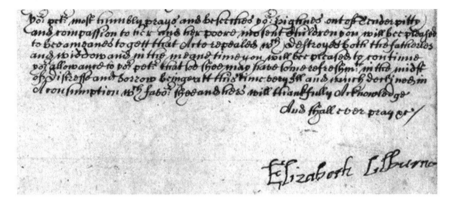

Fig. 8.1. Elizabeth Lilburne's petition with signature (1657)

small pension paid to him—40 shillings per week—and arrears from it. Her small estate was burdened with debts and had been lying under the fine: she needed 'some refreshment in the midst of distresse and sorrow, being att this time very Ill and much declined of A consumption'. In the meantime, William Huntington continued to wrangle with her so that, although Hesilrige had returned control of the estate to her, she said she could receive little benefit by reason of the perverseness of the tenant. Her signature was shaky although bold—a practiced but weakening hand, perhaps (Fig. 8.1).[11] She lived until the mid-1660s, but perhaps in uncertain conditions: we know this because she consulted John Booker, the astrologer, a number of times, particularly in 1664 and 1665, and then again early in 1667. Booker's notes of the questions she asked are sparse, so that she remains tantalizingly out of reach, but she mentions a number of figures from the past. In perhaps the last of her consultations she and her daughter Elizabeth were enquiring about the Duke of Buckingham, who had been friendly with John in exile in the 1650s and was now returned to court favour.[12] Nothing more is known of her.

John's father Richard had himself recovered something of his position during the 1650s, and held a series of local offices, but had lost his youngest son Henry in the second civil war and his middle son John to these serial tribulations. Robert, the elder son, had more success as a military officer and in Durham's committees. He married in 1649 and had children, but was himself a victim of the Restoration regime: sentenced to be hanged, drawn, and quartered for his treason in signing the king's death warrant, he was spared and spent the rest of his life in prison instead, dying in captivity in 1665. John's uncle George does not seem to have benefitted from his nephew's advocacy in the early 1650s, and there is little sign of connection between them after that, but he did prosper during the rest of the decade. At the Restoration he was evidently of sufficient eminence for it to have been worth trying to oust both he and his son from office. George in fact may have been the winner among them all, dying at the ripe age of ninety-nine in 1677.[13]

In general, Lilburne was a better friend to his beliefs than to the people with whom he campaigned for them. He was possessed of admirable, almost inhuman, fortitude, bravery, and strength of purpose, and that clearly rested on a profound belief in the correctness of his convictions. They were clearly inseparable qualities. But his self-belief bordered on self-involvement, despite the fact that it was put to such laudable public purposes: he certainly believed in important things, and prominent among them was a belief in the import-ance of John Lilburne. We do not have many descriptions of him in social situations, but there are glimpses of what was probably a powerful personal charisma. It was evident in the pillory, on the battlefield at Brentford, and in court, but also hinted at in his more casual encounter with four soldiers in 1649, tempted to join him for a drink and political chat in a nearby tavern.

Despite his almost self-annihilating courage, therefore, and the important legal battles that he fought, it is hard to be straightforwardly hagiographic about Lilburne. Even his staunchest fans have been fully aware of his angu-larities—for example Brailsford (who wrote in 1961 that it was his generation's great good fortune to rediscover the Levellers) found him 'lovable though egoistical, garrulous and sure of himself'. Henry Marten, one of the more enduring of his friends, said 'in favour of him, That if there were none living but himself John *would be against* Lilburne, *and* Lilburne *against* John'. This was the theme of a number of contemporary epitaphs not always intended in his favour,[14] while the joke certainly had a harder edge in his trials in 1649 and (particularly) 1653: was he really the champion of English liberties, or just a turbulent spirit eternally spoiling for a fight, who would make trouble whoever was in power? There is a strong case, in other words, for thinking of Lilburne as 'a great trouble-world'[15] rather than a saint; not the man who like a candle lived his life 'accommodating others and consuming himself',[16] but a man whose political sanctity came at the expense of main-taining reasonable personal relationships, a monomaniac who left a trail of broken alliances in his wake.

His stubborn pedantry could be glorious: in 1649 he spent a good por-tion of a day in court questioning what was implied by raising his hand and saying he was John Lilburne. In 1653, when really he had no defence, he questioned whether the court had established that he was the 'Lieutenant Colonel John Lilburne' named in the Act of Banishment, and for the first time since 1645 publications by him and his friends began to refer to him as plain Mr John Lilburne, gent, dropping the military title. It is this tactical cleverness that earned Lilburne a reputation as a kind of trickster hero: he was not simply a suffering saint.[17] But that pedantry, his only defence in these trials for his life, was clearly maddening in other contexts, and to people who also felt they were acting out of high principles. He was frequently moved to protest that he was not an argumentative or turbulent man, but we might think that he who tries to excuse himself actually accuses himself.

★   ★   ★

Although limited for the purposes of biography, the surviving materials provide rich resources for a political life: there is a profusion of evidence about the evolution of his public positions, and about how those emerged from specific conflicts. Lilburne placed a high value on the factual accuracy of these publications—he reproduced documents, and cited sources or other publications in ways that can be verified. He often promised to make good his claims in open disputation before witnesses and judges, and reacted angrily to accusations of inaccuracy; he was punctilious about corrections to known errors. The limitation of the sources lies more in what they leave out, rather than what they include, and at times it is possible to see those sins of omission relatively clearly. This was particularly true in court, of course. His testimony about his trip to Amsterdam in 1637 was clear about what he had not done and who he had not met, but not at all forthcoming about what he had actually been up to. In his 1649 trial he was clear about the limitations of the evidence that he was the author of the words in the indictment, but said nothing about what he had written (much to the apparent disgust of Prideaux, the prosecutor). But it was not just in such highly charged situations, when he felt no obligation to incriminate himself, that he displayed economy with the truth. When citing parliamentary orders relating to him, for example, he often leaves out the parts that do not bear directly on the argument he is presenting, although the rest of the order sometimes provides a better guide to what was in Parliament's mind when it was made.

At many stages there is a problem of attribution in his publications— some texts attributed to him do not carry his name, some that do were probably not by him, while other key texts are clearly collaborative. In the later 1630s the input of Canne and others is hard to gauge, and in the Leveller phase in particular there is some difficulty in disentangling Lilburne's writings from those of Wildman, Walwyn, and Overton, even in parts of the same text. The public Lilburne was clearly not produced simply by the man himself, and yet he is often rather coy about naming people with whom he was working.[18] He was conscious about his manipulation of publicity— writing to Elizabeth about his 'Mode and Method', and how it had been agreed—but most of his publications are tightly focused on him. This was part and parcel of his self-identification as a martyr, of course, but probably also reflected a desire to protect others. Certainly in legal proceedings he consistently refused to answer for the actions of others, or to involve them in accusations made against him. His serial appearances before parliamentary committees during the later 1640s for what had been published over his name served as a caution against revealing who had written or said what.

Nonetheless, these publications do provide a very clear view of Lilburne's public political position and its evolution. Reading forward from 1637 we can see the impact on him of particular people and of his reading. Those early pamphlets drew on the reading he had done in the house of his godly master, but also very directly on Bastwick's writing, and the English Protestant martyrological tradition. His campaigns on leaving the army were heavily inflected by his reading of Magna Carta, the Petition of Right, Parliament's own declarations, and increasingly Coke's *Institutes*. The last was a newly published guide to the common law inheritance which became an increasingly constant companion for him in appearances before committees, at the bar of one House or the other, and in court. His imprisonment in the later 1640s brought him into close contact with Judge Jenkins, greatly strengthening his conviction about that common law inheritance. He was an activist rather than a political thinker, however, and his use of sources is instrumental, and sometimes contradictory. Engaged in a broader polemic, the traces of other writings are always present, for example those of the relatively obscure George Wither.[19] In the wider body of Leveller writings too, other sources are present, and they certainly had an impact on Lilburne. In his writing in the late 1630s he had seen natural law as the limit and test of human law, and from the late 1640s there is a complex relationship between these two things. Other Leveller texts draw on the lessons of Roman history and ideas. However, the more systematic thought about these abstract questions seems to derive from his collaborators, and after 1649 he returned more clearly to his quest to secure specific rights according to an inherited tradition.[20] Flirting with Henry Marten, in opposition to the Rump in 1652,

he did begin to cite classical authors, however—Polybius and Plutarch—
and he had read Machiavelli a little earlier. It is hard, though, to find much
evidence in his writings of a thoroughgoing republicanism informed by
these thinkers. While an unsystematic thinker, he has some claims to have
invented the freeborn Englishman in the course of his campaigning and in
his polemical writing.[21]

Oddly, he said remarkably little about what seems to have been one of his
central impulses and two of the key questions in contemporary life—his
relationship with God and the nature of the true church. His commitment
to freedom of conscience and of religious assembly lay behind many of his
legal and political woes: it drew him into anti-episcopal circles in London
and Amsterdam in the late 1630s leading to his first arrest and imprisonment, and was clearly an important factor in persuading him to take up his
pen in 1645. Freedom of conscience was enshrined in the third *Agreement of
People* as an issue against which the people's representative would not be
able to legislate. Yet Lilburne only set out his views on these issues at the
beginning and end of his public life.

In the later 1630s he had argued that the Church of England was not a
true church. Governed by episcopal authority that ultimately derived from
the papacy it was a work of the Antichrist. As a result, whatever the virtues
of an individual minister their preaching was to be avoided. He seems consistently to have wanted to separate clerical and political authority, and to
have seen the mixing of the two as one of the key features of popery: for
him, there were two states—a civil and a clerical. In England in the 1630s
the current clerical estate was governed by false ordinances given by the
Devil, and that false clerical state was acting also to corrupt the civil state,
which was in principle governed by its own ordinances, developed by
Christian kings in the centuries after Christ.

In taking this line in the 1630s he was writing against bishops in alliance
with people who he later came to regard as being just as great a threat to
the true ecclesiastical state and the proper functioning of the civil state. His
view of the constitution of the primitive church was fundamentally anti-
clerical, not just anti-episcopal, but during the 1640s he had not on the
whole 'in print medled or made with the Controversies of the Church'.[22]
But while he was clearly no friend to Presbyterianism, he also denounced
the 'Independent party', in 1649 and afterward. Here his objection was to
their betrayal of their civil obligations and their false, even hypocritical,
religiosity: like the Anabaptist Knipperdolling they had made the power of

godliness ridiculous by entangling it with their flawed government. The key term here seems to be 'party', and the consistent thread is his sense of the boundary between the ecclesiastical state and civil state: this was his public concern ('in print'). As he suggested in *Rash Oaths Unwarrantable*, there was no 'greater treason committed on earth, by man against Jesus Christ, then to disclaime and renounce him and his absolut Kingship...by swearing that either the Pope, or any King, Parliament, or Potentats, are the head...in all Sperituall or Ecclesiastical things or causes'.[23] By the same token, the civil state should be governed by the established civil constitution, so long as it accorded with the abstract principles of divine and natural law, and reason. This was a bracing, perhaps naïve, solution to a problem that preoccupied many contemporaries—what law should govern the church? On this issue, he was clearly a very long way away from William Prynne, whatever ground they shared in their hostility to bishops.[24] Quakerism appealed in part perhaps because of the clear distinction drawn by Quakers on this issue—whatever else they thought, they had no truck with theocracy.

While freedom of conscience was clearly at issue in his first prosecution and was an important element of the Leveller campaign, what got him into trouble most often after 1645 was opposition to tyranny and corruption in the civil state. Even in 1637 he had spoken first against tyranny, corruption, neglect of the public good, and denial of justice by those entrusted with the people's freedoms; only in the pillory had he spoken about what was in the books he was accused of importing. In 1645 he was drawn into the polemical battle as much by his anger at the betrayal of those who had given loyal service to the parliamentary cause of 1642 as by Presbyterian religious intolerance. The obstructions he encountered in getting what he saw as just reward and reparation manifested a broader betrayal, a falling away of this Parliament from its primitive purity. It was out of that analysis of corruption, oligarchy, and self-interest that the *Agreements of the People* grew, and which drove his campaigns against Sir Arthur Hesilrige. They were connected issues, but he risked death more often for this—in 1642, 1649, and 1653—than explicitly for his separatist sympathies.

From this perspective Lilburne's life did not hinge around the Leveller campaign. In 1647 texts with which he was associated contained new elements. His consistent concerns about legal rights, and access to them, were supplemented by more abstract claims about clerical, economic, and political monopoly powers, and how those represented prerogative infringements on the rights of others. Some Leveller writings also take a clear theological position which is difficult to discern in Lilburne's other publications, at least those after 1641 and before his embrace of Quakerism, and his religious differences with Walwyn were openly acknowledged.[25] Important elements of the secular Leveller language did not survive 1649 either—his defence of his interests as a landlord and of the commoners' rights in Epworth did not draw as much on these arguments, resting instead on narrower claims about the English common law inheritance, although his assault on Hesilrige did carry clear echoes of Leveller language.

This leaves us with an apparent paradox, since he often presented himself in the figure of a Christian martyr. There were many martyrs in the century after the Reformation of course, and while they shared fortitude, conviction, and immense bravery, they died for contrasting causes: Protestant and Catholic, Lutheran and Calvinist, Presbyterian and Anabaptist. Contemporaries were clear, therefore, that it was the cause, not the suffering, that made the true martyr, and there were many who thought Lilburne did not suffer in a righteous cause. Bastwick and others denounced his vanity, even suggesting that he had fallen foul of the authorities in 1637 trying to make money, not to save souls. This charge was picked up by others, as well as the claim that Lilburne was simply a turbulent spirit. Far from being the freeborn Englishman, he was the troublesome neighbour who would never be content. His sufferings were 'vainglorious', as Prynne put it, or simply self-inflicted. As one hostile observer asked, 'Is it any reason that when a man shall willfully set fire on his house and goods, his neighbours should be constrained to make him reparation?' Lilburne's defenders had to resist these claims: Samuel Chidley, for example, did not deny that Lilburne was combative, but said instead 'he is not a man given to complaine, but where the shooe wringeth them; if men will let him alone, he will let them alone'.[26]

To Lilburne, the cause which sanctified his suffering was defence of 'the lawes, liberties, and rights of all the people of this Land'. This he did not only in obedience to God, but 'out of duty to my selfe, and neighbours'.[27] He claimed, in other words, to be doing God's work in preserving the civil constitution, not preserving the true religion. Of course, he cited lavishly from the scriptures both for principle and historical example, and he frequently acknowledged a debt to God for giving him the strength to undergo the trials visited upon him. In a characteristic challenge to Cornelius Holland he offered to 'justifie and make good at his utmost hazard (upon the principles of *Scripture, Law, Reason* and the *Parliaments and Armies ancient Declarations*) his late actions or writings in any or all his *Books*'.[28] By ensuring his rights under the civil constitution he was doing a Christian duty. As a Quaker, then, he was not necessarily embracing political quietism, although his failing health was pushing him that way; his refusal to take an obligation like that taken by Fox reflected another consistency that can be traced back to the 1630s—his Christian duty to perfect both the civil and the clerical states. He could not know whether he might be moved to act in relation to the civil state in the future and it was certainly vain to give a human promise not to. His role as a Christian was to seek the proper ordering of both states, but not to derive one from the other.[29] The English civil authorities had to be subordinate to the laws of the land, which had to be equally accessible to all free men. In the late 1630s it had been anti-Christian bishops who had threatened that legal inheritance; by the mid-1640s he saw that the more general threat was self-interested and self-perpetuating oligarchy and, under the influence of others, became more interested in classical histories and the lessons they held about the corruption of republican virtue.

He was a martyr then not for Independents or Quakers, but for Englishmen. If his attitude to Elizabeth is anything to go by, he did mean men and not people. This was despite the fact that Elizabeth and other women such as Katherine Hadley or Katherine Chidley were clearly of crucial practical importance. Elizabeth was harassed and manhandled at the Commons while awaiting an answer to one of her petitions on his behalf, and such incidents give glimpses of the role played by women in these campaigns—like Katherine Hadley, who had ended up in prison having circulated Lilburne's paper among the apprentices in 1639. Leveller women also figured prominently in the rhetorical presentation of the movement and their status as a community of respectable householders; intrusions into those households and disruption of their relationships were frequently presented as examples of tyranny. Despite this, Lilburne gave no sign that this symbolic and practical importance inflected his notion of citizenship.[30]

If the gendering of 'Englishmen' is clear, the national element is at first glance more ambiguous. Many of his contemporaries thought England a chosen nation, but that many unregenerate sinners lived there. On the other hand, they also thought that there were many godly Christians elsewhere so that, even as Europe was fragmented by religious discord, it became common for people to identify fellow travellers in other kingdoms. Lilburne's own links with puritan networks during the 1630s illustrate this potential: it had made him an internationalist, published by an English press in Amsterdam and on the fringes of the Atlantic exile community, close to those who sympathized with the Scottish Prayer Book rebellion. Over the following twenty years, however, his public campaigns had centred on the English settlement, and on the rights of Englishmen under their laws and constitution. He had become hostile to the Scots, at least in so far as they interfered in the English settlement, but also to the persecuting spirit he saw in their Presbyterianism. Of the Irish he said little, and when he went back to Amsterdam in 1652 he saw it as a threatening place, not just because of the fractured English exile community there, but because of the attitude of the magistracy. His legal campaign really does seem narrowly English, but within that broadly encompassing—not restricted to those whose religious beliefs he shared. It resembles a civic patriotism—a celebration and defence of a civic inheritance shared by people with whom he had profound religious and political disagreements. He defended the rights and liberties of the English civil state, created after the time of Christ but (if rightly governed) fully compatible with divine law and reason. His claim to his juries, particularly in 1653, that his oppression today might be theirs tomorrow, clearly resonated.[31] His apparent silence on what should be done in Ireland and Scotland might reflect sharp limits on his view of these secular rights. In the Low Countries, as war broke out with England in 1652, he was reported to have published in favour not just of 'Liberty of the People' but also 'the Freedom of Nations'. This line of argument apparently gave 'ample satisfaction' to the Dutch.[32] One way of thinking about this is that the ecclesiastical state was not a national institution; the civil state was.[33] He favoured separatism as a Christian in the ecclesiastical sphere, and campaigned for his legal rights as an Englishman in the civil sphere.

This use of the martyrological tradition hints at a shift away from the world of reformation politics (where key questions were, for example, about the nature of the true religion, how that should it be secured, and what should be done with an ungodly ruler) and towards the world of enlightenment politics (more centrally concerned with the nature of a subject's or citizen's rights, and how they should be expressed, guaranteed, and secured). His campaigns protected the rights of people whose religious views he thought deeply mistaken.

John Lilburne and the radical tradition

This political life was of broad significance not least because it was lived out close to the heart of the larger political crisis. Lilburne was a key figure in the religious opposition to Charles I, the reforming days of 1640–2, fought at the battles of Edgehill and Marston Moor, and was a significant player in the rift in the parliamentary coalition which gave rise to the New Modelling of the army, self-denial, and to the anti-Presbyterian mobilization in 1647. Out of that came the campaign for an *Agreement of the People*, in which he was a prime mover, and which he championed (albeit briefly) in the Whitehall debates in the weeks when the army was deciding what to do with, or about, Charles I. His was the second great treason trial of 1649, when the legitimacy of the post-regicidal regime was tested, and he was tried again at the next change of regime in 1653. Lilburne's positions, then as now, help mark out our own position in relation to this great crisis— what we think about Lilburne depends in part on what we think was at stake in the revolution that gave rise to his political career.

By 1700, three rival lines of interpretation of England's mid-seventeenth-century crisis were firmly established. A dominant Whig version saw in the events of the 1640s as a battle for a balanced constitution, which was finally won in the revolution of 1689. The meaning and triumph of the crisis was the restraint of the Crown by Parliament. An alternative Tory view did not so much defend Charles I, his policies, or the early Stuart constitution, as emphasize the dangers of disorder and the imperative need to maintain political order and religious decency. It favoured respect for the church, monarchy, and social hierarchy, and recoiled in horror at the excesses of the mid-century. A third, less influential, strand of radical Whig interpretation emphasized the abstract principles enunciated in the course of these crises— religious toleration, civic rights, republican virtue, and the dangers of executive tyranny. But it also saw in England's revolution unfinished business, and a need to sustain these causes for the future.[34]

After 1700 the zealotry and religious enthusiasm of seventeenth-century radicals made them increasingly alien, or incomprehensible, to their descendants. For example, the memoirs of Edmund Ludlow, a contemporary of Lilburne's who moved in similar circles, had to be heavily edited to be read seriously in the decades after 1690.[35] Lilburne escaped this to some extent, since his public appeal had never rested on claims about his access to the true religion—his secular martyrdom was more easily translated for an eighteenth-century audience. While many of his contemporaries devoted their intellect and energies to controversies that seemed opaque and antique to later generations, Lilburne's arguments, and his avoidance of engagement in the 'Controversies of the Church', made him more relevant to eighteenth-century audiences.

He was of course no hero to moderate Whigs or to Tories, but he did have something of a reputation among radical Whigs as Freeborn John. We know that his writings survived in the libraries of a number of seventeenth-century collectors, not least Ralph Smith, a prison manager whose library in 1674 contained ninety works by Lilburne.[36] His later reception depended on his writing, although its impact may be hidden: some later writers who had clearly read him did not explicitly cite him.[37] Nonetheless, we know that the account of his 1649 trial was republished in 1710, at the time of the Sacheverell trials, and the publisher requested readers to send him copies of other Leveller writings. Perhaps a little oddly, he appeared in Thomas Salmon's 1724 book collecting the biographies of men who had 'died' in the defence of their respective princes, or the liberties of their country. 'Lilburne' was used as a nom de plume for Patriot Whigs, opponents of executive power in the eighteenth century, and he merited extensive treatment in *Biographia Britannica*, which rested on detailed work on original materials and much of which still stands up to scholarly scrutiny.[38]

The familiarity of his claims about popular sovereignty and equality before the law translated directly into the campaigns of others. His model of suffering for the rights of Englishmen—of secular martyrdom—can be seen to have directly informed the political practice of subsequent generations too. Alessandro Venturi, an Italian who visited England in 1766–7, was very struck by an encounter with the radical dissenter Thomas Hollis. At a meeting of the Royal Society, Hollis displayed an image of the crucifixion with the label 'Behold the fate of a reformer', an extension of Lilburne's appropriation of the model of Christ in campaigns for secular reform.[39] John Wilkes, on the eve of his own trial in 1764, was given a copy of *A Christian Mans Triall* and one of the medals struck on Lilburne's acquittal.[40] William Bingley, publisher of the *North Briton* and a Wilkite who was prosecuted for libel, was clearly influenced by Lilburne: he refused to answer potentially self-incriminating interrogatories and was imprisoned for contempt in November 1768. He later demanded liberty to pursue his business while in prison.[41] Lilburne's use of an obscure precedent where the rights of habeas corpus had been extended to a mistreated slave, confirmed in Parliament in 1640, gave publicity to it, and it was cited again in 1772. Charles James Fox quoted the 1649 trial in relation to the 1791 trial involving John Luxford, printer of the *Morning Herald*. In fact, in what sounds like a direct comment on Lilburne's 1653 trial, Fox's Libel Act of 1792 stipulated that in seditious libel trials the jury could give 'a general verdict upon the whole matter put in issue, and shall not be required by the court to find the defendant guilty merely on proof of the publication, and of the sense ascribed to it in the information'.[42]

While he was not exactly a household name, then, he was closely associated with freedom of the press in the eighteenth century, and to some extent he stood as an emblem of liberty more generally. His name or example occurs in writing about the powers of juries in the 1760s and 1780s as well as in discussions at the time of the Libel Act: he was the first to develop the idea of the freeborn Englishman in all these senses. This was important to national identity in the eighteenth century, not least in contrast with the French—a comparison Lilburne himself had made in 1652.[43]

Lilburne's fortunes remained high in the first generation after the French revolution. During the 1790s a jumpy English government suspended habeas corpus and launched a series of prosecutions for seditious libel: words seemed once more to threaten political order. Lilburne, who had suffered almost exclusively for what he had said rather than what he had done, and who had consistently sought the freedom to speak under the protection of Magna Carta and habeas corpus, was again an important model. He was clearly a well-known figure in circles that identified themselves as 'radical'—the world of the London Corresponding Society, for example. Jeremiah Joyce had a bound copy of Lilburne's tracts with him while awaiting trial for high treason in 1794, and that volume later found its way into the hands of William Hone, a radical bookseller. Hone had in fact been profoundly influenced by reading an account of Lilburne's 1653 trial at the age of eleven—an experience for him akin to reading Bunyan. It was reading Lilburne that taught him to hate oppression and to valorise the protections given by the law and by freedom of speech. In 1809, Hone was involved in a publishing scheme to commemorate English liberties—the anniversaries of milestones like the signing of Magna Carta, but also the lives of heroes in that story such as Lilburne. On trial himself in 1817, he modelled his performance in court on Lilburne's in 1649, with similar success. Called to answer an *ex officio* oath, he denounced it as unjust and in court ridiculed the government's interpretation of the words he had printed. The jury acquitted him, revealing the limits of the libel laws as a tool of repression.[44] A familiar image of the 'freeborn Englishman', in chains and with his lips locked shut, resonates directly with the memory of freeborn John, and his serial prosecutions for dangerous writings (Fig. 8.2). There is, then, a fairly direct line of descent from Lilburne to this generation of soldiers in the fight for an Englishman's fundamental freedoms.

A FREEBORN ENGLISHMAN,
the Admiration of the World; the Envy of Surrounding Nations;
&c &c.

Fig. 8.2. The freeborn Englishman in chains (1793–8)

But there was also a Romantic response to the French revolution, of course. For William Godwin, a key figure in these radical circles, and a major historian of the English Revolution, Lilburne was a lesser figure. He was a product of an outdated mode of thinking—that of the mixed constitution, which gave specific legal freedoms to the individual to protect themselves from government. Lilburne was too concerned with this narrow view of liberty—freedom from executive abuse—which encouraged an equally narrow view of human self-realization. At times of revolutionary change a fuller human liberty was offered, beyond the freedom to exercise the individual will and encompassing a more fundamental flourishing. Lilburne, by insisting on established legal rights, in detail, was actually an enemy to the revolutionary possibilities being pursued by those who had taken power in the 1650s, in pursuit of such ideals as religious freedom and republican virtue.[45] In this Godwin shared something with Thomas Carlyle: Lilburne did not express the spirit of a new age, and both Goodwin and Carlyle compared him unfavourably with Cromwell. Carlyle thought him 'A contentious, disloyal, commonplace man; little distinguished save by his ill nature, his blindness to superior worth, and the dark internal fermentation of his own poor angry limited mind'.[46] Carlyle thought nineteenth-century Europe needed a new order, based on new principles rather than tradition. Lilburne stood for the narrowness and inflexibility of constitutionalism in conditions that called for visionary heroes.[47]

The cutting edge of historical writing in the nineteenth century was often idealist in this sense, seeing behind the surface of political events the working out of fundamental ideas and finding in those ideas the driving force of history. For the Victorian philosopher and historian T. H. Green, for example, the revolution represented the triumph of the emancipated Christian spirit: it was the quest for this emancipation that lay behind the actions of influential men. He shared some of this ground with his contemporary, the historian S. R. Gardiner, who saw behind the course of events the pressure generated by motivating values and beliefs, even if they were not always the openly stated reasons for people acting as they did.[48] A related Anglo-American tradition emerged, seeing in this puritan insurgency the origins not just of religious toleration but also of individualism—a liberal and democratic ethic which was gradually revealed by the unfolding crisis. In this more idealist literature Lilburne, who was not a great systematic thinker, or a man of generously broad spirit, fared less well.

The French Revolution also gave rise to an explicitly comparative history, which drew lessons from French and English experience in order to inform understanding of the present and future of European politics, and in particular to illuminate the transition to political modernity. During the nineteenth century, as European power across the globe increased, this transition came to be seen as a matter of world historical importance: the interpretation of England's revolution in terms of the comparative history of modernity has been very influential at various times ever since.

François Guizot was, among many other remarkable things, one of the early comparative historians. During the 1820s he translated letters and documents, and brought knowledge of England's seventeenth century to a French readership still absorbing the long aftershocks of the French revolution. He took a moderate Whig position, celebrating England's constitutional settlement which arose from a revolution lasting sixty-three years—from 1625 to 1688. He contrasted its relatively limited violence and social levelling with the radicalism of the French Revolution: for him the English path was the superior one. It was restrained by religious values and by the desire to restore a constitutional balance, rather than to create a new world. His interpretation was received into English in 1850 in a translation of his short pamphlet, *Pourquoi la revolution d'Angleterre a-t-elle reussi?* and his multivolume history began to appear in translation shortly after.[49] That short statement provoked a scathing review by Karl Marx, who argued instead that England's bourgeois revolution was incomplete: Marx was in a sense a radical Whig, seeing a failed or partial revolution in the incomplete implementation of the bourgeois values celebrated by radical Whigs.[50] Marx's attack was mounted against the background of the revolutions of 1848 and, in England, the Chartist movement, and both writers saw direct lessons in these seventeenth-century events for the future of nineteenth- and twentieth-century society. As Guizot put it, the English Revolution bore a double fruit—the constitutional monarchy in 'England' and the Republic of the United States. France had entered that path sixty years previously, and his purpose was 'to show what are the causes which have crowned constitutional monarchy in England, and republican government in the United States, with that solid and lasting success which France and the rest of Europe are still vainly pursuing'.[51]

This has remained an important theme of discussions of England's seventeenth century—it is an important point of reference in many varieties of American political science, for example—giving rise to a long and productive debate, seeing the English Revolution as one model of a transition to modernity. The English path has often been celebrated in that context as an early and flexible resolution avoiding the bloodshed and instability that marred such transitions elsewhere in Europe (in a variation of the moderate Whig interpretation, perhaps) or regretted as an incomplete, partial revolution (perhaps a mutation of the more radical Whig view).

This comparative history put constitutional theory and practice at the heart of the issue, even if the roots of those things were found in economic and social change (as they were by Marxists and others, including to some extent Guizot). As a result, in most twentieth- and twenty-first-century historiography, it is Lilburne the Leveller who has predominated: it his engagement with constitutional change that has defined him and his place in the revolution, rather than his serial battles for legal protections. The *Agreements of the People* concentrated on executive power and in particular on the reform of Parliament, and in that context Lilburne has often been placed in a democratic tradition. To the extent that this was also an egalitarian view, reflecting the rise of new social classes to influence, he has also been assimilated into a socialist tradition.[52] However, he consistently disavowed the name Leveller and any socially levelling ambition; indeed he explicitly argued that a fully representative Parliament would be a safeguard against social levelling, because it would inevitably protect property—property rights being central to the common law tradition that he championed. The third *Agreement* made measures affecting property a reserved power, one on which the people's representative could not legislate, and he insisted at many points on his own gentry status, and on his rights as a landlord or businessman.

While it is hard to cast him as a forerunner of redistributive politics or social levelling, however, it is relatively easy to see him as a proponent of what we would call the rule of law. He clearly supported a settlement based on the principle of popular sovereignty but he seems more consistently interested in the practical restraint of the executive. He referred to natural law as a test against which to hold the common law, but does not seem to have had a consistent view of the relationship between the two: he certainly does not seem to have had a coherent sense of a state of nature from which government arises and to derive the limits of political power from his view of how that happens. Most political theorists, and some contemporaries, have therefore found his thought inconsistent, or even incoherent.[53] Certainly his appendices to the third *Agreement* are less abstract than the body of the text, and more closely related to the specific legal battles he had fought.

These specific, pragmatic concerns might though have coherence for us as aspects of a generalized commitment to the 'rule of law'. Eight key principles of this conception have been identified by a prominent modern jurist: the law must be accessible and so far as possible, intelligible, clear, and predictable; questions of legal right and liability should ordinarily be resolved by application of the law and not the exercise of discretion; ministers and public officers at all levels must exercise the powers conferred on them in good faith, fairly, for the purpose for which the powers were conferred, without exceeding the limits of such powers, and not unreasonably; the law must afford adequate protection of fundamental human rights; means must be provided for resolving, without prohibitive cost or inordinate delay, bona fide civil disputes which the parties themselves are unable to resolve; adjudicative procedures provided by the state should be fair; the rule of law requires compliance by the state with its obligations in international law as in national law.[54] Lilburne can be thought of as a defender of six of them at least: the two exceptions being that he displayed no obvious interest in an international legal order and that a systematic notion of fundamental human rights would have been news to him, although perhaps he could have accepted much of that too.

The reform of executive power to reflect the sovereignty of the people seems from this perspective a way to secure particular rights and liberties rather than the product of a consistent theory of democratic or natural rights. As Godwin put it, 'His maxim was that that which in a direct and confined view appeared to be right, was the thing to be at all events and instantly done'.[55] In our terms we could see this as a version of a negative liberty—a freedom from active restraint—rather than a fuller, positive liberty to flourish in some broader sense. By insisting on his established rights, Lilburne was an impediment to those trying to create a new order; he was, as Godwin noted in his diary, 'retrograde'.[56]

Histories of political modernity throughout the nineteenth and twentieth centuries emphasized the importance of constitutional arrangements. This gave prominence to the *Agreement of the People* and made Lilburne an important figure, but some of what we might call this Romantic suspicion of his pedantry also survived. Christopher Hill, for example, the leading historian of this period in the decades after 1945 and a man of communist sympathies, clearly had an ambivalent attitude, seeing in Lilburne a defence of bourgeois values, rather than the full radical potential of the revolution, the promise of *The World Turned Upside Down*. Hill tended to prefer Winstanley, who he considered a proponent of primitive or Christian communism.[57] And, of course, Lilburne did more than many to destabilize the only government with any republican credentials in English history: this too was one of the charges made against him by Godwin. Against this broad canvas Lilburne seemed perhaps remarkable rather than heroic—Guizot's praise, for example, might fall into the category of faint: 'there is nothing more indomitable than a narrow, subtle, and vain mind, joined to a brave and honest heart'.[58] Nonetheless, Lilburne had a long run as a champion for secular political principles which we can all recognize to be important to the way we now are; and that 'we', in this comparative history of modernity, had come to mean much more than the Englishmen he had been intent on defending.

Recent writing has not been kind to these progressive histories of the revolution and, naturally enough, Lilburne's career has shared their fate. A concerted effort has been made to understand these events in seventeenth- not twentieth- or twenty-first-century terms. This led many historians to emphasize the role of religion rather than the secular issues more recognizable to us, or the difficulty for Charles of ruling three very different kingdoms while the subjects of each watched what was happening in the others in order to understand what he was really up to. If there was a long-term structural problem underlying the crisis apart from the destabilizing effects of the Reformation it was the difficulty of making the necessary financial adjustment to the escalating costs of war and the reluctance of the political classes to make that adjustment. This, rather than social and economic change, was the key structural force driving constitutional change. The effort to return discussion to terms that would have made sense to contemporaries also involved the commitment to talk about the full range of opinion and not just those strands that sounded most modern—neutrals and Anglicans got airtime along with the atheists, democrats, and republicans. By the same token, more attention was paid to the pre-modern passions of those who sounded like democrats and republicans: we were encouraged to think again about how different from us these people were.[59]

The Levellers were prime targets in this. Once considered something like a modern political party, not just in their ideology but also their organiza- tion, they were now said to be a loose group, not a party or a movement, who were marginal to real politics, and even to the famous Putney Debates, which were placed back into their army context.[60] It was said that for con- temporaries liberty did not mean the absence of subjection, but rather the freedom to submit to God's purposes without interference.[61] Seventeenth-century radicals argued as they did out of a radical puritanism not a secular democratic impulse. Moreover, a more incautious literature had assimilated the Levellers to the people in the sense that 'radical' was seen as a synonym for 'popular'. This presented a double problem in Lilburne's case—as we have seen, he was himself of a gentry background and proud of it, and his specifically Leveller ideas do not appear to have been what most people thought would make a good peace. He was popular with juries and on the streets when championing his rights as a defendant, less obviously popular with the people at large as a champion of popular sovereignty and proto-democracy in the state. Lilburne the radical, born out of the crisis of the 1790s, was, by the 1990s, out of fashion.

Lilburne clearly did contribute to a tradition—primarily a common law tradition championing the rights of the subject against executive tyranny—and provided a direct example to subsequent generations. We need not claim that he reveals the real core of the revolution in order to attach significance to his life and arguments. A second joke about him associated with Henry Marten's household was that he was England's noble Cato—a man of rigid, austere commitment to principle, whose arguments and life were a standing indictment of more pliant politicians, and those who profited from public office. Lilburne himself does not seem to have drawn directly on these classical examples, but his insistence on established rights and the virtues of self-denial, his constant critique of the powerful and corrupt, lent itself to that reading. The eighteenth century liked Cato, the defender of republican values at the time of Rome's transformation into an empire; the nineteenth preferred, perhaps, the vision of Caesar, and in that shift something of Lilburne was lost from our memory. Second, the core of his concerns is not best understood through the campaigns for an *Agreement*, or by considering his views simply as a variety of 'Leveller' thought—he clearly had different concerns, and different inspirations than Walwyn, Overton, and Wildman.[62] Revising the significance of the Levellers to the revolution need not involve downplaying the importance of their Cato for subsequent generations.

The tide has turned a little now from the high-water mark of this historical revisionism, but my main purpose in revisiting Lilburne's life has not been to contribute to those debates. I have tried to broaden our view of him beyond his involvement in the Leveller campaigns by placing that campaign and his role in it in the context of the whole course of his political activism. In one sense that has recovered some of the significance he held for eighteenth- and nineteenth-century audiences. What drove Lilburne's political campaigns was the quest to recover and protect existing native rights, a specific civic inheritance. The turn to a comparative and primarily constitutional history tended to obscure the more alien aspects of his thinking, but also to focus attention quite narrowly on his involvement with the Levellers rather than this broader, and very consistent, practical concern: we might say it tried to place him in the context of a history of democracy rather than of the rule of law and the Englishman's inherited legal rights. That latter context, however, was very familiar, and of urgent importance in the eighteenth and early nineteenth centuries. It is not negligible, either, to the current generation.

John Lilburne and the English Revolution

Equally significantly, his life was one of continuous engagement in serial political battles. The historical significance of his political *practice*, however, which is potentially very great, has also been obscured by an emphasis on his contribution to the intellectual legacies of the revolution. They are not separate issues, of course, since it was the experience of practical politics that led him to the certainties he achieved—his prison reading, collaborative campaigns, personal traumas, conflicts, and reflection. The positions he reached can hardly be said to have been representative or typical responses, but how he came to them was far from unusual: how the pressure of events, of weighty and sometimes deadly dilemmas, acted on his beliefs, forcing him to make alliances, but also to decide what was really at stake for him. Almost everyone confronted these events and arguments in some way, and had to make some kind of sense of them, or at least come to some kind of settlement with the times: in that respect his experience is revealing of a more general experience. There were many people who, like Lilburne, engaged in the conflict and in so doing helped to shape it.

The conditions in which they did so reflected significant changes in social and political life. The fractured world of reformation politics in the sixteenth century had led to an increasingly common appeal to public opinion outside political institutions in order to influence opinion within them. Those close to power circulated rumours, manuscripts, and, increasingly, anonymous publications in order to mobilize support for their position in the partisan religious and political arguments at court or in Parliament. In England this gathered pace in the three generations prior to 1640, and the increasing availability of print helped in that acceleration (or at least many contemporaries feared that it did).[63]

Lilburne was himself a creature of print. First arrested for his suspected involvement in the circulation of seditious books, after 1637 it was his own words, rather than those of others, that got him into trouble. He subsequently used print relentlessly. It was the means to publicize his sufferings and his claims, both in relatively lengthy tracts and shorter petitions and addresses scattered up and down the streets or handed out to anyone who would take them at the door of the House. His incessant, serial autobiography produced insight 'by sudden flashes, without method or sequence': he 'was always thinking aloud as he wrote'.[64] The immediacy of his experience, the burning sense of injustice, constructed through print for a public audience, mobilized the emotional connection that promoted his cause, and on occasion saved his life. His impact on later generations has come through these voluminous writings, produced in the heat of political campaigning, not the calm of the study. The power of that prose, and of the life it portrayed, captured the imagination of Hone, and others. Without print we would have no Lilburne—almost everything we know about him comes from print, put there to promote or undermine the causes he championed. Without print, in fact, Lilburne would not have been what he became—it was central to his political practice.

This use of print both fed, and fed off, a Parliament that exercised extensive powers over life and property, and which was increasingly open both to organized lobbying and to public view. There was a long tradition of active citizenship, particularly in London, which involved participation in government, and regular, informed, engagement with official bodies and formal procedures. This was the culture into which Lilburne had been apprenticed, but in wartime conditions its functioning rapidly became more complex, and more public.[65] That Parliament was in apparently permanent session: Lilburne did not live to see another election after 1640, indeed he never participated in a general election (since he was in prison in 1640), a striking fact which gives his attacks on oligarchy and the provisions of the various *Agreements* an extra charge. That Parliament also quickly developed an elaborate committee structure with unprecedented powers to interfere in local affairs—taxation, the seizure and disposal of property, the ejection of religious ministers, the suspension of legal cases against servants of Parliament, and of course of printing. These committees were increasingly open to public scrutiny. Lilburne, his allies, and enemies all printed accounts of committee discussions, copies of orders and decisions, and publicized the achievements and betrayals of individual politicians in that world. Navigating these committees, and confronting or subverting them, became a highly valued skill, and one which put Lilburne in demand. This was in fact the nearest he came to a full-time career. In 1637 he may have intended a career importing books and he later complained about losses when his books were seized, or the difficulty of making money from print in exile,[66] but the nearest he came to establishing a significant estate seems to have been through his activity as a paid advocate. His expertise in the world of print, in the law, and in the workings of Parliament allowed him in the 1650s to act as a kind of agent for others with a lobby to make, such as the commoners in Lincolnshire or his uncle George. He certainly seems to have done better from print and advocacy than he did in wool, brewing, or soap-making.

Free presses and active political mobilization also allowed for new forms of solidarity which were crucial to Lilburne's career. His shifting alliances were primarily built on shared beliefs, not the more traditional connections of neighbourliness, patronage, or kinship, and they were often formed through print or in the world of practical mobilization, petitions, and lobbying. With the exception of his advocacy for his family or the Lincolnshire commoners, he petitioned for groups who shared a partisan political view rather than a corporate or administrative interest—'the affectors and approvers of the 11 September petition', for example. His introduction to Quakerism came through the presses—he encountered it in books before he was able to join a meeting of Friends.[67] We can also glimpse the existence of partisan social spaces where such solidarities might form—for example in his hostility to Goodwin's congregation, which in 1649 he regarded as a gathering of those who meant him no good, or in the various taverns where he went to (or kept away from) meetings, such as the Windmill, the Nag's Head, or the Whalebone.[68]

Lilburne's political life illuminates the emergence of a new political world, which was greatly accelerated by the crisis of the 1640s. From this perspective his involvement in the mobilization for a peace settlement based on an *Agreement of the People* was one of a series of campaigns: he, Overton, and Walwyn thought different things for different reasons, but could all support the campaign for an *Agreement* in opposition to a personal treaty with the ever-unreliable Charles I. In fact, for Lilburne a peace with Charles would be acceptable if it was based on an *Agreement*, and he had no truck with the regime that betrayed the promise of an *Agreement*. Following the settlement of 1649 the Leveller leaders went on their separate paths once more. To that extent it seems unnecessary to find the real core or theoretical unity of Leveller belief, or to regard them (as Brailsford did) as 'the first model of a democratically organized political party'. That is surely over-stated, but on the other hand, the way they came together and mobilized support reflects the broader possibilities for political action in revolutionary England.[69] The Levellers were wholly exceptional in some ways but shared with many others (including their enemies) these methods of political action. This new world was full of shifting possibilities for political engagement opened up by partisan mobilization, continuous parliamentary sessions, reli-gious diversity, and print; that was the social and political basis of remarkable intellectual creativity, of which Lilburne's ideas give us but one example.

Taken together, this complex social and political crisis therefore also cre-ated the possibility of a new kind of career. Lilburne was a second son of a minor gentry family, with no secure landed estate or trade, and no public office. And yet he exerted enough political influence to make it worth imprisoning him, putting him on trial, or sending him into exile. That pol-itical influence rested not on the traditional sources of political power but on his skill in mobilizing a broader public opinion through print, and in petitioning campaigns; in working the corridors and committees of the par-liamentary regime; and through his confidence in asserting his legal rights in defence of his political interventions (even when he had misunderstood them). He built partisan solidarities through the dramatization of his own struggles, making connections through print or joining organizing commit-tees at tavern meetings with people he had not previously met or did not recognize. Many of his opponents, of course, were operating in the same way. Lilburne's techniques of political mobilization reflected more general features of life in revolutionary England, even if the ends for which he used them, and the skill with which he did so, were more exceptional. Lilburne's career reveals a more general shift in the possibilities for political engage-ment; a shift moreover which was of very long-lasting significance. Other minor gentleman had shaken governments in the past, but they had usually done so at the head of a peasant army. Lilburne's influence was achieved in ways much more familiar to future generations than to his forebears—his career illustrates the new opportunities for political action opened by the English Revolution.

Presumably there were as many intellectual paths through this crisis, as many epiphanies and revelations, as there were people who experienced it. However, by following an individual such as Lilburne we can again see more general features of life in revolutionary England: patterns and shapes in the apparent chaos of religious and political debate; themes and climacterics in the arguments, and the shibboleths which sorted the sheep from the goats at such key moments. It is sometimes difficult to know in advance how any particular individual would jump at any particular point, but we can see patterns in the issues that might make people feel they had to make a jump, and at what points in the unfolding crisis they might feel that it was necessary. For Lilburne the parliamentary cause had been expressed in its entirety in the spring of 1642, and although he took no other state oaths during the wars he had perhaps taken the Protestation. His other experiences were measured against the promise of that spring, and his view of that cause was refined through confrontation. The challenge of the Scots alliance, the Solemn League and Covenant, the Presbyterian mobilization of 1647, what he saw as an army coup in late 1648, and the Engagement controversy refined this commitment for him. These tests, and the debates they gave rise to, led him by stages to support the *Agreement of the People*, and to his subversive definition of the Commonwealth to which he was engaged in 1649 when he took another state oath but with his fingers crossed behind his back, at least metaphorically. These turning points would have been recognizable to many others even as they followed their very different paths.

Lilburne and other 'radicals' have been dismissed as marginal and unrepresentative, a lunatic fringe.[70] It is true that their ideas place them at the margins, and their political influence was often limited, although Lilburne's political significance was sometimes considerable, as his state trials make clear. But in any case these fascinating figures can be brought back to our attention as exemplars of this much more general experience. These decades were marked by unprecedented mobilization of resources and people. That was accompanied by the continuous broadcast of incompatible political certainties: for example that the king's rule was divinely ordained or that political power derived from the people; that religious conscience was sacrosanct or that it was imperative that governments intervene to discipline Christians who had strayed into error. Some of these contradictions caused impossible problems for people at moments when both propositions seemed true, and yet a choice had to be made—for example that English Protestantism was under threat both from popish bishops and from an erosion of the power of bishops. Confronted by incompatible truths which often demanded immediate political action of one kind or another—taking an oath, answering an order or tax demand from one side or another—people sought out new grounds, new ways of establishing reliable foundations for religious and political order. Images like that of gold tried in the fire were common— what was revealed in the crucible of war were the real truths of political and religious life.

It was a war on an appalling scale. Perhaps one in ten men were in arms at some point, perhaps 3 per cent of the English population died (a higher percentage than in the First World War, and it was far worse in the related conflicts in Scotland and Ireland), taxes increased by a dizzying amount, and as much as 20 per cent of the country's urban property was destroyed. This trauma, though, ushered in a period of intense political and cultural creativity. Some of the new certainties were durable too, speaking directly to audiences after the French and then industrial revolutions, and they were products of a new scale of political mobilization in the social and political conditions of traumatic civil war.

Lilburne's experience epitomizes both the trauma and the creativity. He was an activist, not a political theorist, drawing on (and according to his contemporaries and modern experts, misinterpreting) common law rights, engaging in but also transforming a lay, civic tradition of mobilization. This interest should not prevent us from appreciating the foreignness of his world, however—there are good reasons to be cautious about recruiting Lilburne, or the English Revolution, to the service of our arguments. Nonetheless, measured against the modern, largely secular concerns of the twenty-first-century West, Lilburne appears an ambiguous rather than simply alien figure: clearly a child of Reformation politics, his words and actions speak to Enlightenment political practice. There is that fundamental tension in views about his personality too: his courage and certainty, his disregard for his own safety and comfort, continue to inspire. The personal conviction on which they drew, though, clearly made him very difficult to live with, and were combined with an almost monstrous egotism and an apparent misogyny remarkable even for the seventeenth century. I think there is a good case, however, that we are all in his debt: that rather than rebuke him for his failings, we should honour him for his courage.

List of Abbreviations

A&O	*Acts and Ordinances of the Civil War and Interregnum*, eds C. H. Firth and R. S. Rait, 3 vols (London, 1911)
Agas Map	'The Agas Map', The Map of Early Modern London, ed. Janelle Jenstad, 2012, Web. 27 July 2012. Rpt. of Civitas Londinvm. [1562?] <http://mapoflondon.uvic.ca/map.htm>
BBTI	The British Book Trade Index <http://www.bbti.bham.ac.uk/>
Bod. Lib.	Bodleian Library
BL	British Library
Braddick, *God's Fury*	Michael Braddick, *God's Fury, England's Fire: A New History of the English Civil Wars* (London, 2008)
CCAM	*Calendar of the Committee for the Advance of Money, 1642–1656*, ed. Mary Anne Everett Green, 3 vols (London, 1888)
CCC	*Calendar of the Committee for Compounding, &c., 1643–1660*, ed. Mary Anne Everett Green, 5 vols (London, 1889–92)
CCED	Clergy of the Church of England Database <http://theclergydatabase.org.uk/>
CJ	Journals of the House of Commons
Clarendon	Edward Hyde, earl of Clarendon, *The History of the Rebellion and Civil Wars in England*, ed. W. Dunn Macray, 6 vols (Oxford, 1888)
CSPD	*Calendar of State Papers Domestic* (Charles I and interregnum), eds John Bruce, William Douglas Hamilton, Sophia Crawford Lomas, and Mary Anne Everett Green, 36 vols (London, 1858–97)
CSPVen	*Calendar of State Papers and manuscripts, relating to English affairs, existing in the archives and collections of Venice*, vols XXIII to XXXII, ed. Allan B. Hinds (London, 1920–31)
Edwards, *Gangraena*	Thomas Edwards, *Gangraena* (Exeter, 1977)
EHR	*English Historical Review*
ESTC	English Short Title Catalogue <http://estc.bl.uk/F/?func=file&file_name=login-bl-estc>

FD	Fortescue date: date attributed by Fortescue, in his catalogue of the Thomason Tracts
Foxley	Rachel Foxley, *The Levellers: Radical Political Thought in the English Revolution* (Manchester, 2013)
Gardiner, *CD*	S. R. Gardiner, ed., *Constitutional Documents of the English Revolution*, 3rd edition (London, 1906)
Gardiner, *Commonwealth*	S. R. Gardiner, *History of the Commonwealth and Protectorate*, 4 vols (London, 1903)
Gibb	M. A. Gibb, *John Lilburne the Leveller: A Christian Democrat* (London, 1947)
Gregg	Pauline Gregg, *Freeborn John: A Biography of John Lilburne* (London, 1961)
HEH	Henry E. Huntington Library
HJ	*Historical Journal*
JBS	*Journal of British Studies*
HLQ	*Huntington Library Quarterly*
HPT	*History of Political Thought*
LJ	*Journals of the House of Lords*
ODNB	*Oxford Dictionary of National Biography*, 60 vols (Oxford, 2004)
P&P	*Past and Present*
PA	Parliamentary Archives
Rees	John Rees, *The Leveller Revolution: Radical Political Organisation in England, 1640–1650* (London, 2016)
Rushworth	John Rushworth, *Historical Collections of Private Passages of State*, 8 vols (London, 1721)
SR	*Statutes of the Realm: Volume 5, 1628–80*, ed. John Raithby (London, 1819)
STCN	Short Title Catalogue, Netherlands <https://www.kb.nl/en/organisation/research-expertise/for-libraries/short-title-catalogue-netherlands-stcn#>
TD	Thomason date: annotated date by George Thomason of pamphlets in his collection
Thurloe	*A Collection of the State Papers of John Thurloe, Esq*, ed. Thomas Birch, 7 vols (London, 1742)
TNA	The National Archives
Wales and Hartley	*The Visitation of London begun in 1687*, eds T. C. Wales and C. P. Hartley, The Harleian Society, new series, vols 16 and 17 (London, 2004)

Note on Attributions and Citations

For ease of reference for readers I have followed standard attributions of authorship unless I am certain or it has been clearly demonstrated that the attribution is mistaken. Many such attributions for Richard Overton are unsound, while Overton's hand can be seen in works attributed to others or published anonymously. For a guide to these attributions see David Richard Adams, 'Religion and Reason in the Thought of Richard Overton, the Leveller' (PhD dissertation, Cambridge University, 2002). There is no similar work for Lilburne or the many other authors who appear in these pages. For ease of reference I have cited modern anthologies, editions, or calendars where possible but only where citing the original did not seem to add anything to the point I want to make. For the same reason I have included some Thomason call numbers for publications where there are many others with similar titles.

Notes

PREFACE

1. For his place in American legal argument, see this volume, pp. 358–9 n. 2.
2. John Lilburne, *The Innocent Man's second-Proffer* (London, 1649).
3. William Walwyn, *Englands Lamentable Slaverie* (1645) in *The Levellers in the English Revolution*, ed. G. E. Aylmer (London, 1975), p. 64.
4. Geoffrey Bindman, 'My Legal Hero: John Lilburne', *Guardian*, 15 December 2010, accessed online 6 February 2017: <https://www.theguardian.com/law/2010/dec/15/legal-heroes-geoffrey-bindman-john-lilburne>.
5. J. G. A. Pocock, quoted in J. C. Davis, '"Epic Years": The English Revolution and J. G. A. Pocock's Approach to the History of Political Thought', *History of Political Thought*, 29 (2008), pp. 519–42.
6. Gibb; Gregg. There is no anthology of Lilburne's work: he is usually anthologized as part of a corpus of Leveller thought, using writings from that period of his life. See, for example, *The Leveller Tracts 1647–1653*, eds William Haller and Godfrey Davies (Gloucester, Mass., 1964); *Leveller Manifestoes of the Puritan Revolution*, ed. Don M. Wolfe (New York, 1967); *The Levellers*, ed. Aylmer; *The English Levellers*, ed. Andrew Sharp (Cambridge, 1998). For the differences and tensions between his concerns and those of other prominent Levellers, see chs 4–6.
7. H. N. Brailsford, *The Levellers and the English Revolution* (Nottingham, 1961), p. 309.
8. For a good crisp summary of the scholarly state of play, see Foxley, esp. pp. 1–6.

CHAPTER I

1. John Lilburne, THE CHRISTIAN MANS TRIALL, 2nd edition (London, 1641), p. 1; for Hewson's house, John Lilburne, *The Legal Fundamental LIBERTIES Of the People of England*, 2nd edition (London, 1649), TD 4 August 1649, pp. [24]–25; for Wharton's address as Bow Lane, ibid., p. 21; Agas Map.
2. *CSPD, 1635–6*, pp. 81, 468. Sir John Lambe and Lilburne both refer to him as Old Wharton: *CSPD, 1637–8*, p. 2; Lilburne refers to Wharton as a hot presser: CHRISTIAN MANS TRIALL, p. 1. Hot pressing was a technique used in paper making too, and paper making was also depended on a supply of rags, so there were potential connections between the print, paper making, and textile trades. We

know of four hot pressers with connections to the book trade in early seventeenth-century London: BBTI s.n. Christopher Bridge, John Clarke, Jnr,
Edmond Symons, and William Wilson.

3. Lilburne, CHRISTIAN MANS TRIALL, pp. 10–11.

4. Ibid., p. 11. Tantlin's Church is presumably St Antholin's Church on Budge Row.
   It was home to a hot Protestant congregation and was one of the churches in
   which William Kiffin, a close associate of Lilburne's for most of his adult life,
   was first exposed to godly preaching: William Kiffin, *Remarkable Passages in the
   Life of William Kiffin*, ed. William Orme (London, 1823), p. 3.

5. Lilburne, CHRISTIAN MANS TRIALL, pp. 11–12. For the fullest account of the evidence that Chilliburne betrayed him see John Lilburne, A WORKE OF THE BEAST
   ([Amsterdam], 1638), pp. 10–13. He compares Chilliburne's betrayal to that by
   Judas, saying (perhaps with some exaggeration) that it was in some respects
   worse: Lilburne, CHRISTIAN MANS TRIAL, p. 10; see also how he was 'betrayed by
   my pretended bosome friend, John Chilliburne' in Lilburne, *Legal Fundamental
   LIBERTIES*, p. 25.

6. Lilburne, CHRISTIAN MANS TRIALL, pp. 1–2. See also Lilburne, WORKE OF THE
   BEAST, p. 10. Flamsted, or Flamsteed, was active in attempts to police illicit
   printing and seditious words, taking the initiative in one case and facing assault
   charges in another: *CSPD, 1635–6*, p. 239; *CSPD, 1637–8*, p. 64; *CSPD, 1638–9*,
   p. 206; *CSPD, 1641–3*, p. 518.

7. Lilburne, CHRISTIAN MANS TRIALL, pp. 1–2.

8. History of Parliament Trust, London, unpublished article on George Lilburne for
   1640–60 section by David Scott [hereafter, Scott, 'George Lilburne']. I am grateful
   to the History of Parliament Trust for allowing me to see this article in draft.

9. John Lilburne, INNOCENCY AND TRUTH JUSTIFIED (London, [1645]), TD 6 January
   1646, p. 8; Rushworth, V, p. 83. No baptismal record has yet been found: Gibb,
   pp. 1–2; Gregg, pp. 363–5. For the family tradition, see Durham University Library
   Special Collections SB 1614–16: I am grateful to Alex Barber for this reference.

10. Lilburne, INNOCENCY AND TRUTH JUSTIFIED, p. 8.

11. Bod. Lib., MS J Walker c. 1, f. 31r. The published version omits some of this
    detail: John Walker, *An Attempt towards Recovering the Numbers and Sufferings of the
    Clergy of the Church of England . . .* (London, 1714 edition), p. 252. I am grateful
    to John Walter for this reference.

12. TNA, PROB/11/187, ff. 129r.–131v, Thomas Hewson will, made: 12 August
    1641, proved: 5 October 1641, f. 129v, 130r. Hewson died on either 20 or 22
    August: TNA, C142/621/25, C3/423/77.

13. Information can be retrieved from the online records of the Clothworkers'
    Company using search term Hughson: <http://www.londonroll.org/home>.
    A further apprentice, Robert Watson, seems to have been taken on earlier,
    although it is not clear when: his freedom is recorded in 1614. I am grateful to
    Jessica Collins of the Clothworkers' Company for information and advice
    about Hewson's apprentices. Pauline Gregg suggested a family connection

between Hewson/Hughson and Lilburne's maternal family, the Hixon's: Gregg, p. 36.

14. Lilburne, *Legal Fundamental LIBERTIES*, pp. [24]–25.

15. TNA, PROB/11/187, f. 130r.

16. Gibson owed much of his early success to the patronage of Barnaby Potter, who had been master of Queen's College, Cambridge, where Gibson took his MA. This suggests a godly but not necessarily nonconformist outlook. By the late 1630s, however, he seems to have embraced the Laudian programme and was clearly one of its more reliable champions in Lincolnshire: CCED; A. J. Heggarty, 'Potter, Barnaby (*Bap.* 1577, *d.* 1642)', *ODNB*; this volume, pp. 68–9. I am grateful to Kenneth Fincham for his advice about how to interpret Gibson's career.

17. For his Covenanting sympathies see this volume, p. 38. For George's own account of these years see *CCC*, III, pp. 1918, 1920.

18. He was a good friend of Henry Jessey, chaplain to the Gurdons: Murray Tolmie, *The Triumph of the Saints: The Separate Churches of London, 1616–1649* (Cambridge, 1977), pp. 36, 44. His connection with the Montague's may have come through Anne's first marriage to Robert Wyncoll, since Hewson refers to his 'cousin' Thomas Wyncoll in his will: TNA, PROB/11/187, ff. 129v, 130r; Cust, 'Montagu, Edward, first Baron Montagu of Boughton (1562/3–1644)', *ODNB*.

19. Hewson was a member of the Court of Assistants of the Massachusetts Bay Company as well as an investor, and his son John Hewson also supplied materials for the settlements. For his commercial connections to Winthrop see *Winthrop Papers*, Massachusetts Historical Society, 5 vols (Boston, 1929–47), vol. 3, pp. 234–5. See also *Records of the Governor and Company of Massachusetts Bay, I: 1628–1641* (Boston, 1853), ed. Nathaniel B. Shurtleff, pp. 27, 32, 40, 44, 48, 52, 53, 53, 56, 58, 61, 130–2; Frances Rose-Troup, *The Massachusetts Bay Company and its Predecessors* (New York, 1930), pp. 20, 63, 144–5. For Winthrop see Francis J. Bremer, *John Winthrop: America's Forgotten Founding Father* (Oxford, 2003).

20. TNA, PROB/11/187, f. 130r; *A History of the County of Oxford: Volume 10, Banbury Hundred*, ed. Alan Crossley (London, 1972), pp. 48, 63–4, 39; *The 'Bawdy Court' of Banbury: The Act Book of the Peculiar Court of Banbury, Oxfordshire and Northamptonshire, 1628–1648*, ed. E. R. C. Brinkworth and R. K. Gilkes, Banbury Historical Society, 26 (1997), p. 177; *LJ*, IV, p. 108, 11 December 1640 (the petition mentions a number of other transgressions). Vivers was clearly a leading parishioner there, and his father's will suggests extensive landholding. Hewson also left a legacy to Symon Adams, who might have been the rector of nearby Aston Le Walls: TNA, PROB/11/187, f. 129v, CCED.

21. Karen Ordahl Kupperman, *Providence Island 1630–1641: The Other Puritan Colony* (Cambridge, 1993).

22. For Jessey, ibid., pp. 12–19, 36–4, 47; for connections between Gurdon, Jessey and Wincoll see ibid., pp. 44–5, and *Winthrop Papers*, vol. 2, pp. 266n, 296–7, 309; vol. 3, pp. 25, 36–7, 57–8, 61–2, 172–4, 189. Kiffin had been a member of

Jessey's church, probably until late 1643 or early 1644, after which Kiffin's Baptist sympathies led them to take separate paths: Tolmie, *Triumph of the Saints*, pp. 27, 121–2, and, more generally, ch. 3.

23. For Rosier and his subsequent activity, including civic office, which was not always sympathetic to Lilburne, see Tolmie, *Triumph of the Saints*, pp. 36–7, 56, 66, 68, 122, 148, 171, 177, 184, 187; for Kiffin, who also held office in the 1640s, ibid., esp. pp. 28–9, 43–4, 80, 182–4, 194–5.

24. The letters from the 1630s seem mainly to concern apparently uncontroversial commercial matters, although there are some references to dangerous reading materials: see the *CSPD* volumes for the 1630s, *passim*. For his later role see Keith Lindley, *Popular Politics and Religion in Civil War London* (Aldershot, 1997), p. 331; Elliott Vernon, *London Presbyterianism and the Politics of Religion in the British Revolution, c.1638–1663* (forthcoming). I am grateful to Elliot Vernon for discussing Willingham with me.

25. Lilburne, *Legal Fundamental LIBERTIES*, p. 25.

26. 'But in regard my grand adversaries, and their little Beagles in London, doe continually report me to be a man of contention, and one that is never quiet from broyls, nor never content with any Government; but full of self-conceitedness, malice and revenge; it will be very necessary for me to return an effectuall answer to this', ibid., p. 20.

27. John Bastwick, *A IUST DEFENCE OF JOHN BASTWICK* (London, 1645), p. 15.

28. Lilburne, *WORKE OF THE BEAST*, p. 20.

29. Ibid., p. 19.

30. The gibe was Prynne's, who claimed that it was he and Bastwick, men with whom Lilburne was then in conflict, who had originally rescued Lilburne from obscurity: William Prynne, *THE LYAR CONFOUNDED* (London, 1645), p. 2. For their falling out, see this volume, ch. 3. Wood repeats a claim that Lilburne had wanted to enter the law and had in fact been Prynne's servant: Anthony Wood, *Athenæ Oxonienses*, 2 vols (London, 1721 edn), vol. 2, p. 172; the first time Warwick noticed Oliver Cromwell was when he spoke for a servant of Prynne's who had dispersed libels against the Queen's recreations. Gregg thought this was Cromwell's speech on Lilburne's behalf: HEH, HM 41956 p. 71; Gregg, p. 372–3. This may be mistaken: Lilburne had done more than that, and was by that time a name that Warwick perhaps would have known. Lilburne denied that he had been a servant, let alone Prynne's, and I have found no other evidence to support the claim: Lilburne, *INNOCENCY AND TRUTH JUSTIFIED*, pp. 7–8.

31. For an overview see Michael J. Braddick, *State Formation in Early Modern England, c. 1550–1700* (Cambridge, 2000), pp. 292–301.

32. Valerie Pearl, *London and the Outbreak of the Puritan Revolution: City Government and National Politics, 1625–43* (Oxford, 1961), esp. ch. 2; Ian Archer, *The Pursuit of Stability: Social Relations in Elizabethan London* (Cambridge, 1991), esp. ch. 3. For Southwark see Jeremy Boulton, *Neighbourhood and Society: A London Suburb in the Seventeenth Century* (Cambridge, 1987), esp. pp. 141–5; for the political and religious culture of Coleman Street ward see Rees, pp. 46–8; John Coffey,

John Goodwin and the Puritan Revolution: Religion and Intellectual Change in Seventeenth-Century England (Woodbridge, 2006), ch. 2; for Cheapside Cross see David Cressy, *Agnes Bowker's Cat: Travesties and Transgressions in Tudor and Stuart England* (Oxford, 2000), ch. 14.

33. See, in general, Patrick Collinson, *The Religion of Protestants: The Church in English Society 1559–1625* (Oxford, 1982), esp. ch. 6. For the London puritan underground see Stephen Foster, *Notes from the Caroline Underground: Alexander Leighton, the Puritan Triumvirate, and the Laudian Reaction to Nonconformity* (Hamden, Conn., 1978); Peter Lake, *The Boxmaker's Revenge: 'Orthodoxy' and 'Heterodoxy' and the Politics of the Parish in Early Stuart London* (Manchester, 2001), esp. pt 3.

34. Adrian Johns, 'Coleman Street', *HLQ*, 71:1 (2008), 33–54. See Rees, pp. 46–8. For the connections more generally between the gathered churches and Leveller mobilization see ibid., pp. 36–41 and (for Katherine Chidley) 58–61.

35. Lilburne, *Legal Fundamental* LIBERTIES, p. 25. Gregg says it was both Rosier and Hewson who took him to meet Bastwick: Gregg, p. 47. For Bastwick see Frances Condick, 'Bastwick, John (1595?-1654)', *ODNB*.

36. William Lamont, 'Prynne, William (1600–1669)', *ODNB*; Kenneth Gibson, 'Burton, Henry (*bap.* 1578, *d.* 1647/8), *ODNB*. For Burton, see also Tolmie, *Triumph of the Saints*, pp. 66, 91–4, 110–11.

37. Mark Kishlansky, 'Martyrs Tales', *JBS*, 53:2 (2014), 334–55; see also Kishlansky, 'A Whipper Whipped: The Sedition of William Prynne', *HJ*, 56:3 (2013), 603–27.

38. Kevin Sharpe, *The Personal Rule of Charles I* (London, 1992), pp. 758–65, quotation at p. 763; Clarendon, I, pp. 125–6; Gregg, p. 51. For Prynne's injuries see Lamont, 'Prynne'. For the presence of separatists including Jessey see Tolmie, *Triumph of the Saints*, pp. 46–7.

39. Rushworth, III, pp. 306–15, quotation at p. 306.

40. Cited in Brian Quintrell, 'Williams, John (1582–1650), archbishop of York', *ODNB*. Williams shared some ground with Charles and Laud on the value of ceremonial worship, but they had been at odds for much of the previous decade: Sharpe, *Personal Rule*, pp. 330, 333–40, 345, 364, 672, 676–8, 937. Clarendon thought Williams was a difficult character as much as a principled opponent: Clarendon, I, 128–9. In 1641 he was to be raised the Archbishopric of York, when Charles needed friends who might be acceptable to the parliamentary opposition: Quintrell, 'Williams'; Sharpe, *Personal Rule*, p. 935.

41. Ibid., pp. 717–30. Saye, as it happens, had also been keen to provoke a hearing of the issues. For the Lilburne's resistance to ship money, *CSPD, 1640*, pp. 346–7 and John Lilburne, *A* IUST REPROOF *to Haberdashers-Hall* ([London, 1652]), TD August [1652], p. 2.

42. Bastwick, IUST DEFENCE, pp. 11, 29, 30–1. This was after they had fallen out and in response to Lilburne's claim that he had ventured his life for Bastwick: the counter-claim was that Lilburne had been trying to make money.

43. Prynne, LYAR CONFOUNDED, p. 2; Edwards, *Gangraena*, pt 1, p. 96; Lilburne, WORKE OF THE BEAST, p. 10; Bastwick, IUST DEFENCE, pp. 11, 29, 30–1.

44. Lilburne, *Legal Fundamental* LIBERTIES, p. 25.

45. Polly Ha, *English Presbyterianism 1590–1640* (Stanford, 2011); Keith L. Sprunger, *Dutch Puritanism: A History of the English and Scottish Churches of the Netherlands in the Sixteenth and Seventeenth Centuries* (Leiden, 1982). For printing see ibid, pp. 306–18 and Keith L. Sprunger, *Trumpets from the Tower: English Puritan Printing in the Netherlands, 1600–1640* (Leiden, 1994). For book smuggling see the testimony of Matthew Symmons, TNA, SP16/387/79, discussed with additional material in Sprunger, *Trumpets*, pp. 30–1, 159–61.

46. Lilburne, *Legal Fundamental LIBERTIES*, p. 25.

47. Sprunger, *Trumpets*, pp. 42–5, 119–24. For English government pressure on printers working in the United Provinces after 1637 see also Sprunger, *Dutch Protestantism*, pp. 314–17. These measures can be followed in: TNA, SP 84/138, f. 44; SP 84/144, ff. 164v; SP 84/153, ff. 183–90, 271, 293–6; SP 84/154, ff. 17–19, 113–14, 148–9, 150–3, 256; SP 84/155, ff. 32, 93, 102, 136–7, 145, 260.

48. Rushworth, III, p. 306.

49. Lilburne, *CHRISTIAN MAN'S TRIAL*, pp. 9–10.

50. STCN: *The letany of John Bastvvick*, was written from the Gatehouse and as the title page boasted, it was *a full demonstration, that the bishops are neither Christs, nor the Apostles successors, but enemies of Christ and his kingdome, and of the Kings most excellent Majesties prerogative royall* (Leiden, 1637); *The answer of John Bastvvick, Doctor of Phisicke, to the information of Sir Iohn Bancks Knight, Atturney universall. In which there is a sufficient demonstration, that the prelats are invaders of the Kings prerogative royall, contemners and despisers of holy Scripture, advancers of poperie, super-stition, idolatry and prophanesse: also that they abuse the Kings authoritie* (Leiden, 1637); *The ansvver of Iohn Bastwick, Doctor of Phisicke, to the exceptions made against his Letany by a learned gentleman* (Leiden, 1637); *The vanity and mischeife of the old letany* (Leiden, 1637).

51. STCN, ESTC: William Prynne, *The unbishoping of Timothy and Titus* (Amsterdam, 1636), printed by J. F. Stam; *A breviate of the prelates intollerable usurpations, both upon the Kings prerogative royall, and the subjects liberties* (Amsterdam, 1637), printed by J. F. Stam; [William Prynne], *A looking-glasse for all lordly prelates* ([London?], 1636). It seems likely that sixteen queries was *Woodstreet-compters-plea for its prisoner. Or sixteen reasons, which induce mee Nathaniel Wickins . . . to refuse to take the oath ex officio* (Amsterdam, 1638).

52. Lilburne, *CHRISTIAN MANS TRIALL*, pp. 2–3. 'Hargust' was probably Joost Hartgersz, who was active in the news trade, in association with Joost Broersz (publisher of a courant, an early form of news publication), and his father Broer Jansz, a well-known publisher of one of the four newsbooks around that time. Hartgersz published pamphlets in association with both of them and some of this material was controversial: in 1640, Broer Jansz printed a pamphlet for Hartgersz, *St. Nicolaas milde gaven, aen d'Amstelse jonckheyt. Ofte het laetste Quartier der Amsterdamsche Mane-schijn*, which mocked Amsterdam Council, as a result of which Hartgersz was questioned, fined, and paid costs for the trial: I. Prins, 'Amsterdamse schimpdichters vervolgd', *Amstelodamum*, 30 (1933), 189–227. I have found no connection with English puritan publishing during the 1630s,

but he did have an interest in English affairs, and Joost Broers published material sympathetic to the Covenanters: *Verwerpinghe vande episcopale regeeringhe in Schotlant [...] Mitsgaders van all misbruycken ende paepshe ceremonien inghevoert zedert de reformatie* (Amsterdam, 1639). Hartgersz published a well-produced engraving of William Laud following his execution, which is in the National Portrait Gallery Collections, and between 1647 to 1653 his active pamphleteering included a number of titles dealing with the execution of Charles I and the first edition of the *Eikon Basilike*: STCN; his interest in Laud was presumably part of the reassessment in Holland of the trials of Strafford and Laud in the light of the execution of Charles I: Helmer J. Helmers, *The Royalist Republic: Literature, Politics, and Religion in the Anglo-Dutch Public Sphere, 1639–1660* (Cambridge, 2015), pp. 118–20, 128. He also published Constantijn Huygens, who had a very informed interest in English culture and politics: STCN; Hoftijzer, 'British Books Abroad: The Continent', in *The Cambridge History of the Book in Britain*, vol. 4: *1557–1695*, ed. John Barnard and D. F. McKenzie, with the assistance of Maureen Bell (Cambridge, 2002), p. 742. Sprunger makes no mention of Hartgersz, although Joost Broersz was involved in publishing English bibles: *Dutch Puritanism*, p. 310, and was, with Christiaensz and Stam, a target for the English authorities: Sprunger, *Trumpets*, pp. 122–3. I am grateful to Roeland Harms and Helmer Helmers for discussion of Hartgersz.

53. Lilburne, CHRISTIAN MAN'S TRIALL, p. 3. For Chillenden's arrest see *CSPD, 1637*, p. 49, TNA, SP 16/354, f. 379.
54. Lilburne, WORKE OF THE BEAST, p. 10. For Foote and Scottish anti-episcopal hostility to the prayer book, see Sprunger, *Dutch Puritanism*, p. 270.
55. Henry Burton, *The baiting of the Popes bull. Or an vnmasking of the mystery of iniquity* (London, 1627). I have not been able to identify an edition of this work from the 1630s, or one published in Holland.
56. He later claimed on several occasions that Chillenden had sworn falsely to save his own skin, receiving his liberty and £30 for his testimony. He was subsequently a lieutenant in Whaley's regiment of horse, and was captive in Oxford Castle with Lilburne, where the latter showed him considerable kindness: Lilburne, *Legal Fundamental* LIBERTIES, pp. 25–6 (see this volume, pp. 63, 318 n. 74). Chillenden was active in the army revolt with which the Levellers joined in 1647: Ian Gentles, *The New Model Army in England, Ireland and Scotland, 1645–1653* (Oxford, 1992), chs 6–7.
57. Lilburne, CHRISTIAN MAN'S TRIALL, p. 5.
58. Ibid., pp. 5–6.
59. Lilburne, WORKE OF THE BEAST, p. 13. G. R. Elton, *The Tudor Constitution: Documents and Commentary* (Cambridge, 1960), pp. 217–21; J. P. Kenyon, *The Stuart Constitution 1603–1688: Documents and Commentary* (Cambridge, 1966), pp. 176–80; J. H. Baker, *An Introduction to English Legal History*, 3rd edition (London, 1990), p. 152; Sharpe, *Personal Rule*, pp. 374–7.
60. Lilburne, CHRISTIAN MANS TRIAL, p. 8; John Lilburne, *Come out of her my people* ([Amsterdam], 1639), p. 30.

61. *CSPD, 1637–8*, p. 2. He had refused to answer articles against him in the High Commission in 1635 too: *CSPD, 1635–6*, p. 81. Lambe was a jurist and keen supporter of Laud, who sat on the High Commission: J. Fielding, 'Lambe, Sir John (c.1566–1646)', *ODNB*.

62. Lilburne, WORKE OF THE BEAST, p. 10.

63. Ibid., pp. 15–16.

64. Hoftijzer, 'British Books Abroad', p. 739. For Stam and Christiaensz, see Sprunger, *Trumpets*, 102–3, 144–55, 204–7, 215–18; Sprunger, *Dutch Protestantism*, pp. 309–12.

65. Lilburne, WORKE OF THE BEAST, p. 11.

66. The account given here agrees with that in Rushworth, II, pp. 463–6, which includes official records.

67. Lilburne, WORKE OF THE BEAST, pp. 4–6.

68. The testimony is from a later hearing before the House of Lords of Lilburne's claim for reparations: Anon., *A true relation of the material passage of Lieut. Col. Iohn Lilburnes sufferings* (London, [1645]), p. 3. For Lilburne's estimate of 500 strokes: *Legal Fundamental LIBERTIES*, p. 25; Rushworth, also reported that Lilburne had received 500 blows from a three-corded whip with knots, but also that some reports put the number higher: Rushworth, II, p. 469.

69. Anon., *A true relation*, pp. 3, 7. Rushworth reports him stamping and repeats the claim about the humiliation implied by both gagging and the pillory: Rushworth, II, pp. 466, 469. For his loyal declaration see [John Lilburne] *A COPPY OF A LETTER WRITTEN BY JOHN LILBVRNE* ([London], 1640), p. 24. For this testimony about the books see Bod. Lib., Bankes MSS, vol. 18, f. 33. I am grateful to Jason Peacey for this reference.

70. Quoted from Lilburne, CHRISTIAN MANS TRIALL, pp. 38–9. For the official order see TNA, PC 2/49, f. 55v. Bankes was ordered to examine Lilburne about his behaviour in the pillory: Bod. Lib., Bankes MSS, vol. 13, f. 18 (18 April). I am grateful to Jason Peacey for this reference.

71. Reproduced in Lilburne, CHRISTIAN MANS TRIALL, pp. 38–9.

72. He was questioned on this point by John Bankes and Edward Littleton a month later, but he 'would give noe other answare but that he was unwilling to tell it': Bod. Lib., Bankes Mss, vol. 18, f. 33 (17 May). This is presumably the examination ordered on 18 April: Bankes Mss, vol. 13, f. 18. I am grateful to Jason Peacey for these references.

73. Lilburne, *Legal Fundamental LIBERTIES*, p. 26.

74. Roger Lee Brown, *A History of the Fleet Prison, London: The Anatomy of the Fleet* (Lewiston, 1996), pp. 5–9, 313–15; Edward Marston, *Prison: Five Hundred Years of Life Behind Bars* (Kew, 2009), pp. 44–6.

75. Peter Lake, with Michael Questier, *The Antichrist's Lewd Hat: Protestants, Papists and Players in Post-Reformation England* (London, 2002), section II, esp. pp. 193–5; for prison writing see Ruth Ahnert, *The Rise of Prison Literature in the Sixteenth Century* (Cambridge, 2013); and the articles gathered in *HLQ*, 72:2 (2009).

76. Bod. Lib. Bankes Mss 18, f. 33.

77. [John Lilburne], THE POORE MANS CRY ([Amsterdam], 1639), quotation at pp. 4, 6; see also Lilburne, INNOCENCY AND TRUTH JUSTIFIED, p. 74. For the later testimony see Anon., *A true relation*, pp. 4–5, 5–6; Sean Kelsey, 'Bradshaw, John, Lord Bradshaw (bap. 1602, d. 1659)', *ODNB*. Bradshaw was a coming man at the point that he made this representation.

78. Lilburne, POORE MANS CRY, p. 7. He claimed in fact that Laud had tried to use the dispute to pressure Richard into making John submit: Lilburne, INNOCENCY AND TRUTH JUSTIFIED, p. 39. For a summary of the dispute see BL Add Ms 27380, esp. ff. 64v–65r; for the Privy Council interest during the 1630s see ff. 50r–64r. See also Rushworth, II, 789, IV, 356; TNA, C2/Eliz/H17/52; Stac8/200/13; C2/Jas I/L12/65; C2/Chas I/C50/63. The order regulating the battle specified that it 'must proceede til death or yielding', BL, Add Ms 34712 f. 184r. A pardon was issued to those accused of arson *CSPD, 1603–10*, p. 137, and in another dispute that Richard claimed was also affected by losses of records in the fire he did not accuse his enemies of arson: TNA, C2/ChasI/l39/17. The matter went to parliament in 1641 resulting apparently in legislation to end trial by battle: PA HL/PO/JO/10/1/50 ff. 34, 112, HL/PO/JO/10/1/55 f. 21, HL/PO/JO/10/1/60 ff. 83, 84, HL/PO/JO/10/1/62, f. 17, HL/PO/JO/10/1/69, ff. 128–31, HL/PO/JO/10/4/5; *LJ*, IV, p. 208.

79. Braddick, *God's Fury*, pp. 34–6.

80. John Lilburne, A LIGHT FOR THE IGNORANT ([Amsterdam], 1638), quotations at pp. 3, 5–6. It was reprinted in 1641 with minor typographical changes alongside the Glover engraving.

81. Lilburne, A LIGHT FOR THE IGNORANT, p. 6.

82. I owe this point to Peter Lake.

83. For the Bishop's treason: POORE MANS CRY, pp. 9–10. For his obedience to lawful royal authority see for example ibid., pp. 3–4, 5, 11, 12; Lilburne, WORKE OF THE BEAST, p. 16; Lilburne, *Come out of her my people*, pp. 14–15, 27. Nicholas Tyacke has traced a tradition of interpretation of Galatians 5:1, which imposed an obligation on Christians to oppose tyranny in state as well as the church: 'Revolutionary Puritanism in Anglo-American Perspective', *HLQ*, 74:2 (2015), 745–69. Lilburne's arguments are close to this position, but he does not cite this passage prominently in publications from this period, drawing predominantly on Revelations, although he did cite other early chapters of Galatians.

84. Lilburne, WORKE OF THE BEAST, p. 13.

85. Ibid., p. 20.

86. Lilburne, A LIGHT FOR THE IGNORANT, p. 9.

87. Lilburne, *Come out of her my people*, p. 4.

88. Lilburne, A LIGHT FOR THE IGNORANT, p. 20; biblical citations omitted. Interestingly, the 1641 edition varies from this more significantly than other parts of the text, and there are variations in the biblical passages cited: see this volume, p. 87.

89. The fullest discussion is Lilburne, *Come out of her my people*; see Tolmie, *Triumph of the Saints*, pp. 36–7.

90. See this volume, p. 308 n. 50, 51.

91. John Lilburne, *AN ANSWER TO NINE ARGUMENTS Written by T.B.* (London, 1645). It carries the Glover engraving of Lilburne, and the title page says it was written by him 'long since'. There is a preface by 'M.N.' Lilburne claims authorship in Lilburne, *INNOCENCY AND TRUTH JUSTIFIED*, p. 9 and John Lilburne, *THE Oppressed Mans Oppressions declared* ([London, 1647]), p. 15. On these issues in general, and the tensions inherent in the anti-episcopal alliance, see Tolmie, *Triumph of the Saints*, esp. pp. 46–49; and, later, Coffey, *Goodwin*, esp. pp. 139–40.

92. Lilburne, *A LIGHT FOR THE IGNORANT*, epistle to the reader.

93. Sprunger, *Trumpets*, 98–101, 119–24, 151–2, 200–4; Roger Hayden, 'Canne, John (d. 1667?)', *ODNB*. For English government pressure on printers working in the United Provinces after 1637, see this volume, p. 308 n. 47. Christiaensz and Broersz were also in trouble: Sprunger, *Trumpets*, pp. 122–3; Sprunger, *Dutch Protestantism*, p. 315 (Christiaensz).

94. ESTC gives no author; for Lilburne's attribution see Lilburne, *POORE MANS CRY*, pp. 13–14.

95. Lilburne, *WORKE OF THE BEAST*, quotations at title page, pp. 14, 16, sig. A1v.

96. Lilburne, *POORE MANS CRY*, p. 12, quotations at title page, pp. 2, 4.

97. He complained that he could not support himself in prison, since his goods had been 'disposed of: For the Prelates, have already robbed mee of the most part of them; for *Canterburies* Catchpoles took from me the last yeare, at the Custome House, almost two Thousand of my Bookes, as they came from *Amsterdam*': Lilburne, *COPPY OF A LETTER*, p. 4. Print was potentially lucrative business. Print runs of English puritan and other pious works from Dutch presses varied between 1,000 and 5,000, with some reaching 10,000 at a time: Sprunger, *Trumpets*, p. 31. The Star Chamber decree made seized books forfeit under some circumstances, and stipulated that the king should receive half of the proceeds of sale. Particularly dangerous works were to be burnt: Rushworth, III, p. 315.

98. PA HL/PO/JO/10/1/45, petition of Katherine Hadley, 21 December 1640.

99. Lilburne, *INNOCENCY AND TRUTH JUSTIFIED*, p. 74; Rushworth, III, p. 855. For the later printed version of his letter to the apprentices see John Lilburne, *The Prisoners Plea for a Habeas Corpus* ([London,] 1647), pp. [14–16], there dated 10 May 1639, although this seems mistaken.

100. Bod. Lib., MS Clarendon 16, f. 174v; John Fielder, *THE HUMBLE PETITION AND Appeal of John Fielder of Kingston Miller* (London, 1651), TD 14 October 1651, p. 18; Rees, pp. 32–3; Braddick, *God's Fury*, pp. 93–4.

101. Fielder, *PETITION AND Appeal*, pp. 18–19; for her petition see PA HL/PO/JO/10/1/45; the order for her release is the first entry in the journal the following day: *LJ*, IV, p. 113.

102. Lilburne, *POORE MANS CRY*, quotations at pp. 7, 4, 13.

103. Rushworth, II, pp. 467–8.

104. Lilburne, *POORE MANS CRY*, p. 6. Like Lilburne, Grosvenor seems to have thought that opposing corruption in the church and illegal government was the duty of a loyal subject: see Richard Cust, 'Grosvenor, Sir Richard, first

baronet (1585–1645)', *ODNB*; and Richard Cust and P. G. Lake, 'Sir Richard Grosvenor and the rhetoric of magistracy', *Bulletin of the Institute of Historical Research*, 54 (1981), 40–53.

105. Lilburne, POORE MANS CRY, p. 5. For the importance of prison writing in the ensuing decades see Jerome De Groot, 'Prison Writing, Writing Prison during the 1640s and 1650s', *HLQ*, 72:2 (2009), 193–215.

106. Lilburne, *Come out of her my people*, pp. 32–5, quotation at p. 35. He had also asked for a public disputation A LIGHT FOR THE IGNORANT, pp. 3–4.

107. John Adamson, *Noble Revolt: The Overthrow of Charles I* (London, 2007), pp. 21–5, 36–45. See also Braddick, *God's Fury*, ch. 3. For other examples of well-connected English sympathizers with the Scots see David Cressy, *Dangerous Talk: Scandalous, Seditious, and Treasonable Speech in Pre-Modern England* (Oxford, 2010), pp. 181–2.

108. Adamson, *Noble Revolt*, p. 25.

109. Braddick, *God's Fury*, pp. 96–106, Cressy, *Dangerous Talk*, p. 153.

110. *CSPD, 1638–9*, pp. 343, 455, 489, 543. In April, Butler petitioned Laud about the loss of trade consequent on his imprisonment and appearance before the High Commission: *CSPD, 1639*, p. 22. For his relationship with Hewson, TNA, PROB/11/187, f. 130r.

111. *CSPD, 1639–40*, pp. 566, 426, 427, 546.

112. *CSPD, 1640*, p. 347. See also Bod. Lib., MS Clarendon 19, ff. 123r, 274r–275v.

113. Lilburne, ANSWER TO NINE ARGUMENTS, p. 44.

114. Lilburne, COPPY OF A LETTER, p. 4.

115. Ibid., pp. 7, 8. This has not, it seems, survived, but a riposte has: Humfrey Vincent, *The coblers sermon cryed downe, . . . Confuting the matter and confounding the authour of that base-blasphemous pamphlet called The coblers sermon* (London, 1641).

116. Adamson, *Noble Revolt*.

117. Butler was admitted in November 1626, and was active in December 1631, although his quarterage payments ceased in 1634: *The Cardew-Rendle Roll: A Biographical Dictionary of Members of the Honourable Artillery Company from c. 1537–1908*, 2 vols (London, 2013), ed. Kirsty Bennet, vol. 1, p. 490; for the role of the society see Adamson, *Noble Revolt*, pp. 65–72; Rees, pp. 48–51. George Willingham: BL, Sloane Ms 2035B, fos. 5r–5v, 9r–12r.

CHAPTER 2

1. Rushworth, IV, pp. 28–9.

2. Figures cited from David L. Smith, *The Stuart Parliaments 1603–1689* (London, 1999), pp. 36–7; see, in general, James S. Hart, *Justice Upon Petition: The House of Lords and the Reformation of Justice 1621–1675* (London, 1991).

3. Clarendon, I, pp. 267–9, quotation at pp. 268, 269; John Adamson, *The Noble Revolt: The Overthrow of Charles I* (London, 2007), pp. 114–15.

4. Clarendon, I, 267–9, quotations at p. 269.

5. *The Writings and Speeches of Oliver Cromwell, vol 1: 1599–1649*, ed. Wilbur Cortez Abbott (Cambridge, Mass., 1937), pp. 120–1. Cromwell was added to the Committee considering a similar petition from Alexander Leighton, which was now to consider Lilburne's too: *CJ*, II, p. 24; Rushworth, IV, p. 20. The cases of Burton, Bastwick, and Prynne had been raised two days earlier: *CJ*, II, p. 22. Lilburne's petition is reprinted in John Lilburne, INNOCENCY AND TRUTH JUSTI-FIED (London, [1646]), TD 6 January 1646, pp. 66–7.

6. Braddick, *God's Fury*, pp. 122–34.

7. See this volume, pp. 16–17; John Lilburne, *A WORKE OF THE BEAST* ([Amsterdam], 1638), p. 10. For his freedom see <http://www.londonroll.org/home> sn Johes Libborne.

8. Lilburne, INNOCENCY AND TRUTH JUSTIFIED, pp. 22, 38–9, 75. For George's brewing interest see Bod. Lib., MS Clarendon 19, f. 274v. Litigation surrounding Thomas Hewson's will reveals that John Hewson also had brewing interests, some of them shared with Thomas, Lilburne's master: TNA, C/3/436/57, C2/ChasI/H76/35, C2/ChasI/H15/14, C2/ChasI/B49/9. See also C3/423/77.

9. Dewell appears in the Visitation records as a gentleman of Walton on Thames, and servant of Charles I. He is probably, therefore, the surveyor of the King's Highway of that name: Wales and Hartley, II, p. 491; *CSPD, 1637*, pp. 127–8, *1637–8*, p. 341, *1639*, p. 363. There are others of the same name, at least one of whom acted in commissions during the 1640s and 1650s: *A&O*, I, pp. 383–7, II, 1116–22; *CJ*, VII, p. 562.

10. John Lilburne, *L. Colonel JOHN LILBURNE revived* ([Amsterdam?], March 1653), p. (1) [13]; see also John Lilburne, ENGLANDS *weeping spectacle* ([London], 1648), p. 4. For Elizabeth see Ann Hughes, 'Lilburne, Elizabeth (fl. 1641–60)', *ODNB*; Keith Lindley, *Popular Politics and Religion in Civil War London* (Aldershot, 1997), p. 81; for her arrest see TNA, KB 9/823/113. For Spilsbury and his congregation see Murray Tolmie, *The Triumph of the Saints: The Separate Churches of London 1616–1649* (Cambridge, 1977), esp. pp. 24–7, 192–4; Lindley, *Popular Politics*, pp. 81, 82; Rees, pp. 19–20.

11. Adamson, *Noble Revolt*, chs 8–10; Brian Manning, *The English People and the English Revolution* (Harmondsworth, 1978 edition), pp. 20–32.

12. PA BRY/2 ff. 38–9, Deposition of Eusebius Andrewe. I am grateful to John Walter for this reference. Andrewe may have been seeking favour: he was a future royalist, and had been in dispute with the speaker of the Commons, Lenthall: PA HL/PO/JO/10/1/48, ff. 126, 162.

13. [John Lilburne], *A Whip for the present House of Lords* (n.p., n.d.) TD 6 March 1647, p. 18; John Lilburne, *Lieft. Col. I Lilburne his Apologeticall Narration* (Amsterdam, 1652), p. 2; Lilburne, INNOCENCY AND TRUTH JUSTIFIED, pp. 74–5. See also Gibb, p. 79. The Lords' record suggests that the king had a direct interest in seeing Lilburne examined: *LJ*, IV, p. 233.

14. *LJ*, IV, p. 233.

15. *CJ*, II, p. 134. For his place in US constitutional and legal argument, see this volume, pp. 358–9, n. 2.

16. *CJ*, II, p. 134. Rushworth puts all these events together: IV, esp. pp. 249–50. For the abolition of the Star Chamber, see: *SR*, V, p. 110; Gardiner, *CD*, pp. 179–86.

17. Gardiner, *CD*, pp. 155–6, quotation at p, 156; Rushworth, VIII, p. 736.

18. HEH, HM 41956, p. 52; Braddick, 'Prayer Book and Protestation'.

19. The oath, its implementation, and the debate surrounding both are the subject of John Walter, *Covenanting Citizens: The Protestation Oath and Popular Political Culture in the English Revolution* (Cambridge, 2017).

20. John Lilburne, THE PICTURE OF THE *Council of State* ([London], 1649), TD 11 April 1649, p. 10.

21. Manning, *English People*, pp. 29–32.

22. HEH, HM 41956, p. 47.

23. Peter Lake, 'Post-Reformation Politics, or on Not Looking for the Long-Term Causes of the English Civil War', in *The Oxford Handbook of the English Revolution*, ed. Michael J. Braddick (Oxford, 2015), pp. 21–39.

24. Gardiner, *CD*, pp. 163–6 (24 June 1641).

25. Lindley, *Popular Politics*, 104–8; Adamson, *Noble Revolt*, pp. 474–6.

26. John Lilburne, ENGLANDS *weeping spectacle* (London, 1648), p. 3. He says that Lunsford's men drew first: John Lilburne, *The Legal Fundamental LIBERTIES Of the People of England*, 2nd edition (London, 1649), TD 4 August 1649, p. 26; John Lilburne, *The Copy of a LETTER from Lieutenant Colonell JOHN LILBURNE, to a friend* (London, 1645), TD 9 August 1645, pp. 3–4. His reputation as a hot head or turbulent man in 1649 was damaging to his prospects, and it was important to establish that he was simply a committed defender of Parliament's liberties. He conflates it with this appearance before the Lords in May, perhaps for tactical reasons, in Theodorus Verax, THE TRIALL, *Of Lieut. Collonell JOHN LIL-BURNE* (Southwark, [1649]), p. 3. For a report of these events by a sympathetic observer see *The Notebooks of Nehemiah Wallington, 1618–1654: A Selection*, ed. David Booy (Farnham, 2007), pp. 133–4. There is a very full account of these events in Rees, pp. 1–9.

27. For an excellent discussion and further reference see Nicholas Poyntz's blog about Walker: <https://mercuriuspoliticus.wordpress.com/tag/henry-walker/>; Lindley, *Popular Politics*, pp. 147–9.

28. Joad Raymond, 'Walker, Henry (fl. 1638–1660)', *ODNB*.

29. William Kiffin, *Remarkable Passages in the Life of William Kiffin*, ed. William Orme (London, 1823), pp. 1–12. He remembered the preaching Mr Moulin at London Stone, presumably Lewis Du Moulin, the son of one of the authors who had affected Lilburne as a young man: ibid., pp. 7–8; this volume, p. 6. Du Moulin was living at St Martin in the Fields in 1633 but it is not clear that he had an ecclesiastical living in the city: Vivienne Larminie, 'Du Moulin, Peter [Pierre], (1601–1684)', *ODNB*; no living is recorded for this period in CCED.

30. Lilburne, *Legal Fundamental LIBERTIES*, p. 23.

31. John Lilburne, THE CHRISTIAN MANS TRIALL, 2nd edition (London, 1641), FD [December] 1641. There is no Thomason copy of A LIGHT FOR THE IGNORANT, and no other means of more precise dating have yet been suggested. For Larner, Kiffin, and the connections in the London puritan underground which were close to Lilburne's, see Rees, pp. 72–4.

32. Walter, *Covenanting Citizens*, esp. chs 4–6.

33. John Lilburne, *Rash Oaths unwarrantable: And the breaking of them as inexcusable* ([London], 1647); for the Protestation, Vow and Covenant, and Solemn League and Covenant, see pp. 10–11. See also the remonstrance of William Sykes, reproduced in John Lilburne, THE CHARTERS OF LONDON (London, 18 December 1646), sig. K2v. I am grateful to John Walter for this reference.

34. John Lilburne, *An Anatomy of the Lords Tyranny* ([London, November 1646]), pp. 19–20; *The English Levellers*, ed. Andrew Sharp (Cambridge, 1998), pp. 7–8. This separate forms the first part of John Lilburne, ENGLANDS BIRTH-RIGHT *Justified*, see here p. 6; I have here given it Sharp's title.

35. Essex Record Office, X/E 522/14; for a transcription see C. A. Clay, 'Barnston Notes', *Essex Review*, 26 (1916), pp. 92–4. I am grateful to John Walter for this reference. The evidence of the signature is also inconclusive: although the names are recorded in more than one hand, it seems that the return is not signed individually. For good examples of Lilburne's signature see PA HL/PO/ JO/1/1/200, 203; TNA, SP 16/503, f. 125v. I have not been able to establish a connection between Lilburne and any of the other people recorded.

36. *CSPD, 1640–41*, pp. 430, 434, 435, 454; see also *CSPD, 1641–43*, pp. 154, 167; *CSPD Addenda, 1625–49*, p. 633.

37. 'Parishes: Childerditch', in *A History of the County of Essex*, VIII, ed. W. R. Powell, Beryl A. Board, Nancy Briggs, J. L. Fisher, Vanessa A. Harding, Joan Hasler, Norma Knight, and Margaret Parsons (London, 1983), pp. 17–24 <http:// www.british-history.ac.uk/vch/essex/vol8/pp17-24> accessed 3 July 2015.

38. Jason Peacey, '"Fiery Spirits" and Political Propaganda: Uncovering a Radical Press Campaign of 1642', *Publishing History*, 55 (2004), 5–36.

39. Richard Cust, 'Montagu, Edward, first Baron Montagu of Boughton, (1562/ 3–1644)', *ODNB*; for his connection with Hewson see this volume, p. 305 n. 18.

40. Hughes, *Warwickshire*, pp. 136–43, quotation at pp. 139–40.

41. Ibid., pp. 141–8.

42. Kiffin was before Justice Malet, accused of preaching against the king while in White Lyon Prison, and Brooke tried to secure him bail. This was refused, given the seriousness of the charge, but Brooke promised to take up the case once more was known. By a providence Malet was himself then called before the Commons in relation to the controversial Kentish petition, and committed to the Tower by the Lords, which prevented further prosecution of Kiffin: *Remarkable Passages*, ed. Orme, pp. 16–19. The charge against Malet was made on 28 March 1642: *CJ*, II, p. 501, *LJ*, IV, pp. 675–9.

43. TNA, SP 28/1A, f. 193, warrant for payment of ninety-seven troops mustered on 18 August under Captain Lilburne, 24 August 1642. Vivers and Cromwell both seem to have raised troops in the same few days: ibid., ff. 159, 169. See also TNA, SP 16/539/1, f. 190.

44. Lilburne, ENGLANDS *weeping spectacle*, p. 4.

45. Hughes, *Warwickshire*, p. 125; David J. Appleby, 'The Search for George Willingham: The Influence of the London Livery Companies on the Conduct of Holles' Regiment, 1642', *English Civil War Notes & Queries*, 48 (1993), pp. 30–6;

Edward Peacock, *The Army Lists of the Roundheads and Cavaliers*, 2nd edition (London, 1874), p. 34. I am grateful to Ann Hughes and David Appleby for their advice on this point.

46. *CCC*, III, pp. 1918, 1920.

47. Lilburne, ENGLANDS BIRTH-RIGHT *Justified*, pp. 18–21; Lilburne, INNOCENCY AND TRUTH JUSTIFIED, pp. 75–6.

48. TNA, SP 16/539/1, f. 190, written from Cheapside, 24 August.

49. Ismini Pells, 'Wharton, Nehemiah (fl. 1641–1649?)', *ODNB*. The letters are in the state papers, and calendared in *CSPD*, but *Letters from a Subaltern Officer of the Earl of Essex's Army*, ed. Henry Ellis (London, 1854) is more accurate, although not free of errors. I have here quoted from Ellis, generally the more accessible source. While Brooke had tended to draw on his connections among the godly, Holles seems to have worked through the networks of the livery companies: David Appleby, 'George Willingham'. George Willingham seems to have been important to this—Wharton appealed, successfully, for a change of lieutenant colonel, later thanking Willingham for achieving it, and the letters have something of the tone of a report to HQ, rather than simply news: *Letters from a Subaltern Officer*, ed. Ellis, pp. 6, 7, 8. Willingham was a significant player in London politics in the coming decade: Elliott Vernon, *London Presbyterianism and the Politics of Religion in the British Revolution, c.1638–1663* (forthcoming). I have not established any connection between Nehemiah Wharton and his namesake Old John Wharton, although they were clearly near neighbours.

50. *Letters from a Subaltern Officer*, ed. Ellis, p. 10. For his interest in antiquities see for example, pp. 10 (Coventry), 12 (Northampton), 18 (Warwick Castle), 21 (Worcester and its surrounding countryside), 25 (Hereford), 26 (Malvern Church).

51. Ibid., pp. 6–7, 9, 19, 13, 25.

52. Ibid., pp. 6, 11, 15–16. For the more general phenomenon (although primarily dealing with the Scottish wars) see John Walter, '"Abolishing Superstition with Sedition": The Politics of Popular Iconoclasm in England, 1640–1642', *PP*, 183 (2004), 79–123.

53. HEH, HM 41956, p. 60.

54. *Letters from a Subaltern Officer*, ed. Ellis, pp. 8, 10, 13, 15. Deer parks had been attacked in 1640, an early sign of the breakdown of social and political order. In many of those attacks the deer had not been eaten—even more plainly an attack on the badges of gentility: Daniel C. Beaver, *Hunting and the Politics of Violence Before the English Civil War* (Cambridge, 2008).

55. *Letters from a Subaltern Officer*, ed. Ellis, pp. 10–11, 12, 13, 25.

56. Ibid., pp. 10, 20, 24.

57. Ibid., pp. 11, 14, 15, 26.

58. Michael J. Braddick, *State Formation in Early Modern England* (Cambridge, 2000), pp. 68–90; Braddick, 'Loyauté partisane durant la Guerre Civile et histoire des relations sociales en Angleterre', in *Conflits, opinion(s) et politicization de la fin du Moyen Âge au début du xxe siècle*, eds Laurent Bourquin, Philippe Hamon, Pierre Karila-Cohen, and Cédric Michon (Rennes, 2011), pp. 95–114; *The Politics of*

Gesture: Historical Perspectives, ed. Braddick, Past and Present Supplements, New Series, 4 (Oxford 2009), esp. editor's introduction and the essay by John Walter.

59. Lilburne, ENGLANDS *weeping spectacle*, p. 4.

60. Brooke's and Holles's regiments were alongside each other, in Thomas Ballard's brigade: Peter Young, *Edgehill 1642: The Campaign and the Battle* (Kineton, 1967), pp. 102, 250–1; Sir John Maynard, A SPEECH *Spoken in the Honourable House of* COMMONS (London, 11 August 1648), p. 7; Gregg, p. 100. Lilburne claimed to have been plundered at Edgehill too: Lilburne, INNOCENCY AND TRUTH JUSTIFIED, p. 39.

61. Lilburne, ENGLANDS *weeping spectacle*, p. 4.

62. Lilburne, INNOCENCY AND TRUTH JUSTIFIED, pp. 39–41.

63. Ibid., pp. 40–1.

64. Ismini Pells, 'Nehemiah Wharton'. I am grateful to Dr Pells for discussing Wharton with me.

65. For contemporary accounts of the battle see Rushworth, V, p. 59; Clarendon, II, p. 395.

66. Verax, THE TRIALL, p. 3. See also John Lilburne, *The Reasons of Lieu Col. Lilbournes sending his Letter to Mr Prin.* ([London, 1645]), p. 2.

67. THE HUMBLE PETITION OF THE ALL THE INHABITANTS OF THE TOWN OF Old Braintford (London, 27 November 1642); A DECLARATION AND manifestation (1642), TD 17 November 1642; HIS MAJESTIES DECLARATION... Shewing His true Intentions in advancing lately to Brainford (1642), TD 2 December 1642; Clarendon, II, p. 395. See also Rushworth, V, pp. 59 ff.

68. William Felton, THE EXAMINATION AND CONFESSION OF *Captaine Lilbourne and Captaine Viviers* (London, 1642), TD 16 December 1642, sig. A3v.

69. John Morrill, 'Holles, Denzil, first Baron Holles (1598–1680)', ODNB.

70. Peter Young and Richard Holmes, *The English Civil War: A Military History of the Three Civil Wars* (Ware, 2000), pp. 82–3.

71. Lilburne, ENGLANDS *weeping spectacle*, p. 4.

72. They were the earl of Kingston, Lord Dunsmore, Lord Maltravers, and Lord Andevour: John Lilburne, *To the hon[ble]. the House of Commons now Assembled in the high Court of Parliament, the humble petition of John Lilburne Lieft. Colonel. In all humilitie*. See also Lilburne, *The Reasons*, p. 3.

73. For Vivers's connection with Hewson via Banbury, see this volume, pp. 5, 305 n. 20. In the summer of 1642 he was captain of Banbury Castle under John Fiennes, and in August enlisted as captain of a troop of horse in Essex's army. Nathaniel Fiennes claimed that Vivers's troop was one of the first to flee before the royalist charge at Edgehill: Young, *Edgehill*, pp. 319–20.

74. Lilburne later cited his kindness to Chillenden at Oxford as evidence of his own capacity for forgiveness: Lilburne, L. Colonel JOHN LILBURNE *revived*, p. 3. They were together involved in the Leveller campaigns: Lindley, *Popular Politics*, pp. 81–3, 393; H. N. Brailsford, *The Levellers and the English Revolution*, 2nd edition (Nottingham, 1976), pp. 80, 187 and n.; Rees, pp. 80–4.

75. State trials, IV, p. 1272.

76. Felton, EXAMINATION AND CONFESSION, sig. A2v.

77. Rushworth, V, p. 83.

78. Felton, EXAMINATION AND CONFESSION, sig. A2v.

79. A SPEECH, spoken by Prince ROBERT (London, 21 December 1642), sig. A4–A4v.

80. CJ, II, p. 891; see also PA HL/PO/JO/10/1/138; LJ, V, 497.

81. Lilburne, ENGLANDS weeping spectacle, p. 4–5.

82. A true and most sad RELATION OF The hard usage and extrem cruelty (London, 13 February 1642), pp. 6–7. For later accounts of conditions for prisoners in Oxford see Chillenden, THE INHUMANITY of the King's Prison-Keeper at OXFORD (London, 1643), TD 4 August 1643; see also Chillenden, A PITIFVLL RELATION OF THE KINGS PRISON KEEPER AT OXFORD (London, 1643); CJ, III, p. 98.

83. For a summary of the negotiations see David L. Smith, Constitutional Royalism and the Search for Settlement, c. 1640–1649 (Cambridge, 1994), pp. 112–14.

84. Lilburne, The reasons, p. 3; A letter sent from Captaine Lilburne to divers of his frinds, citizens, and others of good account in London, p. 7; Lilburne, Apologeticall Narration, p. 3; Lilburne, INNOCENCY AND TRUTH JUSTIFIED, p. 41.

85. Lilburne, Legal fundamental LIBERTIES, p. 27.

86. Michael J. Braddick, 'History, Liberty, Reformation and the Cause: Parliamentarian Military and Ideological Escalation in 1643', in The Experience of Revolution in Stuart Britain and Ireland: Essays for John Morrill, eds Michael J. Braddick and David L. Smith (Cambridge, 2011), 117–34.

87. See this volume, p. 31.

88. Manchester was closely associated with Saye and Lord Brooke, with both of whom Lilburne had at least a slight connection. His uncle was the husband of Lady Anne Montagu, a close friend of Lilburne's master. He would have refused to fight in the Bishop's Wars but for his father's threat to disinherit him: Ian J. Gentles, 'Montagu, Edward, Second Earl of Manchester (1602–1671)', ODNB; and this volume, pp. 4–5. Lilburne, INNOCENCY AND TRUTH JUSTIFIED, pp. 41–2; Lilburne, Legal fundamental LIBERTIES, p. 27.

89. Lilburne, Apologeticall Narration, pp. 3–4.

90. Clive Holmes, 'Colonel King and Lincolnshire Politics, 1642–1646', HJ, 16 (1973), 451–84. See also Holmes, The Eastern Association in the English Civil War (Cambridge, 1974), p. 188 and Holmes, Seventeenth-Century Lincolnshire (Lincoln, 1980), p. 184.

91. Holmes, Eastern Association, p. 200; Lilburne, INNOCENCY AND TRUTH JUSTIFIED, pp. 41–2.

92. Holmes, Lincoln, p. 198.

93. Lilburne, INNOCENCY AND TRUTH JUSTIFIED, pp. 41–2.

94. Bod. Lib., MS J Walker c. 1, f. 31r. The published version omits much of this detail: John Walker, An Attempt towards Recovering the Numbers and Sufferings of the Clergy of the Church of England... (London, 1714), p. 252. The manuscript account dates from 1704 but the circumstantial details tally with what is known of Gibson's career and with those of Lilburne's: CCED.

95. Gregg, pp. 108–9; Lilburne, INNOCENCY AND TRUTH JUSTIFIED, p. 25; Rushworth, V, pp. 307–8.

96. Holmes, 'Colonel King', p. 463.

97. *LJ*, VI, pp. 531, 536, 581, 595–6, 605, 611, 612 (April–July, 1644). King was also involved in conflict over conduct at Lincoln throughout 1647 and 1648 (*CJ*, V, p. 307, and *passim*) and in October 1648 'information of dangerous consequence' was reported to the Commons: Rushworth, VII, p. 1301. For the full context, see Holmes, 'Colonel King'.

98. Gregg, p. 109.

99. For the incident see Peter Wenham, *The Siege of York 1644* (York, 1994), pp. 59–63.

100. Maynard, *A* SPEECH *Spoken in the Honourable House of* COMMONS, p. 8; Lilburne, INNOCENCY AND TRUTH JUSTIFIED, p. 25.

101. Holmes, 'Colonel King', pp. 463–4.

102. Lilburne, ENGLANDS *weeping spectacle*, p. 5.

103. Gentles, 'Manchester', *ODNB*; Holmes, *Eastern Association*, p. 198.

104. Lilburne, *Legal Fundamental* LIBERTIES, p. 27.

105. Lilburne, INNOCENCY AND TRUTH JUSTIFIED, pp. 22–3. The following account is taken from this vivid narrative. It agrees in all essential detail with Lilburne's formal testimony to Parliament about Manchester's conduct on 30 November 1644: *CSPD, 1644–5*, pp. 148–9. For the original see TNA, SP 16/503, f. 125r–v.

106. Lilburne, INNOCENCY AND TRUTH JUSTIFIED, pp. 23–4.

107. Lilburne, INNOCENCY AND TRUTH JUSTIFIED, p. 24. In his formal testimony he named the quartermaster general as having endorsed his interpretation of Manchester's view, and who also said it was the general view: TNA, SP 16/503, f. 125. In print, it seems, Lilburne was careful to protect those with no direct stake in the argument.

108. Lilburne, INNOCENCY AND TRUTH JUSTIFIED, pp. 24–5.

109. Ibid., p. 25.

110. *The Quarrel between the Earl of Manchester and Oliver Cromwell*, ed. David Masson, Camden Society, New Series, 12 (1875), pp. 2, 80–1.

111. Lilburne, INNOCENCY AND TRUTH JUSTIFIED, p. 26.

112. Holmes, *Eastern Association*, pp. 199–205.

113. Gentles, 'Manchester', *ODNB*.

114. Quoted in Braddick, *God's Fury*, p. 334.

115. Lilburne, *Legal Fundamental* LIBERTIES, p. 27.

116. Lilburne, ENGLANDS *weeping spectacle*, p. 5; Lilburne, INNOCENCY AND TRUTH JUSTIFIED, p. 22.

117. Lilburne, INNOCENCY AND TRUTH JUSTIFIED, p. 25. See also Lilburne *Apologeticall Narration*, pp. 4–5.

118. Lilburne, INNOCENCY AND TRUTH JUSTIFIED, p. 46.

119. Lilburne, *Legal Fundamental* LIBERTIES, p. 27; Lilburne, ENGLANDS *weeping spectacle*, p. 7. Cromwell, he said, continued to press him to serve in Fairfax's army: Lilburne, *Legal Fundamental* LIBERTIES, pp. 27–8.

CHAPTER 3

1. Ann Hughes, *Gangraena and the Struggle for the English Revolution* (Oxford, 2004), pp. 34–7.

2. Cheney Culpeper, 'The Letters and Papers of Sir Cheney Culpeper, 1641–1657', ed. Michael J. Braddick and Mark Greengrass, in *Camden Miscellany*, 33, Camden 5th series, 7 (Cambridge 1996), 105–402, quotation at p. 209.

3. F. J. Bremer, 'Williams, Roger (c. 1606–1683)', *ODNB*, following Bremer's summary of *The Bloudy Tenent*.

4. Gordon Campbell, 'Milton, John (1608–1674)', *ODNB*.

5. David Richard Adams, 'Religion and Reason in the Thought of Richard Overton, the Leveller' (PhD dissertation, Cambridge University, 2002), esp. chs 3 and 4.

6. Michael Mendle, 'De Facto Freedom, de Facto Authority: Press and Parliament, 1640–1643', *HJ*, 38 (1995), pp. 307–32.

7. There are fragments of evidence of other raids at this time: David Como, 'Print, Censorship, and Ideological Escalation in the English Civil War', *JBS*, 51 (2012), pp. 820–57, at p. 825.

8. David Como, 'Secret Printing, the Crisis of 1640, and the Origins of Civil-War Radicalism', *P&P*, 196 (2007), pp. 37–82; Como, 'Print, Censorship and Ideological Escalation', p. 823.

9. For Writer see Jason Peacey, 'Reviving the Radicals: Clement Writer and the Historiography of the English Revolution', *Prose Studies*, 36 (2014), pp. 243–55.

10. Como, 'Print, Censorship and Ideological Escalation', pp. 829–36.

11. *CJ*, III, p. 606.

12. Como, 'Print, Censorship and Ideological Escalation', p. 838.

13. Ibid., pp. 836–8, 842–5.

14. John Lilburne, INNOCENCY AND TRUTH JUSTIFIED (London, [1646]), TD 6 January 1646, pp. 38–9.

15. Ibid., p. 62.

16. Ibid., pp. 21–2; John Lilburne, *To the Honble the House of Commons now assembled* (1646?).

17. John Lilburne, *The Copy of a LETTER . . . to a freind* ([London: Larner's press at Goodman's Fields, 1645]), TD 9 August 1645, p. 11. Page references here from Huntington Library copy: there are slight variations in the copy held at the British Library.

18. Lilburne, *The Copy of a LETTER . . . to a freind*, pp. 10–11; Lilburne, *The Reasons of Lieu Col. Lilbournes sending his Letter to Mr Prin* ([London, 1645]), TD 13 June 1645, p. 3; Lilburne, *To the Honble the House of Commons*; Lilburne, INNOCENCY AND TRUTH JUSTIFIED, pp. 43–6.

19. Lilburne, INNOCENCY AND TRUTH JUSTIFIED, pp. 46–7; John Lilburne, *London's Liberty In Chains discovered* (London, Oct 1646), quotation at p. 22.

20. For example, Lilburne, INNOCENCY AND TRUTH JUSTIFIED, pp. 22, 44–6; Lilburne, *To the Honble the House of Commons*.

21. Richard had been appointed to a committee in Durham managing relations with the occupying Scottish army in 1640: Rushworth, III, p. 1274. He was appointed by the House of Lords to hear witnesses in a dispute between a minister and his parishioners in Aycliffe (Hewson's home parish) in July 1645 and was an assessment and militia commissioner in 1648: *LJ*, VII, p. 511; *LJ*, X, pp. 52, 278; *A&O*, I, p. 1081. George had been mayor of Sunderland before 1640. He was named a commissioner for the £400,000 subsidy in 1640 and to a commission to disarm recusants in August 1641: *SR*, V, pp. 145–69; *LJ*, IV, p. 386. He was a deputy lieutenant in 1644, and with Richard was witness to the appointment of Sheriffs in 1646, 1647, and 1648: *CJ*, III, p. 593; *A&O*, I, pp. 831–3; *LJ*, VIII, p. 176; *LJ*, VIII, p. 716; *LJ*, X, pp. 105–6. He was added to the Militia Commission in 1648: *A&O*, I, p. 1236. Both served on the Durham Sequestration committee too. For Robert Lilburne's career, which really took off over the following decade, see Barry Coward, 'Lilburne, Robert (bap. 1614, d. 1665)', *ODNB*. John's younger brother, Henry, became governor of Tynmouth Castle, but this was to end in his death, when he took the king's side in the second civil war in 1648.

22. See this volume, p. 57.

23. Lilburne, INNOCENCY AND TRUTH JUSTIFIED, pp. 75–6.

24. Lilburne, *The Reasons*, pp. 5–7; Lilburne, *The Copy of a LETTER … to a freind*, pp. 10–12; this volume, p. 68.

25. Lilburne, *The Reasons*, p. 3.

26. Ibid., pp. 3–5; Lilburne, *The Copy of a LETTER … to a freind*, pp. 11–12.

27. William Prynne, TRVTH TRIVMPHING OVER FALSEHOOD, ANTIQVITY Over NOVELTY (London, 1645), p. 1.

28. Prynne, TRVTH TRIVMPHING, p. [iv]. For Prynne's views see William Lamont, 'Prynne, William (1600–1669)', *ODNB* and, more generally, *Marginal Prynne*.

29. [J. Goodwin], *Innocency and Truth triumphing together* (London, 1646), TD 8 January 1645. For Goodwin's role in these controversies, see John Coffey, *John Goodwin and the Puritan Revolution: Religion and Intellectual Change in Seventeenth-Century England* (Woodbridge, 2006), ch. 4; and for his connection with Lilburne and Walwyn see esp. pp. 121–2.

30. See for example, William Prynne, THE LYAR CONFOUNDED (London, 1645); John Bastwick, A IVST DEFENCE, (London, 1645), pp. 31–2.

31. [John Lilburne], ENGLANDS *weeping spectacle* (1648), TD 29 June 1649, p. [6].

32. John Lilburne, A COPIE OF A LETTER, *Written by John Lilburne, Leut. Collonell, to Mr William Prinne Esq* ([London, 1645]), p. 2.

33. John Lilburne, ENGLANDS BIRTH RIGHT *Justified* ([London, 1645]), pp. 10–11.

34. Gardiner, *CD*, pp. 267–71.

35. Lilburne, A COPIE OF A LETTER, quotations pp. 2, 6.

36. David R. Adams, 'The Secret Printing and Publishing Career of Richard Overton the Leveller, 1644–46', *The Library*, 7th Series, 11:1 (2010), pp. 3–88. This expands and corrects the pioneering study by H. R. Plomer, 'Secret Printing During the Civil War', *The Library*, 2nd Series, 5 (1904), pp. 374–403.

For Walwyn, Paine, and Lilburne see David Como, 'An Unattributed Pamphlet by William Walwyn: New Light on the Prehistory Of the Leveller Movement', *HLQ*, 69:3 (2006), pp. 353–82.

37. Adams, 'Religion and Reason', ch. 5.

38. Elliot Vernon and Philip Baker, 'What Was the First Agreement of the People?', *HJ*, 53 (2010), pp. 39–59, at p. 43.

39. The relevant passages are each on the final page at p. 20. It is difficult to interpret exactly what these emendations might mean, not least because there is no precise date for the 1641 edition—there is no copy in the Thomason collection. I am grateful to John Coffey, John Morrill, and Hunter Powell for discussing this point with me.

40. John Lilburne, *The Copy of a LETTER . . . to a friend* (London, 1645), TD 9 April 1645, p. 12.

41. Lilburne, *A COPIE OF A LETTER*, p. 7.

42. Lilburne, *INNOCENCY AND TRUTH JUSTIFIED*, pp. 9–10; John Lilburne, *The Oppressed Mans Oppressions Declared* (London, 1647), p. 15.

43. Lilburne, *A COPIE OF A LETTER*, pp. 4–5.

44. Lilburne, *ENGLANDS BIRTH RIGHT Justified*, p. 12.

45. Lilburne, *The Copy of a LETTER . . . to a freind*, p. 12.

46. Lilburne, *ENGLANDS BIRTH RIGHT Justified*, p. 12.

47. Lilburne, *A COPIE OF A LETTER*, p. 2.

48. Adams, 'Secret printing', pp. 33–9; *LJ*, VII, 116, 142; PA HL/PO/JO/10/1/180, f. 146; Gregg, pp. 115–16.

49. Andrew Sharp, 'Lilburne, John (1615?–1657)', *ODNB*; J. T. Peacey, 'John Lilburne and the Long Parliament', *HJ*, 43 (2000), pp. 625–45 at p. 630.

50. Lilburne, *INNOCENCY AND TRUTH JUSTIFIED*, p. 9.

51. Prynne, *LYAR CONFOUNDED*, pp. 4, 9.

52. Adams, 'Secret Printing', pp. 48–54.

53. Rees, pp. 85–100.

54. See, in general, Jason Peacey, *Print and Public Politics in the English Revolution* (Cambridge, 2013); Rees.

55. Lilburne, *INNOCENCY AND TRUTH JUSTIFIED*, pp. 4–6; see also Edwards, *Gangraena*, pt 1, p. 96. For the wider world of partisan petitioning and public mobilization see Peacey, *Print and Public Politics*; David Zaret, *Origins of Democratic Culture: Printing, Petitions, and the Public Sphere in Early-Modern England* (Princeton, 2000).

56. Edwards, *Gangraena*, pt 2, p. 154.

57. John Lilburne, *The Legal Fundamental LIBERTIES Of the People of England*, 2nd edition (London, 1649), TD 4 August 1649, p. 28; Lilburne, *The Copy of a LETTER . . . to a freind*, p. 6. The letter was reproduced in a number of places. For his account of the battle and advice about military civilian relations see *A more full relation of the great battell fought betweene Sir Tho: Fairfax, and Goring. on Thursday last, 1645.* (London, 1645).

58. Lilburne, *The Copy of a LETTER . . . to a freind*, p. 6.

59. Ibid., pp. 15–16.

60. Prynne, LYAR CONFOUNDED, quotation at p. 4; John Vicars, THE PICTURE OF INDE-PENDENCY (London, 1645), quotation at p. 9; Edwards, *Gangraena*, pt 1, p. 70 [pagination inconsistent]; II, p. 104. Lilburne does not seem to have made any reference to this at the time, although he did mention the resulting problems in his appearance before the Committee of Examinations on 8 February 1647: John Lilburne, *The resolved mans Resolution* ([London], 1647), TD 24 May 1647, p. 11: 'I have but one good eye to see with, and yet for that, I am forced to the use the help of spectacles'.

61. Edwards, *Gangraena*, pt 1, p. 96; pt 2, pp. 29–30, 40, 103.

62. Lilburne, INNOCENCY AND TRUTH JUSTIFIED, p. 10.

63. Lilburne, *The Copy of a LETTER . . . to a freind*, pp. 1–2, 6–8; John Lilburne, THE IUST MANS IUSTIFICATION: or A Letter by way of Plea in Barre, ([London, 1646]), TD 10 June 1645, pp. 2–3. For the counter-charges see Prynne, LYAR CONFOUNDED; Bastwick, IVST DEFENCE.

64. Lilburne, INNOCENCY AND TRUTH JUSTIFIED, pp. 10–11, 27–8; Lilburne, *The Copy of a LETTER . . . to a freind*, pp. 5–8, quotation at p. 8. Cromwell's letter is repro-duced in *Writings and Speeches of Oliver Cromwell*, 4 vols (Cambridge, Mass., 1937–47), vol. 1, pp. 363–4.

65. The order is reproduced in Lilburne, *The Copy of a LETTER . . . to a freind*, p. 8, and Lilburne, INNOCENCY AND TRUTH JUSTIFIED, p. 13.

66. Gregg, pp. 119–20.

67. Lilburne, *The Copy of a LETTER . . . to a friend*, esp. p. 10; Adams, 'Secret Printing', pp. 41–5. See also Lilburne, INNOCENCY AND TRUTH JUSTIFIED, pp. 13–15.

68. Lilburne, *The Copy of a LETTER . . . to a friend*, pp. 2, 6.

69. Adams, 'Secret Printing', pp. 41–5.

70. Reprinted in *The English Levellers*, ed. Andrew Sharp (Cambridge, 1998), pp. 3–8, quotation at p. 3.

71. Andrew Sharp, 'John Lilburne and the Long Parliament's Book of Declarations: A Radical's Exploitation of the Words of Authorities', *History of Political Thought*, 9 (1988), pp. 19–44, at pp. 19, 22.

72. *English Levellers*, ed. Sharp, quotations at p. 7; the Protestation, which would have committed those who took it to 'oppose, and by all good ways and means endeavour to bring to condign punishment all such as shall by force, practice, counsels, plots, conspiracies or otherwise, do anything to the contrary in this present Protestation contained': Gardiner, *CD*, pp. 155–6, quotation at p. 156. Again his point is that Parliament itself imposed these obligations through the Protestation: he does not quite here say that he himself took it. For Lilburne and the Protestation see this volume, pp. 53–4.

73. Lilburne, *The Copy of a LETTER . . . to a freind*, p. 5.

74. For a similar analysis see Rachel Foxley, 'John Lilburne and the Citizenship of the Free-Born Englishman', *HJ*, 47 (2004), pp. 849–74.

75. Lilburne, INNOCENCY AND TRUTH JUSTIFIED, pp. 15–17; Gregg, p. 122.

76. Lilburne, INNOCENCY AND TRUTH JUSTIFIED, pp. 28–9.

77. Lilburne, ENGLANDS BIRTH-RIGHT Justified, p. 42.

78. Edwards, *Gangraena*, pt 1, pp. 40. For Knowles and this congregation see also pt 1, pp. 97–8; and for sectaries' sympathy for Lilburne's attacks on civil powers, pt 2, p. 157.

79. Lilburne, INNOCENCY AND TRUTH JUSTIFIED, 29–30.

80. In 1649 he claimed that Rosier had been his '*pastor or teacher*' in late 1644 and early 1645: Lilburne, *Legal Fundamental* LIBERTIES, pp. 23, 28.

81. Prynne challenged him to say how many nights he had been in prison, with what diet, and having paid how much in fees: LYAR CONFOUNDED, p. 10.

82. Lilburne, ENGLANDS BIRTH-RIGHT Justified, quotation at p. 12.

83. Alan Craig Houston, '"A Way of Settlement": The Levellers, Monopolies and the Public Interest', *HPT*, 14 (1993), pp. 381–420.

84. Lilburne, INNOCENCY AND TRUTH JUSTIFIED, p. 75.

85. Adams, 'Secret Printing', pp. 45–8.

86. Foxley, 'The Levellers: John Lilburne, Richard Overton and William Walwyn', in *The Oxford Handbook of Literature and the English Revolution*, ed. Laura Lunger Knoppers (Oxford, 2012), pp. 272–86; Samuel Dennis Glover, 'The Putney Debates: Popular versus Elitist Republicanism', *P&P*, 164 (1999), pp. 47–80; Nicholas McDowell, 'Ideas of Creation in the Writings of Richard Overton the Leveller and *Paradise Lost*', *Journal of the History of Ideas*, 66 (2005), pp. 59–78; Iain Hampsher-Monk, 'The Political Theory of the Levellers: Putney, Property and Professor Macpherson', *Political Studies*, 24 (1976), pp. 397–422, esp. pp. 412–22.

87. Lilburne, ENGLANDS *weeping spectacle*, p. 7.

88. Ibid., p. 7; Lilburne, INNOCENCY AND TRUTH JUSTIFIED, pp. 29–34.

89. *CJ*, IV, p. 338; *LJ*, VII, p. 73; Peacey, 'John Lilburne and the Long Parliament'.

90. Lilburne, INNOCENCY AND TRUTH JUSTIFIED, pp. 63–4, 68–70, quotation at p. 68.

91. *CJ*, IV, p. 418; PA HL/PO/JO/10/1/200, 2 February 1646 [folios inconsistently numbered]; *LJ*, VIII, pp. 127, 139, 152, 164–5; Anon., *A true relation of the materiall passages of Lieut. Col.* Iohn Lilburnes *sufferings* (London, [1645]), quotation at p. 9

92. *LJ*, VIII, 167, 201, 217, 234, 272, 278, 286; PA HL/PO/JO/10/1/203, f. 58; Anon., *True relation*, pp. 8–9; Lilburne, INNOCENCY AND TRUTH JUSTIFIED, p. 75; John Lilburne, A PREPARATIVE TO AN HUE AND CRY AFTER SIR ARTHUR HASLERIG ([London, 1649]), TD 13 September 1649, pp. 17–18. In this later account Lilburne gets some dates slightly wrong, and also claims he was awarded £10,000, but this seems clearly mistaken. He does not mention that an ordinance for reparations for Bastwick was making its way through at the same time. For George Lilburne and Henry Vane see also this volume, pp. 57, 216–18.

93. Adams, 'Secret Printing', pp. 48–54.

94. Lilburne, IUST MANS IUSTIFICATION, quotation at p. 2.

95. For Lilburne, Overton, and Walwyn: Edwards, *Gangraena*, pt 1, p. 96, sig. a 3, pp. 29, 33, 171; for bookshop conversation and Westminster Hall sales: pt 1, pp. 111, 148–9; for plans for Lilburne election, pt 1, pp. 53; for partisan advantage and opposition to civil magistracy see, for example, pt 1, pp. 63, 67, 108–9. Milton's views on divorce also figure as error number 154, pt 1, p. 34.

96. Edwards, *Gangraena*, pt 2, pp. 28–9 (Peter), quotation at p. 183; Walwyn: *The Writings of William Walwyn*, eds Jack R. McMichael and Barbara Taft (Athens, GA, 1989), chs 8–17, quotation at p. 177. For the political and religious context of the publication see Hughes, *Gangraena*, esp. ch. 5.

97. Lilburne, IUST MANS IUSTIFICATION, quotation at p. 9. The Lords proceedings include annotated copies of the IUST MANS IUSTIFICATION and John Lilburne, THE FREE-MANS FREEDOME VINDICATED (London, 1646), TD 23 June 1646, with particular attention to legal and jurisdictional claims, as well as manuscript copies of the Protestation and his letter to Wollaston: PA HL/PO/JO/10/1/203, 210.

98. Lilburne, FREE-MANS FREEDOME VINDICATED, pp. 3–4; *LJ*,VIII, p. 370.

99. The text of the Protestation, which is signed by Lilburne, does appear to have been more hastily written, but there are few interlineations or corrections, suggesting that what was said had been quite carefully thought through before this version was written out: PA HL/PO/JO/10/1/203, ff. 100–4.

100. Lilburne, *FREE-MANS FREEDOME VINDICATED*, quotations at pp. 6, 8.

101. John Lilburne, *To the right Honourable the chosen and Representative body of England Assembled in Parliament* (np, nd), p. 11.

102. Martin Dzelzainis, 'History and Ideology: Milton, the Levellers and the Council of State in 1649', *HLQ*, 68 (2005), pp. 269–87, for Hugh Peter's observations about Lilburne's inconsistency, pp. 284–5. Foxley is persuasive on the relationship between natural law and common law in Leveller writings: 'Sovereignty'; see also Foxley, 'The Levellers', esp. pp. 282–4. For the importance of understanding their writing as polemic see Glenn Burgess, 'Protestant Polemic: The Leveller Pamphlets', *Parergon*, 11:2 (1993), pp. 45–67.

103. Glenn Burgess, *British Political Thought 1500–1660: The Politics of the Post-Reformation* (Basingstoke, 2009), pp. 246–7.

104. John Lilburne, *A coppy of a Letter sent by Liev. Col. John Lilburne to Mr Wollaston Keeper of Newgate or his Deputy* ([London, 1645]), TD London, 24 June 1645.

105. Michael J. Braddick, *State Formation in Early Modern England c. 1550–1700* (Cambridge, 2000), esp. pp. 68–90; Braddick, 'Administrative Performance: The Representation of Political Authority in Early Modern England', in *Negotiating Power in Early Modern Society: Order, Hierarchy and Subordination in Britain and Ireland*, eds Michael J. Braddick and John Walter (Cambridge, 2001), pp. 166–87; Braddick, 'Civility and Authority', in *The British Atlantic World, 1500–1800*, 2nd edition, eds Michael J. Braddick and David Armitage (Basingstoke, 2009), pp. 113–32; Michael J. Braddick, 'Introduction: The Politics of Gesture', in *The Politics of Gesture: Historical Perspectives*, ed. Braddick, Past and Present Supplements, New Series, 4 (Oxford, 2009), pp. 9–35; Braddick, 'Face, légitimaté et identité partisane dans la négociation du pouvoir de l'État en Angleterre (1558–1660)', in *Le pouvoir contourné. Infléchir et subvertir l'autorité a l'âge moderne*, ed. Héloïse Hermant (Paris, 2016), pp. 193–221; John Walter, 'Gesturing at Authority: Deciphering the Gestural Code of Early Modern England', in *Politics of Gesture*, ed. Braddick, pp. 96–127; Walter, 'Body Politics in the English Revolution', in *The Nature of the English Revolution Revisited*, ed. Stephen Taylor

and Grant Tapsell (Woodbrige, 2013), pp. 81–102. The theatre of Lilburne's appearances before the Lords is discussed in detail in Jonathan Vallerius, 'Radical Movements and Body Politics in the English Revolution' (PhD dissertation, University of Essex, 2014), ch. 4. For Lilburne's encounter with Banks see this volume, pp. 18–19.

106. Lilburne, *Coppy of a Letter sent by Liev. Col. John Lilburne.*

107. Lilburne, *London's Liberty In Chains*, p. 26; John Lilburne, *An Anatomy of Lords Tyranny* ([London, 1646]), p. 6.

108. Lilburne, *London's Liberty In Chains*, pp. 31–2 (for Elizabeth's petition see pp. 65–70).

109. Lilburne, *An Anatomy of Lords Tyranny*, pp. 12–18, quotation at p. 15.

110. Ibid., pp. 12–18; PA HL/PO/JO/10/1/210, ff. 114–15; HL/PO/JO/10/4/8, f. 32; HL/PO/JO/10/1/213, ff. 69–81; HL/PO/JO/10/3/181/8; *LJ*, VIII, pp. 429–30, 432–3, 435, 494; Valerius, 'Radical Movements', ch. 4. See also Gregg, p. 142.

111. See, in general: Keith Thomas, *The Ends of Life: Roads to Fulfilment in Early Modern England* (Oxford, 2009), chs 2, 5 and Richard Cust, 'Honour and Politics in Early Stuart England: The Case of Beaumont v. Hastings', *P&P*, 149 (1995), pp. 57–94; and in the civil war context in particular, Barbara Donagan, 'Codes and Conduct in the English Civil War', *P&P*, 118 (1988), pp. 65–95; Donagan, 'The Web of Honour: Soldiers, Christians, and Gentlemen in the English Civil War', *HJ*, 44 (2001), pp. 363–89.

112. BL, Sloane 1519, f. 135; Bod. Lib., MS Clarendon 97, ff. 38v–39r; MS Clarendon 28, f. 110; MS Clarendon 29, f. 183r.

113. Richard Overton, *A DEFIANCE AGAINST ALL ARBITRARY USURPATIONS* ([London], 1646), TD 9 September 1646, pp. 8–14; Gregg, pp. 144–5; PA HL/PO/JO/10/1/212, ff. 2–36 (which includes a manuscript copy of *An alarum*, with printer's marks); Adams, 'Secret Printing', pp. 55–6.

114. Richard Overton, *An Arrow against all Tyrants* (London, 1646), excerpts reprinted in *The Levellers in the English Revolution*, ed. G. E. Aylmer (London, 1975), pp. 68–70, quotation at p. 69. For very similar phrases attributed to Lilburne see this volume pp. 106–7.

115. Reprinted in *Levellers*, ed. Aylmer, pp. 63–7, quotations at pp. 64, 65–6.

116. Glover, 'Putney Debates', esp. pp. 65–71.

117. *English Levellers*, ed. Sharp, pp. viii–ix. For a succinct account of the differing intellectual interests of Lilburne, Walwyn, and Overton, and also of what drew them together, see Foxley, 'The Levellers'.

118. Overton, *A DEFIANCE AGAINST ALL ARBITRARY USURPATIONS*, p. 1.

119. A case made clearly in *ENGLAND'S MISERIE, AND REMEDIE IN A JVDICIOVS LETTER from an Utter-Barrister to his speciall Friend* (London, 1645). TD 19 September 1645, Thomason note 'Lilburnes owne'.

120. *English Levellers*, ed. Sharp, p. ix. The remonstrance is reprinted at pp. 33–53, quotation at p. 34; excerpts also appear in *Writings of William Walwyn*, ed. McMichael and Taft, pp. 223–6. For doubts about Overton's authorship see Adams, 'Religion and Reason', appendix.

121. Rees, p. 147, and see also p. 165. For the tensions between this developing mobilization and some of the separatist congregations see Murray Tolmie, *The Triumph of the Saints: The Separate Churches of London 1616–1649* (Cambridge, 1977), esp. ch. 7.

122. Bod. Lib., MS Clarendon 29, f. 10 (December 1646).

CHAPTER 4

1. See table in David L. Smith, 'The Impact on Government', in *The Impact of the English Civil War*, ed. John Morrill (London, 1991), pp. 32–49, at p. 45.

2. Anon., THE APOLOGIE OF THE *Common Souldiers of his* EXCELLENCIE S^{IR} THO. *FAIRFAXES ARMY* (London, 3 May 1647), quotation at p. 3.

3. Eduard Bernstein, *Cromwell and Communism: Socialism and Democracy in the Great English Revolution* (Nottingham, 1980); Henry Holorenshaw [Christopher Hill], *The Levellers and the English Revolution* (London, 1939); H. N. Brailsford, *The Levellers and the English Revolution*, 2nd edition (Nottingham, 1976). Gregg refers to Lilburne as a 'party leader' around this time: ch. 19.

4. See, for example, Rachel Foxley, 'John Lilburne and the Citizenship of the Free-Born Englishman', *HJ*, 47 (2004), pp. 849–74; Glenn Burgess, 'Protestant Polemic: The Leveller Pamphlets', *Parergon*, 11:2 (1993), pp. 45–67; Norah Carlin, 'The Levellers and the Conquest of Ireland in 1649', *Historical Journal*, 30 (1987), pp. 269–88, at p. 272.

5. Rees, esp. pp. 339–43; Elliot Vernon and Philip Baker, 'What was the First *Agreement of the People*?', *HJ*, 53 (2010), pp. 39–59; Jonathan Scott, 'Radicalism and Restoration: The Shape of the Stuart Experience', *HJ*, 31 (1988), pp. 453–67, esp. p. 455. See also the discussion of Lawrence Clarkson's career in *Political Ideas of the English civil wars 1641–1649*, ed. Andrew Sharp (New York, 1983), p. 185.

6. For a similar view of Lilburne's role see Jonathan Scott, *England's Troubles: Seventeenth-Century English Political Instability in European Context* (Cambridge, 2000), ch. 10, esp. p. 285. See also Richard Tuck, *Philosophy and Government 1572–1651* (Cambridge, 1993), pp. 241–5.

7. For his comments on Lilburne and Overton in particular see Edwards, *Gangraena*, pt 3, pp. 148–60, 262. For the broader context see Ann Hughes, *Gangraena and the Struggle for the English Revolution* (Oxford, 2004), pp. 360–7.

8. Rees, pp. 162–4; see also Gibb, pp. 157–8; Philip Baker, 'Londons Liberty in Chains Discovered: The Levellers, the Civic Past, and Popular Protest in Civil War London', *HLQ*, 76 (2013), pp. 559–87.

9. John Lilburne, *Londons Liberty In Chains discovered* (London, Oct 1646), TD 2 November 1646; John Lilburne, *An Anatomy of the Lords Tyranny* ([London, November 1646]), pp. 19–20; John Lilburne, THE CHARTERS OF LONDON (London, 18 December 1646), p. 4. Lilburne claimed authorship of both in John Lilburne, THE *Oppressed Mans Oppressions declared* ([London, 1647]), p. 12.

10. Lilburne, *Charters of London*. The annotations are reminiscent of those to *The Kings Cabinet opened* (1645), which had republished the king's captured letters

with annotations attesting to the accuracy of the transcription: see Braddick, *God's Fury*, 380–3.

11. [John Lilburne], ENGLANDS BIRTH-RIGHT *Justified* ([London, 1645]), pp. 43–5. For the riot and its context see Michael J. Braddick, 'Popular Politics and Public Policy: The Excise Riot and Smithfield in February 1647 and its aftermath', *HJ*, 34 (1991), pp. 597–626, Braddick, *God's Fury*, pp. 481–5.

12. Quoted in *The Levellers in the English Revolution*, ed. G. E. Aylmer (London, 1975), pp. 22–3. A petition on behalf of Lilburne and Wildman had been laid aside by the Commons on 21 February 1647: Rushworth, VII, p. 1004.

13. *The Levellers*, ed. Aylmer, pp. 76–81, quotations at pp. 76–7, 78. See also *[T]o the right Honourable…The humble Petition of the Inhabitants of* Buckingham-shire *and* Hartfo[rd]shire ([London], 1647), 669. f.10[115], TD 1 March 1647. A postscript by Overton claims that it had 10,000 signatures and was presented by 500 people.

14. Austin Woolrych, *Soldiers and Statesmen: The General Council of the Army and its Debates 1647–1648* (Oxford, 2002), ch. 3.

15. Ibid.; Mark Kishlansky, 'Ideology and Politics in the Parliamentary Armies, 1645–9', in *Reactions to the English Civil War 1642–1649*, ed. John Morrill (Basingstoke, 1982), pp. 163–83, 241–2, Mark A. Kishlansky, 'The Army and the Levellers: The Roads to Putney', *HJ*, 22 (1979), pp. 795–824; John Morrill, 'The Army Revolt of 1647', reprinted in *The Nature of the English Revolution*, ed. John Morrill (Harlow, 1993), pp. 307–31; Michael A. Norris, 'Edward Sexby, John Reynolds and Edmund Chillenden: Agitators, "Sectarian Grandees" and the Relations of the New Model Army with London in the Spring of 1647', *Historical Research*, 76 (2003), pp. 30–52.

16. A central theme of Mark A. Kishlansky, *The Rise of the New Model Army* (Cambridge, 1979).

17. Woolrych, *Soldiers and Statesmen*.

18. Richard Baxter, *Reliquiae Baxterianae: OR, Mr* RICHARD BAXTER'S *NARRATIVE OF The Most Memorable Passages* OF HIS LIFE, ed. Matthew Sylvester (London, 1696), pp. 53–4. We should also note, however, that he distinguished between Lilburne and still wilder writers decrying all ministry and all authority except the express words of scripture. For Baxter it was this latter group that were the 'levellers'. More recent scholarship has accepted this distinction between Lilburne and his like and 'true Levellers', although drawing the distinctions differently: Christopher Hill, *The World Turned Upside Down: Radical Ideas During the English Revolution* (London, 1972).

19. 'The Tower of London Letter-Book of Sir Lewis Dyve, 1646–47', ed. H. G. Tibbutt, *Bedfordshire Historical Society*, vol. 38 (1958), pp. 49–96, at pp. 94–5, 95–6. Sexby was holding Lilburne's books in July 1647, see John Lilburne, THE IVGLERS DISCOVERED ([London, 1647]), pp. 1–2. For Lilburne's interest in the March petitions see John Lilburne, IONAHS *Cry out of the Whales belly* ([London, 1647]), pp. 3–4: Lilburne had been informed about events 'by an Officer out of the Army, and by another knowing man yesterday, that came a purpose to me out of the Army' (p. 3).

20. Gregg, p. 165; Lilburne, *IVGLERS DISCOVERED*, p. 3.

21. Lilburne, *IVGLERS DISCOVERED*, p. 3, letter to Fairfax, 22 July 1647.

22. Bod. Lib., Ashmole MS 420, f. 267 (29 April 1647).

23. Rees, p. 177; John Coffey, *John Goodwin and the Puritan Revolution: Religion and Intellectual Change in Seventeenth-Century England* (Woodbridge, 2006), pp. 130, 139–40. See more generally Murray Tolmie, *The Triumph of the Saints: The Separate Churches of London 1616–1649* (Cambridge, 1977), esp. ch. 7.

24. Anon., *A New Found STRATAGEM* (1647), TD 18 April 1647, quotations at pp. 7, 9, 10.

25. David R. Adams, 'The Secret Printing and Publishing Career of Richard Overton the Leveller, 1644–46', *The Library*, 7th Series, 11 (2010), pp. 3–88 at pp. 33–9, 70–1, 76–7. For Tew see this volume, pp. 10, 89.

26. John Lilburne, *Rash Oaths unwarrantable* ([London], May 1647), pp. 28–54; for tithes and the Solemn League and Covenant see p. 26.

27. Walwyn, *Gold Tried in the Fire; or, The Burnt Petitions Revived* (1647), reprinted in *The Writings of William Walwyn*, eds Jack R. McMichael and Barbara Taft (Athens, GA, 1989), pp. 275–93, quotation at p. 279.

28. [John Lilburne?], *Plaine Truth without FEARE OR FLATTERY* ([London?], 1647), quotation at sig. C3–C3v. A contemporary annotation attributes the pamphlet to Lilburne, but ESTC does not accept this.

29. Gregg, pp. 181–2; for Chillenden see this volume, pp. 19, 21–2, 63, 318 n. 74.

30. For discussion of the evidence about who did or did not authorize Joyce's action see Woolrych, *Soldiers and Statesmen*, pp. 105–10.

31. Reprinted in *Puritanism and Liberty*, 2nd edition, ed. A. S. P. Woodhouse (London, 1974), pp. 401–3, quotation at p. 402.

32. Gregg, p. 192.

33. *LJ*, IX, pp. 244, 340. See also Rushworth, VI, p. 629; *CSPVen*, XXVIII, p. 9; Christopher W. Brooks, 'Jenkins, David (1582–1663)', *ODNB*. Dyve thought it was principally Lilburne that they were concerned about: 'Letter book of Dyve', ed. Tibbutt, p. 69.

34. Wales and Hartley, pp. 491 and 495 n. 13.

35. Brailsford, *Levellers*, pp. 205–6; John White, *IOHN WHITES DEFENCE* (London, 1646), TD 15 September 1646; Rees, pp. 203, 215. For a cautionary note about the evidence for Lilburne's direct influence see Vernon and Baker, 'The First Agreement', p. 42–3.

36. *The Notebooks of Nehemiah Wallington, 1618–1654: A Selection*, ed. David Booy (Farnham, 2007), p. 228.

37. I owe this insight to Rachel Foxley.

38. Recounted in John Lilburne, *The resolved mans Resolution* ([London], 1647), TD 24 May 1647, esp. pp. 2–11.

39. Anon., *Regall Tyrannie discovered* (London, 1647), p. 11, 40–1. For the attribution see Lilburne, *Oppressed Man's Oppressions declared*, pp. 10, 12. In that pamphlet he says that his own last pamphlet was *An Anatomy*: p. 13. For Lilburne's disavowals of social-levelling see this volume, pp. 168–9, 210, 212–13, 237.

40. Lilburne, *Resolved mans Resolution*, title page.

41. Anon., *Regall Tyrannie*, p. 100.
42. Lilburne, *Resolved mans Resolution*; for Vane, see esp. pp. 13–18.
43. Anon., THE RECANTATION *Of Lieutenant Collonel John Lilburne* ([London], 1647), TD 13 May 1647.
44. Lilburne, *Resolved mans Resolution*, p. 20.
45. John Lilburne, A COPY OF A LETTER WRITTEN *to Collonell Henry Marten . . . Iuly 20. 1647* ([London, 1647]); John Lilburne, TWO LETTERS: THE ONE FROM LIEVTENANT COLONELL *Iohn Lilbourne* TO COLONEL HENRY MARTIN ([London, 1647]), TD 22 July 1647; Lilburne, *IONAHS Cry*. The rift was soon mended (Rees, pp. 168–9), and during the 1650s Lilburne clearly placed a lot of trust in Marten.
46. Lilburne, IVGLERS DISCOVERED, p. 5.
47. Lilburne, IONAHS *Cry*, p. 13.
48. For the consensual rhetoric see Kishlansky, 'Ideology and Politics'.
49. Rushworth, VII, p. 790; Gregg, p. 191.
50. 'Letter book of Dyve', ed. Tebbutt, pp. 85–7; John Lilburne, *The additionall Plea of Lievt. Col. Iohn Lilburne* ([London, 1647]), TD 9 November 1647, p. 24; Jason Peacey, 'The Hunting of the Leveller: The Sophistication of Parliamentarian Propaganda, 1647–53', *Historical Research*, 78 (2005), pp. 15–42, at p. 18.
51. *CJ*, V, pp. 294, 296, 297, 301; Rushworth, VII, 804, 805, 811. Gregg states that this was on Cromwell's motion, but it is not clear that the cited sources support that claim: Gregg, p. 195 and p. 382 n.31.
52. Bod. Lib., MS Clarendon 30, ff. 67v, 125r.
53. Brooks, 'Jenkins, David'.
54. D. Alan Orr, 'Law, Liberty, and the English Civil War: John Lilburne's Prison Experience, the Levellers and Freedom', in *The Experience of Revolution in Stuart Britain and Ireland*, ed. Michael J. Braddick and David L. Smith (Cambridge, 2011), pp. 154–71, at pp. 158–9.
55. John Gurney, 'Maynard, Sir John (1592–1658)', *ODNB*.
56. Anon., THE CASE OF THE ARMIE *Truly stated* (London, 1647), TD 19 October 1647
57. Kishlansky, 'Army and the Levellers'; Vernon and Baker, 'The First *Agreement*'.
58. David Wootton 'Leveller Democracy and the Puritan revolution', in *The Cambridge History of Political Thought 1450–1700*, ed. J. H. Burns with Mark Goldie (Cambridge, 1991), pp. 412–42, p. 412. Wootton adds a third key principle—that there should be no property qualification for the franchise, although quite what was proposed is not agreed among scholars.
59. Reprinted in *Divine Right and Democracy: An Anthology of Political Writing in Stuart England*, ed. David Wootton (London, 1986), pp. 283–5.
60. John Lilburne, L. COLONEL JOHN LIBVRNS APOLOGETISCH VERHAEL/L. COLONEL JOHN LILBVRNE HIS APOLOGETICAL NARRATION (Amsterdam, April 1652), p. 8.
61. *The Putney Debates of 1647: The Army, The Levellers and the English State* (Cambridge, 2001), ed. Michael Mendle, esp. John Morrill and Philip Baker, 'The Case of the Armie Truly Re-stated', pp. 103–24; Kishlansky, 'Army and the Levellers'; Mark A. Kishlansky, 'Politics and the Structure of Debate at Putney', *JBS*, 20 (1981), pp. 50–69. For the franchise debate see Philip Baker, 'The

Franchise Debate Revisited: The Levellers and the Army', in *Nature of the English Revolution Revisited*, eds Taylor and Tapsell, pp. 103–22, and the works cited there.

62. For the discussions of *Agreements*, see Elliot Vernon and Philip Baker, 'Introduction: The History and Historiography of the *Agreements of the People*', in *The Agreements of the People, the Levellers and the Constitutional Crisis of the English Revolution*, eds Philip Baker and Elliot Vernon (Basingstoke, 2012), pp. 3–6.

63. See this volume, pp. 168–9, 210, 212–13, 237; Bod. Lib., MS Clarendon 29, f. 10, MS Clarendon 30, f. 175r (my emphasis); Lilburne, APOLOGETICAL NARRATION, pp. 68–9; for the nickname see for example, John Lilburne, *A PREPARATIVE TO AN HUE AND CRY AFTER SIR ARTHUR HASLERIG* ([London, 1649]), TD 13 September 1649, pp. 10, 30. It has generally been accepted that its use as a noun dates from the time of the Putney Debates, which fits Lilburne's recollections too: Blair Worden, 'The Levellers in History and Memory, c. 1660–1960', in *The Putney Debates*, ed. Mendle, pp. 256–82 at pp. 262–3, 280–2.

64. The question is posed clearly by Wootton, 'Leveller Democracy', p. 413. For natural law see Rachel Foxley, 'Problems of Sovereignty in Leveller Writings', *History of Political Thought*, 28 (2007), pp. 642–60, and the literature cited there. For the franchise debate see Baker, 'The Franchise Debate Revisited', and the literature cited there.

65. David Richard Adams, 'Religion and Reason in the Thought of Richard Overton, the Leveller' (PhD dissertation, Cambridge University, 2002), pp. 238–40; Paul Halliday, *Habeas Corpus: From England to Empire* (Cambridge, Mass., 2010), p. 195; Edward Vallance, 'Oaths, Covenants, Associations and the Origins of the *Agreements of the People*: The Road to and from Putney', in *The Agreements of the People*, eds Baker and Vernon, pp. 28–49, at p. 43.

66. Orr, 'Law, Liberty, and the English Civil War'.

67. John Lilburne, *The Proposition of Liev. Col. John Lilburne* ([London, 1647]), 2 October 1647.

68. Rushworth, VII, pp. 844, 848, 858.

69. Gregg, p. 201; Rushworth, VII, p. 868; *LJ*, IX, p. 511; *CJ*, V, p. 353; John Lilburne, *The grand Plea of Lievt. Col. John Lilburne* ([London, 1647]).

70. Vernon and Baker, 'The First *Agreement*', p. 59.

71. Gregg, pp. 222–3; *Mercurius Anti-Pragmaticus*, 18–25 November 1647, p. 4, quoted in Gregg, pp. 384–5.

72. Mark Kishlansky reconstructed much of what actually happened, and argued that there was in fact no mutiny: 'What happened at Ware?', *HJ*, 25 (1982), pp. 827–39. This latter view has found little favour among other historians: Ian Gentles, *The New Model Army in England, Ireland and Scotland, 1645–1653* (Oxford, 1992), pp. 219–26; Woolrych, *Soldiers and Statesmen*, pp. 284–5.

73. Bod. Lib., MS Clarendon 30, ff. 175r, 180r, 193r.

74. Gregg, pp. 203–4; [Sir John Wildman], PUTNEY PROIECTS. Or the Old SERPENT In a new Forme (London, 1647), TD 30 December 1647, p. 2.

75. 14 December 1648, Gardiner, *CD*, pp. 335–47.

76. 26 December 1648, ibid., pp. 347–52, with additional articles at p. 353; quotation at p. 349.
77. His answer to the Four Bills is in ibid., pp. 353–6.
78. Ibid., p. 356.
79. *CJ*, V, pp. 387, 388; Rushworth, II, p. 958.
80. George Masterson, *The Triumph stain'd* (London, 1647), pp. 20–4. These events are discussed at length in Rees, pp. 223–31.
81. [John Lilburne], *A Whip for the present House of Lords* ([London, 1648]), TD 6 March 1647[8], p. 11.
82. *CJ*, V, pp. 436–7; Masterson, *Triumph stain'd*, pp. 9–14. Henry Marten may have been the rumoured would-be assassin: Vernon and Baker, 'The First *Agreement*', p. 48. For a (not very flattering) biography of Masterson see E. S. De Beer, 'The Reverend George Masterson', *Notes and Queries* (7 February 1948), pp. 57–9. The Nag's Head may have been another place associated with Independents and radicals: it was the site of a famous sermon by Samuel How in 1639, in favour of lay preaching: Tolmie, *Triumph of the Saints*, p. 39; and other meetings of such circles during the 1640s: this volume, pp. 91–2, 151, 173, 183, 256, 269.
83. Masterson, *Triumph stain'd*, p. 10; Lilburne, *A Whip*, p. 11. For the varying accounts of what had happened see John Wildman, *Truths triumph* (London, 1 February 1647[8]); Anon., *A DECLARATION Of some PROCEEDINGS of Lt. Col. Iohn Lilburn* (London, 1647[8]), TD 14 February 1648; John Harris, *A Lash for Lyar* (London, 1648).
84. Lilburne, *A Whip*, pp. 11–18 for his evasion about the assassination rumours, see p. 17. See also [John Lilburne], *AN IMPEACHMENT OF HIGH TREASON AGAINST Oliver Cromwell* (London, 1649), pp. 10–16.
85. *LJ*, IX, p. 666; *CJ*, V, pp. 436–7; Rushworth, VII, p. 969.
86. *CSPD*, 1648–9, pp. 14, 15; TNA, SP 21/9, f. 15; SP 21/24, f. 9.
87. *CJ*, V, pp. 437–8, quotations at pp. 437, 438. Lilburne recounted his appearance in detail in Lilburne, *A Whip*, pp. 9–18. See also *Mercurius Pragmaticus* (18–25 January 1648), sig. T4–4v.
88. *CJ*, V, pp. 437–8; *CSPD*, 1648–9, p. 5; Rushworth, VII, pp. 969–70; Bod. Lib. MS Clarendon 30, f. 269r. Wildman's testimony is reprinted in Wildman, *Truths triumph*. For Lilburne's lack of meekness, see Anon., *A DECLARATION Of some PROCEEDINGS*.
89. BL, Stowe 189, f. 39r.
90. See this volume, p. 141.
91. Bod. Lib., MS Clarendon 30, f. 279r.
92. This point is also made by Norah Carlin, 'Leveller Organisation in London', *HJ*, 27 (1984), pp. 955–60.
93. John Walter, 'Confessional Politics in Pre-Civil War Essex: Prayer Books, Profanations and Petitions', *HJ*, 44 (2001), pp. 677–701.
94. David Zaret, *Origins of Democratic Culture: Printing, Petitions, and the Public Sphere in Early-Modern England* (Princeton, 2000).
95. Jason Peacey, *Print and Public Politics in the English Revolution* (Cambridge, 2013).

96. Holorenshaw, *Levellers*, ch. 3; Jürgen Diethe, 'The Moderate: Politics and Allegiances of a Revolutionary Newspaper', *HPT*, 4 (1983), pp. 247–79.

97. Austin Woolrych, *Britain in Revolution 1625–1660* (Oxford, 2002), pp. 418–19; see this volume, pp. 160–1.

98. *CJ*, V, p. 536; Gregg, pp. 242, 244.

99. Halliday, *Habeas Corpus*, pp. 193–7.

100. Sir John Maynard, *A SPEECH Spoken in the Honourable House of COMMONS* (London, 11 August 1648); *To THE HONOURABLE the COMMONS of England assembled in PARLIAMENT* (London, 1648), TD 8 August 1648; Rushworth, VII, p. 1212; *CJ*, V, p. 657; *LJ*, X, p. 407. The speech was delivered on 27 July. Firth suggested that Lilburne had been released because he might have been willing to help impeach Cromwell: he wrote to Cromwell at this time saying that he would not strike him while he was low, *The Memoirs of Edmund Ludlow*, ed. C. H. Firth (Oxford, 1894), p. 200 n. 2. Wildman was released the following day since his offence had been the same as Lilburne's: Rushworth, VII, p. 1213.

101. Lilburne, *PREPARATIVE TO AN HUE AND CRY*, pp. 18–26. See also *CJ*, V, pp. 679, 689, 692; VI, pp. 6, 7, 8; *LJ*, X, pp. 637–8; *CSPD*, 1648–9, p. 341; Rushworth, VII, pp. 1249, 1252–3 (Rushworth notes an order to absent members to obey a Call to Members, suggesting that the house was, indeed, thin). The warrant for £300 had been issued in September: *CCC*, pt 1, p. 808; PA HL/PO/JO/10/1/272, f. 34.

102. Lilburne, *PREPARATIVE TO AN HUE AND CRY*, pp. 26–9, quotations at pp. 27, 29; Anon., *CERTAINE OBSERVATIONS ON THE TRYALL Of Leiut. Col, JOHN LILBURNE* ([London, 1649]), pp. 15–16; Gregg, pp. 248–9, 261–2; J. T. Peacey, 'Blakiston, John (bap. 1603, d. 1649)', *ODNB*. The stories of Bellingham, Bowes, and Gibb reveal how politically sensitive issues of delinquency were and, by extension, how Lilburne was right to be wary about the security of title. Bellingham had stayed in Parliament until 1643, and was named to the Westmorland and Durham committees in the spring and summer of that year, but had then gone to the Oxford Parliament and was disabled from sitting at Westminster. He had been sequestered, but no proceedings had been taken on the order by May 1647. He joined the royalist rising in 1648, claiming that he had no other way of protecting his estate, and in early 1649 he was protected from all further action until his fine was set by Parliament. He had died by September 1651: *A&O*, I, pp. 95, 117, 151, 236; *CJ*, IV, p. 305; *CCC*, II, pp. 1136–8; *CCAM*, II, p. 821; *CCAM*, III, p. 1380. Bowes had been named to the militia committee as late as May 1648: *LJ*, X, p. 278. Gibb (or Gibbs) too had only recently been identified as a delinquent, his lands sequestered in August 1648 amid a raft of such orders following the capture of the Duke of Hamilton. He had not been named to the militia commission in May of that year, however, although he had been in the commission in 1644. A number of claims were immediately placed on his lands, but he appealed, and so did his wife who petitioned to protect her share of the estate. When he died in April 1650 the sequestration was discharged and his widow secured control of the lands: *LJ*, X, pp. 278, 476; *CJ*, III, p. 593; *CJ*, V, pp. 689, 692; Rushworth, VII, pp. 1242; *CCC*, III, pp. 2239–40.

103. Lilburne, *PREPARATIVE TO AN HUE AND CRY*, p. 30.

104. S. R. Gardiner, *History of the Great Civil War*, 4 vols (London, 1893), vol. 3, p. 480.

105. For example, John Lilburne, *THE PICTURE OF THE Council of State* ([London?], 1649), TD 11 April 1649, p. 3.

106. Vernon and Baker, 'Introduction', pp. 4–6.

107. Woolrych, *Britain in Revolution*, pp. 421–2. The petition is reproduced in *The English Levellers*, ed. Andrew Sharp (Cambridge, 1998), pp. 131–9. See Rees, pp. 271–6.

108. Braddick, *God's Fury*, p. 556.

109. Quoted in Woolrych, *Britain in Revolution*, p. 423.

110. Quoted ibid., p. 426.

111. Gregg, pp. 252–3. For Rainsborough's death see Rees, pp. 259–71.

112. Worden, *The Rump Parliament 1648–1653* (Cambridge 1974). For the attendance figures cited here see p. 1.

113. Gregg, p. 250.

114. For Tichborne's career and previous connections with Walwyn (and Henry Marten) in the Salter's Hall Committee see Keith Lindley, 'Tichborne, Robert (1610/11–1682), *ODNB*.

115. Vernon and Baker, 'Introduction', pp. 4–5.

116. Quentin Skinner, 'Rethinking Political Liberty', *History Workshop Journal*, 61 (2006), pp. 156–70; Skinner, *Liberty Before Liberalism* (Cambridge, 1998).

117. Barbara Taft, 'The Council of Officers' *Agreement of the People, 1648/9'*, *HJ*, 28 (1985), pp. 169–85; Carolyn Polizzotto, 'What Really Happened at the Whitehall Debates? A New Source', *HJ*, 57 (2014), pp. 33–51; Polizzotto, 'Liberty of Conscience in the Whitehall Debates of 1648–9', *Journal of Ecclesiastical History*, 28:1 (1975), pp. 69–82; Wootton, 'Leveller Democracy', pp. 440–2.

118. Vernon and Baker, 'Introduction', pp. 6–7.

119. Ibid.

120. Lilburne, *PREPARATIVE TO AN HUE AND CRY*, pp. 31–4; John Lilburne, *The Legal Fundamental LIBERTIES Of the People of England*, 2nd edition (London, 1649), TD 4 August 1649, pp. 45–6; Gregg, pp. 258–60.

121. Quoted in Woolrych, *Britain in Revolution*, p. 431.

122. Frances Henderson, 'Drafting the Officers' *Agreement of the People, 1648–49: A Reappraisal'*, in *The Agreements of the People*, ed. Baker and Vernon, pp. 163–94.

123. Gardiner, *CD*, pp. 359–71.

124. See, for example, Rees, pp. 282–3.

125. Adams, 'Religion and Reason', pp. 259–60.

126. Ian Gentles, 'The Politics of Fairfax's Army, 1645–9', in *The English Civil War*, ed. John Adamson (Basingstoke, 2009), pp. 175–201, 288–94, esp. pp. 186–94; Gentles, 'The Agreements of the People and their Political Contexts, 1647–1649', in *The Putney Debates*, ed. Mendle, pp. 148–74, esp. 156–64; Barbara Taft, 'From Reading to Whitehall: Henry Ireton's Journey', in ibid., 175–93; Glenn Burgess, *British Political Thought 1500–1660: The Politics of the Post-Reformation* (Basingstoke, 2009), pp. 255–71; Polizzoto, 'What Really Happened at Whitehall'.

127. The regicide is currently the subject of academic controversy: for an overview and further reference see Philip Baker, 'The Regicide', in *The Oxford Handbook of the English Revolution*, ed. Michael J. Braddick (Oxford, 2015), pp. 154–69. .

128. *Levellers*, ed. Aylmer, p. 41; Gregg, p. 264. This language, of Machiavelli and the perpetual parliament, owes something to the lay republicanism of wider Leveller circles: Samuel Dennis Glover, 'The Putney Debates: Popular versus Elitist Republicanism', *P&P*, 164 (1999), pp. 47–80.

CHAPTER 5

1. Austin Woolrych, *Britain in Revolution 1625–1660* (Oxford, 2002), pp. 434–8, 453–6; Blair Worden, *The Rump Parliament 1648–53* (Cambridge, 1974), esp. pt 1.

2. J. C. Davis and J. D. Alsop, 'Winstanley, Gerrard (*bap.* 1609, *d.* 1676)', *ODNB*; Ariel Hessayon, 'Totney, Thomas [later Theaurau John Tany] (*bap.* 1608, *d.* 1659)', *ODNB*; Leo F. Solt, 'Winstanley, Lilburne and the Case of John Fielder', *HLQ*, 45:2 (1982), pp. 119–36.

3. Richard L. Greaves, 'Wildman, Sir John (1622/3–1693)', *ODNB*; Derek Hirst, 'A Happier Man: The Refashioning of Wiliam Walwyn', *The Seventeenth Century*, 27 (2012), pp. 54–78.

4. Clarendon, IV, p. 499; *CJ*, VI, pp. 131, 136.

5. Clarendon, IV, p. 500.

6. Ibid., p. 500.

7. Gardiner, *Commonwealth*, I, p. 10.

8. Clarendon, IV, p. 503.

9. Ibid., p. 507. The votes in most cases, including Owen's, were actually quite close, *CJ*, VI, pp. 159–60.

10. Clarendon, IV, p. 511.

11. John Lilburne, *The Legal Fundamental LIBERTIES Of the People of England*, 2nd edition (London, 1649), TD 4 August 1649, pp. 46, 54[68]–70 [irregular pagination].

12. *The English Levellers*, ed. Andrew Sharp (Cambridge, 1998), pp. 140–57. Although usually attributed to Lilburne, this was probably the work of several hands. Lilburne later said that '*being chosen by my . . . friends*' he had presented it at the bar of the Parliament '*a large representation of their sad apprehensions, whereunto an abundance of their names were annexed*'. This '*we called in print* Englands new chaines discovered': John Lilburne, L COLONEL JOHN LILBURNS APOLOGETISCH VERHAEL/L. COLONEL JOHN LILBURNE HIS APOLOGETICAL NARRATION (Amsterdam, 1652), p. 9, emphasis added. The supporters of the 11 September 1648 petition had petitioned the new regime on 11 January calling it to its representative obligation: TO THE RIGHT HONOURABLE, THE SUPREME AUTHORITY OF THIS NATION, THE COMMONS OF ENGLAND ([London, 1649]), BL, 669.f.13[73]. Foxley suggests that in these months the Levellers had in general been waiting to see what happened: Foxley, pp. 161–4.

13. These four phases are set out in John Lilburne, *The Innocent Man's second Proffer* ([London, 1649]), which includes a bibliography of forty-five publications to that date, under each of these four headings: see appendix. His breach with the

regime was really over the Council of State and parliamentary sovereignty, and not the franchise. On this point see also Richard Tuck, *Philosophy and Government 1572–1651* (Cambridge, 1993), p. 251.

14. Quoted from *English Levellers*, ed. Sharp, p. 149—spelling and punctuation modernized there.

15. John Lilburne, AN IMPEACHMENT OF HIGH TREASON AGAINST *Oliver Cromwell and his Son in Law Henry Ireton* (London, 1649), p. 9.

16. Quoted from *English Levellers*, ed. Sharp, p. 152—spelling and punctuation modernized there.

17. John Lilburne, *A* IUST REPROOF TO *Haberdashers-Hall*, ([London, 1651]), pp. 4–6. For the wider conflicts between Vane, Hesilrige, and others with the Lilburne family see this volume, pp. 215–19.

18. Christopher Durston, 'Hesilrige [Haselrig], Sir Arthur, Second Baronet (1601–1661)', *ODNB*.

19. Gardiner, *Commonwealth*, I, pp. 31–1, quotation at p. 31.

20. Ibid., I, pp. 31–2.

21. Robert Ward, Thomas Watson, Simon Graunt, George Jellis, and William Sawyer, *The Hunting of the Foxes* ([London], 1649), TD 21 March 1649, quotation at p. 4; Gardiner, *Commonwealth*, I, pp. 32–3.

22. Ward et al., *Hunting of the Foxes*, quotations pp. 6, 9, 12.

23. Ibid., p. 14.

24. Lilburne, APOLOGETICAL NARRATION, p. 9.

25. John Lilburne, *The second Part of* ENGLANDS NEW-CHAINS DISCOVERED ([London, 1649]), quotations at pp. 3–4.

26. See, for example, Anon., *A* DECLARATION *Of the proceedings of the Prince of VVales* (London, 30 March 1649).

27. Lilburne, *Legal Fundamental* LIBERTIES, p. 75.

28. *CSPD*, 1649–50, pp. 59–60. See also *CJ*, VI, pp. 174–5, published as *A* DECLAR-ATION OF THE COMMONS *Assembled in* PARLIAMENT *Against a Scandalous Book entituled The Second Part of Englands new Chains discovered* (London, 1649) BL, 669.f.14[13]. Walwyn's arrest had been associated with scandal. His landlord, Mr Devenish, was at that time sleeping with his lodger since his wife was nursing a baby. When soldiers found Walwyn half dressed in a bed that had been occupied by two people they accused him of sleeping with Mrs Devenish, causing offence to Walwyn, his landlord, and landlady. Details of the arrests of Lilburne, Walwyn, and Prince in John Lilburne, THE PICTURE OF THE *Council of State* ([London], 1649), TD 11 April 1649, pp. 1–3, 25–8, 49–51.

29. *CSPD*, 1649–50, pp. 57–8.

30. Lilburne, THE PICTURE OF THE *Council of State*, quotations at pp. 4, 6, 16, 17.

31. Ibid., quotations at pp. 15, 17; *CJ*, VI, pp. 174–5; *CSPD*, 1649–50, pp. 57–8, 59–60.

32. Gardiner, *Commonwealth*, I, pp. 42, 44; Margaret George, *Women in the First Capitalist Society: Experiences in Seventeenth-Century England* (Urbana, 1988), pp. 64–6; TO THE *Supream authority of this Nation ...The humble* PETITION *Of divers wel-affected* WOMEN (London, 1649), TD 24 April 1649, for the organization, p. 8.

33. John Lilburne, William Walwyn, Thomas Prince, and Richard Overton, *A Manifestation* ([London], 1649), TD 16 April 1649, p. 5. The suggestion about the Diggers is made by Gibbs, p. 264.

34. *A DECLARATION OF THE PARLIAMENT OF ENGLAND Expressing the Grounds of their late PROCEEDINGS And of setling the present GOVERNMENT In the way of A Free State* (London, 12 March 1649); [John Canne], *The Discoverer. WHEREIN IS SET FORTH . . . the reall plots and stratagems of [Lilburne, Walwyn, Prince and Overton]* (London, 1649) and *The Discoverer. Being and Answer to a Book entituled ENGLANDS NEW CHAIN* [*sic*] (London, 1649). See, in general, Jason Peacey, 'The Hunting of the Leveller: The Sophistication of Parliamentarian Propaganda, 1647–53', *Historical Research*, 78 (2005), pp. 15–42, at pp. 23–9; and, for Milton, Martin Dzelzainis, 'History and Ideology: Milton, the Levellers and the Council of State in 1649', *HLQ*, 68:1/2 (2005), pp. 269–87. For Canne and Simmons see this volume, pp. 10, 33, 233, 308 n. 45.

35. John Lilburne, et al., *A Manifestation*, p. 5. See also Lilburne, *APOLOGETICAL NARRATION*, pp. 68–71.

36. Clement Walker, *THE COMPLEAT HISTORY OF Independencie* (London, 1661), p. 197.

37. Lilburne, *Legal Fundamental LIBERTIES*, p. 75. He blames the calumny on 'The Discoverer'. In fact, on the day of the publication of *A Manifestation* the Council of State ordered Fairfax to St George's Hill to break up the Digger colony.

38. Ian Gentles, *The New Model Army in England, Ireland and Scotland, 1645–53* (Oxford, 1992), pp. 326–9.

39. Anon., *The Army's Martyr* (London, 1649), TD 30 April 1649.

40. John Lilburne and Richard Overton, *The Copie of a Letter, Written to the General* ([London], 27 April 1649).

41. Gardiner, *Commonwealth*, I, pp. 46–7.

42. John Lilburne, William Walwyn, Thomas Prince, and Richard Overton, *AN AGREE-MENT OF THE Free People of England* ([London], 1649), quotations at pp. 1, 2, 7.

43. William Thompson, *ENGLANDS Standard Advanced* ([London], 1649), TD 12 May 1649, sig. A1v.

44. *A&O*, II, pp. 120–1; *CJ*, VI, p. 209.

45. Elliot Vernon and Philip Baker, 'Introduction: The History and Historiography of the *Agreements of the People*', in *The Agreements of the People, the Levellers and the Constitutional Crisis of the English Revolution*, eds Philip Baker and Elliot Vernon (Basingstoke, 2012), p. 9, see also pp. 262–6; and William Beik, *Urban Protest in Seventeenth-Century France: The Culture of Retribution* (Cambridge, 1997), p. 247.

46. *THE Thankfull Acknowledgement and Congratulation OF Divers well-affected Apprentices* ([London, 1649]), 669.f.14[30]; *THE RESOLVED APPRENTICES OR A reply to the well-affected Apprentices* ([London, 1649]), 669.f.14[32]; *CJ*, VI, pp. 200, 210.

47. Lilburne, *Legal Fundamental LIBERTIES*, p. 75 [Here and elsewhere I have cited from the second edition, published in August]; for the offer of a 'place' see also p. 47.

48. John Lilburne, *To all the Affectors and Approvers in England, of the* London *Petition of the eleventh of* September *1648* ([London, 1649]), quotations at pp. 5, 7, 8.

49. *CJ*, VI, p. 264; *Kingdoms Weekly Intelligencer* (17–24 July 1649), 18 July; Lilburne, AN IMPEACHMENT OF HIGH TREASON, 'The Author *to the Courteous Reader*'.

50. Lilburne, AN IMPEACHMENT OF HIGH TREASON, title page.

51. For the second act: *A&O*, II, pp. 193–4; *CJ*, VI, p. 262.

52. Lilburne, AN IMPEACHMENT OF HIGH TREASON, quotation at p. 30, for Cromwell and Ireton's apostacy see pp. 29–34.

53. See David Underdown, *Royalist Conspiracy in England 1649–1660* (New Haven, 1960), pp. 24–5.

54. Bod. Lib., MS Clarendon 37, f. 22v: the rumour was obviously circulating and a matter of discussion in royalist circles.

55. Lilburne, AN IMPEACHMENT OF HIGH TREASON, p. 8. The plot is laid out in detail in John Lilburne, *A* PREPARATIVE TO AN HUE AND CRY AFTER SIR ARTHUR HASLERIG ([London, 1649]), pp. 8–14.

56. Lilburne, AN IMPEACHMENT OF HIGH TREASON, p. 8. The same passage appears in Lilburne, *To all the Affectors and Approvers*, p. 8.

57. Quoted in Andrew Sharp, 'The Levellers and the End of Charles I', in *The Regicides and the Execution of Charles I*, ed. Jason Peacey (Basingstoke, 2001), pp. 181–201.

58. Bod. Lib., MS Clarendon 37, f. 32r.

59. Lilburne, AN IMPEACHMENT OF HIGH TREASON, p. 34.

60. Anon., *VValwins vviles* (London, 23 April 1649); Rees, pp. 289–90; Murray Tolmie, *The Triumph of the Saints: The Separate Churches of London 1616–1649* (Cambridge, 1977), esp. ch. 8. For Goodwin's attitudes see John Coffey, *John Goodwin and the Puritan Revolution: Religion and Intellectual Change in Seventeenth-Century England* (Woodbridge, 2006), pp. 147–54. Goodwin had supported Pride's Purge, and the new regime, seeing it as a guarantee of freedom of conscience. Three of his congregation had been members of the court that tried the royalist prisoners: ibid., ch. 6, esp. pp. 169–70, 185–7.

61. *CSPD, 1649–50*, pp. 540, 544.

62. Lilburne, AN IMPEACHMENT OF HIGH TREASON, p. 7.

63. *CCC*, pt I, p. 811.

64. Lilburne, *The Legal Fundamental* LIBERTIES, p. 75.

65. Lilburne, THE PICTURE OF THE Council *of State*, p. 20; John Lilburne, *A* DISCOURSE *Betwixt* LIEUTENANT COLONEL IOHN LILBURN . . . *AND* Mr HUGH PETER (London, 1649), TD 29 May 1649.

66. Ibid., p. 8.

67. *A&O*, II, pp. 193–4; *CJ*, VI, p. 262.

68. [Charles Collins et al], AN OUTCRY *Of the* Youngmen *and* Apprentices *of* London ([London, 1649]), quotations at pp. 9, 11.

69. [John Wood et al], THE LEVELLERS *(Falsly so called)* VINDICATED ([London, 1649]), p. 9.

70. *CSPD, 1649–50*, pp. 340–1; p. 549.

71. *A&O*, II, pp. 245–54; *CJ*, VI, p. 298.

72. Gregg, p. 293.
73. John Lilburne, *Strength out of Weaknesse* (London, 1649), quotation at p. 1; Lilburne, *A PREPARATIVE TO AN HUE AND CRY*, quotation at p. 8.
74. Lilburne, *Strength out of Weaknesse*, quotation at p. 14.
75. Ibid., pp. 2, 13.
76. *CSPD, 1649–50*, p. 314.
77. Ibid., pp. 291, 522.
78. Ibid., pp. 334, 335, 340–1, 549.
79. *A DECLARATION OF THE Parliament of England, In Vindication of their PROCEEDINGS and Discovering the Dangerous Practices of several INTERESTS* (London, 1649), printed by order of Commons 27 September, TD 3 October 1649.
80. John Lilburne, *The Innocent Man's first Proffer* ([London, 1649]), reprinted in Theodorus Verax, *THE TRIALL, Of Lieut. Collonell JOHN LILBURNE* (Southwark, [1649]), pp. 155–8. Heveningham was a regicide and sat on the Council of State, but he was sceptical about the Engagement and sympathetic to army demands. It seems that he wanted to defend Parliament, and therefore to mollify the army was one means to do that. In that sense he was perhaps a plausible ally for Lilburne: Daniel Webster Hollis, III, 'Heveningham, William (1604–1678)', *ODNB*; Worden, *Rump Parliament*, p. 45.
81. Verax, *THE TRIALL*, pp. 14, 158; *A DECLARATION OF THE Parliament of England, In Vindication of their PROCEEDINGS . . . 27 Sept 1649*, pp. 21–32; H. N. Brailsford, *The Levellers and the English Revolution*, 2nd edition (Nottingham, 1976), p. 577, citing *Perfect Weekly Account* (26 September–3 October 1649), see pp. 617, 623. For Thomas May's role see also *Mercurius Pragmaticus* (23–30 October 1649), sig. Dd2. Lilburne also claimed that Henry Walker had calumniated him at this time: Lilburne, *A PREPARATIVE TO AN HUE AND CRY*, p. 38.
82. Verax, *THE TRIALL*, p. 14.
83. *CJ*, VI, p. 306.
84. Cuthbert Sydenham, *AN ANATOMY OF Lievt Colonel John Lilburn's SPIRIT and PAMPHLETS* (London, 1649), TD 16 October 1649, title page, pp. 1, 4. It was printed by John Maycock, who had published pamphlets by Prynne, Bastwick, and Vicars attacking Lilburne (among others) in 1646. There is a preface addressed to Parliament, signed T.M. I am grateful to Gary Rivett for discussion of May's involvement in this campaign. For Sydenham, Hesilrige, and Lilburne: Anon., *CERTAINE OBSERVATIONS ON THE TRYALL Of Leiut. Col, JOHN LILBURNE* ([London, 1649]), p. 16. The bulk of Sydenham's entry in Wood's *Athenæ Oxonienses* is actually concerned with Lilburne: Anthony Wood, *Athenæ Oxonienses*, 2 vols (London, 1721), II, pp. 173–4.
85. Peacey, 'Hunting the Leveller', pp. 29–32.
86. Verax, *THE TRIALL*, pp. 159–61; Lilburne, *Innocent Mans second Proffer*, also appeared separately. This is presumably what the council heard when Robert was called in 'to hear what he has to propound' on 22 October: *CSPD, 1649–50*, p. 356.
87. Verax, *THE TRIALL*, pp. 161–[67].

88. *CSPD, 1649–50*, pp. 356, 357.

89. *Mercurius Pragmaticus* (23–30 October 1649), sig. Ddv–Dd2.

90. John Lilburne, *A Salva Libertate* ([London, 1649]).

91. Lilburne, *Strength out of Weaknesse*, p. 25.

92. Verax, THE TRIALL, p. 146.

93. Ibid., pp. [167–8].

94. *CSPD, 1649–50*, pp. 357, 361.

95. Lilburne had been in correspondence with Rigby in August, referring to him then as colonel. He had been made a baron of the exchequer by the Rump, and Prideaux had caught Lilburne out referring to him by that title, although Lilburne claimed that the Rump had no power to make such elevations: Lilburne, *Strength out of Weaknesse*, pp. 22–3. Rigby was a major landowner in Lancashire, and MP for Wigan. He had been very active in the war in Lancashire, seeking vigorous action, and an assiduous member of many committees. He went along with the purge of Parliament in December 1648 but did not take his seat at the king's trial. He had been elevated to the Bench in June 1649: Lilburne wrote to him as 'Colonel' two months later: Malcolm Gratton, 'Rigby, Alexander (*bap.* 1594, *d.* 1650)', *ODNB*.

96. Anon., *The First Dayes Proceedings, at the Tryal of Lieut. Col. John Lilburne* ([London, 1649]), p. 2.

97. It is reprinted in Anon., *The First Dayes Proceedings*, with hostile marginal comment, pp. 3–9. See also Anon., THE SECOND PART *Of the Triall of Lieut. Col. John Lilburn* (London, 1649/50) for a full discussion of Lilburne's view of the issues.

98. For the legal record of the commission and indictment see TNA, KB33/1/1/ii.

99. Verax, THE TRIALL, pp. 2–6, quotation at p. 6.

100. J. H. Baker, *An Introduction to English Legal History*, 3rd edition (London, 1990), ch. 2, esp. pp. 20, 25, 29–30.

101. Verax, THE TRIALL, pp. 6–16.

102. Ibid., pp. 16–25, quotation at p. 17.

103. Ibid., pp. 56–66, quotations at pp. 65–6.

104. Ibid., pp. 26–47, quotation at p. 28.

105. Ibid., p. 49.

106. Anon., *The First Dayes Proceedings*, pp. 10–12. See also *Mercurius Pragmaticus* (23–30 October 1649), sig Dd3v; *Mercurius Elencticus* (22–9 October 1649), p. 208. The account in THE TRIALL does not contain these details, but does record that Lilburne asked to speak to the Grand Jury at the start of the second day's hearing, having heard that they had not found him guilty of treason and 'conceive themselves wronged by some words yesterday': Verax, THE TRIALL, p. 53.

107. Ibid., at pp. 60–1, 66.

108. Paul H. Hardacre, 'Eyre [Eyres, Ayres], William (fl. 1634–1675)', *ODNB*. The significance of Eyres to Lilburne's trial has not I think been generally acknowledged: it is not mentioned in Gibb, Gregg, Brailsford, *Levellers*, or Rees, nor in Hardacre, 'Eyre'.

109. Verax, *THE TRIALL*, quotation at p. 82.

110. Ibid., p. 120, Anon., *TRUTHS VICTORY Over TYRANTS AND TYRANNY* ([London], 1649), p. 6.

111. Verax, *THE TRIALL*, pp. 122–3.

112. Ibid., pp. 117–19.

113. Ibid., pp. 139, 141.

114. Ibid., p. 145.

115. Ibid., p. 151; John Lilburne, *L. Col JOHN LILBURNE revived* ([London], 1653), p. 4.

116. *The Man in the Moon* (24–31 October 1649), p. 222.

117. Lilburne, *APOLOGETICAL NARRATION*, pp. 11–12.

118. Verax, *THE TRIALL*, p. 153.

119. Anon., *TRUTHS VICTORY*, p. 7; *Mercurius Pragmaticus* (23–30 October 1649), sig [Dd4].

120. Ibid.

121. Gregg, pp. 301–2; *CSPD, 1649–50*, p. 552.

122. See this volume, ch. 8.

123. Verax, *THE TRIALL*, p. [168]; *Mercurius Elencticus* (22–9 October 1649), pp. [207]–8. See also Anon., *The First Dayes Proceedings*, and Anon., *THE SECOND PART Of the Triall*, which give more procedural detail with more extensive legal commentary. For the Engagement see this volume, pp. 182, 198–200.

124. Tai Liu, 'The Trial of John Lilburne: A Study of the Jurymen', *The National Chengchi University Journal of History*, 5 (1987), 203–21.

125. Verax, *THE TRIALL*, title page, p. 154. Lilburne vouched for its accuracy, and its fairness to him and the court, in a preface. Two subsequent publications seem to be these promised improvements: Anon., *THE SECOND PART Of the Triall*, which in some editions incorporates the Anon., *First Dayes Proceedings*, which was also published separately. Both contain hostile commentary on legal matters, and Anon., *THE SECOND PART Of the Triall* has a lengthy vindication of the power of juries.

126. Anon., *TRUTHS VICTORY*, p. 3. A John Hinde, also referred to as 'Captain Hinde' was a member of the Grand Jury, one of those most vocally put out by Jermyn's gloss on what they had found true in the indictment, referring to his own notes of what had been said the previous day: Anon., *First Dayes Proceedings*, pp. 3, 11. This is probably the man who was captain in the city militia, until purged in 1648. A Presbyterian and enthusiastic parliamentarian, one of the leading parishioners of St Christopher Le Stocks who appears as signatory to a number of Presbyterian petitions. One of his close colleagues, Vaughan, was involved in the Love plot (Tai Liu, *Puritan London: A Study of Religion and Society in the City Parishes* (Newark, NJ, 1986), pp. 80–1; Keith Lindley, *Popular Politics and Religion in Civil War London* (Aldershot, 1997), pp. 144 n. 186, 207 n. 42, 231 n. 163, 378 n. 123).

127. Verax, *THE TRIALL*, p. 65.

128. *CSPD, 1649–50*, pp. 376, 381; *Mercurius Pragmaticus* (23–30 October 1649), sig. [Dd4], [Dd4v].

129. *CSPD, 1649–50*, p. 558.

130. Anon., *A brief DISCOURSE Of the present power of Magistracy and Iustice* (London, 1649), TD 26 October 1649. The debate about Lilburne's legal arguments was

taken up the following year by Henry Parker among others: [Henry Parker], *A LETTER OF DUE CENSURE, AND REDARGVTION TO Lieut: Coll: JOHN LILBURNE* (London, 1650), TD 21 June 1650 (the attribution to Parker is Thomason's). It and others were answered by John Jones, *JURORS JUDGES OF LAW and FACT* (London, 1650), TD 2 August 1650.

131. See Clement Walker, *THE COMPLEAT HISTORY OF Independency* (London, 1661), pt 1 (which includes a long list of MPs enjoying public office and spoils despite the Self-Denying Ordinance), pt 3 was titled *THE High Court OF JUSTICE or CROMWELS New Slaughter House*; David Underdown, 'Walker, Clement [*pseud.* Theodorus Verax] (d. 1651)', *ODNB*. See also Underdown, *Somerset in the Civil War and Interregnum* (Newton Abbot, 1973). Publishing as Theodorus Verax, the second part cites *England's new Chains discovered*: *HISTORY OF Independency*, pt 2, p. 31.

132. For the legislation, see Joad Raymond, *The Invention of the Newspaper: English Newsbooks 1641–1649* (Oxford, 1996), pp. 69–79; for the silence of the official press see also Brailsford, *Levellers*, pp. 603–4.

133. *Mercurius Pragmaticus* (23–30 October 1649), sig. Dd–[Dd4v]; *Mercurius Elencticus* (22–9 October 1649), pp. [207]-8; *The Man in the Moon* (24–31 October 1649), pp. 219–20. For the more generally divided response of royalist press to the Levellers in 1649 see Amos Tubb, 'Mixed Messages: Royalist Newsbook Reports of Charles I's Execution and of the Leveller Uprising', *HLQ*, 67:1 (2004), pp. 59–74.

CHAPTER 6

1. *A&O*, II, 325–9, at p. 325. The Engagement itself is reproduced in Gardiner, *CD*, p. 391. For a succinct account of the issues at stake see Quentin Skinner, 'Conquest and Consent: Thomas Hobbes and the Engagement Controversy', in *The Interregnum: The Quest for Settlement*, ed. G. E. Aylmer (London, 1972), pp. 79–98.

2. *CSPD, 1649–50*, p. 552.

3. G. E. Aylmer and Jerrard Winstanley, 'England's Spirit Unfoulded, or an Incouragement to Take the Engagement', *P&P*, 40 (1968), pp. 3–15.

4. See this volume, pp. 174–5.

5. John Lilburne, *THE ENGAGEMENT Vindicated & Explained* (London, 1650), pp. 1–2.

6. Ibid., quotations at pp. 2–3, 4, 5, 6.

7. *CJ*, VI, pp. 337–8. I have not been able to find a printed or manuscript version of this petition: I am grateful to David Luck, of the London Metropolitan Archives, for his advice about this. There is some evidence of Chetwin's earlier opposition to the Presbyterian influence in the City: Reginald R. Sharpe, *London and the Kingdom*, 3 vols (London, 1895), pp. 276, 292–3, 319.

8. Lilburne, *THE ENGAGEMENT Vindicated*, p. 1.

9. Ibid., title page.

10. John Lilburne, *L COLONEL JOHN LILBURNS APOLOGETISCH VERHAEL/L. COLONEL JOHN LILBURNE HIS APOLOGETICAL NARRATION* (Amsterdam, 1652), pp. 13–14.

11. John Lilburne, *Strength* out of *VVeaknesse* (London, 1649), p. 21.

12. Gregg, p. 357.

13. Ibid., pp. 108, 116, 135.

14. Ann Hughes, *Gender and the English Revolution* (London, 2012), p. 58.

15. Gregg, pp. 283, 304. For his emotional response to the children's illness see John Lilburne, A PREPARATIVE TO AN HUE AND CRY AFTER SIR ARTHUR HASLERIG ([London, 1649]), pp. 38–9. Elizabeth gave birth to her ninth child in 1654, Benomy: Gregg, p. 334. John was only apparently survived by four children: Wales and Hartley, XVII, p. 491. See this volume, p. 272. For Elizabeth see also Ann Hughes, 'Lilburne [*nee* Dewell], Elizabeth, (*fl.* 1641–1660)', ODNB.

16. John Lilburne, L. COLONEL IOHN LILBVRNE *His letter to his dearely beloved wife* ([Amsterdam, 1652]), sig. A3.

17. TNA, SP 18/99 f. 235r.

18. John Lilburne, A IUST REPROOF to *Haberdashers-Hall* ([London, 1651]), TD August [1651], p. 40.

19. Anon., CERTAINE OBSERVATIONS UPON THE TRYALL *Of Leiut. Col.* JOHN LILBURNE ([London, 1649]), pp. 16, 18. It is not clear that this is an accurate account of the decisions in relation to Bellingham and Bowes: CCC, II, p. 1136; CCC, I, p. 203.

20. Lilburne, IUST REPROOF, p. 6.

21. Lilburne, APOLOGETICAL NARRATION, pp. 12–13; Gregg, p. 304.

22. CCC, I, p. 813; CJ, VI, pp. 430, 441, 444, 445, 447. For the printed version see: *An Act for satisfying Lieutenant-Colonel John Lilburne* (London, 1650), BL, 669.f.15[44]. For the Dean and Chapter lands see A&O, II, pp. 81–104; CJ, VI, p. 197–8. Although it should be said that, as with other legislation during 1649, this measure seems rushed, and some tidying up followed: A&O, II, pp. 152–4; CJ, VI, p. 238. The contractors needed advice on how to prioritize claims on Dean and Chapter lands in September—it is clear that this new resource was quickly committed: CJ, VI, pp. 461–2.

23. Kiffin also petitioned against the monopoly: CSPD, *1653–4*, pp. 99–100. For Lilburne's earlier attempt to set up in soap boiling see this volume, p. 172.

24. John Hayes et al., *To the supreme Authority the Parliament of the Common-wealth of* ENGLAND ([London, 1650]), TD 2 November 1650; see also THE SOAPMAKERS COMPLAINT (London, 1650), TD 23 October 1650. The petition is not recorded in the Commons Journals. The Commons had considered the new excise earlier, and this argument that the tax fell both on soap and the materials from which it was made: CJ, VI, p. 471.

25. Michael J. Braddick, *The Nerves of State: Taxation and the Financing of the English State, 1558–1714* (Manchester, 1996), pp. 36–8, 60–5, 99–100, 106–7.

26. John Lilburne, *To every individuall Member of the supreme authority of the Parliament of the Commonwealth of England* ([London, 1650]), TD 7 November 1650, BL, 669.f.15[64].

27. Anon., CERTAINE OBSERVATIONS, pp. 17–18.

28. Lilburne, L. COLONEL IOHN LILBURNE *His letter to his dearely beloved wife*, sig. A3.

29. Jason Peacey, 'The Hunting of the Leveller: The Sophistication of Parliamentarian Propaganda, 1647–53', *Historical Research*, 78 (2005), pp. 15–42, at p. 23; Lilburne,

Just defence, quoted in Leo F. Solt, 'Winstanley, Lilburne and the Case of John Fielder', *HLQ*, 45:2 (1982), pp. 119–36 at p. 124.

30. Jason Peacey, *Print and Public Politics in the English Revolution* (Cambridge, 2013), pp. 294–5; John Poyntz, *To the supreme Authority . . . the humble Petition of John Poyntz* (London [1650]), TD November 1650, BL, 669.f.15[66].

31. Joy Lloyd, 'The Communities of the Manor of Epworth in the Seventeenth Century', (PhD dissertation, University of Sheffield, 1998); John Lilburne, THE CASE OF THE TENANTS OF THE MANNOR OF EPWORTH (London, 1651), pp. 1–2. The broader history of the drainage, and the story of the disputes in Axholme, can be followed in Keith Lindley, *Fenland Riots and the English Revolution* (London, 1982); Clive Holmes, *Seventeenth-Century Lincolnshire* (Lincoln, 1980); and Holmes, 'Drainers and Fenmen: The Problem of Popular Political Consciousness in the Seventeenth Century', in *Order and Disorder in Early Modern England*, eds Anthony Fletcher and John Stevenson (Cambridge, 1985), pp. 166–95.

32. Lilburne, CASE OF THE TENANTS, p. 2. For the costs of the improvements in Epworth specifically see TNA, SP 18/37, f. 13.

33. Lloyd, 'Epworth', pp. 243–4.

34. Ibid., pp. 25–56; Lilburne, CASE OF THE TENANTS, pp. 2–3. Some were willing to say in testimony before the King's Bench that earlier agreements had been coerced: Lloyd, 'Epworth', p. 250.

35. Ibid., pp. 256–8. The whereabouts of the deeds was of interest in the 1670s, when it was asserted that Daniel Nodell had it: TNA, C22/687/42, interrogatory no. 7 and responses.

36. TNA, SP 18/37, ff. 14, 58–9, 75–9 and, for wages, ff. 59–61.

37. Lloyd, 'Epworth', pp. 23–5, 259; Lindley, *Fenland Riots*, pp. 140–2; Lilburne, CASE OF THE TENANTS, p. 4. For testimony about the orders to open the sluices see TNA, SP 18/37, ff. 72–4, 84–5.

38. PA HL/PO/JO/10/1/196.

39. *LJ*, VIII, p. 36; see also in PA HL/PO/JO/10/1/239.

40. PA HL/PO/JO/10/1/200 (6 February); 202 (21 March).

41. Lilburne, CASE OF THE TENANTS, p. 4.

42. Lindley, *Fenland Riots*, pp. 140–1. Nodell was socially mobile—his father was described as a yeoman. There is some indication of his estate in litigation relating to his inheritance: TNA, C10/105/121.

43. PA HL/PO/JO/10/1/239. See also TNA, KB/9/838/528, KB/9/839, 199–200, KB/29/297/27. For Nodell's defence, and counter-accusations about Gibbon, the representative of the proprietor, see TNA, SP 18/37, ff. 25–32.

44. Lloyd, 'Epworth', pp. 264–5.

45. PA HL/PO/JO/10/1/244.

46. Lloyd, 'Epworth', p. 265–6, TNA, KB/9/869/288; TNA, SP 18/37, ff. 51–57.

47. Lindley, *Fenland Riots*, pp. 140–1. Nodell served in Fairfax's army under Captain Robert Dyneley: TNA, SP 18/37, ff. 66–7. Dyneley was a relatively important and well-connected man, who testified on Nodell's behalf. He held a number of important civilian positions—commissioner for the Isle of Man, and a commissioner for the ejection of scandalous ministers and for the assessment in

Yorkshire: see John Callow, 'In So Shifting a Scene':Thomas Fairfax as Lord of the Isle of Man, 1651–60', in *England's Fortress: New Perspectives on Thomas, 3rd Lord Fairfax*, eds Andrew Hopper and Philip Major (Farnham, 2014), pp. 21–52, at pp. 29–30; *A&O*, II, p. 970, 1067; Hopper 'A Directory of Parliamentarian Allegiance in Yorkshire During the Civil Wars', *Yorkshire Archaeological Journal*, 73 (2001), pp. 85–122, at p. 116. He seems to have had clear puritan sympathies: *Stuart England*, ed. Blair Worden (Oxford, 1986), pp. 114–15. For Eastern Association troops in the Isle see, for example,TNA, SP 28/26, f. 606 (Colonel Russell's troop).

48. Lilburne, *CASE OF THE TENANTS*, p. 4; see also TNA, SP 18/37, f. 66.

49. Lloyd, 'Epworth', pp. 266–7; Lindley, *Fenland Riots*, p. 199; TNA, SP 18/37, ff. 62–3.

50. TNA, SP 18/37, ff. 46–48, 55–6, 61–2, quotations at ff. 55, 56.

51. Lilburne, *CASE OF THE TENANTS*, p. 4.

52. Lloyd, 'Epworth', ch. 6; Holmes, 'Drainers', pp. 180–1.

53. Lilburne, *CASE OF THE TENANTS*, p. 4; TNA, E 134/1&2 James II/H. 25, f. 30; E 134/2 James II/E. 31; Lloyd, 'Epworth', p. 269; Lindley, *Fenland Riots*, pp. 204–5.

54. TNA, SP 18/37, ff. 46–51; Lloyd, 'Epworth', p. 269; Lindley, *Fenland Riots*, p. 208.

55. TNA, SP 18/37, ff. 45, 46, 68, 84.

56. Ibid., ff. 66–74.

57. Ibid., f. 45; for the division into parishes ff. 48–51. Lloyd reaches a similar conclusion: 'Epworth', p. 271. One of the secondary causes of conflict in the dispute was the payment of church rates—the tenants paying to their own church as well as to the others in the manor: Lloyd, 'Epworth', pp. 259–60. For the importance of quiet possession see, for example,TNA, SP 18/37, ff. 22, 24, 59–61. For Richard Lilburne's dispute see this volume, pp. 29, 311 n. 78. One witness also said that Nodell had tried to restrain riot, thinking that disorder was to their political disadvantage:TNA, SP 18/27, ff. 63–3.

58. Lilburne, *CASE OF THE TENANTS*, p. 4.

59. John Fielder, *THE HUMBLE PETITION AND Appeal of John Fielder* (London, 1651), TD 14 October 51. See also Solt, 'Winstanley, Lilburne and Fielder'; John Gurney, *Brave Community: The Digger Movement in the English Revolution* (Manchester, 2007), esp. pp. 76–8.

60. Anon., *TWO PETITIONS Presented to the Supreame Authority OF THE NATION* (London, 1650), attributed to Lilburne by Thomason.

61. Quoted from Lindley, *Fenland Riots*, p. 211. For Crowle see TNA, SP 18/37, ff. 57–8; for Nodell quotation f. 66.

62. Ibid., ff. 46, 62–3, 65–6, 80; *CSPD, 1651*, 12 July 1651, p. 286.

63. Lindley, *Fenland Riots*, p. 180, 208.

64. TNA, SP 18/37, f. 46.

65. Lilburne, *CASE OF THE TENANTS*, p. 7. For the tuning of the Commoners' rhetoric (elsewhere) see Holmes, 'Drainers', p. 170.

66. TNA, SP 18/37, quotations ff. 82, 66. For the promise offered by changes of regime, see f. 63.

67. Nodell's hopes of a lucrative career seem to have been disappointed, and he later sued to recover charges and fees from the many commoners he had represented: TNA, C9/409/18, C10/104/59, C6/49/51.
68. TNA, C 5/399/176; Bod. Lib., MS Clarendon 19, f. 274v.
69. *CCC*, III, pp. 1918, 1920; History of Parliament Trust, London, unpublished article on George Lilburne for 1640–60, section by David Scott [hereafter, Scott, 'George Lilburne']. I am grateful to the History of Parliament Trust for allowing me to see this article in draft.
70. Lilburne, *PREPARATIVE TO AN HUE AND CRY*, pp. 17–18.
71. Ibid., p. 17.
72. Scott, 'George Lilburne'; for the accusations about Vane's conduct in 1642 see this volume, p. 57.
73. Scott, 'George Lilburne'; Lilburne, *IUST REPROOF*, pp. 2–4.
74. John Lilburne, *ENGLANDS BIRTH-RIGHT Justified* ([London, 1645]), pp. 20–1.
75. TNA, C2/ChasI/B71/30, C5/606/35, C5/403/176.
76. Lilburne, *IUST REPROOF*, pp. 2–5; Gregg, pp. 305–6.
77. Scott, 'George Lilburne'; he gave a certificate of his interests in Lumley and Lambton in August 1644—*CSPD, 1644*, p. 393; TNA, SP16/502, f. 145. For Blakiston and John see this volume, p. 148.
78. Edward Colston, *To the Supreame Authority of ENLAND* [*sic*] ... *THE VINDICATION OF EDWARD COLSTON* (London, 1649). This publication does not appear in Early English Books Online <http://eebo.chadwyck.com/home?instit1=centeuro& instit2=welcome> (paywall): I am grateful to Jason Peacey for showing me his copy. Musgrave: Peacey, *Print and Public Politics*, p. 390.
79. Lilburne, *IUST REPROOF*, pp. 3–4.
80. Ibid., pp. 2–5; Gregg, pp. 305–6.
81. *CSPD, 1644–45*, pp. 328–9.
82. Scott, 'George Lilburne'; *CCAM*, pp. 1762–3; *CCC*, III, pp. 1917–18, 1919, 1920, 2128. His conduct in relation to Ford had been raised by an enemy in 1640 too: Bod. Lib., MS Clarendon 19, f. 275r.
83. Lilburne, *IUST REPROOF*, pp. 7ff; Scott, 'George Lilburne'.
84. Lilburne, *PREPARATIVE TO AN HUE AND CRY*, p. 33.
85. Ibid., p. 37.
86. John Lilburne, *A LETTER OF Lieutenant Colonel John Lilburns, written to Mr John Price* ([London, 1651]), TD 8 April 1651, p. 3.
87. Longleat House, PO/VOL. II, Autograph Letters of celebrities, with other select papers, 35: Lilburne to Cromwell, 13 January 1651/2, ff. 89–90. For rumours in early 1651 about Lilburne, Wildman, Marten, and royalist conspiracy see Gibb, p. 301.
88. *CCAM*, III, pp. 1339, 1344.
89. *CCC*, III, p. 2128.
90. Ibid., p. 1921; *CJ*, VI, p. 598.
91. Lilburne, *IUST REPROOF*, quotations at pp. 37, 38, 39–40.
92. *CCC*, III, p. 2129.

93. The Council of State ordered that £100 be paid to Lieutenant Colonel Lilburne for being in the action and bringing the good news of Colonel Lilburne's victory over the earl of Derby's forces in Lancashire: *CSPD, 1651*, p. 389. Robert's letters to Cromwell and the Speaker of the House of Commons do not mention his brother, but the letter reporting the news to the Speaker notes that 'This bearer was all the while in the engagement, and is able to give you a fuller relation': *Memorials of the Great Civil War*, ed. Henry Cary, 2 vols, (London, 1842), quotation at p. 344.

94. John Lilburne, *A DEFENSIVE DECLARATION OF Lieut. Col. John Lilburne* (London, 1653]), TD 22 June 1653, p. 9.

95. Lilburne, *TO EVERY INDIVIDUALL MEMBER of the Supream Authority of the Parliament . . . 26 November 1651* (London, 1651), BL, E.647[7]; Huntington's petition is reprinted at pp. 7–8.

96. Ibid., pp. 2–6.

97. Ibid., quotations at pp. 7–8. The charges were repeated in Eden Gascoyne, *A True NARRATIVE Concerning Sir Arthur Haslerigs Possessing of Lieutenant-Colonel John Lilburnes Estate* (London, 1653).

98. John Lilburne, *AS YOU WERE* ([Amsterdam?], May 1652), p. 30.

99. See this volume, pp. 182–3.

100. Lilburne, *TO EVERY INDIVIDUALL MEMBER of the Supream Authority of the Parliament . . . 26 November 1651*, pp. 6, 8–9, 10.

101. Lilburne, *TO EVERY INDIVIDUALL MEMBER . . . 26 November 1651*, pp. 11–12; *CCC*, III, p. 2129.

102. *CJ*, VII, p. 55. The text is reproduced in a later entry: *CJ*, VII, pp. 71–2, 15 January 1652.

103. Ibid., p. 55, 23 December 1651.

104. Ibid., p. 64, 6 January 1651. Henry Marten counted the votes against.

105. Ibid., pp. 71–3, 15 January 1652.

106. Ibid.

107. Lilburne, *AS YOU WERE*, p. 2. Primatt was apparently free by this time.

108. *CJ*, VII, p. 73, 16 January 1652.

109. TNA, SP 18/37, ff. 13–85; Fielder, *THE HUMBLE PETITION AND Appeal*.

110. *CJ*, VII, pp. 74–5, 20 January 1652.

111. John Lilburne, *A REMONSTRANCE OF Lieut. Col John Lilburn* (London, 1652), TD 28 January 1652, quotation at p. 8. For the petition: *TO THE SUPREAME AUTHORITY The Parliament of the Common-wealth of England . . . highly concerned in the sentence against Lieutenant Col. JOHN LILBURN* (London, 1652), BL, 669.f.16[37].

112. *CJ*, VII, p. 79. It appears in Firth and Rait's table of Acts but with no text, dated 30 January, citing CJ: *A&O*, III, p. lxxxvii. Lilburne reproduced the text in one of his pamphlets, citing *Mercurius Politicus* as his source: Lilburne, *APOLOGETICAL NARRATION*, pp. 61–3. A later parchment copy survives, endorsed by Henry Scobell, parliamentary clerk, returned to a writ from the Attorney General in June 1653 in preparation for Lilburne's trial: TNA, C202/37/4.

113. Lilburne, *APOLOGETICAL NARRATION*, p. 19. At the end of the 1650s, when it was repealed an element of the parliamentary debate had been whether a formal Act of appeal might retrospectively legitimate a hurried, or perhaps illegal Act: Rutt: *Diaries of Thomas Burton, Esq*, vol. 3: *January–March 1659*, ed. J. T. Rutt (London, 1828), pp. 503–9.
114. Gregg, pp. 310–11.
115. See this volume, p. 222.
116. Lilburne, *L. COLONEL IOHN LILBURNE His letter to his dearely beloved wife*, sig. A3v.
117. Blair Worden, *The Rump Parliament 1648–53* (Cambridge, 1974), pp. 292–3; for Hesilrige and the Rump see also Christopher Durston, 'Hesilrige [Haselrig], Sir Arthur, Second Baronet (1601–1661)', *ODNB*.
118. Lilburne, *A DEFENSIVE DECLARATION*, pp. 2–3; Lilburne, *AS YOU WERE*, p. 1; Lilburne, *APOLOGETICAL NARRATION*, p. 59.

CHAPTER 7

1. John Lilburne, *L. COLONEL JOHN LILBURNS APOLOGETISCH VERHAEL/L. COLONEL JOHN LILBURNE HIS APOLOGETICAL NARRATION* (Amsterdam, 1652), p. 1.
2. John Lilburne, *L. COLONEL IOHN LILBVRNE His letter to his dearely beloved wife* ([Amsterdam, 1652]), sig. Ar.
3. John Lilburne, *A DECLARATION Of Lieutenant-Colonel JOHN LILBURNE* (London, 1652), TD 22 January 1652, pp. 5–6.
4. Overton: 'I am a free-man by Birth, so I am resolved to live and die, both in heart, word and deed, in substance and in shew': John Lilburne, *A REMONSTRANCE Of Lieut. Col. JOHN LILBURN* (London, 1652), TD 28 January 1652, pp. 7–8; *A REMONSTRANCE* is reproduced in part in Lilburne, *A DECLARATION*, pp. 6–8.
5. Lilburne, *A REMONSTRANCE*, p. 6.
6. Lilburne, *L. COLONEL IOHN LILBVRNE His letter to his dearely beloved wife*, sig. A1v, A3v. It later emerged in fact that none of those to whom Lilburne's fines were awarded had claimed their money—it was in general caution money—but it was a huge liability on a limited estate: the fine was still lying on Elizabeth's estate in 1657, TNA, SP18/157A. For the defence of Hesilrige see Eden Gascoyne, *A True NARRATIVE Concerning Sir Arthur Haslerigs possessing of Lieutenant-Colonel JOHN LILBURNES ESTATE* (London, 1653).
7. John Lilburne, *L. Colonel JOHN LILBURNE revived* ([Amsterdam?], 1653), esp. letter to a friend in Scotland, 8 January 1653, English-style quotations at pp. 1, 2, 3; Lilburne, *L. COLONEL IOHN LILBVRNE His letter to his dearely beloved wife*, sig A2v.
8. Lilburne, *APOLOGETICAL NARRATION*, quotations at pp. 2, 21.
9. Lilburne, *L. COLONEL IOHN LILBVRNE His letter to his dearely beloved wife*, sig. [A4r].
10. I am grateful to Harmen Snel for his advice on Elizabeth Bezar, based on the notarial records in the Amsterdam City Archives.
11. See this volume, pp. 10, 33, 233, 308 n. 45.
12. Lilburne, *APOLOGETICAL NARRATION*, pp. 21, 22.
13. Ibid., p. 21.

14. C. H. Firth, rev. Sean Kelsey, 'Scott [Scot], Thomas (d. 1660), Politician and Regicide', *ODNB*; Firth, 'Thomas Scot's Account of his Actions as Intelligencer During the Commonwealth', *EHR*, 12 (1897), pp. 116–26; see also BL, Stowe MS 189, ff. 72–3.

15. Firth, 'Thomas Scot's Account', p. 118.

16. Ibid., pp. 120–1. Riley was, according to Lilburne, a former Irish rebel who had served as quartermaster to Sir Charles Lucas at the siege of Colchester in the second civil war, and such a notorious turncoat and renegade that he had barely escaped hanging several times. There is certainly no sign that Lilburne was ever in doubt about him or threatened by him, although his claims had damaged Lilburne's reputation: John Lilburne, *A DEFENSIVE DECLARATION* ([London, 1653]), TD 22 June 1653, pp. 6–7.

17. Bedfordshire and Luton Archives Service, ABCP 35, 36, 37, 38 (although the interrogatories and depositions concentrate closely on what dues Oxford was liable for, and do not reveal any obviously principled objection to tithes or the religion practised in Potton); *LJ*, V, p. 222; Edward Peacock, *The Army Lists of the Roundheads and Cavaliers*, 2nd edition (London, 1874), p. 34; Peter Young, *Edgehill 1642: The Campaign and the Battle* (Kineton, 1967), p. 250; TNA, SP 21/24, f. 329. He was probably active in 1648 too, securing a horse from a defeated royalist: *CSPD, 1648–49*, p. 145.

18. TNA, SP 21/24, f. 329.

19. *CCAM*, II, pp. 832–3; *CCAM*, III, p. 1318; *CJ*, VI, pp. 591–2; *CJ*, VIII, pp. 75, 76. Lilburne suggested that his punishment had been part of his cover story: Lilburne, *A DEFENSIVE DECLARATION*, pp. 13–14.

20. Firth, 'Thomas Scot's Account', p. 121.

21. Lilburne, *A DECLARATION*, p. 4.

22. Lilburne, *APOLOGETICAL NARRATION*, p. 43.

23. Lilburne, *L. COLONEL IOHN LILBVRNE His letter to his dearely beloved wife*, sig. A2.

24. Bod. Lib., MS Clarendon 42, f. 383v.

25. Lilburne, *APOLOGETICAL NARRATION*; for Cromwell the banishment and the plot to become king see pp. 19–21; for the Levellers, pp. 68–71. For his comment to Elizabeth see Lilburne, *L. COLONEL IOHN LILBVRNE His letter to his dearely beloved wife*, sig A2v.

26. John Lilburne, *AS YOU WERE* ([Amsterdam?], May 1652), pp. 31, 32–3; Lilburne, *APOLOGETICAL NARRATION*, p. 71.

27. Lilburne, *AS YOU WERE*, pp. 32, 33. I am grateful to Helmer Helmers for a discussion of Vianen's independent status under the Lords of Brederode, which included the power to issue its own coinage. Its history as a place of refuge is discussed in Marijke Gijswijt-Hofstra, *Wijkplaatsen voor vervolgden: asielverlening in Culemborg, Vianen, Buren, Leerdam en IJsselstein van de 16de tot eind 18de eeuw* (Dieren, 1984).

28. Lilburne, *L. Colonel JOHN LILBURNE revived*, p. 12; Anon, *A LETTER Sent from the STATES OF HOLLAND TO THE KING OF SCOTS* (London, 1652), p. 5.

29. Lilburne, *AS YOU WERE*, pp. 1–2, 9–10. He noted the extent of Scot's networks in Lilburne, *APOLOGETICAL NARRATION*, p. 45. See also Lilburne, *L. Colonel JOHN LILBURNE revived*, pp. 10–11; Lilburne, *A DEFENSIVE DECLARATION*, pp. 5–7, 13–14.

30. BL, Stowe MS 189, f. 73r.

31. Jason Peacey, 'The Hunting of the Leveller: The Sophistication of Parliamentarian Propaganda, 1647–53', *Historical Research*, 78 (2005), pp. 15–42, at p. 34; *CSPD, 1651–2*, p. 204.

32. Austin Woolrych, 'Moyer, Samuel (*c.* 1609–1683)', *ODNB*; G. E. Aylmer, *The State's Servants: The Civil Service of the English Republic 1649–1660* (London, 1973), pp. 214–16.

33. *CSPD*, 1651–2, p. 287; Anon., *A DECLARATION OF THE PROCEEDINGS OF Major General Massy, Sir Marmaduke Langdale, and Lieut. Col. John Lilburn* (London, 1652), TD 22 December 1652, p. 5.

34. Anon., *BLOUDY NEWES FROM HOLLAND* (London, 1652), TD 17 March 1652.

35. Gregg, p. 315. Clarendon referred to him apparently sarcastically as Nicholas's friend on a number of occasions: Bod. Lib., MS Clarendon 29, f. 183r; MS Clarendon 46, f. 89v; and commiserated with Nicholas about his new neighbour (although preferable perhaps to the Earl of Roxborough) in Paris: MS Clarendon 43, f. 4v.

36. Firth, 'Thomas Scot's Account', p. 121. For the £100,000 figure see: Bod. Lib., MS Clarendon 46, f. 9v. For his intimacy with Buckingham in 1652 and the misgivings about that among other royalists see MS Clarendon 43, ff. 217r, 277v.

37. For Lilburne's account of this relationship see Lilburne, *A DEFENSIVE DECLARATION*, pp. 16–18. For contemporary hostile testimony about his relationship with the royalists see Isaac Berkenhead, *SEVERALL INFORMATIONS AND EXAMINATIONS Taken concerning Lieutenant Colonell Iohn Lilburn* (London, 1653), TD 13 July 1653.

38. Bod. Lib., MS Clarendon 43, ff. 4v, 139r.

39. Ibid., f. 217r.

40. Ibid., f. 277v.

41. Ibid., f. 303v.

42. Gregg, pp. 317–18; Berkenhead, *SEVERALL INFORMATIONS*; *The Nicholas Papers, vol II: Jan. 1653–June, 1655*, ed. George F. Warner, Camden Society, New Series, vol. 50 (1892), p. 13. For context see Geoffrey Smith, *The Cavaliers in Exile, 1640–1660* (Basingstoke, 2003).

43. Lilburne, *APOLOGETICAL NARRATION*, pp. 44–5. For his evident distaste for Scot's methods see Lilburne, *A DEFENSIVE DECLARATION*, p. 19.

44. Lilburne, *AS YOU WERE*, pp. 10–11.

45. It is set out particularly clearly in his letter to William Kiffin: Lilburne, *AS YOU WERE*, esp. pp. 11ff.

46. Firth, 'Thomas Scot's Account', p. 121. The standard accounts of royalist conspiracy and of the royalist exile community certainly give little or no space to Lilburne. For the general context, and the potential of a Leveller-Royalist

alliance, see David Underdown, *Royalist Conspiracy in England 1649–1660* (New Haven, 1960), esp. pp. 5–6, 24–5, 123–4, 159–60, 192–4, 197–8. Lilburne does not figure as an active player in this unlike, for example, Wildman or Sexby; suspicion also attached to Henry Marten, Thurloe, I, p. 711; Sarah Barber, *A Revolutionary Rogue: Henry Marten and the English Republic* (Sutton, 2000), esp. ch. 2. For the exile community see Geoffrey Smith, *Royalist Agents, Conspirators and Spies: Their Role in the British Civil Wars, 1640–1660* (Farnham, 2011); Smith, *Cavaliers in Exile*.

47. Gregg, p. 313.

48. BL, Add MS 71533, f. 8.

49. Lilburne, *L. Colonel JOHN LILBURNE revived*, Letter to D.D., quotation at p. 7, For the report of his death see p. 10; for the accusations made by Oxford see ibid., Letter to friend in Scotland, pp. 4–5. Oxford published two apparently royalist pamphlets in Holland: *A prospective for King and subjects* (Leyden, 1652) and *The unexpected life, and wished for death, of the thing cal'd Parliament in England* ([Delft], 1652). His answer to Lilburne was published in London, however: *Vincit qui patitur or Lieutenant Colonel John Lylborne decyphered* (London, 1653). The title page claims that Lilburne's pamphlet had been published in Bruges and Vianen.

50. Lilburne, *L. Colonel JOHN LILBURNE revived*, letter to Henry Marten, quotations at pp. 10, 11–12. This suggestion clearly echoes the policy of the recently passed navigation acts—to make London Europe's entrepôt by binding colonial trades to export through London, under English naval protection.

51. Barber, *Revolutionary Rogue*, for his relationship with Lilburne see esp. pp. 15, 24, 29, 56–60, 73–6; *Aubrey's Brief Lives*, ed. Oliver Lawson Dick (Harmondsworth, 1972), p. 354. See also Sarah Barber, 'Marten [Martin], Henry [Harry] (1601/2–1680)', *ODNB*.

52. For the influence of classical republicanism on Leveller thinking see Samuel Dennis Glover, 'The Putney Debates: Popular versus Elitist Republicanism', *P&P*, 164 (1999), 47–80. Glover's account emphasizes Wildman's importance in this respect. Lilburne seems also to have been arguing in close parallel to Clement Walker, HISTORY OF *Independency*, at this point. Walker's epigraphs include Polybius, Pliny, and Thucydides; see this volume, pp. 112–13, 136–7.

53. Lilburne, *L. Colonel JOHN LILBURNE revived*, letter to Henry Martin, p. 23.

54. Lilburne, *A DEFENSIVE DECLARATION*, p. 6. He found *The Prince* worth more 'than its weight in beaten Gold': John Lilburne, *The Upright Mans Vindication* ([London, 1653]), TD 5 August 1653, pp. 7–9, quotation at p. 7.

55. Barry Coward, *The Stuart Age: England 1603–1714*, 2nd edition (Harlow, 1994), pp. 252–3, 259–60; Blair Worden, *The English Civil Wars 1640–1660* (London, 2009), pp. 125–7.

56. Quoted in Coward, *Stuart Age*, p. 253.

57. *CSPD, 1652–3*, p. 436.

58. Lilburne, *A DEFENSIVE DECLARATION*, for Oxford see pp. 5–7.

59. Lilburne, *Upright Man's Vindication*, for Elizabeth's hopes see pp. 5–7.

60. John Lilburne, *The Banished mans suit for Protection* (London, 1653), TD 15 July 1653; John Lilburne, *A Second Address directed to his Excellency the Lord Generall Cromwell* (London, [1653]) (quotation); John Lilburne, *A Third Address directed to his Excellency the Lord Generall Cromwell* (London, 1653) (quotation). All three single-page addresses were published by Thomas Newcombe. See also Gregg, p. 321.

61. Bod. Lib., MS Clarendon 46, ff. 9r–9v, 89v; TNA, SP 18/37, ff. 13–85; *CJ*, VII, p. 73.

62. Lilburne, *A DEFENSIVE DECLARATION*, pp. 9–20, esp. pp. 13–14, 16–18, 19, 20.

63. Bod. Lib., MS Clarendon 45, ff. 442v, 499v; MS Clarendon 46, ff. 9v, 15v, 34r.

64. *CSPD, 1652–3*, p. 420.

65. Austin Woolrych, *Commonwealth to Protectorate* (Oxford, 1982), pp. 141–2; Blair Worden, *The Rump Parliament* (Cambridge, 1974), pp. 215–16.

66. Bod. Lib., MS Clarendon 46, ff. 9r–9v.

67. TNA, C 202/37/4.

68. *CSPD, 1652–3*, pp. 410, 415, 436.

69. Ibid., quotation at p. 420.

70. John Lilburne, *The PRISONER'S Most mournful Cry* ([London, 1653]), p. 3.

71. *CSPD, 1652–3*, p. 423.

72. John Lilburne, *Lieu. Col. Lilburn's Plea in Law*, 2nd edition ([London], 2 July 1653); John Lilburne, *The Second LETTER FROM JOHN LILBURN Esquire . . . to the Right Honourable JOHN FOWKE* (London, 1653), TD 21 July 1653. The letter is dated 10 July.

73. Woolrych, *Commonwealth*, p. 258. Woolrych suggests that a charge of treason based on his dealings with the royalists might have served Cromwell's purposes better, but given the ambiguities of that evidence, Lilburne's clear contravention of the Act of Banishment must have seemed a better bet.

74. *CSPD, 1652–3*, p. 436; Gascoyne, *A True NARRATIVE*; Thurloe, I, p. 320. Most observers before and during the trial thought he was doomed: see for example, Bod. Lib., MS Clarendon 46, ff. 82r, 113r, 208r.

75. Lilburne, *PRISONER'S Most mournful Cry*, p. 2.

76. Thurloe, I, p. 324. It is striking that, despite Lilburne's sense of his profile in Holland, the Dutch ambassadors do not seem to have assumed he would be known there, referring to him as 'One lieut. col. Lilburne'. Two petitions survive from 24 and 25 June (TD): a reissued version of the rejected petition *To the supreme Authority . . . The humble Petition of divers well-affected People inhabiting the Cities of London, Westminster, the Borough of Southwark* (London, 1650 [sic]), BL 669.f.17[24]; and *TO THE PARLIAMENT OF THE COMMON-VVEALTH OF ENGLAND. The humble Petition of diuerse afflicted WOMEN* (London, 1653), 669.f.17[26].

77. Quoted in Coward, *Stuart Age*, p. 259.

78. *CSPD, 1653–4*, p. 22; *CJ*, VII, p. 284.

79. Woolrych, *Commonwealth*, pp. 235, 250, 268–9; *CJ*, VII, pp. 285; *Diaries of Thomas Burton, Esq*, vol. 1: *July 1653–April 1657*, ed. J. T. Rutt (London, 1828), p. ii.

80. Gregg, pp. 326–7. For the trial as a public controversy and focus for hostility to Barebones see Woolrych, *Commonwealth*, pp. 250–61.

81. Berkenhead, SEVERALL INFORMATIONS; Anon., *A Conference with the Souldiers* ([London, 1653]), TD 18 July 1653, pp. 3–4.

82. Anon., THE TRIALL OF Mr JOHN LILBURN *Prisoner in Newgate* (London, 1653), TD 28 July 53. This is a distinct publication from Anon., THE TRYALL OF Mr *Iohn Lilburn at The Sessions House* (London, 1653), TD 25 August 1653. Thomason noted on this second publication 'difrent from the former'. The text of the Act is in fact difficult to find: see this volume, p. 348 n. 112.

83. Bod. Lib., MS Clarendon 46, f. 86r; see also f. 109v.

84. Ibid., f. 109v.

85. Ibid.; Anon., THE TRIALL, quotations at pp. 17, 24.

86. Bod. Lib., MS Clarendon 46, f. 82r.

87. Anon., THE TRIALL, pp. 20, 25. For his leaving the country as a free man, see Anon., THE TRYALL OF *L. Col. Iohn Lilburn* (London, 1653), TD 22 August 1653, p. 5. The pamphlets published during the trial refer to him as Mr John Lilburne, a departure from the usual practice of using his military rank, which the latter pamphlet, published after the verdict, resumed. A pamphlet usually attributed to Richard Overton had in fact placed some stress on the military rank, which was being denied to Lilburne in the House of Lords proceedings against him, in 1646: Richard Overton, AN ALARUM to the House of LORDS (London, 1646), pp. 3–4. For the rejection of this attribution see David Richard Adams, 'Religion and Reason in the Thought of Richard Overton, the Leveller' (PhD dissertation, Cambridge University, 2002), pp. 330–3.

88. Thurloe, I, pp. 367, 368, 369; Bod. Lib., MS Clarendon 46, f. 109v, see also ff. 82r, 112v–13r.

89. Thurloe, I, p. 385.

90. Ibid., p. 387; *CSPD, 1653–4*, p. 50.

91. *Unto every individual Member of Parliament* (London, 1653), TD 29 July 1653, BL, 669.f.17[36]; Bod. Lib., Clarendon MS 46, ff. 131v–132r. For the Chidleys see Ian Gentles, 'London Levellers in the English Revolution: The Chidleys and their Circle', *Journal of Ecclesiastical History*, 29:3 (1978), pp. 281–309; Gentles, 'Chidley, Katherine (fl. 1616–1653)', *ODNB*; Gentles, 'Chidley, Samuel (b. 1616, d. in or after 1672)', *ODNB*. Samuel also published a defence of Lilburne: Samuel Chidley, AN ADDITIONAL REMONSTRANCE to the Valiant and wel-deserving SOULDIER (London, 1653).

92. CJ, VII, p. 294; *Diary of Thomas Burton*, ed. Rutt, vol. 1, p. vi; *CSPD, 1653–4*, pp. 65, 66. For the content of the petition: Bod. Lib., MS Clarendon 46, f. 159v.

93. *CSPD, 1653–4*, pp. 65, 66.

94. Ibid., p. 88.

95. John Lilburne, *Malice detected* (London, 1653), TD 15 July 1653, quotation at p. 4; Lilburne, *Upright Mans Vindication*, p. 2. Anon., *Conference with the Souldiers*, addressed the soldiers directly, saying that their presence made Lilburne's case much harder to make, pp. 1–2.

96. Bod. Lib., MS Clarendon 46, f. 160r.

97. Anon., THE TRIALL, reported on the hearings on 13–16 July; John Lilburne, THE EXCEPTIONS of John Lilburne Gent. (London, 1653), TD 16 July 1653.

98. Lilburne, *Upright Mans Vindication*, p. 29. See, for example: Anon., *A Caveat to those that shall resolve, whether right or wrong, to destroy J.L.* ([1653]); Anon, *Oyes, Oyes, Oyes* ([1653]), TD 23 July 1653; Anon., *A PLEA at large For JOHN LILBURN* ([London], 6 August 1653); Ralph Willis et al., *A Voyce from the Heavenly Word of God* (London, 10 August 1653).

99. *CSPD, 1653–4*, p. 50; *CSPVen*, XXIX, p. 109.

100. Thurloe, I, p. 441.

101. Anon., THE TRYALL, pp. 5–6; Anon., *The humble and further Demand of* Iohn Lilburn, *Gent* ([London, 1653]); Bod. Lib., MS Clarendon 46, f. 207v; Anon., *A Word to the JURY in the behalfe of JOHN LILBURN* ([London, 1653]), TD 11 August 1653.

102. *CSPVen*, XXIX, p. 119.

103. Anon., THE TRYALL, p. 6.

104. Anon., MORE LIGHT TO *Mr John Lilburnes JURY* (London, 16 August 1653), quotation at p. 8.

105. Thurloe, I, p. 427.

106. Ibid., p. 429, see also p. 430.

107. Anon., THE TRYALL OF *L. Col. Iohn Lilburn*, p. 1.

108. Bod. Lib., Ashmole MS 385, f. 240.

109. Anon., THE TRYALL OF *L. Col. Iohn Lilburn*, p. 4, the speech is summarized, pp. 4–6; Bod. Lib., MS Clarendon 46, ff. 208r–208v; Thurloe, I, p. 435.

110. Anon., THE TRYALL OF *L. Col. Iohn Lilburn*, p. 6.

111. Ibid., p. 4.

112. Gregg, p. 332; Bod. Lib., MS Clarendon 46, f. 208v; Thurloe, I, p. 442; *CSPVen*, XXIX, p. 122.

113. Ibid.

114. Bod. Lib., MS Clarendon 46, f. 208v.

115. *CSPD, 1653–4*, p. 98; for the windmill meeting, Woolrych, *Commonwealth*, p. 257; Bod. Lib., MS Clarendon 46, f. 208v.

116. Woolrych, *Commonwealth*, pp. 294–5.

117. Thurloe, I, p. 435; see also *CSPVen*, XXIX, pp. 122, 125; Bod. Lib., MS Clarendon 46, ff. 208v, 239v.

118. *CSPD, 1653–4*, p. 100–1.

119. Ibid., pp. 102, 114, 117.

120. Ibid., p. 131. Lilburne's leadership of the attack on Sandtoft was raised again the following August, along with Wildman's involvement: *CSPD, 1654*, pp. 309–10. Petition of John Gibbon and the participants in the level of Hatfield Chace, cos. York, Lincoln, and Notts, to the Protector. The intention was clearly to try to prevent Wildman being accepted as an MP. See also *CSPVen*, XXIX, p. 122.

121. *CSPD, 1653–4*, pp. 105, 107; Thurloe, I, pp. 441, 442, 451, 453. See also *CSPVen*, XXIX, p. 125; *Diary of Thomas Burton*, ed. Rutt, vol. 1, p. x. The letter in Thurloe, II, p. 582 appears to misdated—it seems to belong to September 1653 not 1654.

122. John Lilburne, THE JUST DEFENCE OF JOHN LILBURN, *Against Such as charge him with Turbulency of Spirit* ([London, 1653]), TD 25 August 1653.

123. Thurloe, I, pp. 449, 475, 628; *CSPVen*, XXIX, p. 122; Underdown, *Royalist Conspiracy*, pp. 66–70.

124. Thurloe, I, p. 451; Bod. Lib., MS Clarendon 46, f. 230r.

125. John Lilburne, *An Hue- and Cry AFTER THE Fundamental Lawes and Liberties of ENGLAND* (Europe, [1653]), TD 26 September 1653. The standard attribution to Lilburne is questionable.

126. Anon., *LIEUT. COLONEL J. LILBURN TRYED AND CAST* (London, 1653): it claimed to be published '*by AUTHORITY*'.

127. *CSPD, 1653–4*, pp. 242–3, 254; *CJ*, VII, p. 358; The keeper of the gatehouse was given similar orders in relation to Streater who had also been suing habeas corpus in relation to his detention for seditious publishing: *CSPD, 1653–4*, p. 243. These were important legal questions, discussed in Anon., *Clavis ad aperiendum Carceris Ostia OR, The High Point of the WRIT of Habeas Corpus DISCUSSED* (London, 1654). The key issue is the relationship between powers of judicial review and commitment orders from Parliament or the Council of State: Paul Halliday, *Habeas Corpus: From England to Empire* (Cambridge, Mass., 2010), pp. 226–31.

128. *CSPD, 1653–4*, p. 262. For Barkstead's expenses in taking Lilburne to and from the Upper Bench see ibid., p. 311.

129. Ibid., p. 344, approved by the Lord Protector on 10 January.

130. Worden, *Civil War*, pp. 127–8; Worden, 'Oliver Cromwell and the Instrument of Government', in *The Nature of the English Revolution Revisited*, eds Stephen Taylor and Grant Tapsell (Woodbridge, 2013), pp. 123–50.

131. Gregg, p. 334.

132. *The Writings and Speeches of Oliver Cromwell*, ed. W. C. Abbott, 4 vols (Cambridge, Mass., 1937–1947), III, pp. 216–17. The belief was apparently mistaken: Halliday, *Habeas Corpus*, pp. 227–8; *CSPD, 1654*, pp. 16, 33–4, 44, 46, 50. He had arrived in Portsmouth by 2 April: ibid., p. 470. For the related expenses see ibid., pp. 446, 452, 456.

133. Bod. Lib., MS Clarendon 48, f. 186r.

134. Slingsby Bethel, *THE WORLD'S MISTAKE IN Oliver Cromwell* (London, 1668), p. 12. The injustice of this last imprisonment is also assumed in, for example, [John Gough, William Sewell and others], *The History of the People Called Quakers*, 2 vols (London, 1799), I, pp. 69–70. For the doubts about the legality of the 1651 Act among MPs later in the 1650s see this volume, p. 349 n. 113.

135. Lilburne, *JUST DEFENCE*, p. 11.

136. Gregg, pp. 336–7; Thurloe, III, p. 629; *CSPD, 1655*, pp. 126, 128; *CSPD, 1656–7*, pp. 21, 47, 62.

137. *CSPVen*, XXIX, p. 217; Anon., *The Last Will & Testament of Lieutenant Col. John Lilburn* ([London], 1654), TD 27 May 1654. Clarendon had heard and discounted the rumour: Bod. Lib., MS Clarendon 48, f. 251v.

138. *CSPD, 1654*, p. 195.

139. For the broader significance of this language of slavery see Quentin Skinner, 'Rethinking Political Liberty', *History Workshop Journal*, 61 (2006), pp. 156–70; Skinner, *Liberty Before Liberalism* (Cambridge, 1998).

140. Thurloe, III, pp. 512, 629.

141. TNA, SP 18/99, f. 235r.

142. Ibid., f. 236r. Richard was born on 4 July 1583: Wales and Hartley, p. 494 n.4.

143. *CSPD, 1655*, p. 556; for the Cinque Ports and habeas corpus see Halliday, *Habeas Corpus*, esp. pp. 85, 368 n.103, 433 n.4.

144. Gregg, pp. 339–40.

145. His conversion is discussed in Ariel Hessayon, 'The Resurrection of John Lilburne, Quaker', in *John Lilburne and the Levellers: Reappraising the Roots of English Radicalism 400 Years on*, ed. John Rees (Abingdon, 2018), pp. 95–116. We reach broadly similar conclusions. I am grateful to Ariel Hessayon for allowing me to see his chapter before publication.

146. Gregg, p. 343; *The First Publishers of Truth*, ed. Norman Penney (London, 1907), pp. 144–5.

147. See this volume, pp. 31–2, 88.

148. Glenn Burgess, 'Radicalism and the English Revolution', in *English Radicalism, 1550–1850*, ed. Glenn Burgess and Matthew Festenstein (Cambridge, 2007), 63–86, at pp. 74–5.

149. Lilburne, *L. Colonel JOHN LILBURNE revived*, postscript to letter to Scotland, pp. 9–10. Clement Walker, who published the fullest account of Lilburne's 1649 trial, made a similar argument, including the comparison between Cromwell and the Münster Anabaptists: Clement Walker, THE COMPLEAT HISTORY OF *Independency* (London, 1661), pt 1, p. 85; see John Lilburne, AN ANSWER TO NINE ARGUMENTS *Written by T.B.* (London, 1645) esp. pp. 31–5. Comparison had been made between Cromwell and John of Leyden as early as 1647: Henry Holorenshaw [Christopher Hill], *The Levellers and the English Revolution* (London, 1939), p. 55. Edwards had by contrast made the same charge against sectaries, including Lilburne and other Leveller leaders: see for example, *Gangraena*, pt 3, pp. 151, 262.

150. Gibb has a similar view of the consistency of his conversion to Quakerism with his earlier beliefs: ch. 14.

151. Clive Holmes, *Seventeenth-Century Lincolnshire* (Lincoln, 1980), p. 205; see this volume, p. 209.

152. *The Complete Works of Gerrard Winstanley*, ed. Thomas N. Corns, Ann Hughes, and David Loewenstein, 2 vols (Oxford, 2009), II, p. 448; see this volume, pp. 213–14.

153. Gregg, p. 339.

154. Kate Peters, *Print Culture and the Early Quakers* (Cambridge, 2009); for Calvert see esp. pp. 50–64.

155. John Lilburne, THE RESURRECTION OF JOHN LILBURNE (London, 1656), quotations at pp. 7, 18. The Huntington Library copy appears to be the first edition, containing only pages 1–14.

156. Lilburne, THE RESURRECTION, quotations at p. 1.

157. Ibid., quotations at p. 4.

158. Ibid., quotations at pp. 4, 5, 6, 7–8.

159. Ibid., quotations at p. 1.

160. Thomas Winterton, *The chasing the YOUNG QUAKING HARLOT Out of the CITY* (London, 1656), quotation at pp. 4, 9.

161. For the early Quakers see Adrian Davies, *The Quakers and English Society 1655–1725* (Oxford, 2000).

162. David Loewenstein, *Representing Revolution in Milton and his Contemporaries: Religion, Politics and Polemics in Radical Puritanism* (Cambridge, 2001), ch. 1, esp. 29–31.

163. Anon., THE *Selfe Afflictor* (London, 1657), p. 12.

164. *Diary of Thomas Burton*, ed. Rutt, vol. 1, pp. 156–7.

165. Lilburne, THE RESURRECTION, quotations at p. 10.

166. Ibid., quotation at pp. 13–14.

167. [Gough, Sewell], *History of the Quakers*, I, p. 70.

168. Richard Hubberthorn, THE HORN OF THE *He-goat broken* (London, 1656), p. 10.

169. *CSPD, 1653–4*, p. 120; Thurloe, III, p. 365.

170. Lilburne to Margaret Fell, 1657, reprinted in *Journal of the Friends' Historical Society*, 9:1 (1912), 53–9, quotation at p. 58.

171. Lilburne, THE RESURRECTION, quotation at p. 14.

172. [Sewell], *History of the Quakers*, I, p. 70. It should be noted, however, that this account is inaccurate in other respects, stating for example that Lilburne died in 1660. This narrative, of confinement and personal redemption, was a standard form in Quaker writing.

173. Library of the Society of Friends, London, Swarthmore Mss 355, item 14, Letter from Richard Hubberthone to George Fox, 1657.

174. TNA, SP 18/157A, f. 129a; the child was presumably Bethia: Wales and Hartley, p. 491. For his preaching see Anthony Wood, *Athenæ Oxonienses*, 2 vols (London, 1721), II, p. 173; Bethel, THE WORLD'S MISTAKE, p. 12.

175. Anon., *Selfe Afflictor*, quotation at p. 13; *Mercurius Politicus* (27 August–3 September 1657), pp. 1597–8; Rushworth, II, p. 468; Wood, *Athenæ Oxonienses*, II, p. 174.

CHAPTER 8

1. The quotation in the heading is from H. N. Brailsford, *The Levellers and the English Revolution*, 2nd edition (Nottingham, 1976), p. 578.

2. Paul D. Halliday, *Habeas Corpus: From England to Empire* (Cambridge, Mass., 2010), quotation at p. 193. For Lilburne and the right against self-incrimination under the Fifth Amendment and other constitutional rights see: Leonard W. Levy, *Origins of the Fifth Amendment: The Right Against Self-Incrimination* (Chicago, 1968), pp. 271–313; Harold W. Wolfram, 'John Lilburne: Democracy's Pillar of Fire', *Syracuse Law Review*, 3 (1952), 213–58. Others, however, have disputed Lilburne's significance: John H. Langbein, 'The Privilege and Common-Law Criminal Procedure: The Sixteenth to Eighteenth Centuries', in *The Privilege Against Self-Incrimination: Its Origin and Development*, ed. R. H. Helmholz et al. (Chicago, 1997), pp. 82–108. Lilburne has been cited several times by the US Supreme Court on the right to a public trial. See, e.g., Gannett Co., Inc. v. DePasquale, 443 U.S. 368, 387 n.18 (1979); Barenblatt v. United States, 360 U.S. 109, 160–2 (1959)

(Black, J., dissenting). For Justice Hugo Black's affinity for Lilburne, see Edward G. Hudon, 'John Lilburne, the Levellers, and Mr. Justice Black', *American Bar Association Journal*, 60 (1974), 686–8. For the continuing relevance of Leveller legal and constitutional ideas see Martin Loughlin, 'The Constitutional Thought of the Levellers', *Current Legal Problems*, 60 (2007), pp. 1–29; Diane Parkin-Speer, 'A Revolutionary Interprets Statutes and Common Law Due Process', *Law and History Review*, 1 (1983), pp. 276–96. I am very grateful to Paul Halliday and Kent Olson for their advice on this point.

3. Thomas A. Green, *Verdict According to Conscience: Perspectives on the English Criminal Trial Jury, 1200–1800* (Chicago, 1985), esp. ch. 5. See also Edward Vallance, 'Reborn John? The Eighteenth-Century Afterlife of John Lilburne', *History Workshop Journal*, 74 (2012), pp. 1–26, p. 18.

4. *CSPD, 1653–4*, p. 120; Thurloe, III, p. 394; Clement Walker, THE COMPLEAT HISTORY OF *Independency* (London, 1661), pt 3, p. 31. For Fox, see this volume, pp. 284–5.

5. John Lilburne, *A COPY OF A LETTER WRITTEN to Collonell* Henry Marten ([London, 1647]).

6. Margaret George, *Women in the First Capitalist Society: Experiences in Seventeenth-Century England* (Urbana, 1988), ch. 4 draws this material together as the fullest account of her life. The image of the footnote is hers, at pp. 69–70.

7. John Lilburne, *AS YOU WERE* ([London], May 1652), p. 32. The juxtaposition of fear and flattery perhaps recalls Machiavelli, whose maxims Lilburne accuses Cromwell of following: p. 4. Brailsford was drawn to a similar, but slightly distinct, speculation about John's taste for arbitration and about the connection between his relationship with his father and other hero figures such as, for example, Bastwick or Cromwell: *Levellers*, pp. 237–8.

8. Wales and Hartley, p. 491.

9. His spoof will provided that 'My Trade of Soap-boyling, I leave to all those variable Mechanicks, that being weary of one Trade resolve to try another, though it be never so much to their loss and prejudice': *The Last VVill & Testament of Lieutenant Col. John Lilburn* (London, 1654), p. 5.

10. *A&O*, III, p. cvi. The Act repealed both the Act of 1653 and the execution of judgement on it, apparently accepting that it had been a legal Act, although perhaps a bad one.

11. TNA, SP 18/157A, f. 129a. The pension was continued through 1659 to March 1660 with, evidently, some further complications: *CJ*, VII, pp. 682–3, 751, 760, 776, 879; *CSPD, 1658–9*, pp. 260–1; *CSPD, 1659–60*, pp. 183, 593, 594. Huntington initiated a Chancery suit over disputed tithes in April 1659, but she did not answer (this is not necessarily unusual): TNA, C7/176/5.

12. Bod. Lib., Ashmole MSS, 347, ff. 71v, 75v (Buckingham), 77; 428, ff. 192v, 200, 214v, 222v, 241v, 254v, 259, 260v, 262, 268v, 269v.

13. Barry Coward, 'Lilburne, Robert (*bap.* 1614, *d.* 1665)', *ODNB*; History of Parliament Trust, London, unpublished article on George Lilburne for 1640–60 section by David Scott. I am grateful to the History of Parliament Trust for allowing me to see this article in draft; TNA, SP 29/7, f. 77; Wales and Hartley, p. 492.

14. Rushworth, II, p. 468; Wood attributed the joke to Judge Jenkins, Anthony Wood, *Athenæ Oxonienses*, 2 vols (London, 1721), II, p. 174. For other examples see: Anon., THE *Selfe Afflictor* (London, 1657), pp. 13–14; Anon., *The Last VVill & Testament*.

15. Wood, *Athenæ Oxonienses*, II, p. 172.

16. Samuel Chidley, quoted from Gregg, pp. 355–6.

17. Thomas N. Corns, '"I Have Writ, I Have Acted, I Have Peace": The Personal and the Political in the Writing of Winstanley and some Contemporaries', *Prose Studies*, 36 (2014), pp. 43–51, at p. 44; Rachel Foxley, 'The Levellers: John Lilburne, Richard Overton and William Walwyn', in *The Oxford Handbook of Literature and the English Revolution*, ed. Laura Lunger Knoppers (Oxford, 2012), pp. 272–86, at p. 277.

18. This was partly for their own protection, of course: '(but in regard I abhor to be a betrayer, or a mischievous accuser, I shal not dare without leave from themselves to name their names', [John Lilburne], AN IMPEACHMENT OF HIGH TREASON AGAINST *Oliver Cromwell* (London, 1649), p. 22.

19. Jason Peacey, 'The People of the *Agreements*: The Levellers, Civil War Radicalism and Political Participation', in *The Agreements of the People, the Levellers and the Constitutional Crisis of the English Revolution*, eds Philip Baker and Elliot Vernon (Basingstoke, 2012), pp. 50–75, at pp. 62–3.

20. The relationship between the civic law and natural law or the state of nature is ambiguous in his writing: Parker-Speer, 'Revolutionary'; Rachel Foxley, 'Problems of Sovereignty in Leveller Writings', *History of Political Thought*, 28 (2007), pp. 642–60. This is partly because he wrote as a polemicist, for immediate effect, rather than as a theorist: Glenn Burgess, 'Protestant Polemic: The Leveller Pamphlets', *Parergon*, 11:2 (1993), pp. 45–67. Overton, for example, is clearer on such abstract matters: Nicholas McDowell, 'Ideas of Creation in the Writings of Richard Overton the Leveller and *Paradise Lost*', *Journal of the History of Ideas*, 66 (2005), pp. 59–78. Those seeking system in 'Leveller thought' often cite preponderantly from Overton, Walwyn, or Wildman: see for example Iain Hampsher-Monk, 'The Political Theory of the Levellers: Putney, Property and Professor Macpherson', *Political Studies*, 24: 4 (1976), pp. 397–422 (for Overton see esp. pp. 412–22); Samuel Dennis Glover, 'The Putney Debates: Popular versus Elitist Republicanism', *P&P*, 164 (1999), pp. 47–80 (Wildman). See also the general verdicts of Jonathan Scott, *England's Troubles: Seventeenth-Century English Political Instability in European Context* (Cambridge, 2000), p. 285 and D. Alan Orr, 'Law, Liberty, and the English Civil War: John Lilburne's Prison Experience, the Levellers and Freedom', in *The Experience of Revolution in Stuart Britain and Ireland*, eds Michael J. Braddick and David L. Smith (Cambridge, 2011), pp. 154–71 at pp. 170–1.

21. Foxley, ch. 3, esp. pp. 92–9.

22. John Lilburne, *The Copy of a* LETTER . . . *to a freind* (London, 1645), TD 9 August 1645, p. 12.

23. John Lilburne, *Rash Oaths unwarrantable* ([London], 1647), p. 15.

24. Charles W. A. Prior, *A Confusion of Tongues: Britain's Wars of Reformation, 1625–1642* (Oxford, 2012).

25. See this volume, p. 112.

26. John Downame contrasted Lilburne's sufferings with Prynne's, drawing a clear distinction between them: John Downame, *A REVIEW Of a certain PAMPHLET* (London, 1645), p. 1. The charge that he was trying to make money in 1637 is repeated for example in S[amuel] Shepheard, *THE FAMERS FAMED* (London, 1646), p. 11; Gregg, p. 355; Samuel Chidley, *The Dissembling SCOT set forth in is COVLOVRS* ([London], 1652), p. 5.

27. John Lilburne, *Londons Liberty in Chains* (London, 1646), p. 20.

28. Lilburne, *AN IMPEACHMENT*, title page.

29. For a similar analysis see Glenn Burgess, 'Radicalism and the English Revolution', in *English Radicalism, 1550–1850*, eds Glenn Burgess and Matthew Festenstein (Cambridge, 2007), pp. 63–86. J. C. Davis argues that Lilburne thought God dealt directly with Christians via their conscience and not via the church, and that there was therefore a sphere of life outside civic regulation; and also that there was a civic sphere immune from the immediate intervention of God. Hence, for Lilburne, 'Civil freedom was to live under the known and consistent laws of a lawfully derived authority and not to be subject to arbitrary and willful government': J. C. Davis, 'Religion and the Struggle for Freedom in the English Revolution', *HJ*, 35 (1992), pp. 507–30, at pp. 526–7.

30. Ann Hughes, 'Gender and Politics in Leveller Literature', in *Political Culture and Cultural Politics in Early Modern Europe*, eds Susan D. Amussen and Mark A. Kishlansky (Manchester, 1995), pp. 162–88; Melissa Mowry, '"Commoners Wives who Stand for their Freedom and Liberty": Leveller Women and the Hermeneutics of Collectivities', *Huntington Library Quarterly*, 77:3 (2014), pp. 305–29; see also George, *Women in the First Capitalist Society*, ch. 3. For the relationship to notions of citizenship see Keith Thomas, 'The Levellers and the Franchise' *The Interregnum: The Quest for Settlement*, ed. G. E. Aylmer (London, 1972), pp. 57–78, esp. p. 77; Patricia Crawford, '"The Poorest She": Women and Citizenship in Early Modern England', in *The Putney Debates of 1647: The Army, The Levellers and the English State*, ed. Michael Mendle (Cambridge, 2001), pp. 197–218; Rachel Foxley, 'John Lilburne and the Citizenship of "Free-Born Englishmen"', *HJ*, 47 (2004), pp. 849–74, at pp. 870–1.

31. Foxley, 'Lilburne and Citizenship': he was arguing for the uniform legal rights of denizens. There was very little comment in Leveller writing on Ireland, although there was some indication of more internationalist sympathies, and a capacity to identify with the rights of the Irish: Norah Carlin, 'The Levellers and the Conquest of Ireland in 1649', *HJ*, 30 (1987), pp. 269–88. See also, Christopher Hill, 'Seventeenth-Century English Radicals and Ireland', in *Radicals, Rebels and Establishments*, ed. P. J. Corish (Belfast, 1985), 33–49.

32. Anon., *A DECLARATION OF THE PROCEEDINGS OF Major General Massy, Sir Marmaduke Langdale, and Lieut. Col. John Lilburn* (London, 1652), TD 22 December 1652, p. 5.

33. I have not found a formulation of this last point quite as explicitly in these terms in Lilburne's own writing, but it is put this way in a posthumous publication setting out his views for use in the summer of 1659: Anon, *LILBURNS GHOST* (London, 1659), TD 22 August 1659, pp. 2–3. For the denial of a national basis for the ecclesiastical state see the argument that Christ had left his power 'in the bodies of his particular (not Nationall) Churches': John Lilburne, *Come out of her my people* ([Amsterdam], 1639), p. 4.

34. For a similar view see Steve Pincus, *1688: The First Modern Revolution* (New Haven and London, 2009), ch. 1.

35. Blair Worden, *Roundhead Reputations: The English Civil Wars and the Passions of Posterity* (London, 2001), chs 1–4.

36. Jason Peacey, *Print and Public Politics in the English Revolution* (Cambridge, 2013), p. 36. Others were collecting his work earlier: ibid., pp. 37, 40, 46, 53–4, 74.

37. Jason McGelligott, 'William Hone (1780–1842), Print-Culture, and the Nature of Radicalism', in *Varieties of Seventeenth- and Early Eighteenth-Century English Radicalism in Context*, eds Ariel Hessayon and David Finnegan (Farnham, 2011), pp. 241–60, at pp. 257–8.

38. F. K. Donnelly, 'The Levellers and Early Nineteenth-Century Radicalism', *Bulletin of the Society for the Study of Labour History*, 49 (1984), pp. 24–8, at pp. 24–5; Thomas Salmon, *The characters of the several noblemen and gentlemen that have died in the defence of their respective princes, or the liberties of their country* (London, 1724); ['John Lilburn'], *An epistle from Col. John Lilburn, In the shades, to John Wilkes, Esq; late A Colonel in the Buckinghamshire Militia* (London, [1765?]); Vallance, 'Reborn John', pp. 3, 15–16; *Biographia Britannica*, ed. William Oldys (London, 6 vols, 1747–66), p. [2938].

39. Franco Venturi, *The End of the Old Regime in Europe, 1786–76: The First Crisis* (Princeton, 1989), p. 393. Innes sees this as part of a longer tradition of radical apologetic: Joanna Innes, '"Reform" in English Public Life: The Fortunes of a Word', in *Rethinking the Age of Reform: Britain 1780–1850*, eds Arthur Burns and Joanna Innes (Cambridge, 2003), p. 81.

40. Vallance, 'Reborn John', pp. 15–16.

41. John Brewer, 'The Wilkites and the Law, 1763–74: A Study of Radical Notions of Governance', in *An Ungovernable People: The English and their Law in the Seventeenth and Eighteenth Centuries*, eds John Brewer and John Styles (London, 1980), pp. 128–71, at pp. 161–3, 381 n. 83; Peter D. G. Thomas, *John Wilkes: A Friend to Liberty* (Oxford, 1996), pp. 123–4. Bingley cited Lilburne in William Bingley, *The case of William Bingley, bookseller, Who was Two Years imprisoned by the Court of King's-Bench, without Trial, Conviction, or Sentence* (London, 1773) (see pp. 54–5 for examination by interrogatory). He also published *A guide to the knowledge of the rights and privileges of Englishmen. Containing commentaries on I. King John's Magna Charta; II. Henry III's* (London, 1771), in which Lilburne favourites such as Magna Carta, the Petition of Right, habeas corpus, and the power of grand juries feature prominently. I am grateful to Joanna Innes for her advice on the later reception of Lilburne.

42. Vallance, 'Reborn John', pp. 17–18; 30 Geo III, *c.* 60: <http://www.legislation. gov.uk/apgb/Geo3/32/60>. The parallel with Fox's Act is also drawn by Rutt: *Diaries of Thomas Burton, Esq,* vol. 3: *January–March 1659,* ed. J. T. Rutt (London, 1828), p. 506n; for a celebration of the 1649 trial see Wolfram, 'Democracy's Pillar of Fire'.

43. Vallance, 'Reborn John', pp. 18–19; Foxley, 'Lilburne and Citizenship', pp. 851–2. For the cautionary note see Blair Worden, 'The Levellers in History and Memory, c. 1660–1960', in *The Putney Debates of 1647: The Army, The Levellers and the English State,* ed. Michael Mendle (Cambridge, 2001), pp. 256–82, at p. 269.

44. Donnelly, 'Levellers and Early Nineteenth-Century Radicalism', p. 26; McGelligott, 'William Hone', pp. 253–5; Philip Harling, 'The Law of Libel and the Limits of Repression, 1790–1832', *HJ,* 44 (2001), pp. 107–34, at pp. 113, 128–34; Ben Wilson, *The Laughter of Triumph: William Hone and the Fight for the Free Press* (London, 2005), pp. 32–4, 60.

45. William Godwin, *History of the Commonwealth of England,* 4 vols (London, 1824–28), vol. 2, book 1, ch. 20; book 2, ch. 13. This brief discussion follows the interpretation of John Morrow, 'Republicanism and Public Virtue: William Godwin's *History of the Commonwealth of England*', *HJ,* 34 (1991), pp. 645–64.

46. Carlyle letters online, Thomas Carlyle to Thomas Wise Jr, 21 February 1648: <http://carlyleletters.dukejournals.org/cgi/content/full/22/1/ lt-18480221-TC-TWJR-01>. Rather alarmingly for the present author he went on: 'does not seem to me an apt hero for a "Life and Times."—Provided also some Bookseller will undertake to publish such a work, when once after long toil it is got completed?'

47. John Morrow, 'Heroes and Constitutionalists: The Ideological Significance of Thomas Carlyle's Treatment of the English Revolution', *History of Political Thought,* 14 (1993), pp. 205–23; Morrow, *Thomas Carlyle* (London, 2006), ch. 7.

48. Duncan Kelly, 'Idealism and Revolution: T. H. Green's Four Lectures On The English Commonwealth', *HPT,* 27 (2006), pp. 505–42; Mark Nixon, *Samuel Rawson Gardiner and the Idea of History* (Woodbridge, 2010).

49. M. Guizot, *On the causes of the success of the English revolution of 1640–1688* (London, 1850); it coincided with the publication in French of the first volume of *Histoire de la révolution d'Angleterre* (Paris, 1850).

50. Karl Marx, 'England's 17th Century Revolution', first published in Politisch-Ökonomische Revue, No. 2, February 1850: <https://www.marxists.org/archive/ marx/works/1850/02/english-revolution.htm>.

51. Guizot, *Success of the English revolution,* p. 1.

52. Henry Holorenshaw [Christopher Hill], *The Levellers and the English Revolution* (London, 1939), esp. pp. 12–13, 93–4. See also Eduard Bernstein, *Cromwell and Communism: Socialism and Democracy in the Great English Revolution* (Nottingham, 1980); Brailsford, *Levellers;* Gregg. It should be noted, though, that Hill (publishing as Holorenshaw and in his later work), as well as Bernstein, tended to assimilate

Lilburne to a democratic tradition, seeing in Winstanley and the True Levellers the roots of the native socialist tradition.

53. Foxley, 'Problems of Sovereignty'; Foxley, 'Lilburne and Citizenship'; Hampsher-Monk, 'Political Theory of the Levellers'; Halliday, *Habeas Corpus*, pp. 193–7.

54. Tom Bingham, *The Rule of Law* (London, 2010), pp. 37, 48, 55, 60, 66, 85, 90, 110.

55. Godwin, *History*, II, p. 423.

56. For Lilburne and negative liberty see Orr, 'Law, Liberty and the English Civil War'; Godwin diary, entry for 3 August 1825. The diary makes clear the extent to which Lilburne captured Godwin's attention: <http://godwindiary.bodleian. ox.ac.uk/index2.html>. For an analysis of more fundamental reflections on liberty in the mid-seventeenth century see Quentin Skinner, 'Rethinking Political Liberty', *History Workshop Journal*, 61 (2006), pp. 156–70; Skinner, *Liberty Before Liberalism* (Cambridge, 1998).

57. Rachel Foxley, 'The Logic of Ideas in Christopher Hill's English Revolution', *Prose Studies*, 36 (2014), pp. 199–208, at pp. 203–5. See also the verdict of Keith Thomas, that Leveller thought was constitutionally interesting, but that they were not harbingers of a new social order: Thomas, 'Levellers and the Franchise', esp. p. 77.

58. M. Guizot, *History of Oliver Cromwell and the English Republic* (London, 1854), p. 60.

59. The literature on revisionism is extensive. The structural issues included the functional breakdown of English government (Conrad Russell), the Wars of Religion (John Morrill), and the British problem/problem of the Three (or multiple) Kingdoms (Morrill and Russell). For a recent overviews see: Thomas Cogswell, Richard Cust, and Peter Lake, 'Revisionism and its Legacies: The Work of Conrad Russell', in *Politics, Religion and Popularity in Early Stuart Britain: Essays in Honour of Conrad Russell*, eds Cogwell, Cust, and Lake (Cambridge, 2002), pp. 1–17; John Adamson, 'Introduction: High Roads and Blind Alleys—The English Civil War and its Historiography', in *The English Civil War: Conflict and Contexts*, ed. Adamson (Basingstoke, 2009), pp. 1–35; and the works cited there. For the passions of those other than the radicals, see John Morrill, *Revolt in the Provinces: The People of England and the Tragedies of War, 1630–1648*, 2nd edition (Harlow, 1999).

60. Key interventions were Mark A. Kishlansky, 'The Army and the Levellers: The Roads to Putney', *HJ*, 22 (1979), pp. 795–824; Kishlansky, 'Ideology and Politics in the Parliamentary Armies, 1645–9', in *Reactions to the English Civil War 1642–1649*, ed. John Morrill (Basingstoke, 1982), pp. 163–83; John Morrill, 'Mutiny and Discontent in English Provincial Armies, 1645–1647', reprinted in *The Nature of the English Revolution: Essays by John Morrill*, ed. Morrill (Harlow, 1993), pp. 332–58.

61. Davis, 'Religion and the Struggle for Freedom'.

62. For their contrasting trajectories into and out of the campaigns for an *Agreement* see Barbara Taft, 'Walwyn, William (*bap.* 1600, *d.* 1681)', *ODNB*; Derek Hirst,

'A Happier Man: The Refashioning of William Walwyn', *The Seventeenth Century*, 27 (2012), pp. 54–78; Richard L. Greaves, 'Wildman, Sir John (1622/3–1693)', *ODNB*; B. J. Gibbons, 'Overton, Richard (*fl.* 1640–1663)', *ODNB*; and, in general, Rachel Foxley, 'The Levellers: John Lilburne, Richard Overton and William Walwyn'.

63. Peter Lake, 'Post-Reformation Politics, or on Not Looking for the Long-Term Causes of the English Civil War', in *The Oxford Handbook of the English Civil War*, ed. Michael J. Braddick (Oxford, 2015), pp. 21–39.

64. Brailsford, *Levellers*, pp. 56, 115.

65. The point was made by Thomas, 'Levellers and the Franchise'; for fuller recent treatments see Philip Baker, '*Londons Liberty in Chains Discovered*: The Levellers, The Civic Past, and Popular Protest in Civil War London', *HLQ*, 76 (2013), pp. 559–87; Baker, 'The Levellers, Decentralisation and the *Agreements of the People*', in *The Agreements of the People*, eds Baker and Vernon, pp. 97–116; Phil Withington, 'Urban Citizens and England's Civil Wars', in *Handbook of the English Revolution*, ed. Braddick, pp. 312–29.

66. Overton may have had a viable printing business: David R. Adams, 'The Secret Printing and Publishing Career of Richard Overton the Leveller, 1644–46', *The Library*, 7th series, 11 (2010), pp. 3–88, at pp. 73–5.

67. For the importance of print to the development Quakerism more generally see Kate Peters, *Print Culture and the Early Quakers* (Cambridge, 2009).

68. For his avoidance of meetings as evidence that he had no subversive intentions see John Lilburne, L COLONEL JOHN LILBURNS APOLOGETISCH VERHAEL/L. COLONEL JOHN LILBURNE HIS APOLOGETICAL NARRATION (Amsterdam, 1652), p. 14.

69. This emphasis on the Levellers as an alliance of fellow travellers rather than a party, bringing together people with a variety of commitments, offers a similar approach to recent work on Leveller political thought and political organization: Foxley, Rees.

70. Famously by Kenyon in his review of Christopher Hill's *World Turned Upside Down*: quoted in John Morrill, 'John Phillips Kenyon', *Proceedings of the British Academy*, 101 (1999), pp. 441–64, at p. 452.

Picture Acknowledgements

Index